LADY GREGORY

LADY GREGORY

The Woman Behind the Irish Renaissance

Mary Lou Kohfeldt

ANDRE DEUTSCH

First published in Great Britain 1985 by
André Deutsch Limited
105 Great Russell Street London WC1

British Library Cataloguing in Publication Data

Kohfeldt, Mary Lou
    Lady Gregory: the woman behind the Irish
renaissance.
    1. Gregory, Isabella Augusta, *Lady*
    2. Authors, Irish—20th century—Biography
    822′.912   PR4728.G5Z/

ISBN 0-233-97793-7

Printed in Great Britain by
St Edmundsbury Press, Bury St Edmunds

Phil, Tara, Philip Forest

Acknowledgments

First and warmest thanks to Weldon Thornton, professor of English at the University of North Carolina at Chapel Hill, and Colin Smythe, publisher of *The Coole Edition of the Works of Lady Gregory*, for innumerable facts supplied, errors corrected, and contacts made.

Thanks to the late Major Richard Gregory and Bobbie Gregory for their kind hospitality.

Thanks to Susan Gilbert, Meredith College, Raleigh, North Carolina, for praise, corrections, and brilliant suggestions. And to Robin Dent, Pendleton and Jill Herring, Chris Armitage, Joseph Flora, Connie Eble, and Margaret O'Connor, the last four professors of English at the University of North Carolina, for reading and reactions. Thanks to Lt. Col. John Stewart Eyre, John S. Kelly of St. John's College, Oxford; Ann Saddlemyer and Gretchen L. Schwenker for helpful information supplied.

Special thanks to Benjamin L. Reid for the picture of John Quinn that appears in this book and for permission to quote from his *The Man from New York: John Quinn and His Friends*.

Thanks to Merry Weed for sharing with me her notes on the Persse family from the Folklore Archives, University College Dublin, which I also thank.

Thanks to Dr. Lola Szladits, curator, and Brian McInerney, assistant, at the Berg Collection of the New York Public Library, and to Dr. Paul Woudhuysen, Keeper of Manuscripts & Printed Books at the Fitzwilliam Museum, Cambridge, for their help and courtesy.

Thanks to my agent Rosalie Siegel, my editor at Atheneum, Judith

Kern, and indexer Phyllis Marchand—all of whom were a pleasure to work with.

And thanks to Carolee Lane, Irit Harris, and Doris Petrie for help with the rest of my life while I was writing this biography.

Thanks to Colin Smythe Limited on behalf of Anne de Winton and Catherine Kennedy for permission to quote unpublished works by Lady Gregory as well as copyrighted material from the following works: *Irish Folk History Plays*: *Dervorgilla, Kincora, Grania, The White Cockade, The Canavans*, and *The Deliverer* (copyright 1912 by Lady Gregory, renewed 1940); *Our Irish Theatre* (copyright 1913 by Lady Gregory, renewed 1941); *New Comedies*: *The Bogie Men, Damer's Gold, The Full Moon, Coats*, and *McDonough's Wife* (copyright 1913 by Lady Gregory, renewed 1941); *The Golden Apple* (copyright 1916 by Lady Gregory, renewed 1943); *Visions and Beliefs in the West of Ireland* (copyright 1920 by Lady Gregory, renewed 1947); *The Kiltartan Poetry Book* (copyright 1918, renewed 1946); *Three Wonder Plays*: *The Jester, Aristotle's Bellows*, and *The Dragon* (copyright 1922, renewed 1950); *The Image and Other Plays*: *The Image, The Wrens, Shanwalla*, and *Hanrahan's Oath* (copyright 1922, renewed 1949); *Mirandolina* (copyright 1924, renewed 1952); *Three Last Plays*: *Sancho's Master, Dave*, and *The Would-Be Gentleman* (copyright 1928, renewed 1955); *The Dragon* (copyright 1920, renewed 1947). All renewals are in the names of Richard Graham Gregory, Anne Gregory, and Catherine Frances Kennedy.

Thanks to Colin Smythe Limited on behalf of Anne de Winton for permission to quote from *Me and Nu: Childhood at Coole* (copyright 1970 by Anne de Winton).

Thanks to Colin Smythe Limited for permission to quote from *Theatre Business*, edited by Anne Saddlemyer (copyright 1982 by Michael B. Yeats and Anne Yeats, Anne Saddlemyer, and the Lady Gregory Estate).

Grateful acknowledgment is made to Michael and Anne Yeats for permission to quote from the unpublished letters of W. B. Yeats to Lady Gregory in the Berg Collection of the New York Public Library.

Thanks to the Macmillan Publishing Co., Inc., for permission to quote from *The Autobiography of William Butler Yeats* (copyright 1916, 1926 by Macmillan Publishing Co., Inc., renewed 1944, 1964 by Bertha Georgie Yeats); from *Essays and Introductions* by William Butler Yeats (copyright Mrs. W. B. Yeats, 1961); from *Explorations* by William Butler Yeats (copyright Mrs. W. B. Yeats, 1962); from *A Vision* by William Butler Yeats (copyright 1937 by W. B. Yeats, renewed 1965 by Bertha Georgie Yeats and Anne Butler Yeats); from "In the Seven Woods" from *The Poems of W. B. Yeats* edited by Richard Finneran (New York: Macmillan, 1983); from *The Letters of W. B. Yeats*, edited by Allan Wade (copyright 1953, 1954 by Anne Butler Yeats); from *The Collected Plays of W. B. Yeats* (copyright 1934, 1952 by Macmillan Publishing Co., Inc.); from *The Variorum Edition of the Poems of W. B. Yeats*, edited by Peter Allt and Russell K. Alspach (copyright 1957 by Macmillan Publishing Co., Inc.); and from *The Poems of W. B. Yeats*, edited by Richard J. Finneran (copyright 1912, 1919, 1933 by Macmillan Publishing Co., Inc., renewed 1940, 1947, 1961 by Bertha Georgie Yeats. Copyright 1940 by Georgia Yeats, renewed 1968 by Bertha Georgie Yeats, Michael Butler Yeats, and Anne Yeats).

Thanks to The Henry W. and Albert A. Berg Collection, The New York Public Library, Astor, Lenox and Tilden Foundations, for permission for extensive quotations from the Lady Gregory archives; to The John Quinn Memorial Collection, Rare Books and Manuscripts Division, The New York Public Library, Astor, Lenox and Tilden Foundations, for permission to quote from the correspondence of Lady Gregory and John Quinn; to the Special Collections department, The Robert W. Woodruff Library, Emory University, for permission to quote from Lady Gregory's diary, dated 4 March 1880 through 24 May 1882; to the Special Collections department, Morris Library, University of Southern Illinois at Carbondale, for permission to quote from Lady Gregory's letters to Lennox Robinson in the Lennox Robinson Abbey Theatre papers; to the Syndics of the Fitzwilliam Museum, Cambridge, for permission to quote from Lady Gregory's poems to Wilfrid Blunt in prison.

Thanks to Mr. T. Coghill for permission to quote from the letters of Violet Martin to Lady Gregory in the Berg Collection; to Weidenfeld & Nicolson and Curtis Brown for permission to quote from *A Pilgrimage of Passion: The Life of Wilfrid Scawen Blunt* by Elizabeth Longford (copyright 1979 by Elizabeth Longford); to Harvard University Press for permission to quote from *Letters to Molly* by J. M. Synge, edited by Ann Saddlemyer; to The Boston Herald for permission to quote from excerpts from articles reprinted in *Lady Gregory: Interviews and Recollections* by E. H. Mikhail; to Macmillan Pubishing Co., Inc., for permission to quote from *Inishfallen, Fare Thee Well* by Sean O'Casey (copyright 1949 by Sean O'Casey, renewed 1977 by Eileen O'Casey, Breon O'Casey and Shivaun O'Casey); to E. P. Dutton, Inc., for permission to quote from *Hail and Farewell* by George

Moore (copyright 1911 by D. Appleton & Co., renewed 1959 by Charles Douglas Medley); to Alfred A. Knopf for permission to quote from *My Diaries: Being A Personal Narrative of Events, 1888–1914*, by Wilfrid Scawen Blunt (copyright 1921 by Wilfrid Scawen Blunt); to Samuel French for permission to quote from *Dave* by Lady Gregory appearing in *One Act Plays for Stage and Study, Third Series*; to Dr. Thomas F. Conroy for permission to quote from the letters of John Quinn; to Joseph Hone for permission to quote from *W. B. Yeats* (copyright 1943 by Joseph Hone), and to Mrs. Pauline Hague for permission to quote from Sara Allgood's unpublished memoirs.

Thanks to the Folklore Archives, University College, Dublin, for permission to quote material from their files; to Michael B. Yeats and Macmillan London, Ltd for permission to quote from the works of W. B. Yeats; and to Macmillan London, Ltd for permission to quote from *Inishfallen, Fare Thee Well* by Sean O'Casey.

Every effort has been made to trace quotations to their ultimate source and to obtain the copyright owners' permission to use the material concerned. The author and publishers apologize for any inadvertant omissions and will be pleased to receive any information that would enable these omissions to be rectified in a future edition.

Contents

INTRODUCTION: *The Road to the Renaissance*   3

  I   *Last Days in the West*
     CHILDHOOD AND YOUTH: 1852–1880   8

 II   *The Seductions of Union*
     MARRIAGE: 1880–1892   45

III   *The Rediscovery of Ireland*
     WIDOWHOOD: 1892–1897   90

 IV   *Hitching Her Wagon to a Star*
     YEATS COMES TO COOLE: 1897–1898   109

  V   *Living off the Land*
     THE IRISH EPICS AND *Cathleen ni*
       Houlihan: 1899–1902   133

 VI   *Laughing at Last*
     FIRST PLAYS: 1902–1904   152

VII   *Prolific at the Abbey*
     THEATER MANAGER AND PLAYWRIGHT: 1904–1908   173

VIII   *A New Lease on Life*
     CHANGING—A LITTLE: 1908–1911   203

CONTENTS

IX *Triumph in America*
    TOURING WITH THE ABBEY: 1911–1913   223

 X *The Swallows Scatter*
    PARTING AND DEATH: 1914–1922   243

XI *The End of the Renaissance*
    PERSISTENCE—*Con Spirito*: 1920–1927   265

XII *The Happy Servant*
    LAST YEARS: 1927–1932   290

    CHRONOLOGY   307
    NOTES   313
    BIBLLIOGRAPHY   345
    INDEX   357

Illustrations

The castellated entrance to Roxborough, the Persse family estate
(COURTESY COLIN SMYTHE)
Augusta Gregory, as she appeared at the time of her wedding
(COURTESY COLIN SMYTHE)

Sir William Gregory caricatured in *Vanity Fair*
(COURTESY COLIN SMYTHE)
and as he actually appeared (COURTESY COLIN SMYTHE)
The dashing Wilfred Scawen Blunt (COURTESY COLIN SMYTHE)

Robert Gregory, at the age of twenty-one (COURTESY COLIN SMYTHE)
William Butler Yeats, the young poet, at the time he met Lady
Gregory (COURTESY THE BETTMANN ARCHIVE/BBC HULTON)

Sean O'Casey (COURTESY THE BETTMANN ARCHIVE/BBC HULTON)
A drawing of John M. Synge done by John Butler Yeats
(COURTESY THE BETTMANN ARCHIVE/BBC HULTON)

Lady Gregory, on the frontispiece for *Our Irish Theatre*
(COURTESY COLIN SMYTHE)
Robert Gregory in RFC uniform (COURTESY COLIN SMYTHE)

The library at Coole (COURTESY COLIN SMYTHE)
Coole Park, photographed by George Bernard Shaw
(COURTESY COLIN SMYTHE)

Lady Gregory at the height of her career
(COURTESY THE BETTMANN ARCHIVE/BBC HULTON)
John Quinn at the age of fifty-one (COURTESY B. L. REID)
Augusta sitting under the catalpa tree at Coole
(COURTESY IRISH TOURIST BOARD)

LADY GREGORY

INTRODUCTION

The Road to the Renaissance

*I notice that when anybody here writes
a play it always works out, whatever the
ideas of the writer, into a cry for a more
abundant and a more intense life.*

W. B. YEATS, *Letters*

RENAISSANCE is a beautiful word. We use it even when we are
not sure what has been reborn, as in the Irish Renaissance, because it combines the unexpected delight of creativity with the satisfying stability of the establishment. The breathtaking nerviness of
Christ's "I come that you may have life and have it more abundantly"
is transformed into the predictable magic of birth.

Ireland had a renaissance beginning in the 1890's and lasting until
the 1920's. Augusta Gregory had just such a controlled and exhilarating flowering in her fifties, lasting through her seventies. Intersecting
with the time of the Irish Renaissance, her creativity had causes not
purely personal. Like other excited Irish people discovering abilities
they did not know they had, she too was invigorated by the particular
moment in Irish history.

In the 1890's the Irish people, turning away from the quarrels and
confusion following the death of their leader Charles Stewart Parnell,
looked for a nationality apart from politics and turned to the ancient
Celtic culture to create for themselves the myth of a heroic past. Augusta, with her retelling of the ancient Irish epics, helped create the
myth. It turned out to be not such a good or useful inheritance, but the
Irish people who had so long seen their identity as a function of their

3

subordinate relationship to England were exhilarated, momentarily touched and ennobled, to feel themselves inheritors at all.

There had been other backward looks, other aborted flowerings, in Irish history. This one came at a time when the Irish people were also breathing in a surprised realization of their possible freedom. Excitement about the past turned into excitement about the future, making the participants feel there was some great tangible good to result from their activity. They felt they were bringing a nation to birth.

For six hundred years Ireland had been a seedbed of patriotic passion, both invigorating and cozy, because its situation offered the opportunity to unite against an oppressor on whom all evil could be projected, who was, in addition, so powerful there was no danger of actually attaining freedom or responsibility. Then in the nineteenth century the immovable barrier against which the Irish people had routinely hurled themselves began to move. The granting to Catholics the right to hold office in 1829, the British reform bills of 1832 and 1867 broadening the electorate, the local-government bill of 1898 taking local affairs out of the hands of the landlords, and the land bills at the end of the century and the beginning of the next granting tenants more rights slowly pushed the landlords out of their position of power. The most astute among them knew their days were numbered, but most, having no special abilities, sat very still and did or did not succeed in living within their dwindling incomes.

The makers of the Irish Renaissance—chief among them W. B. Yeats, Augusta Gregory, John Synge, Douglas Hyde, George Moore— were the more talented, energetic, and less economically fortunate members of the landed gentry—sometimes one or two generations away from the great estate—who, pushed or leaping from their shrinking lives, made the quantum jump from a social to an artistic identity. The foot soldiers of the renaissance were the lower classes, chiefly Catholics, who directed the energy of their long resistance into artistic acitvity and literary appreciation. The Irish Renaissance was made by the surprised energy of a class on the way up meeting the dying flare of a class on the way down.

Augusta Gregory rose through the renaissance to become one of its leaders because she—though her appearance and manner belied the relationship—had more in common with the Irish people than did other upper-class renaissance makers. The neglect and domination of her family had shaped her in the same fashion as the Celtic past, the Catholic Church, and the mismanagement and overlordship of England had shaped the Irish people.

Augusta Persse was buying the literature of rebel Ireland by the time she was tall enough to push her sixpence across the counter of the dark, dirty stationer's shop in the little market town near her family's great estate. This literature, like that of most subject peoples, is an attempt to make up for the huge injury of having had, in a national sense, bad parents. It suited Augusta well. She was one of sixteen children of a powerful, greedy, unstable father and a frivolous, pretty mother whose chief interest in life was evangelical religion, who preferred her sons to her daughters, her pretty daughters to her plain ones, and who liked Augusta least of all. The rebel literature with its intense love of Ireland, its stories of resistance and loyalty, its mourning for lost leaders, gave a warmth and a width and a passion to Augusta's obscure but urgent feeling of neglect.

Like Augusta's parents, those in authority over the Irish people had for hundreds of years deprived them of a sense of their value or power. The result, along with their feeling a lack of personal freedom, was a diminution of personal passions and an accentuation of abstract ones. The power of the church was intensified. The Catholic Church in the case of the Irish people, the Protestant Church of Ireland in Augusta's case, produced a sense of living in a vast hierarchy stretching beyond the boundaries of the visible world, a sense of being watched and judged from all quarters of the sky by—as Augusta called them—"the unseen watchers," "the cloud of witnesses." It was a mind-set created by oppression that, while it gave passion and meaning, also created a deeper internal oppression. It was a dark inheritance, though Augusta escaped the darkest part—the irresponsibility of the oppressed and the love of death for the cause—because of her sense of duty, her innate sanity and balance.

When the truce was signed in 1921, ending the last fighting between Irish and English in the south of Ireland, young Irishmen out in the hills refused to lay down their arms because, "Why wouldn't we have a chance to die for Ireland?" (They created their chance in the civil war that followed.) Just before the truce Augusta wrote, "I seem possessed with the passion for Ireland, for my country. . . . I wish to put myself on the side of the people, I wish to go to prison, I think even to execution." Then she added with her usual practicality and dutifulness, "I think my name would serve the 'rebels' better than my life."

The circumstances of her childhood, the teaching of family, church, and class all told her that her role as a female was to serve others. She believed it; duty was the lifeline from which she hung all her actions and achievements. Her life is dazzlingly instructive in the utility of those drab virtues within command of the will: self-restraint, tenacity, hard work, devotion. But she also had fairy gifts: a great, long-term vitality, a soldier's courage, and a detachment that—taking away from love—brought laughter. She had luck, the power to make things happen that belongs to those who commit themselves completely to a goal, clearly defined but subconscious. Underneath the conviction that she must serve, the feeling of being constantly judged, was the child's passionate wish to be centerstage, to be loved, admired, acclaimed, the wish for, as W. H. Auden put it, "Not universal love/ But to be loved alone." The fascination of her life, the delighted admiration one feels for her character, and her sneakiness, derive from the manner in which she turned the straight and narrow into an ascending arc.

First she served her brothers as junior nursemaid and later as housekeeper. She served the poor on her family's estate far in the west of Ireland. There was not much future in it. Then when she was twenty-seven she captured the catch of the Irish marriage market, sixty-three-year-old Sir William Gregory, master of neighboring Coole Park, a former colonial governor of Ceylon, a delightful and cultured gentleman who moved in the highest social circles in Ireland and England. She was, she wrote, "happy in the thought of being with him, of serving him." At his death when she was forty, she put on mourning and continued to wear it, long after her sorrow was gone, for the remaining forty years of her life. It was the appropriate costume for her role as a dutiful woman. She edited several books about her husband's family, she collected folklore for Ireland, and she again captured the one man in Ireland who could do her the most good, the thirty-one-year-old poet William Butler Yeats, poor, overworked, and ready for all the good she could do him.

She looked after him at Coole Park, she loaned him money, bought furniture for his flat in London, sympathized with his hopeless love for Maud Gonne, collected folklore for his collections, wrote pleasant dialogue for his plays, founded the Irish theater with him. . . . Their relationship, as complex, rewarding, and limiting as a marriage, was the masterstroke of her life—and immensely important to his. As he wrote, "I doubt I should have done much with my life but for her firmness and care." And, as she wrote him on her deathbed, "I have had a full life & except for grief of parting with those who have gone, a happy one. I do think I have been of use to the country. & for that in great part I thank you." Serving him, founding the Abbey Theatre with him, she found at last the broadest, most congenial and rewarding objects of service: Ireland and literature.

But there was a break in the continuity of her service. When she

6

was fifty, in the middle of a renaissance, when she was busier and happier than she had ever been, in the service of Yeats, the Irish theater, Ireland, and literature, she set out to write plays. Unlike Yeats, who was continually making the night sea-journey through his soul, she was suddenly dunked into her subconscious—and discovered her creativity. She came up gasping, "*Sein fein,* 'we ourselves'—is well enough for the day's bread, but is not *Mise Fein*—'I myself'—the last word in Art?"

Her short comedies are explosions of laughter. Her patriotic plays touch immediately a deep tribal identification with the Irish people united against an oppressor. All her plays provide a satisfying, touching demonstration of the power of the psyche to balance itself, to supply in one form the love and freedom denied in another. Many of her plays were very popular. She never stood centerstage at the Abbey, spread her arms, and exulted, "I made it!" But she did smile and bow. Drama scholar Una Ellis-Fermor wrote of her creativity: "Few men or women have had so rich a flowering so late in life and kept unsuspected by themselves or others, so rich a genius unused and yet unsoured. Truly she could say with Hans Andersen, 'My life has been a wonderful fairly tale.' "

I

Last Days in the West

CHILDHOOD AND YOUTH: 1852–1880

> *Everyone is used in Ireland to the trag-*
> *edy that is bound up with the lives of*
> *the farmers and fishing people; but in*
> *this garden one seemed to feel the trag-*
> *edy of the landlord class also.*
>
> J. M. SYNGE, *Journals*

ISABELLA Augusta Persse was born at midnight on March 15, 1852, the twelfth in a family of sixteen children of Protestant land-owners in the west of Ireland. She was descended from nearly every party to the wavelike history of conquest and resistance that had been Ireland's history for seven hundred years. The O'Gradys, her maternal grandmother's family, were native Irish—turned Protestant in the early eighteenth century to escape the restrictions placed on Catholics. The Barrys, her maternal grandfather's family, were the oldest English invaders. One ancestor arrived as a military officer with the Earl of Essex to suppress Hugh O'Neill's rebellion against Queen Elizabeth. Another was Lord Deputy of Ireland under Charles I—until he was thrown into prison; yet another led the Irish armies against Cromwell. Augusta Persse was not interested in ancestors; the one of whom she was most proud was a French Huguenot great-great-grandmother from whom she received a diamond Maltese cross and

8

a Bible inscribed "Frances Algoin her Book—Ist January 1724/5."

The great estate upon which she was born had been bought by her great-great-great-great-grandfather Dudley Persse, a successful and favored Church of Ireland clergyman, in the late seventeenth century. This gentleman held five profitable church appointments and received large land grants from Charles II and James II. The family fortune was thus founded on royal favor and tithes of Catholic tenants to a church they abhorred. Augusta never looked back and figured out her past; she merely said, acquiescing in her fall, "God knows many of my ancestors and forerunners have eaten and planted sour grapes and we must not repine if our teeth are set on edge."

The estate had originally been called by the Irish name of Cregroostha. Dudley Persse changed it to Roxborough and gave Scots Border names to other places on the land—calling the hunting lodge in the mountains Chevy Chase—in honor of his descent from the Persses of Northumberland. (Hotspur, young Henry Percy of *Henry IV* fame, was an ancestor.)

The descendants of Dudley Persse married sons and daughters of neighboring landowners, the Parsons, Croftons, Ormsbys, Blakeneys, and Wades. Local government was under their control. During the eighteenth century the Blakeneys held the post of High Sheriff for County Galway six times, the Persses three times. These families also held the post of Deputy Lieutenant for County Galway, the local representative of the Lord Lieutenant of Ireland appointed by the English crown. Thus Catholic tenants who cut turf in their landlord's bog, or let their cattle graze in their landlord's field, or burned their landlord's house (as Castle Blakeney was burned), were almost always judged by a Protestant landlord—a system of justice which reinforced the traditional Celtic inclination to regard lawbreakers as heroes. (In 1900 Augusta wrote an article called "The Felons of Our Land" for an English magazine in which she stated, "I have known the hillsides ablaze with bonfires when prisoners were released, not because they were believed to be innocent, but because they were believed to be guilty.")

Irish affairs, in so much as the Irish were permitted to manage their own affairs, were under control of her ancestors. Six Blakeneys, two of them married to Persses, held the same seat in the Irish Parliament during almost all of the eighteenth century. In the 1770's her great-grandfather William Persse organized and paid for his own small army, the Roxborough Volunteers, as part of a widespread movement to force England to grant Ireland more self-government. (William Persse was a correspondent of George Washington; there was a stuffed

9

turkey in a glass case at Roxborough to prove it.) When England, whose armies were busy in America, did, temporarily, grant Ireland its own Parliament, William Persse erected a plaque, the lichen-grown letters of which his great-granddaughter traced thoughtfully: "IN MEMORY OF IRELAND'S EMANCIPATION FROM FOREIGN JURISDIC-TION"—which meant something far more revolutionary in her day than in his. In her day "emancipation" encompassed, as it did not in his, the emancipation of the Irish tenant from the Irish landlord.

The huge estate of Roxborough was at times a rallying point for tenant hatred. In 1820 "Ribbonmen"—one of the secret tenant socie-ties pledged to revenge themselves on landlords for the injustices for which they could not obtain legal redress—attacked Roxborough. Masked men gathered under a large oak tree on the lawn and fired at the house. Augusta's father and his younger brothers—their father was away—fired back. The masked men slowly dispersed. In the morning the household, family and servants, came out to look at trails of blood leading away from the tree.

The economic position of those landlords—the Persses among them—who did not concern themselves with their tenants' welfare was improved by the great famine of 1845 to 1847. Their neighbor Lord Gort at Lough Cutra, on the other hand, bankrupted himself feed-ing the poor. Robert Gregory, father of Augusta's future husband, died of famine fever working among them. (William Gregory described the scene when he returned to Coole at his father's death: "I well re-member the poor wretches being housed up against my demesne wall in wigwams of fir branches. . . . There was nothing I ever saw so hor-rible as the appearance of those who were suffering from starvation. The skin seemed drawn tight like a drum to the face, which became covered with small light-coloured hairs like a gooseberry. This, and their hollow voices, I can never forget.") Death and emigration took one fourth of the population, and many landlords, including the Pers-ses, realized that raising sheep and cattle was more profitable than collecting rent.

Tenants who had not abandoned their holdings were evicted. In later years another secret society was formed to obtain revenge, this time against Augusta's father, Dudley, whose own father had given him the management of Roxborough upon his first marriage. The plotters were betrayed and a list of their names was put into Dudley's hands. Dudley went to his father in a fury, swearing he would have them all arrested and transported. His father merely reached over, took the list from his hand, and threw it on the fire. The conspiracy also faded like smoke. The feeling of being inferior, of being constantly watched by priest, God, and Mary, or by one's fellow conspirators, was so close to the feeling of being watched by the incalculable hostile power of the landlord that continual confusion resulted as conspirators, in a panic, suddenly felt exposed and bound to their former enemy. Informers and traitors, irresolution and inaction appear nearly as often in the story of Irish resistance as stories of courage, loyalty, and effective action.

Dudley Persse had married the Honorable Katherine O'Grady in 1826—"Honorable" because she was the daughter of a baron, Standish O'Grady, who was Viscount Guillamore, Baron of Rockbarton, and for many years Lord Chief Baron of the Exchequer in Ireland. Katherine's younger brother William O'Grady also came with his sister as Archdeacon of the diocese of Kilmacduagh near Roxborough. Son of a baron or not, he had to have a profession. Church revenues came chiefly from Catholic tenants, as tithes were payable not by the owner of the land, but by those who farmed it. Land in pasturage for sheep and cattle was—since landlords had most of this land and they were making the law—exempt from church tithes. (When William Gregory, then a member of Parliament, voted with the majority in 1869 to disestablish the Church of Ireland and abolish its tithes, he commented, "I had no objection to a State Church both in England and Ireland, but I had the strongest objection to a State Church of a minority.")

Katherine Persse lived less than three years after her marriage. Her brother christened her children in the little Killinane church on the estate, first Katherine, then Maria, then Dudley, the all-important male heir to whom she gave birth five weeks before she died.

Four years later Dudley Persse, then thirty-one, handsome and rich, married his first wife's first cousin Frances Barry of Castle Cor, co-heir with her brother to their father's considerable estate in County Cork. (Her brother also married a Persse, a daughter of Burton Persse of Moyode.) Frances Barry was seventeen, "bright and strong," when she became the stepmother of three children aged four, five, and six. William Gregory, a year younger than his future mother-in-law, told of seeing her for the first time at a rowdy house party, "a very pretty woman not long married, dressed in white of an evening with pearl decorations." Frances Persse, like her daughter Augusta, had long-term staying power. Over the next twenty-six years she would bear thirteen children at the more leisurely pace of one every two years.

Dudley Persse and Frances Barry were well suited to each other. They both loved movement for its own sake. They visited Dudley's

11

father at his Galway house. They stayed at their house near the sea at the Burren (called Mount Vernon after the family friendship with George Washington), they stayed at their fishing cottage on Lough Corrib, spent summers at Newcastle, their estate near Galway on the River Corrib, and held shooting meets at their hunting lodge on Slieve Echtge.

They both had the harshness of the secure who yet feel threatened. Dudley Persse was greedy. When his father died in 1850 leaving Roxborough to him and the adjoining estate of Castleboy to his brother Robert Henry, he started a long, acrimonious lawsuit to obtain the estate from his brother. The suit kept him poor for many years, but it ruined his brother, and eventually he got what he wanted.

Though tenacious, he was short-sighted. He set up a sawmill and began cutting timber. The money went to lawyers and many passing flings at the Kildare Street Club in Dublin. His oldest son and heir objected so violently to the cutting of what he considered his trees that he left home and joined the army.

Dudley Persse ate and drank excessively, and continued to do so even after gout deprived him of the use of his legs.

He continued to give such offense to his tenants that a sniper once lay in wait for him along the route he was to take to Galway to preside at the Assizes as High Sheriff. An attack of gout had kept him safe at home. (An Irish judge commented on the shooting of landlords: "I never met an instance of a landlord being killed, who did not deserve—I don't say to be hanged, as I am a judge—but I do say, a case of the kind never came before me that the landlord did not deserve to be *damned!*")

Dudley's wife, however, had a remedy. She was a disciple of an evangelical preacher, the Reverend John Cuming of Scotland, whose books had an enormous popularity at the time, and whose message was: "Tremble at sin. Plague, pestilence, famine are nothing to sin. These scathe the body, it blasts the soul. These have but a temporary effect, while sin creates an eternal woe. But through Christ I am washed from my sins by that precious blood, alike from their curse, their condemnation, and all their penal consequences." Augusta later remarked that her mother had taught her father the lessons of her evangelical religion so well that he believed "You might be greedy, untruthful, uncharitable, dishonest—in moderation—that did not really matter, you would be 'washed in the blood' at last."

The complicity between mother and father did not, however, include equality. Dudley Persse did as he liked, paying his wife compliments or giving her dresses to pacify her. Not having any real con-

12

trol over her life, Frances Persse took it upon herself to change the lives of those around her. She, her two stepdaughters, and her own oldest daughter, Elizabeth, all considered converting Catholics of prime importance to their own salvation. Maria was rumored to have offered a suit of clothes and a half-sovereign to anyone who would spit on a picture of the Virgin Mary. Katie once engaged in a hand-to-hand struggle with a priest over the raising of an orphan, each of them holding on to an arm of the bewildered child. Katie, who married and went to England in 1862, was remembered for years afterward by the country people, the subject of a satiric poem about her supposed attempt to convert an ass to Protestantism, ending:

> This orange rip she raised her whip, to knock the donkey down
> When a multitude of asses soon her did surround.
> They tore her flounces to rags, to set their brother free,
> So here's a glass for every ass who fights for Popery!

The country people endured the attempt to convert them with more good humor than the Persse women had in making it. Though Frances and her daughters were concerned with souls, they were well aware of the huge imbalance in numbers between Catholic and Protestant; the 1862 census revealed it to be twenty-four to one in the west of Ireland. Feeling themselves to be a tiny minority holding their privileged position in the vast darkness of Catholic Ireland, their attempt at conversion contained a good deal of aggression, self-interest, and fear.

Frances Persse first gave birth to Richard Dudley, then William Norton, then Edward, then Elizabeth, Adelaide, Algernon, Gertrude, and Arabella. Becoming pregnant with her ninth child in June of 1851 was not a special event. During her pregnancy she and her husband made their first journey outside Ireland since their honeymoon trip to Germany twenty-one years and eight children earlier. They visited Bath, where they made friends with a Miss Isabella Augusta Brown. "Isabella Augusta" had the sonority of the family names, which had been exhausted, and was remembered when the Persses returned to Roxborough.

At midnight of March 15, 1852, the planet Jupiter stood at midheaven. The moon was rising. The planets Jupiter, Uranus and the sun together, and Mars formed a great triangle in the sky, the "grand trine" of astrologers, promising success, power, and prosperity. Though the stars were welcoming, the mother was not. Frances Persse, passionate in what might be thought a matter of indifference, was bit-

13

terly disappointed the new baby was not a boy. The baby girl was laid aside and temporarily forgotten. When the baby was remembered, she was nearly dead. A quilt had accidentally been thrown over her. After everyone was sure the baby would live, her mother remarked that she "would have been sorry for such a loss, because the other children would have been disappointed at not having a new baby to play with." That was the only welcome Augusta ever got.

She was taken to the little Killinane church to be christened "Isabella Augusta" by her cousin William O'Grady. (The family brought their *famille rose* christening basin, as the plain white one in the church was cracked.) The little girl hated the name "Isabella" and was teased by her brothers and sisters with a long rhyming poem about "Isabella and her gingham umbrella." She disliked "Augusta" as being too dignified—but no one called her anything else, and as the years passed, she accepted the instruction and became very dignified indeed. From the first she missed that vital internal reciprocity, that sense of being at ease and pleased with herself.

One of her first memories was of the nurse telling her, with neither indignation nor comfort, the story of her birth, her near-death, and her mother's comment, which Augusta seemed to interpret as a kind of conditional salvation. Though every female child of her time and class was taught she was to live for others, Augusta believed it more than most. (She also, all her life, preferred boys to girls.) Never greeted with delight for herself, she looked for value in the circle around her rather than the center inside herself.

Augusta and Arabella, her sister just two years older, were looked after by Mary Sheridan, a Catholic, Gaelic-speaking nurse. Mary had two daughters of her own, one dearly loved, who had emigrated to America. Reversing the relationship between parents left at home and every other daughter or son who emigrated, every month Mary sent part of her wages to her children.

Augusta was the seventeenth child of Mary's nursing career, which had included, before coming to Roxborough, the ten children of the famous rebel Hamilton Rowan. Augusta was Mary's seventh Persse baby, but twenty-five months after she arrived, Francis Fitz Adelm arrived; seventeen months later Henry was born; twenty-three months after that, Gerald Dillon arrived; and eighteen months later Alfred Lovaine was born—the last of Frances Persse's thirteen children. Mary had little time for Augusta, who in any case described her as "that proud old nurse."

All her life Augusta was looking after someone. She started with her four younger brothers. She shared their secrets, played their

14

games, accompanied them everywhere, until the increasing distinctions of sex kept her at home while they were free to roam. They did not return her care; she did not tell them her secrets. The pattern was set early for the relative isolation in which she passed her life—surrounded by people who were either inferiors or superiors, but by none who returned her glance as an equal or gave her a sense of herself as an individual. In fact, when she came to write her autobiography, she was unable to remember or imagine herself as a young child and finally wrote the first chapter in the third person, referring to herself not as "I" but as "she" and "this little-welcomed girl."

The younger children lived in the girls' and boys' nurseries, separated by a wide, dusky passage, up under the high eaves on the third floor. In realms below were the older sisters, Gertrude, Adelaide, and Elizabeth. Beyond them were the older boys, William, Richard, Edward, and Algernon, who, only seven years older than Augusta, occasionally joined the younger children at their games. Her half-brother, Dudley, wounded at the Battle of Alma in the Crimea two years after she was born, was only a legend. The two half-sisters, Katie and Maria, hardly impinged on her consciousness; to her they were merely "elder daughters of the house."

The house itself, continuously occupied by prolific and quarrelsome Persses for 160 years, was part of her parentage. Augusta thought it "not beautiful, quite the reverse," yet she was obviously proud of the commanding social statement it made to the surrounding countryside. It was very large, three stories high, with many wings, and no particular architectural pretensions except two pseudo-Gothic towers, matching the pseudo-Gothic gatehouse added early in the century. The roof was slate, the walls whitewashed stucco. In Augusta's day there were flowerboxes at the windows. The house gave, and Augusta accepted, an impression of well-worn wealth and solidity.

Outside, a wide lawn sloped down to a lake. The creek from it flowed under the Volunteer Memorial Bridge and through the deer park. Sallies, bullrushes, coots, and wild fowl lived, and otters played, along its bank. The children played in a bed of soft mud. The stream then divided, one branch going underground, the other flowing by the villages on the estate, past more wide lawns covered in spring with daffodils, and finally to the high road, where it passed out of the Persse demesne.

Near the house was the three-acre garden surrounded by walls ten feet high, designed not so much to prevent thievery as to cut the high winds that, during severe storms, dashed salt water on the windows of the house from the Atlantic many miles to the west. Fruit trees were

15

espaliered on the inside walls of the garden; the paths were lined with gooseberry bushes and strawberries. Flowers and vegetables grew together, violets and artichokes, lilies and asparagus, in great profusion.

Behind the house and garden and farm buildings rose the gentle, heather-covered slopes of Slieve Echtge. Often one looked at them through mist or rain; Augusta called it "not rain but foggy dew on my cheek." (Her father's acquaintance, the novelist Charles Lever, had a more severe description of the Irish rain:"that steady persistence, that persevering monotony of down-pour, which, not satisfied with wetting you to the skin, seems bent upon converting your very blood into water.") Looking at the hills, especially in the morning, Augusta could see herds of "quickly startled deer."

The house and grounds were alive with servants, most of them country people from nearby villages. The Persses did not travel enough to acquire, as did their neighbors the Gregorys, a French maid or an Italian butler. The Persse servants were Catholic and Gaelic-speaking. One Protestant, an enthusiastic convert, was in charge of the main avenue leading to the house. Anxious to keep it from being turned into a tow-path, he called out to the barefoot women bringing their husbands potatoes and milk for dinner, and called out to the gentry too, "Ladies and gentlemen, you're welcome to pass, but walk on the gravel, not on the grass!"

Servants were also in charge of the plumbing. Water from the lake was brought to the house in barrels and carried in buckets to reservoirs on each landing. Under every bed was a chamberpot, emptied by a servant every morning and evening.

Housekeeping at Roxborough was a complex and exuberant affair. The household consumed a sheep a week and a cow a month. There was fish from the lake, venison, woodcock, pheasant, and rabbit from the hillsides. The garden provided fruits and vegetables. Waste timber from the sawmill was stacked in sheds, and turf for cutting lay in the bog. That his household was able to live off the fruits of his estate was a tribute to Dudley Persse's effectiveness as a manager. Many Irish landlords found it cheaper to live abroad—order lamb chops at the *table d'hote* and pay accordingly—than to supervise the slaughter and efficient use of the whole beast at home.

All around the house stood the outbuildings necessary to a great working estate: cow barns, dairies, stables, kennels, blacksmith shop, carpenter shop, carriage house. On the stream was the infamous sawmill with its great black boiler attended by engineers and turners. Every morning the laborers filed through the yard to their work.

16

There were gardeners, herdsmen, dairy maids, smiths, carpenters, gamekeepers, and trappers. Sheep, cows, and goats were also led through the yard. Besides his horses and hounds for hunting, the Gordon setters, retrievers, and greyhounds, Dudley Persse kept an Irish deerhound, larger than a young pony, which accompanied him everywhere. To Augusta it was "a hive of life." Her father, the Master, sat in the middle in his wheeled chair, supervising it all. Augusta never saw him walk.

Even in a wheelchair, with a rug around his legs that looked like a skirt, her father was, as a countryman described him, "a fierce looking man to look at." He had side whiskers, huge teeth, bright eyes—a face made to glower. When not in his chair, he rode his tall white horse or drove a little donkey cart, for which paths with wicket gates had been laid out all over the estate. He always carried a shotgun, and the back of the cart would be full of the birds and rabbits he shot as he went about his business. Augusta seems never to have talked with him. His words were orders to be obeyed instantly. Looking back on his death in 1878, just before the beginning of the land troubles, she wrote, "I am glad he did not see them. The breaking of his absolute power would have been a hard work."

Her relationship with her mother, whom everyone, servants and children, called "the Mistress," was perhaps even more unsatisfactory because her denigration was more personal. One of Augusta's earliest memories was of a wonderful painted wooden bird she bought with her pocket money. When her mother saw it, she exclaimed, "You don't mean to say you have been throwing away your money on that rubbish!" To Augusta "her words were the breaking of a happy dream." She spent the day in dread that her mother would scold her again at dinner in front of all the brothers and sisters.

Augusta's family subscribed fully to the prevalent doctrine that a woman's right to be loved depended upon her beauty. Augusta was considered very plain, and she grew so slowly it was many years before she could see her eyes in the mirror over the dining-room fireplace and check for herself. She was frail, never recovering completely from an early attack of whooping cough. But she had an attentive, intelligent face, dark eyes, and straight, dark hair. (William Gregory later insisted he had seen her as a child and said to her mother, "That is the prettiest of all your daughters.") In her youth her beautiful hands, of which she was later touchingly proud, were disfigured by chilblains and she kept them out of sight.

In spite of the stacked timber, the bog full of peat, and sea coal which sold for fifteen shillings a ton, Roxborough was a cold house.

17

Augusta wrote that her mother "would not willingly allow a fire to be lighted in the schoolroom until the dahlias had been cut down by frost."

Except for the fire, no one paid much attention to what went on in the schoolroom. The girls were taught by a series of "amiable, incompetent" governesses. These young women also seem to have been lonely, depressed, and socially humiliated, but Augusta never had much sympathy with female distress. She wrote, "I don't think our first governess, Miss W——, knew much. She was from Dublin, very pretty in a straw bonnet with a bunch of faded magenta ribbons. When we went for a walk she liked going a mile or so towards Athenry, and would look longingly down the road and say, '115 miles to Dublin.'" Another governess was a Miss C——, "whose father had been an officer . . . and who had a photograph of herself dressed up for a fairy ball as 'Night' with a crown of stars." The governesses exercised their emotions by having crushes on the local curates.

Augusta was slow to learn to read, and the Wesleyan clerk who tutored them would say soothingly when the others laughed and she blushed with shame, "Augusta's steady, slow and sure." She was also slow at arithmetic, partly because her brothers were so good they did her work for her. But she had one triumphant moment proving the Rule of Three, and she remembered Arabella, usually ahead of her, ruffling her hair, with tears in her eyes, exclaiming despairingly, "Will it be more? Or will it be less?"

A French tutor was hired for the boys, and as long as he was there, the girls were permitted to learn from him too. The girls were taught everything else out of a few standard history texts. When the governesses asked for more books, the Mistress would ask if the girls could answer all the questions in the old ones. They never could. The Mistress's idea of education was simple: "Religion and courtesy, and holding themselves straight, these were to her mind the three things needful." Augusta was scolded frequently for tilting her head when she got excited. (Jacob Epstein captured the same tilt in his bust of her done in 1911.)

The Mistress herself provided an example in courtesy, "having fine manners." Not liking to give her mother credit for anything, Augusta thought they were "inherited perhaps from that French ancestress Frances Algoin." The French tutor later told Augusta, and she recounted in her autobiography, how he had arrived at Roxborough, "a frightened stranger, after a nine miles drive along a dreary road," when "a tall lady in black velvet and diamonds had come to the open hall door and welcomed him to Ireland with a friendliness he remembered through half a hundred years." (The Mistress also tried to convert him while he was at Roxborough, though he told her he was a Protestant, translating from an open Bible in her hand, "Babylon est *tombé, tombé, tombé*.") Frances Persse's friendliness did not necessarily mean she felt friendly, as it was a point of pride with her never "to appear impatient with the dullness or ill-manners of a guest."

Augusta's early life, passed in the midst of continual activity and great natural beauty, was achingly unsatisfactory. But there were so many distractions, she hardly realized it. In summer the whole family went to Newcastle, their grandfather's old estate north of Galway on the River Corrib between the lake and the sea. They had a whole fleet of boats there and would row up the river to the lake, where their father fished for trout, or down the river to Galway town, where their mother shopped. The children played jacks on the wide porch or hide-and-seek in the half-ruined distillery adjoining the house. (One branch of the family was in the brewing business.)

Every day at Newcastle two servants sat at a little table covered with scraps of silk and feathers, tying flies for the trout and salmon fishing. Augusta sat with them to tie flies for her brothers. The children were also taken to Galway town to watch the men fishing for salmon in the river. At first Augusta could see nothing; then, looking straight down, she saw "one fish, then another, then hundreds and thousands of the great shoal, each fish keeping its place in the current." One bridge over the river was by Galway jail, and Augusta, as she watched her father and brothers, occasionally looked up and wondered what it would be like to be inside.

The Master once told them to expect a small package at the post office, and on arriving, they found a horse-drawn omnibus. The older children clambered inside, the younger ones swarmed over the roof. Thereafter the omnibus carried them about the estate and took them to the ocean for sea bathing. Old Sibby, who looked after them at Newcastle, believed in the efficacy of tobacco smoke to prevent colds, so before going into the water they each had to take three puffs from her pipe. (When Augusta was in Egypt after her marriage and saw an elegant lady take out a cigarette and light it, she had a sudden vision of Old Sibby in the surf with her red petticoats tucked up and her short black pipe in her mouth. The vision remained: "I have seen a queen and an empress puff their cigarettes and could not forget Sibby.")

Once a week at Newcastle a cart arrived with provisions from Roxborough, and the children ran shrieking to meet it.

Newcastle was a place of general relaxation. Augusta remembered the Master testing a younger brother to see if he had memorized the Bible verse and could be given his weekly sixpence.

"In the beginning," said my father.
"In the beginning," said the child.
"God created the heavens and earth."
"Yes."
"Good boy! A prize!"

Augusta, who had a very good memory, was once refused her sixpence because of some slight slip. When she bought a trinket a few weeks later on credit, she passed days in terror lest she again fail to get her sixpence and be unable to pay her debt. During the long church service before the weekly recitation, she had visions of herself persecuted like their neighbor Sir Val Blake, called "Sunday" Blake because he could not leave his castle except on Sundays for fear of bailiffs. Augusta said her Bible verse perfectly, got her sixpence, paid her debt. The pattern was set. She went on paying debts—not so much for herself as for her family, husband, and friends, really paying the dues of her declining class—for the rest of her life.

The few weeks spent at Chevy Chase in the mountains were a time of even greater parental relaxation. The children were permitted to go alone with only a few maids and the old caretaker to supervise them. The old hunting lodge with its deerhorn decorations and moss-covered walls was a beautiful place to Augusta. The flashing streams and the deer moving past in the moonlight were even more delightful. For Augusta, who was at ease only with the younger brothers, it was a time of absolute happiness.

Life at Roxborough was more constrained. She had the sense of always being in a crowd and under examination. Every day her mother read the Bible to family and servants, a chapter of the Old Testament in the morning, the New Testament in the evening. The genealogies were skipped, but everything else was read unexpurgated, "giving," as Augusta said, "no offense to our ignorance." She was all her life grateful for the "driving force, the training to the ear, the moving of the imagination, the kindling of the spiritual side of nature through much listening to the English of the Bible." After the reading the children were examined on what they had heard. They stood around the Mistress, who sat beside the dining-room fire; they were not permitted to come closer than the edge of the hearthrug.

On Sundays they attended church twice. The stressfulness of the

20

Mistress's proselytizing was in strange contrast to the hominess of their church. "The friendly little Killinane church," as Augusta called it, was attended by neighbors from two or three estates; and there was the customary greeting and gossip before and after service. The creaking harmonium was covered by a blanket to keep out the damp, until the sexton took the blanket home to his bed and the harmonium creaked even more. During the service the sexton would bring in an armload of twigs and dump them in the stove. The fire crackled cozily. The children sat in their upholstered pews with a view of the young pheasants playing in the nettles outside. When brother Richard, taking himself seriously as a law student and future judge, told the sexton to mow the nettles, the sexton, who knew who had power in God's house, refused indignantly: "And what would the Master say if I was to cut them before the young pheasants were reared?"

On Sundays the children could not work or play. They were read to out of instructive books for children. Being told that "This is Sunday Sabbath Day; This is why we must not play," the boys would whisper, "This is Sunday Sabbath night; This is why we'll have a fight." For a time the children were examined every evening from a card beginning, "What sin have I this day committed in thought, word or deed?" But they were so much more anxious to tell on each other than to remember their own "sins" that the questioning was given up. Though Augusta would later refer with great solemnity to "the cloud of witnesses" whom she felt watched and judged her, that sense of being watched had its beginning not in religion but in her early experience of being surrounded by a cloud of eager little tattletales. Though she was, she later insisted, "very good," she was often scolded.

After dinner and prayers the family sat in the drawing room. In Augusta's youth, landlords did not fear their tenants, and light from their lamp streamed out on the lawn through the open windows. The Mistress made tea and sometimes read an article from the *Times* aloud. Except for her reading and Gertrude's piano playing, they sat in silence. Only gradually did Augusta begin to sort out the crowd of older brothers and sisters. Gertrude was "the musical, the gay one." Adelaide was the beauty. She did needlework in the evenings. Augusta's oldest sister, Elizabeth, was "the clever one"; she too did needlework. Arabella was the agreeable one. She seems to have wanted to be Augusta's friend, but Augusta, who had learned early that boys were more important, was not interested in companions from "the weaker side." Arabella, whom Augusta always considered especially intelligent, perhaps because she was always two years ahead as they

21

were growing up, would pick up the *Times* and look at it also. Augusta was too shy to do anything but sit and be part of the circle and turn the pages of a few display books that lay on the table.

Her half-brother, Dudley, still kept away, living in lodgings and at the Kildare Street Club in Dublin, waiting to inherit Roxborough. On one of his few visits she saw that he was "very quiet in manner, very kind, very handsome, with fair hair and beard and blue eyes." He gave her the first pound note she ever had to spend at a bazaar. Richard, her oldest full brother, second in line to inherit, was studying law in Dublin. On visits home he "seemed to look with disapproval on the younger brothers and sisters." Shy Augusta, who suffered most from his sarcasm, was the special butt of his dissatisfaction.

Besides her brothers and sisters, she was surrounded in every direction by relatives. There were six branches of Persses living on country estates in Galway; the Blakeneys were her cousins many times over; Lord and Lady Clanmorris were both cousins. In addition, the similarity of interests among the landlord class was so great that the class itself was almost an extension of the family. There was much socializing. Every year the Persses held a great three-day shooting meet with a fourth day at Chevy Chase on Slieve Echtge. The younger children followed the hunters and beaters and keepers on foot, nibbling sandwiches as they went.

Remembering stories of the moonlight attack on Roxborough, Augusta wanted very much to learn to shoot. Though the Master permitted the gamekeeper to put a shotgun in her hands, he never permitted her to fire anything but a copper cap.

Though it was considered a social asset in other great houses, at Roxborough girls were not permitted to hunt. As Augusta's brothers grew older, they rode with the famous pack of hounds bred by their cousin Burton Persse at Moyode Castle, who remained Master of Fox Hounds for thirty-three years. Those who rode with them called themselves the Galway Blazers because one of their early festivities was so enthusiastic that the hotel where it was being held burned down. Their riding was enthusiastic too, over stone walls set so close together, around such small fields, they could feel they were in the air most of the time. Irish novelist Charles Lever once heard the Marquis of Clanricarde call out to Dudley Presse, who had just cleared a high wall that hid a steep drop, "What's on the other side, Dudley?" and heard the answer come up from below, "I am, thank God."

Augusta, who said she felt little attraction for this "jolly county society," nevertheless wanted very much to hunt. She accompanied her four younger brothers on their rambles about the estate and occasionally managed a horseback ride with them and the pack of harriers. Once they took the foxhounds, which, after a thrilling run across fields and creeks, over walls and fences, led them to the lawn in front of Roxborough, in full sight of her astonished father, who ordered her off her horse at once. Augusta never rode again.

Her first love was not for people, but for the beautiful land around her, the heather-covered slopes of Slieve Echtge, the gray-green fields, the wide view to the west of the sun on the sea. She wrote to her grandchildren when she was old, "I don't know if you will ever love Coole with the strength of passion with which I loved Roxborough." Only outside, alone, unsupervised, was she enough of a person to have the power to love.

The beloved land did not long remain unpersonified. She began to love "Ireland," not the Ireland of the family who weighed upon her, but the Ireland that was, like her, oppressed. She caught every flash of rebellion in the atmosphere around her. Once she heard her nurse Mary Sheridan, who avowed her loyalty to the landlord class, in eager conversation with a white-haired beggar woman telling how, as a child, she had been in a theater when news was brought that the French had landed at Killala and all the people had suddenly stood up and shouted. The beggar woman remembered Killala too. And from that shred of conversation, animating Mary Sheridan, who "so seldom condescended," bridging the gap between the highest and lowest of the servant class, Augusta understood something of the poignant and vital bond that brought together those united against an oppressor.

Another time Mary told the children about her former employer Hamilton Rowan, who was a Protestant landlord like the Persses. He was forced to flee Ireland with a price on his head because of his active membership in the United Irishmen, a Belfast-based organization for an independent Ireland. Augusta was moved by the story "of his escape from prison in which he was aided by his heroic wife and of the boatmen from whom he tried to hide his face until they said, 'We know you very well, Mr. Rowan, and the reward that's on your head and there is no fear that we will betray you.' " Here—instead of a wife teaching her husband to be greedy, a father destroying his son's patrimony, parents limiting their child's experiences, ignoring their child's individuality—here was recognition, approval, and a wide and encompassing loyalty.

Mary Sheridan also told of how she had seen Hamilton Rowan— reading in the newspaper about a trial that angered him—suddenly fling a knife at a portrait of Lord Norbury, the judge, which hung most

23

opportunely on the wall of the breakfast room in front of him. Here was resistance. Walking about the estate, Augusta paused reverently before the plaque erected by her great-grandfather: "IN MEMORY OF IRELAND'S EMANCIPATION FROM FOREIGN JURISDICTION." Here was some sort of sanction for rebellion. . . .

Her great-grandfather and Hamilton Rowan were particularly safe heroes. William Persse had been, for his time at least, on the winning side. Hamilton Rowan had been pardoned by the King; he returned to his beautiful estate in Ireland to live in peace and comfort, there to father the many children cared for by Nurse Sheridan.

Augusta soon found the literature that reinforced the emotion of rebellion. It was sold in the little stationer's shop in Loughrea. Indeed, shopkeepers in market towns all over Ireland were doing a brisk trade in the songs of Young Ireland, which they usually called "Fenian" literature—giving the name of the current resistance movement to the previous one.

The Young Irelanders were an intellectual and literary group, mostly Protestants, who in the early 1840's set out to arouse national feeling by an emotional call for the unity of the Irish people, a great race with a great past and a great future, against the oppressor. Their movement was a prefiguration of the Irish Renaissance without its literary genius or hope of tangible success. Their legacy to the emotion of Irish rebellion was their songs.

The songs are those of brave, intelligent, passionate children—orphans trying to make themselves adults without the protection or guidance of parents. When Augusta wrote of them, she chose the last verse of Thomas Davis's "Lament for the Death of Eogan Roe O'Neill" as representative of them all:

We thought you would not die—we were sure you would not go
And leave us in our utmost need to Cromwell's cruel blow;
Sheep without a shepherd when the snow shuts out the sky,
O why did you leave us, Owen? Why did you die?

It is an orphan's lament. The last line, which she does not quote, is: "But we're slaves, we're orphans—Owen! why did you die?" The history of the Irish resistance to England was so full of lost leaders—defeated by the English, betrayed by their own people, abandoning their own people—that the real issue for the Irish became self-confidence, self-respect, and self-healing. But the presence of England confused and deflected this need. The necessity of unity against and resistance to the outside oppressor became paramount.

Though Augusta's immersion in the literature of Irish resistance expanded her life, teaching richer and kinder emotions than those learned from her family, in essence the role of Irish rebel called for the same subordination of the individual to the group that she experienced in her family. The great difference was that this subordination was made with joy, was rewarded with a rich feeling of group unity, and was made for a great purpose. A far light shone for freedom.

Though the Loughrea bookseller declared that "I look to Miss Augusta to buy all my Fenian books," her infatuation with rebel Ireland was mostly a private affair, known but unimportant to her brothers and sisters. Arabella, who was watching though she did not follow, gave her for her birthday a shilling copy of all the songs collected in *The Spirit of the Nation*. In their self-sufficient blindness the Master and Mistress knew nothing of Augusta's quiet rebellion.

Augusta's love of rebel Ireland called for no change in her attitude to the country people on the estate. Men and women lived, and begat children, in sheds hardly fit for animals. Manure was piled by the door of each cottage; the family slept on a pile of straw and animal hides inside. The tenants' animals, their chickens and pigs and goats, often lived inside with them. Tenants without a lease could be evicted on short notice and without cause; if they could not go to relatives, they could go to the workhouse, take to the roads, or emigrate to England or America. One of Augusta's contemporaries remembered "how they used to go away by train from Claremorris in great batches bawling like animals. There is no denying that we looked upon our tenants as animals, and that they looked on us as kings." Augusta saw the same sights, but she was not interested in economic oppression.

Neither was she interested in political oppression. Not all tenants were miserably poor, and under the Reform Bill of 1832 tenants paying over £50 per year in rent could vote. In the west of Ireland they voted as their landlords told them. William Gregory, who served during the years of Augusta's youth as member of Parliament for County Galway, could easily ascertain that he would be reelected simply by adding up the number of eligible tenants of each landlord who promised to support him. Augusta heard of another landlord who took his tenants to Galway, locked them in a barn for the night, and let them out to vote in the morning.

However, it was not possible to be a secret rebel without being touched by outside events. At first it was simply exciting. When Augusta was thirteen, her sister Adelaide, attending the balls and parties of the viceregal season in Dublin, wrote her family that in the intervals of a dance Lord S—— had told her to tell her family to send all their guns to the police barracks, as there were going to be Fenian raids on country houses to collect guns for the rebellion. The Persses did nothing, and neither did the Fenians; there was no rising.

A few months later, on September 15, 1865, the office of the *Irish People*, the newspaper of this supposedly secret society, was raided and editors arrested. James Stephens, the founder of the Fenians, escaped, was captured, was imprisoned, and escaped again within two weeks. According to one literary historian, "All witnesses reported that in surprise, excitement, and popular identification with the object of a hue and cry, Stephens's jailbreak was one of the high emotional peaks of Irish history." Augusta was surprised, excited, and moved to look for other sources of excitement.

Religion, with which she had been bombarded all her life, supplied the same spaciousness and rich emotions she got from her allegiance to rebel Ireland, but there were many drawbacks. She immediately rejected the aspect of it which impelled her mother and older sisters to proselytize Catholics. But she could not immediately reject Archdeacon Burkett, closer representative of religion, who had succeeded her cousin as rector at the Killinane church and whom neither she nor any of the children could respect because of his Waterford accent.

He encouraged the Mistress in her inclination to constrict life. He advised her not to let the children have dancing lessons. When they wanted to give a play of Cinderella, he advised against it, not because he saw any harm in it, but because "You can't tell where it might lead to!" (The children continued making up elaborate charades. Arabella with "her gift of mimicry and humour" was the star; Augusta was producer and director. Sometimes, "with a round cap and a waterproof," she played a policeman with credit. But more than any specific activity it was her family itself that trained Augusta as a playwright, that created her need for continuous attention to the changing reactions of the group.)

The children revenged themselves on Archdeacon Burkett by mimicking him. They imagined him being late to dinner at Roxborough and saying in his heavy Waterford accent, which Arabella reproduced to perfection, "Oive got an excuse! Oive had a bath! Oi don't approve of dirt!" Or they parodied his talks on the Holy Land, picturing him on a high, rolling camel with a little dissenting minister looking up at him and asking, "How do you feel now, Hoigh Church?"

They had an even more pleasant revenge when the Master, missing his trout fishing, had a water cart full of live trout brought from the River Corrib to the lake in front of the house. A few days later Archdeacon Burkett, who had permission to fish on the estate, landed fifty of them. According to Augusta, "we heard the Master's voice raised in anger."

An even greater difficulty posed by religion was the Athanasian Creed, read several times a year, which begins and ends with the stern warning: "Which faith except everyone keep whole and undefiled, without doubt, he shall perish everlastingly." The congregation also regularly sang the hymn "There is a dreadful hell, With everlasting pains, Where sinners must with devils dwell in darkness, fire and chains." And as this was a Protestant church, there was no possibility of Purgatory, no repentance or conversion at leisure. Augusta preferred not to get involved.

Being involved with the Fenians became more difficult also. In November 1867, when she was fifteen, an attempt was made to rescue two Fenian prisoners from a police van in Manchester. A policeman was shot in the attempt and three young Irishmen were convicted and hanged for his murder. The song inspired by their death was sung everywhere:

"God save Ireland," said the martyrs,
"God save Ireland," say we all,
"Whether on the scaffold high, or the battle field we die,
No matter if for Ireland dear we fall!"

Augusta began to draw away from the Irish rebels. She caught a whiff of what Ernest Hemingway called "the cheap Irish love of defeat." She knew she had something better to do with her life than die for her country. Religion, at least, offered a longer perspective.

After the attempt to free the Fenian prisoners in Manchester, an attempt was made to free other Fenians from Clerkenwell Prison in London. A huge charge of dynamite blew out the prison wall, blew out the side of the tenement across the street, killed twelve people, injured 120 others, and would have killed the Fenian prisoners had they been on that side of the jail. Augusta began to wonder if she was saved.

She wanted to know "What was the wall between her and heaven; the closed door between her and Christ? She would break it open by prayer; she would earn its unclosing by a blameless day. . . ." She never succeeded in having what she considered a blameless day, but she concentrated so hard she got sick and was taken to a doctor in Dublin. The doctor lifted her thin arm and declared that he had seen nothing like it since famine times. He prescribed travel.

She was sent to the family fishing lodge on Lake Corrib. There she continued to concentrate so hard on her problem that she solved it.

27

One morning "she rose up from her bed at peace with God. All doubts and fears had gone, she was one of His children, His angels were her friends."

Her conversion at fifteen was the first revelation of her creativity. She heaved off the huge weight of scrutinizing disapproval; by the subconscious transforming power of her psyche, she turned it into acceptance. As part of her conversion she specifically rejected rebel Ireland: "The ballads, the poems and patriotic songs had become as ashes." Her act of conversion was a replica of her birth scene, her near-death under the coverlet and her salvation because—as she interpreted it—her mother said the other children would be disappointed at not having another baby to play with. This time her salvation was no longer conditional. She still believed service to others was all-important, but now "She need no longer strive to do His will, it was her delight to do it."

Aside from salvation, the chief advantage of this arrangement, as well as its chief defect, was that other people did not count. The whole conduct of her life was a matter between herself and God and his angels. George Moore, the Irish writer, who in fact knew several of Augusta's brothers and sisters, wrote, "I imagine her without a mother, or father, or sisters, or brothers, *sans attaché*." Augusta wrote, "My first real memory of myself is at fifteen." She had found a way to distinguish herself from the crowd of brothers and sisters.

What immersion in the grievances of Ireland did not do, Christianity accomplished. Augusta felt the poverty of the country people around her. She took the poorest village on the estate as her special care: "going day after day the couple of miles on foot with food and comforts, saving her pocket money for such purposes, she visited the sick and clothed the children, and tended the dying." And never seems to have been aware of the irony of devoting her dress allowance of £30 per year to ameliorate conditions created by a system that permitted generations of Persses to take hundreds of pounds out of this same poor village. She was sometimes suspected of trying to convert the people she aided, and when she paid a teacher to teach sewing to the young girls on the estate, the priest ordered them to keep away. He did not change his mind even when she promised to have in attendance, not herself, but one of the Catholic Miss Dalys of Castle Daly.

Her charities, though important, were neither intellectually nor emotionally satisfying. She saw Arabella as "more gifted as I think by nature than myself, but one who for conscience sake surrounded herself with ministers and preachers without intellectual force or train-

28

ing." Augusta was not going to sacrifice her expansive intelligence to her narrow religion.

When Augusta was sixteen, the last governess was dismissed. Arabella was now "out" in society and it did not seem worthwhile to keep a governess for Augusta alone. Augusta's only formal lessons were drawing classes in Galway, but her education had been so negligent as to leave unimpaired her great natural desire for learning. Her self-education accelerated.

Though the Mistress was not enthusiastic about buying books, books nevertheless found their way into the house. One Christmas a large box arrived as a gift for the children to choose from. Gertrude (the gay, musical one) said frankly she did not care for reading but would choose the biggest, and took and laid on the drawing-room table the two volumes of Chambers's *Encyclopedia of English Literature*. For Augusta this was "the breaking of a new day, the discovering of a new world." She read the books straight through and then went back to read her favorite authors again and again. She knew now what to ask for at Christmas or, she added, "from a brother in good humour." (The boys always had more money than the girls because they were given a penny for each crow they shot, and, being very good shots, "they made a fortune.")

Mostly through her brothers and their friends, Augusta acquired Herbert's poems, Scott's poems (novels were not allowed), Burns, Montaigne, Arnold's essays, Clough, Hood, Keats, each new volume of Tennyson as it came out, and, "beyond all most enduring of joys, Malory's *Morte d'Arthur*." One Christmas she persuaded her mother to give her a six-volume edition of Browning, the poet "most understanding of us, the one who gives the heaven in and around us." After reading an article in the *Times* that made her think Browning might be an infidel, her mother was sorry she had given it. But for Augusta her favorite authors became, as had been the leaders of the Irish rebellions, a band of heroes devoted to freeing their readers from limited lives and narrow sympathies.

Augusta's special friend was Katherine Martin of Ross, whose special attraction was that she had for a friend the president of Queens College, Galway, who got her books from the college library which she passed on to Augusta. (Katherine Martin was an older sister of Violet Martin, like Augusta the youngest of many daughters, who with her cousin Edith Somerville was to write stories of the Irish gentry under the name of Somerville and Ross.)

Augusta began to learn German with a grammar and a German Bible. When neighbors hired a real German governess, Augusta went to stay with them. The patriotic songs were not ashes. She was elated on first penetrating the meaning of Heine's *Zwei Grenadier*, not realizing she was reacting to a poem that could have come straight out of *The Spirit of the Nation*.

Gradually the literature of rebel Ireland reoccupied its old place in her affections, seeming not to conflict after all with God and His angels. She decided she wanted to learn Gaelic. (She had the committed linguist's belief that the secret of life is in code—just about to be cracked.) Her edition of *The Spirit of the Nation* had a small dictionary of Irish phrases used in the songs, but this was not enough. She asked to have lessons from an old Scripture reader—a Protestant who had learned Gaelic in the hope of converting Catholics in their own language. It seemed a strange request and her family ignored it.

Gaelic, however, was not foreign to the family, as Frances Persse soon learned. Her cousin Standish Hayes O'Grady came visiting, just back from adventuring in America. He was a Gaelic scholar; the most absorbing activity of his life was translating the ancient epics. Believing he was interested in one of her daughters, Frances Persse sent him away, declaring that she "had a great dislike to the marriage of cousins." She also had a great dislike to marriage with young men with no money. A few years later O'Grady was off to Australia working on a sailing ship; a few years after that he was in London cataloguing the Irish manuscripts in the British Museum. In 1892 he published *Silva Gadelica*, his translations of old Irish literature.

Frances Persse's second cousin Standish James O'Grady was also leaving the traditional attitudes and occupations of his class and would become one of its severest critics, a popularizer of the Irish legends, a journalist, and an inspiration to W. B. Yeats, who, in a moment of exaggeration, called him the father of the Irish Renaissance. This O'Grady, along with his cousin Augusta, ended up in the same poem by Yeats, "Beautiful Lofty Things," described as "supporting himself between the tables / Speaking to a drunken audience high nonsensical words."

All three O'Grady cousins, Standish Hayes O'Grady, Standish James O'Grady, and Augusta Persse Gregory, were, if not the fathers and mother of the Irish Renaissance, among its first participants because they discovered, or rediscovered, a path to glory besides that of futile rebellion, on which so many high-spirited Irish people had perished.

Augusta wrote in a draft of her autobiography, "Those three—what shall I call them? passions, incentives, influences—which have dominated my life, love of country, faith in the spiritual life, delight in poetry and literature, had taken possession of me I think before I entered my seventeenth year." Augusta was busy and happy. No longer delicate, she had a vitality that would last, with only occasional lapses, for the rest of her life. Her brothers, meanwhile, were suffering severely from the traditional Irish occupation of having nothing to do.

An old countryman said of Dudley Persse, "He reared his family bad and had five blackguards of sons." Augusta's younger brothers alternated between Roxborough and their lackadaisical pursuit of higher education in Dublin. At Roxborough they spent their time at fairs and races, roaming the countryside hunting rabbits, birds, and—as they grew older—women. There were rumors of the seduction of maids and country women. Her brother Frank was said to have boasted "that he did everything that could be done out of the way, except kill a man." Another brother, excluded from a hunt ball because of previous misconduct, turned a hose on the guests. This same brother once walked into a public house and put a bullet through every number of the clock.

The Persse brothers were also accomplished pranksters. The old countryman told with delight how they dressed a tenant as a priest: "They used to throw an old sheet around Roland—that was to take the place o' the stole you know—and make the other tenants go up in turn and tell their sins. Whichever tenant told the 'funniest sins' and made the best jokes was to get a big prize and plenty of whiskey and drink!"

Indulged by their mother, excluded from the management of the estate by their father, Augusta's brothers had no goals and few responsibilities. Their family had not taught them to seek, and their class and country had not provided a way for them to find, any challenging outlet for their energies and abilities.

The girls at least knew what was expected of them. Augusta's half-sister Katie married when Augusta was ten. Her oldest sister, Eliza, married when she was twelve—going only ten miles away to Castle Taylor as wife of the young master. All the Persse sisters were constantly going to and participating in weddings. Once, as a bridesmaid, Augusta was drooping from the heat when a whisper from the pews that she herself was languishing for the bridegroom made her straighten in indignant denial. As the years went by, the list of her "fellow bridesmaids" grew longer and longer.

Adelaide and Gertrude attended several sessions of the Irish marriage market, the viceregal season in Dublin at which the Viceroy received, and kissed, the new debutantes. Arabella and Augusta, left at home, watched their adventures from afar and puzzled over their letters describing dances and clothes; a "rose and apple-green peplum" seemed particularly far from their experience. Adelaide "got religion" and wanted to nurse the poor, an activity she was forbidden. Gertrude was looking for love, declaring expansively, "I have enough of everything but that." The sisters conferred together on what was required in a husband. Adelaide said she would never marry a minister, which she did; Arabella that she would never marry a widower, which she did; and Augusta that she would never marry anyone "for whom she had to make small talk."

Augusta, under orders, did not consider herself a candidate for romantic love. She wrote that she "might have been more tempted by dress and society had I nursed any expectation of being admired." The Mistress, however, still did not like her and told her plainly that "I was not to think myself the equal of beautiful Adelaide, of tall gay musical Gertrude or agreeable Arabella." Augusta accepted the verdict: "and this was true enough."

In addition, Augusta began to see that this emphasis on romantic love was simply a dangerous diversion allowed young women whose real business was to make a socially correct marriage. When Adelaide finally fell in love, her family was horrified. Her choice was John Lane, a divinity student at Trinity College six years her junior. He was from a professional family from Cork. Not only had nobody in her family ever married anybody in his family, they had never heard of it. The younger brothers and sisters were scandalized, whispering among themselves, "Who is he? He may be the son of an attorney!"—which he was. Nurse Sheridan had darker suspicions, muttering, "I don't like those sort of names, Lane and Street and Field. They are apt to be given to foundlings."

"The Authorities," as Augusta referred to her mother and father in this case, at first forbade the marriage completely. Then they relented and decided that if Adelaide and John Lane did not see each other for three years, during which time they could exchange one censored letter per year, and still wanted to marry, they could. After two years the Authorities gave up and let them marry—their petty cruelty decreeing that Adelaide could not be married in the Killinane church on the estate. Her marriage in the neighboring parish symbolized her semi-exclusion from the family.

When Augusta was eighteen, she had her own brush with the Master and Mistress. Her brother Frank, temporarily a medical student in Dublin, whom she referred to as "a wild son of the house," brought home a friend, Mr. Henry Hart, whom she described as "a wild undergraduate of Trinity College." This friend was very fond of literature. He was also, she wrote, "extremely handsome with the Grecian profile and an athlete, manly."

Augusta liked wild men. She had too intimate knowledge of her brothers not to feel at ease with them. She had too restricted a life not to feel exhilarated by them. She was, however, insulated from the great attractions of Mr. Hart by her involvement with Shakspeare, which she was just permitted to read on turning eighteen. She was learning the sonnets at her dressing table and reading the plays during long hours lying in the heather. Henry Hart spent his days with her brothers in the open air, on horseback and at fairs. Every evening they met in the drawing room and talked about literature; "those delightful conversations in which one or the other of the great poets or writers was ever a third." Then one evening her brother Frank touched Henry on the shoulder and led him out of the room. Though Augusta had not noticed it, Frank (who had done everything out of the way except kill a man) considered his friend had had too much to drink to talk to his sister.

A day or two later Augusta and Mr. Hart happened to meet in the garden. They sat down on the grass and talked about the violets she had in her hand. Her father, crossing the garden in his wheeled chair, was not pleased to see them together. Next day the Mistress told her she was to go to Castle Taylor. Rather than upset the arrangements of an unsuitable suitor who was Frank's friend, the Mistress preferred to remove Augusta. Augusta agreed cheerfully: "I was exultant about my books, and happy if I took them with me." She insisted that "I am sure that no thought of love or flirtation had crossed my mind." She did have the pleasure of hearing a neighbor say, "I could tell by the sound of that young man's voice when he was talking that he was in love with Augusta."

Years later she learned that Henry Hart had written to her and that the letter had been opened by "the Authorities": the Master, the Mistress, and Archdeacon Burkett. The letter was brief, its only purpose to tell her the authorship of a once-discussed quotation: "Among the faithless faithful only he."

Three years after Adelaide's imprudent marriage Gertrude, then twenty-five, made a proper match with a forty-year-old landlord of Cornwall who was, like her father, High Sheriff and Deputy Lieutenant of his county. Her husband's first wife, a sister of her cousin Burton Persse of Moyode, had died after one child and fourteen years of marriage. Gertrude lived less than three years after her marriage, giving birth to three daughters in thirty-three months. Her husband remarried fifteen months later and had four more children. Augusta

33

could not help realizing that marrying a man old enough to be one's father greatly increased one's chances for a long life.

During the three years of Gertrude's married life Augusta visited her often. When she was in Cornwall, she taught Sunday school, visited the poor, and read to a blind man. After her first visit she returned to Roxborough with a greater appreciation and love of the Irish country people, for when the young people of that decaying mining area of Cornwall left home for America, their old parents were virtually abandoned. Letters seldom came and money never. In contrast, at Roxborough Augusta and her mother were in constant demand to read and reply to letters from America. Once, going into a garden shed, Augusta noticed the gardener carefully potting several sprigs of ivy and was told that his daughter visiting from America would be taking them back with her "so she would never be without a bit of Ireland."

In 1875, during one of her visits to Gertrude in Cornwall, Augusta heard that her brother Richard was sick in lodgings in Dublin. She went at once and stayed with him, and though he was still rude to her, he did have one redeeming feature. He was the only one of her brothers and sisters interested in a wider world. He and his friends cared about art and literature. His friends became Augusta's friends. Her favorite was Mr. Henry West, a Dublin barrister, who told her, in what must have seemed a flight of fancy at the time, that Coole "was the only house in the county that would make a right setting for you."

Richard was Recorder of Galway town, a semi-judicial position on the city council. Augusta's relations continued to play a large role in local government. Her cousin Burton Persse was High Sheriff of County Galway in 1862. His brother was High Sheriff of Galway town in 1868, the same year her brother-in-law Walter Shawe-Taylor was High Sheriff of County Galway. The landlords' power, however, was on the wane.

William Gregory of Coole had been member of Parliament for the county since 1857, to the great satisfaction of his constituency, both Catholic and Protestant, so much so that he asserted that "I am quite sure the mob would have broken the heads of any supporters of a rival candidate, should any such have presented himself during my Parliamentary career." In 1870 he voted, with great misgivings, for Gladstone's tenants'-rights bill, which he feared was the opening wedge in the destruction of the landlord class in Ireland, but which guaranteed essential rights: that departing tenants be reimbursed for improvements they themselves had made, and that tenants evicted without cause be compensated for the "disturbance."

But by 1870 William Gregory had had enough of the rising tide of democracy. The Reform Bill of 1868 had lowered property requirements for voting and doubled the number of those eligible to vote. When he realized he would not be elected again, he told his friend Lady Waldegrave, one of the brilliant and powerful society ladies with whom he was a favorite, that he would like to be Governor of Ceylon. She told her friend Lord Grenville, the Foreign Secretary, and when the post became vacant two years later, he appointed William Gregory.

Gregory was then fifty-four and unmarried, having been in love with a married woman, the daughter of a colleague in the House of Commons, for many years. He described her briefly in his autobiography, in words that would apply equally to Augusta, as "a woman of many accomplishments, a good linguist, extremely fond of art, and remarkably well read." She was also very much in love with him. Just months before his departure would have separated them, her husband died. Gregory put off his departure. Nine months later they were married and left almost immediately for Ceylon. They had only seventeen months together. Elizabeth Gregory died in Ceylon of a fever caused by overexposure to the sun. For William Gregory it was "the greatest sorrow of my life. . . . My life was terrible for some time in the deserted, mournful Queen's House at Colombo."

For Augusta Persse and for his constituents in Galway, Gregory's resignation from Parliament was more interesting than his marriage. In the election that followed, between a landlord's son and a middle-class Catholic, the landlord was defeated four to one. The number of tenants eligible to vote had reached a critical mass; *en masse* they passed from one pole to the other—ordered to vote against the landlords by a powerful local priest. The landlords, having one more weapon, disputed the election in court, alleging "priestly intimidation," but the result was unchanged.

Augusta, now twenty-three, was spending her time as women were supposed to—at the disposal of others. Richard, suffering from tuberculosis, was told to spend winters on the Riviera. The Mistress, who continued to have a low opinion of Augusta's marriage prospects, chose her to accompany him as nurse and companion. Augusta did not want to leave Roxborough, "the large household, the comradeship of the boys, the great plenty, the fireside comfort, the winter shooting parties, the wide demesne." She did not like Richard, but, not being self-centered, felt her dislike only as discomfort, enduring "monotonous walks beside the invalid's chair on dusty roads; the companionship of one that she had never intimately known, so much was he her elder, and whose turn for satire had increased the shy tremors of her early days." Richard, in his early forties, nearing the end of a dreary and empty life, was as unpleasant as ever.

Cannes was dreary. According to Augusta, it was "not France, had no history, no national life, no language but a patois." Augusta read books from the small lending library. She had three lessons in mathematics, after which she saw her tutor collapse in church, from which he was carried raving to a madhouse. "I am never quite sure that my lessons may not have been the last straw."

In the evenings she joined the other guests at the hotel around a large table in the lounge. Augusta, used to the silence of her family's evening circle, was amazed to find that these people entertained themselves by talking to each other. Everyone "put something in the pot." The other guests liked her conversation; they said that "*Chaque mot porte*"—an inestimable gift for a future dramatist.

At the end of the winter she was rewarded by a trip to Italy, "the journey through olive groves to the palaces of Genoa." She had begun to learn Italian, and her studies "were alive now, and every moment was filling my hands with treasure." With a grammar, a dictionary, and "the audacity of the young," she read Dante. First using a French translation and then "making her own, she wrote it out to the very end of the Purgatorio and the triple stars. And the beautiful sound of the language was added to the other unbounded joys of those blossoming Italian Aprils." She called the Divine Comedy "part of the luminous background of my life." The second winter at Cannes was better than the first. She hired tutors and spent most of her time studying French and Italian.

In the summer and autumn, life continued at Roxborough, where she was taking a greater interest in the country people and servants. When she began to write about them after her marriage, she told of her mother looking through the open door of the old butler's room to see several friends around the table and him kneeling at a chair, "his hands devoutly folded looking over his shoulder and saying, 'Ye go on dealing out the cards while I say a few prayers.' The Mistress was a discreet woman and quietly withdrew." Augusta was moved by the story of a young girl, grieving for her dead brother, who died exactly one year later. She remembered overhearing an old man say to his wife, with the supreme sense of male prerogative prevalent in all classes, "Bad luck to you, Biddy, I never knew the likes of you. Bad luck to you for not stirring the sugar in me tea."

She began to realize the poverty of the people more keenly. A young man who went to America wrote an excited account of his success there and finished with "and to think that while I lived at home, the height of my ambition was that I might someday drive my own ass and cart!" This same young man, returning and attempting to describe the wonders he had seen, told the country people that an elephant was "about the one size and shape as my father's house in Moneen."

Augusta also watched Mary Sheridan, who was still grieving for her daughters in America. The Master finally agreed to pay their passage home and that of the aunt who had emigrated with them. Mary got a message that the oldest daughter was dead. "That was a sharp grief but not a lasting one, for the younger one was her favourite and all her desire centered on the approaching meeting with her." But when the cart drove up to Roxborough, there was only "the wizened, half-foolish but wholy wide-awake old woman, the aunt of the poor dead girls, who had concealed until now the fact that both were dead, lest the passage money should by some means have been taken from her and her old bones not thought worth bringing home." Augusta sympathized with Mary. "I think in the next few hours she went through such a bewildering agony of grief that neither joy nor pain could ever touch her again."

The next winter at Cannes, Augusta got word that Mary was dead. She fretted bitterly. "She had been a part of our life, always full of sympathy." She wrote ominously in her journal opposite the news of her death: "Taken away from the evil to come."

That winter a Dutch baron with an invalid son went walking with her, but Richard became alarmed and wrote home that the baron "meant business." Augusta was commanded to end the friendship.

The next spring, in 1877, she made an acquaintance no one would dream of sending away, as he was the greatest catch on the Irish marriage market, the sixty-one-year-old Sir William Gregory, back from Ceylon, where he had been widowed and knighted. They met at a cricket match at Roxborough. She was acting as hostess for the buffet laid out on the long table in the dining room when he arrived late and was put into the last vacant place. She came up and welcomed him. "Most likely I blushed as was then my habit, but I think I must have been looking rather nice in a Paris dress and a Mrs. Heath hat

37

. . . a black and white straw with bunches of corn ears and poppies." They spent the afternoon talking about Ceylon because, as Augusta explained, "my brother Harry had thought of going there."

A short time after their afternoon talk about Ceylon, Augusta received a sudden invitation to dinner at the Maxwells', the Persses' neighbor and Sir William's cousin. The helpful hostess told Augusta that just before dinner Sir William had mentioned Augusta Persse "in a way that made her certain he liked me; and she had sent her messenger at once."

A few days later she and Richard were invited to Coole to dine and sleep. When Richard was asked how he enjoyed the visit, he replied "rather discontentedly" that Sir William had "talked more to Augusta than to me." Sir William drove them through the Seven Woods, famous even before their Gaelic names appeared like incantations in Yeats's poetry: Kyle Na No (nut wood), Shanwalla (old homestead), Kyle Dortha (dark wood), Pairc Na Tarav (bull field), Pairc Na Carraig (rocky field), Pairc Na Lee (calf field), and Inchy (river meadow). They were shown the lake that occasionally disappeared through an underground passage to the sea. It was no great rarity, the Persses' lake did the same. But wild swans visited the lake of Coole, and it was famous in local mythology, though Augusta did not yet know it, because the pregnant mother of Saint Colman, patron of the district, had been thrown into it by a jealous king.

Sir William showed them the large walled garden, which Augusta secretly compared unfavorably to the garden at Roxborough. As a child she had visited the garden with her sister Eliza. Mrs. Gregory, Sir William's mother, had proudly showed them a huge mulberry tree covered with berries—and offered them none. By the time of her second visit, both the tree and Sir William's mother were gone. Mrs. Gregory died before her son returned from Ceylon, holding in her hand the telegram, just received, announcing his knighthood.

As they left, Sir William gave Augusta a pearl ring. When she got home, her mother brought out and showed her a Maltese shawl he had given *her* on his return from a trip to the Mediterranean. Her contempt for Augusta, however, began to waver.

Augusta was now twenty-five. She and Arabella were the only two daughters left at home. Adelaide's marriage had turned out unhappily after all. John Lane was disappointed that he had not gained access to the aristocracy and had to see his beautiful wife "with but the background of a curate's lodging in a smoky English town." Adelaide hated being a minister's wife, hated "the change from the easy luxury to the narrow cares of a home that had upon it the critical eyes of churchworkers." Her first child died; others came in quick succession. One child, Hugh, was delicate, and Adelaide wrote home constantly asking for game or fowl, "a bird of some kind," for him. Gertrude's marriage was over. Meanwhile, Augusta, busy and useful, never experienced the shame of being an old maid or the fear of the future that might have seemed appropriate. She was somehow, she felt, on track.

When she was twenty-six, she was nursing her brother Gerald through an attack of pleurisy at Roxborough and overheard the servants saying they had heard the banshee crying for a death. Though she had always considered tales of the banshee to be superstition, she felt a sudden dread and watched Gerald anxiously all night. As she was going out on the landing to reprove some of the servants for talking too loudly, her father's servant came up the stairs to her and said in a hushed voice, "The Master is dead."

Her father's death was devastating, more for social and economic reasons than emotional ones. His power over her she would never shake completely, but she feared to lose the position he had given her. At fifty, her half-brother, Dudley, had at last inherited. All the younger brothers and sisters were shaken: "Must we leave it all? Where would we go? Were we who had been rich now poor?" Her father had left £10,000 to be divided among the twelve surviving children of his second marriage. Augusta did not have to be good at arithmetic to know how little she had.

The Mistress, with no realm over which to preside, was "wonderfully brave." She also had money of her own. She took a house in Dublin for the younger children, and before she left Roxborough she had an auction of things she did not want to move and Dudley did not want to keep. The shock of seeing household items spread out over the lawn for strangers to bid on and carry off was part of the experience of second families moving down in the world. But it was also symptomatic of the decline of the landlord class. Their neighbors near Newcastle, the Burkes of Danesfield, were now living less expensively abroad than they could on their estate. At Ross the front door was barred; Robert Martin, the heir, was working as a journalist in London. His mother and five of her eleven daughters were in Dublin to welcome Mrs. Persse to the reduced circumstances of a townhouse on Merrion Square. Augusta, however, was saved from having to choose between dependence on her mother in Dublin or her half-brother at Roxborough by again accompanying Richard to Cannes.

Sir William was staying at the Grand Hotel and came often to visit, now finding the girl he had first met with corn ears and poppies on her head all in black mourning for her father. They talked about literature; he read her quotations from his favorite authors. "I married you," he told her afterward, "because you were a good listener." Except for the fact that he was past his prime and she not yet into hers, they each had the qualities the other most admired in the opposite sex.

Augusta liked wildness, liked intelligence, and liked power, both personal and social. Though she could see few signs of wildness in the genial, graying, lordly man who sat before her, his career was well known. After his early success at Harrow and Oxford, he had left without taking a degree. After a brief term as member of Parliament for Dublin, he devoted ten years of his life and the income from Coole to raising horses, racing them, hiring trainers, and making book for himself and his friends. He fought a duel with a man whose unsportsmanlike conduct caused him to lose money betting. Finally he had to sell two thirds of the estate to pay his debts. Chastened, knowing his own mind, he was elected to Parliament from Galway and resumed his life as a useful and popular member of the ruling class. At twenty-seven Augusta, from the west of Ireland, was wise in the ways of masculine sexual extravagance, and if she had heard anything of love affairs before his first marriage, they did not bother her.

Sir William liked powerful and intelligent women. Though the kind of woman Augusta Gregory became after his death was a little too unorthodox for his taste, when he met her she was just right. She was intelligent, bright, eager to serve, and anxious to learn. He had had his great love, and she was not looking for hers.

Augusta, though she did not realize she was looking for anything, was seeking the same sort of controlled relationship she had with her parents, only with a pleasanter person and in a wider world. Parent-ridden as she was, she was more prepared for the wifely subordination of nineteenth-century marriages than more indulged young women, to whom it came as a shock. So when their marriage was made, the ties that held it together were more formal, more social, than personal.

Augusta's mother, keeping an eye on the situation, joined Richard and Augusta at Cannes. When they moved on to Rome in the spring, Sir William followed them. He invited Augusta and her mother to stay at his London house when they returned from Italy. Augusta later wrote, "I cannot say the idea of marriage did not occur to me—I lived in too large and irreverent a family for that detachment of mind—yet it did not fit into the life that seemed planned out for me."

Without giving a thought to sharing Arabella's husband-hunting life at their mother's Dublin townhouse, Augusta returned to the wide spaces and the wild brothers of Roxborough. The life she planned centered on what she saw as her duty: to help with the housekeeping and to care for the charming, poverty-stricken country people. But at Roxborough "the hive of life" was now very quiet. Of her fifteen brothers and sisters, Gertrude was dead and Richard was dying. Her half-sister Katie was a widow in England. Her half-sister Maria lived on a property of her own at Aughrim. William was in the Royal Artillery in England and the father of six children. Edward was a major in the 9th Native Infantry in India and also the father of six children (eventually to be the father of eleven). Eliza was married at Castle Taylor and a mother of three. Adelaide was unhappily married here and there in England and Ireland. The younger boys, Frank, Harry, Gerald, and Alfred, were also here and there, between Roxborough and their mother's house in Dublin. Frank was no longer in medical school. Harry was still thinking of going to the colonies, but never passed the foreign-service examination. Gerald, her favorite, was drinking.

Death coming when it did spared Dudley Persse the breaking of his absolute power, but it put his children in control at a time when everything beyond their control went wrong. Algernon was acting as his half-brother's agent for a fee of five percent of the rents—a common and handy provision for younger brothers, but it was difficult just then to collect any rent. Augusta wrote only that Algernon "had gone through a hard and anxious time and was glad of my help."

Irish harvests had been bad for three years. The winter of 1879–80 was the coldest in memory, and when the ground began to thaw, the liver-fluke disease attacked the sheep. Agricultural prices, responding to abundant European harvests, were lower than they had been for many years. The cold and rain continued and pastureland deteriorated. Tenants demanded reductions in rent. When these were denied, evictions and bankruptcies followed. Herdsmen and laborers were hard to manage. Augusta set up a cricket tent and served food outside the fairgrounds at Ballinasloe to keep the herdsmen out of the public houses. She brought in supplies of tea, sugar, flour, and bacon and sold them at the steward's lodge on Friday afternoons when wages were paid. Catholics saw it as a plot, believing Protestants were charged lower prices. The Protestants also saw a plot, and Miss Samuella, sister of the archdeacon with the Waterford accent, accused Augusta of trying to ruin "the respectable Protestant shopkeepers of Kilchriest." Augusta asked her where she got her supplies, and Miss Samuella confessed to shopping in Dublin.

Housekeeping in reduced circumstances at Roxborough was an unpopular job because "there were some of the old servants who were used to the old wasteful times, the lavish killing of beasts, the masses of meat for all in the house and yard and stable, the beer barrels, the large household, and all this had to be changed and brought within bounds." (An old servant defined "a grand house" as one where as much was thrown out as was used.)

Later Augusta looked back and remembered herself "ministering to the poor and then wishing to leave Roxborough." But she also thought, "I must have had some belief in a future life, a full one, on this earth, for I don't think I ever fretted or flagged." When she was old, her grandchildren called "He Who Would Valiant Be" from *Pilgrim's Progress* "Grandmamma's hymn":

> Who beset him round
> With dismal stories
> Do but themselves confound.
> His strength the more is.

Unfortunately, the methods at her disposal for relieving distress—temperance tents and estate shops—were insignificant as well as insultingly feudal.

The country people could think of more effective relief: the eventual ownership of the land. In County Mayo in April of 1879 a series of evictions on an estate owned by Father Burke, a Catholic priest, led to the formation of the National Land League of Mayo. Michael Davitt, recently released from seven brutal years in prison for Fenian activity, whose family had been evicted from their Mayo holding when he was a child, who had lost his right arm in a Lancashire mill when he was eleven, organized a great demonstration protesting rents which was attended by over 10,000 people. The meeting caused Father Burke to lower his rents and encouraged tenants in all the adjoining counties to join the agitation. By October the Irish National Land League was founded in Dublin with Charles Stewart Parnell, a young member of Parliament from County Wicklow, as its president. The following year Parnell was elected head of the Irish parliamentary party, thus combining agrarian agitation for ownership of the land with parliamentary agitation for Home Rule.

Augusta Persse, fighting wasteful expenditure, drunkenness, low prices, and bad weather, had no time for romantic love of country. Her brother Richard died on September 8, 1879, a year and a day after their father's death. She, Algernon, and their cousin Burton Persse went on foot to see him laid in the unmown Killinane graveyard.

As she stood by his grave, she had no comforting thought of an afterlife for him, or for herself, or any belief "in anything outside the walls of the world." Richard's intelligence, his sarcasm, the wider world she had seen in her travels, and the day-to-day troubles at home had broken down her old beliefs.

At the family gathering at Roxborough after the funeral, she felt faint and nearly fell. Eliza cried, "Oh, Augusta, *you* must not break down!" Her half-brother, Dudley, was already well into a breakdown of his own. Not used to responsibility or discouragement, he took little part in managing the estate, but spent his time drinking with cronies from his club days in Dublin. A few days after Richard's funeral Augusta got him into the carriage and to a doctor in Dublin. She believed, probably correctly, that she had saved his life, and, probably incorrectly, that he was ever afterward very grateful to her.

Sir William was at Coole during this dreary time. He heard from the local doctor about meeting Augusta at the bedside of a dying boy whom she visited daily because he would take food only from her hand. On a visit to Dublin, Sir William protested to her mother about the life of self-sacrifice she was leading at Roxborough.

At Christmas, Algernon went for a two-day shooting party at Coole and returned with a book for her, *Roderick Hudson* by Sir William's friend Henry James. Algernon was "half sarcastic, I don't think he, or the others, yet believed I could really enjoy reading." Shortly after Christmas, Sir William came to lunch to say goodbye; he was going abroad for the rest of the winter. "He looked ill and was, I thought, depressed, and when he said goodbye, I felt sad and lonely." He got as far as his London house and wrote asking her to marry him.

Getting something for herself might have been difficult for one so committed to serving others, but for Augusta it was easy. She felt "extraordinarily happy and serene, happy in the thought of being with him, of serving him, of learning from him." She was reading George Eliot's *Middlemarch* at the time and thought that Dorothea's exalted feelings when the elderly, scholarly Causabon asked to marry her were "something like mine." Dorothea thought: "How good of him—nay, it would be almost as if a winged messenger had suddenly stood beside her path and held out his hand towards her!" Augusta was also happy that Coole was only seven miles from Roxborough, but she thought she could not marry until there was someone else to look after the estate. She wrote Sir William that she could not marry until Algernon found a wife (which he did not do for seven years).

Sir William wrote back angrily. "He had determined I should go with him on the journey he had planned for the spring to Rome,

Athens and Constantinople, and he thought I was being made too much use of by my family!" He took the boat back to Ireland. Augusta took the train to Dublin. They met at her mother's house, and a solution was found. A widowed aunt and her widowed daughter were invited to Roxborough to look after the housekeeping.

Then began the delicious thrills of social triumph. "All my family were pleased," she wrote, "some of them astonished." She had a rare laugh at her mother, who she said was "never quite sure he had not married me as a compliment to her." The brothers were pleased to "think of all the shooting that would run together." They could now hunt from Roxborough, to Coole, to the Shawe-Taylors' woods. Frank went so far as to hope Arabella would marry their Catholic neighbor Edward Martyn "because then they could shoot the whole country-side without a break." The old steward Rick Burke, who in her childhood had given her pennies on fair-days, now "took off his hat with a great sweep" whenever he met her.

Old Mrs. Hardy asked Algernon, "How did that little thing get the big man?" Mrs. Galbraith, who was famous for always having the news first and having it wrong, had heard nothing until her husband burst in with the question "Who do you think Augusta Persse is marrying?" Mrs. Galbraith made a wrong guess. "No, my dear, but William Henry!" When Mrs. Galbraith tried to tell her son, he said he had heard it three days earlier from the postman.

They said they did not want wedding presents, but they received a phaeton from her half-brother, Dudley, and a green vase that kept reappearing in spite of Sir William's instructions, "Boswell, take this downstairs, and don't bring it up again!"

They were married in Dublin at St. Matthias Church on the 4th of March, 1880, eleven days before her twenty-eighth birthday. Sir William was sixty-three. Augusta did not wear white but a gray traveling dress and hat. "I had been so long in mourning for my father and for Richard I did not like to change colours. But I have always been rather sorry I did not, however quiet the wedding, wear white, with wreath and veil. I felt it was a break of tradition, something missed out of my life; or perhaps, I should like to remember myself in bride's attire." After the wedding there was a small party at her mother's house in Merrion Square, and after that they left for England.

II

The Seductions of Union

MARRIAGE: 1880–1892

Perchance not so in heaven above
But here, a woman may not love.
AUGUSTA GREGORY, *Diary*

T H E independent Irish parliament which Augusta's great-grand-father helped bring about amalgamated itself with the English Parliament on January 1, 1800—an abdication of independence facilitated by heavy bribes of land and titles. Augusta's marriage to Sir William, who was an Irish landlord but an English gentleman, was her Act of Union by which she, gaining much, temporarily lost independence of mind and her allegiance to Ireland.

Augusta—Lady Gregory—was a different person during the twelve years of her marriage than she had been before or would be afterward. She was more ordinary. Her wifely duty to Sir William coincided so well with her sense of performing before God and His angels that little else was required. Serving Sir William permitted her to do almost everything she wanted to do. She was like a bird let out of a cage into a room, so delighted by the relative freedom, and so interested in the bric-a-brac, that only rarely did she remember her longing for the great spaces.

After their wedding Sir William and Augusta traveled from Kingstown on the night boat to England, took the train to London, and arrived in the morning at her new home at 3 St. George's Place, Hyde

Park Corner. The house was tall and narrow, "so gay in its outlook on the riders and carriages in the Park," so fashionable in its address, and with a view of the Surrey hills from the upstairs windows. Elizabeth Gregory having left for Ceylon almost immediately after her marriage, Augusta was its first real mistress.

The first thing the new Lady Gregory did was get herself some new clothes. Sir William, who liked and respected Augusta, was now also amused by her, writing his friend Sir Henry Layard, "My wife, who was quite a student, is now plunged among *chiffons* and *modistes*, and I am bound to admit that she bears the infliction with a resignation which is rather alarming, excusing her new-fangled interest in dress on the grounds of pleasing me."

Sir Henry, the English Ambassador at Constantinople, invited Sir William and his new wife to visit. Sir William accepted, "and I can assure you my wife actually jumped for joy at the delightful prospect of nightingales, roses and boats on the Bosphorus."

For Augusta there were many subsidiary pleasures. At her last fitting she asked for the bill, took out her checkbook, and paid the dressmaker, "who was so astonished she cried." Augusta attributed her prompt payment to her dislike of debt—but there was something also to be said for the newfound pleasure of wielding a checkbook.

Part of her regalia was necessary for her presentation to the Queen. Wearing train and veil, plumes and feathers, she was ushered into the presence of Queen Victoria, then sixty-one, in the forty-third year of her long reign. Several young men in uniform seized Augusta's four-yard train and pulled it out. She advanced, making five curtsies, kissed the Queen's hand, and withdrew without mishap. She reported that the Queen had a "sweet smile," and the Queen told someone who told her that she was pleased with Lady Gregory's appearance, especially her hair. The fashion was frizzed bangs, but Augusta wore her hair pulled back on either side of her forehead and tucked into a knot in back—just like the Queen.

She would have met Disraeli, who was standing by the Queen, but Sir William, who could have introduced her, hurried away to a meeting of the Arundel Society, leaving her in the charge of an old neighbor from Galway whom she had never met. Lady Geary was a Burke of Danesfield, but, being Catholic, the family had never been visited by the Persses. Augusta realized that indeed she was in a wider world.

After Augusta's presentation at Court, the Gregorys moved on to Rome, where they found, as was usual wherever they went, a great many people Sir William knew. Augusta, who had spent most of her

life shy and blushing except with her younger brothers, had much
to learn. Her first formal dinner, after years of county society at Roxborough and second-class hotels on the Riviera, was at the English
Embassy in honor of Queen Victoria's daughter, the Crown Princess
of Prussia. Augusta rose to the occasion. "I did not feel shy," she wrote,
"I liked the flowers and the lighted rooms." She wore white satin and
old lace—a dress fit for a bride—and was at ease about her appearance
because the wife of the Ambassador and one of the duchesses present
also wore white.

When she was presented to the Crown Princess, the Princess
touched the bracelet made of replicas of old Greek coins that Augusta
was wearing, examined each coin, and named its city. Sir William
told Augusta afterward he had been watching her "very closely but he
need never do it again, for I had been brought up to manners and
entertaining."

At Athens they were cordially received by the Prime Minister,
Kharilaos Trikoupis, in gratitude for Sir William's friendship for
Greece while he was in Parliament. They were entertained by Dr.
Heinrich Schliemann, who gave Augusta a terra-cotta "whorl" from
the ruins of Troy. And finally, at Constantinople they were guests of
Sir Henry Layard, Sir William's closest friend, and his wife, Enid,
who became Augusta's closest woman friend.

Sir William and Sir Henry had served together in Parliament; they
were both trustees of the National Gallery. Their great loves behind
them, they had both married younger women. Sir Henry, who had
possibly been in love with his wife's mother—the remarkable Lady
Charlotte Guest, wife of a wealthy Welsh iron manufacturer, translator of the old Welsh tales of the *Mabinogion*—had married her
eighteen-year-old daughter when he was fifty. In addition to the simi-
larities between their husbands, Augusta and Enid had in common
the pleasant experience of coming out of a great crowd where they had
been little regarded into a position of respect and even power. Enid
was the eighth of her mother's ten children, and though Augusta described her as a "great lady," Enid Layard was also the closest to an
equal she had ever known.

Augusta soon saw Sir Henry—as she saw her husband—as an "Authority," a wiser, older, and more experienced man who nevertheless
occupied the same dominant position in her mind as had her parents.
Sir Henry's name had even been known at Roxborough; as the discov-
erer of the ruins of ancient Nineveh, he had been hailed as "the man
that made the Bible true." Augusta was at first afraid of him because at

mealtimes he kept up "a sort of humourous grumble at Lady Layard, rather disconcerting to a stranger." However, as he got to know her, "I found myself treated in somewhat the same way."

Sir Henry and Sir William were about to have in common their retirement from positions of great power. Gladstone's election in April had put an end to Sir Henry's diplomatic career, and even as he shared with the Gregorys the enjoyment of the ambassadorial palace, his replacement was *en route*.

The Gregorys returned to London for the brief social season, "dinners, receptions, the Marlborough House Garden Party, the Queen's Ball, the friendly faces of my husband's friends." The friends were delighted to meet her, but quickly returned to the guaranteed charm of Sir William's conversation, leaving her out of exchanges that were "cut to the bone, quick firing. . . . The little dinners used to remind me of the Pool of Bethesda; he only who was prompt to leap in at the right moment had any chance of success." Sir William, "half-vexed, half-amused," quoted what was said of Oliver Goldsmith as a talker—"That he had a thousand pounds in the bank but not a penny of small change in his pocket."

She got braver, and when James A. Froude, an apologist for the British empire, remarked to her, "Everyone nowadays is so commonplace," she replied, "Not where I come from," and launched into a description of Roxborough. Froude, who did not have a high opinion of the Irish, wrote the next day, "It was a delight to meet you!"

In July they returned to Coole. The little market town of Gort was decorated, the Catholic priest and Protestant archdeacon were there to welcome them. A great bonfire blazed at the gate by an arch with the Irish greeting: "CÉAD MILE FÁILTE." Everyone was delighted that Sir William had at last brought a bride home to Coole; and they were particularly delighted she was Augusta Persse of the neighborhood.

Sir William gave a dinner for his tenants at which he made a speech, as he wrote Sir Henry, "reprobating the evil doings of agitators and communists, which was well received. After dinner, the wives and daughters had tea, cake, and a plum-pudding [the men of course had whiskey], and then they danced till five in the morning. Nothing can be better than the spirit apparently of the people about here, but I dread that all may be changed in a day by some of these violent agitators, who lash the tenant classes into a fury even against the best landlords." (He was right, and the next year was writing to Sir Henry that his tenants "have been so persecuted and abused they have almost all joined [the Land League] within one week.")

Augusta was now looking at the county from a different angle—

48

surrounded by more reminders of the great world than she had been at Roxborough. There had always been, Augusta wrote, "a certain distinction about Coole." The estate had been bought and the house built in the 1770's by Sir William's great-grandfather who had made a fortune in India, served in the English Parliament, and been a director and chairman of the East India Company.

Robert Gregory began the extensive plantings which changed the character of the landscape from the gray-green openness of Roxborough to the green gloom of the Seven Woods. Robert Gregory also began the tradition of concern for the country people that had first shown itself in India and that was emulated by Edmund Burke, who wrote him, "Certainly you must begin with the natives. This was always your fundamental maxim, and be assured it will be mine." This letter was subsequently framed, and Augusta showed it proudly to visitors.

Coole was inherited by Robert Gregory's second son. He had told his oldest son, who had lost a good deal of money betting on cockfights, that he would disinherit him if he ever took part in a cockfight again. This son, left in India when his father returned to England, ignored the warning, but his father, walking down the Strand in London, saw in a shop window a print of a picture by Zoffany of the great cock-match between the Nabob of Oudh and Colonel Mordaunt. Standing in a prominent place in the picture and holding a white cock under his arm was his oldest son. Augusta subsequently bought a print of the picture and hung it over the fireplace in the drawing room at Coole. She understood and was attuned perfectly to the resonance of objects, the making of tradition through things.

Richard Gregory, who inherited Coole, added to the romance of the place by his most improbable love affair with a young woman whom he carried off from school, kept concealed in the steward's lodge, and married upon his father's death. When she died, he married her maid. It was he more than any other who made Coole into the house that was a "right setting" for Augusta Gregory. He collected rare books and brought statues from Italy. The bust of Maecenas in the garden and the fine naked Venus which was eventually brought inside because it embarrassed the country people were, according to local tradition, dragged across Europe by oxcart at his instructions. He died without children, and the inheritance passed to his younger brother, William Gregory, grandfather of Augusta's Sir William.

This William Gregory served from 1813 until 1832 as Under-Secretary for Ireland, third in command under six successive Irish viceroys and their chief secretaries. He was, according to Sir William,

49

"the real Governor of Ireland, except, of course, where measures that had to pass through Parliament were concerned."

His son, Robert Gregory, Sir William's father, was the first Gregory to see Coole not as a place of recreation or retreat from the big world, but as his home. (Like Augusta's father, he served for a time as Deputy Lieutenant for County Galway.) But even he lived part of the time at his father's house, the Under-Secretary's Lodge in Phoenix Park, Dublin, and it was there that his only child was born.

Sir William's mother, though she was the daughter of a local family, chose not to make herself part of the neighborhood, exchanging visits only with a few of the neighbors—Augusta's mother and sister Eliza among them. And though Coole was Sir William's inheritance, his real home, the center of the social standards by which he lived and judged himself, was London.

It is also a fact that Sir William, who was universally considered a good landlord, had probably caused his tenants more suffering than someone like Dudley Persse, who was not only considered a bad landlord, but whose life was occasionally threatened. (Charles Lever's estimate of the Irish people applies: "I have never read of a race, who in great poverty and many privations, attaches a higher value to the consideration that is bestowed on them than to the actual material boons, and feels such a seeming disproportioned gratitude for kind words and generous actions.") William Gregory had always assured his tenants that he would be "a robber and ashamed to look you in the face" if he raised their rents because of improvements they themselves had made. The tenants, in turn, had so much confidence in him that they did not ask for leases. However, in the 1850's when he was forced to sell two thirds of the estate to pay his racing debts. "I was so occupied with other matters that I quite forgot their danger." He was planting a pinetum in the nut wood at Coole, ransacking the nurseries of England for "all the specimens that were invented and got up by ingenious nurserymen for the benefit of Coniferomaniacs, as we were then called." Once the pinetum was planted, he went to Egypt for the winter. When the sale was made, the purchasers doubled the rents, and in a few years most of the tenants were ruined. Sir William was pleased to meet some of them on a later trip to America.

By the time Augusta arrived, Coole was no longer a working estate. The groceries came from Gort, not from a home farm. And though there was a gamekeeper and assistant to look after the woods, and gardeners to look after the garden, and maids to look after the house, the relative lack of servants was one reason the Gregorys could come to Coole to economize. Compared to Roxborough, even the diminished Roxborough of later days, it was very quiet.

Augusta did not at first particularly like the thick woods, the unreliable lake, or the large, plain white house, and she never loved them with the passion she felt for Roxborough. Her attachment came through their associations, many of which she created, so that Coole became a work of art to which she herself made the greatest contribution. She began to care about Coole only when she saw it as her son's inheritance.

In August of 1880, five months after their marriage, Augusta and William started the baby that would make such a difference to her. (Augusta said very little about sex in her writings, but it can be assumed that, as part of her duty, she accepted it like a soldier.) She had not thought much about having children. With her thoughts focused on herself and her cloud of witnesses, they seemed an irrelevance. But the coming birth made her realize that if the baby were a boy, she would have a firm position in the social structure that until then had dominated her life without guaranteeing her anything in return.

The Gregorys returned to London for the winter social season, and Augusta again took up her education, this time no longer in books but in society. She had not realized the depth and breadth of Sir William's acquaintance. He had been a favorite of London society for many years before she was born, the confidant of several great ladies, and a member of the most fashionable clubs.

Lady Waldegrave, the charming and powerful hostess who had got him his governorship, was dead. But Lady Molesworth, like Lady Waldegrave a powerful society hostess, was very much alive and, as far as Augusta was concerned, very much of an annoyance. The Gregorys called on her often; for years they ate Christmas dinner at her home. She was then the widow of Sir William Molesworth, a baronet, who had founded the *London Review*, later merged with the *Westminster Review*, which he edited with John Stuart Mill. Augusta considered her (as she considered Lady Waldegrave) an adventuress because she had entered society as an actress and because, before she married either Sir William Molesworth or her previous husband, she had tried to marry Sir William Gregory's uncle on his deathbed—prevented only by a determined servant who locked her out.

Lady Dorothy Nevill, another charming society woman, wrote that Lady Molesworth had "a mysterious power of drawing out clever people by making them talk—a social quality of the highest possible value"—and one that Augusta herself would eventually acquire. But at the time Lady Molesworth saw no need to exercise her charm on the shy, pregnant wife of her old friend.

Lady Dorothy was another of Sir William's old friends. (When he left for Ceylon he had promised her "to enter into relations with mercenary and desperate men to steal a tom cat from the palace of the King of Siam . . . as a comfort to your Siamese tabby"—then a rarity in England.) Though the Gregorys lunched frequently with Lady Dorothy, Augusta did not succeed in being mentioned once in that lady's five volumes of reminiscences.

Augusta succeeded better with men, who were charmed by her youth and her willingness to learn. She practiced "drawing men out," and later confided to an acquaintance that one of her methods was to ask them about their walking sticks. "Their walking sticks?" "Yes," she replied, "I find men are very interested in their walking sticks." After a thoughtful pause her friend replied, "Now *I* have a very interesting walking stick that was given to me by King Edward, another that was lent to me by Queen Alexandra when I was lame at Sandringham at one time, and another . . ." "Yes," said Augusta, "I knew my recipe would not fail," and burst out laughing.

She met many of her literary heroes. The poet Lord Houghton, whom she later called "Dicky Milnes," became a delightful companion. His book of poems *Strangers Yet* had impressed her, but that interest "was absorbed into a stronger one, for he spoke of having known Heine at the end of his life. And to have even touched that paralyzed hand seemed a wonderful thing to me." She visited Robert Browning. Henry James came to visit on Sunday afternoons. (The Gregorys had first met him in Rome, where Sir William had told how closely his gift of *Roderick Hudson* had preceded his proposal, but as for Augusta, "my shyness kept me dumb.") Augusta was no longer dumb, but she was still a good listener. Henry James confided to her, speaking of Isabel in *The Portrait of a Lady*, that "it is delightful to a poor man being able to bestow large fortunes on his heroines." She heard Tennyson reading his poetry, like the "booming of a gun." Alexander Kinglake, author of *Eothen*, her brother Richard's favorite book, lived just around the corner and became touchingly dependent on her as he sickened with the illness that killed him. William Lecky and James A. Froude were no longer distant heroes but dinner companions.

She met Sir Frederic Burton, the director of the National Gallery, an Irishman who believed in English rule but who had, nevertheless, drawn the frontispiece for *The Spirit of the Nation* out of friendship for Thomas Davis. Sir Frederic first noticed Augusta when someone, admiring a painting of Mary Magdalen, remarked that she did not look very repentant, and Augusta murmured, "Perhaps she did not grow quite good at once." Sir Frederic "turned and looked at me through his spectacles in an intent way I was to learn to know, as if giving attention to some offered painting or puzzling over a new signature, and then burst into his sudden delighted laugh, and I blushed disconcerted."

Her husband's friend Frank Lawley wrote that "her little *salon* at 3 St. George's Place, Hyde Park Corner, soon became one of the most agreeable in London." She collected people and had her famous acquaintances autograph the staves of an ivory fan. These included William Gladstone, Robert Browning, Alfred Tennyson, James Whistler, John Millais, Frederic Harrison, Ernest Renan, Randolph Churchill, Wilfrid Blunt, Arthur Sullivan, John Bright, Lord Houghton, Lord Rosebery, Alexander Kinglake, George Trevelyan, William E. Forster, James Russell Lowell, and Henry Layard.

Not everyone was impressed. George Moore, her exact contemporary, showed up in her drawing room and described her "air of mixed humility and restrained anxiety to say or do nothing that would jar. . . . Her eyes were always full of questions, and her Protestant highschool air became her greatly and estranged me from her." Moore had, in fact, entered her drawing room just as she was asking Sir Edwin Arnold, author of *The Light of Asia*, to autograph her fan. She had not asked Moore, though, as he said, "I had already written *A Modern Lover*."

George Moore was a County Mayo landlord who had left his estate in the care of his younger brother and gone to Paris to be an artist. The Land League's successful efforts to lower his rents had brought him back to London to earn his living as a writer. Self-consciously vain, he developed an unpleasant personal manner that stood in contrast to the genuine understanding of and sympathy with the oppressed that he showed in his writings. His middle name, which he detested, was Augustus. He would appear in Augusta's life again.

The other side of Augusta's life, one of the few things she did whose ostensible object was not pleasing her husband, was her service to the London poor—who were much more depressing than the cheerful, quick-witted paupers of Ireland. She adopted the poor parish of St. George the Martyr, and provided tea, cakes, and entertainment for mothers' meetings. (Once she had the bright idea of asking some of the audience to sing, and "They seemed delighted at some of their own number being called up, 'It is as good as half a sovereign to us.' ") She provided a tree and a Christmas party for many years, and in doing so also succeeded in pleasing Sir William, who wrote Sir Henry about her great organizational ability: "I really think had she been alive in the terrible times of the Crimea she would have brought order into the Commissariat."

She eventually adopted an even poorer parish, St. Stephen's, Southwark, and from both these parishes she made a practice of taking little boys (and, very rarely, little girls) to the Natural History Museum, the Colonial Exhibition, and the zoo. These trips proved wonderful practice in holding an audience, as she found she had to give a running monologue on snakes, birds, and crocodiles, for "if the youngsters' attention flagged but for a moment they would begin to fiddle with the cases or finger the specimens, but while they were kept amused they never left my side."

Though Augusta did indeed have a genius for organizing people, one misses again and again any sense of native kindness toward the objects of her charity. The assurance of being saved, which she had received when she was fifteen, did not last at full strength, and she felt constantly under a certain pressure to prove her goodness. She also insisted on going to church every Sunday. Sir William, who liked variety, agreed to accompany her if she would go to a different church every week. Her diaries are full of summaries of sermons, but her early opinion of Archdeacon Burkett had set the pattern for her reactions to the earthly representatives of her religion: she was rarely satisfied with them.

When the Gregorys were not going out, they entertained at home. Housekeeping in London was at first more difficult than in Ireland. Servants were not stranded by poverty at Hyde Park Corner as they had been at Roxborough. They left more frequently. More was demanded of them, especially the cook, and they were much more expensive. Soon, however, Augusta was reporting to her diary on her success.

Charles Gregory told her that his meal at Hyde Park Corner was "the best dinner he had in his life." He was a special challenge because her marriage to his cousin and her pregnancy were about to put him out, as she phrased it, of "the doubtful good of succeeding to an Irish estate." Though Augusta did not yet know it, Charles Gregory had loaned his cousin many thousands of pounds and taken in exchange a mortgage on Coole, which Sir William, never expecting to have any children, never expected to pay.

Augusta's labor pains started on the afternoon of May 20, 1881, as she sat at lunch with acquaintances and in-laws from Ireland. After her guests left, she went upstairs and had her baby. Her diary entry

54

for the day reads in its entirety: "Luncheon party, Bowers, Oranmores, Mr. Gough, Power Trench, A. Moore, F. O'Hara. At 9:00 Baby was born." Augusta's heart did not leap to meet her son. He belonged to the system, somewhat estranged from her by his social portentiousness, his importance as male heir. She did not know him physically. She did not nurse him. She hardly had time to hold him—so that the incongruity between his social importance and his physical insignificance resulted, among other things, in her inability to call him anything but "Baby" for the first several years of his life.

Though her somewhat fearful love for him was far deeper than calculation, it was reinforced by the deepest self-interest. Her baby was her tie to the great structure of the world. Rejected because she was not a boy, she had at last produced a boy. Playing by the rules of the game, she had won and received "life's best gift to me." (And with the birth of the future heir of Coole Park, Augusta's mother at last recognized her for what she was, the ablest and most fortunate of her daughters.)

William Robert Gregory was christened at fashionable St. George's Church, Hanover Square (where Sir William had married his first wife). Sir Henry Layard was his godfather. A week after his christening, "Baby," then two months old, was sent off to Ireland, and Sir William took his wife to the Continent to look at pictures in museums. Sir William had no intention of letting his child interfere with the purpose for which he had married its mother, which was to be a charming companion to him. Though Augusta never permitted herself a critical reevaluation of her husband's character, she did once remark, "The weak point in marriage is that it legitimizes selfishness."

Augusta dutifully went to the Netherlands, Belgium, and Germany to look at pictures, filling page after page of her diary with detailed, lifeless descriptions of them in accordance with Sir William's belief that she was as fond of art as he was. In September they went briefly to Coole, and Augusta caught a second glimpse of her son before they left again for London and the winter in Egypt.

In Ireland the Gregorys found they no longer knew their country. The disorder caused by tenants demanding rent reductions had been so great that in February 1881 a coercion bill was passed giving authorities special powers to quiet disturbances, to ban meetings, and to imprison suspected troublemakers without the usual legal proceedings. Then in April, following the typical English policy of coercion alternating with conciliation, Gladstone had a new land act passed giving the tenants what they asked for: fair rent fixed by arbitration, protection from eviction without cause, and freedom to sell one's lease at a fair price. Michael Davitt, founder of the Land League, considered that this bill had reduced the landlord to an annuitant, "but still carrying in his maimed position as a landlord enough of the odium attached to an evil system to keep Celtic hatred of it alive and active."

The Irish problem had always been two-pronged: the ownership of the land and the overlordship of England. Augusta had never sympathized with land reform, which meant, after all, taking it away from brother, husband, and son. And for this period of her life she believed, without thinking about it, along with most Irish landlords who did not think about it either (and who were wrong), that England's continued rule over Ireland protected their economic position.

As far as Augusta was concerned, Charles Stewart Parnell, leader of the movement for both land reform and Home Rule, was a traitor to his class, busy cutting the ground from under his feet. (As indeed he was. His supporters later collected £37,000 for him to make up for the great decline in the rents from his County Wicklow estate occasioned by the successful agitation of the Land League.) Parnell warned tenants against using the new land courts established to set fair rents until their fairness could be tested by carefully selected cases. William Forster, the Chief Secretary of Ireland, widely mistaking the character of the Irish people, decided Parnell's attitude was obstructive and imprisoned him—making him an immediate hero. Parnell's arrest was followed by new waves of violence.

The Gregory genius for face-to-face kindness made Coole an island of safety surrounded by "an absolute reign of terror." (The Gregorys' neighbor, the Marquis of Clanricarde, a notoriously high-handed landlord, wrote from London to his agent in Galway—on a postcard so the whole county would get the message—"Tell the people they cannot hope to intimidate *me* by shooting *you*.") Sir William described the disorder to Sir Henry in his cheerful, orderly prose: "Besides assassinations successful and assassinations incomplete, there is cutting off ears, and desperate assaults, and mutilation of cattle, and orders, which dare not be resisted, to servants to leave their masters' houses, and to shepherds to leave their flocks." (The land campaign introduced the boycott as one of its most effective weapons.) Much of the violence was, in fact, directed against the tenants themselves to keep them in line. As Sir William wrote, "A single emissary of the Land League exercises more terror and authority over a whole district than all the magistrates, police, and *priests* put together." Not paying the rent exposed a tenant to eviction; paying the rent to a landlord proscribed by the league exposed him to assassination: "Threatening notices of murders are flying like snowflakes . . . and in every house you visit terror prevails, lest the corpse of one of its inmates be brought back in the evening."

The Gregorys, all their sympathies with the landlords and with England, spent the winter of 1881 in Egypt, where, as Augusta put it lightly, they "tumbled into a revolution," which was similar to their own in Ireland except that they sympathized with the other side. At that time Egypt was ruled by the Sultan in Constantinople as head of the Muslim faith, by the Sultan's viceroy in Egypt, Khedive Twefik, and—more directly—by the Khedive's legion of Circassian officials. The English and French, as principal holders of the Egyptian debt, also had their input into Egyptian government. Arabi Pasha, a peasant who had risen through the ranks in the army, was a kind of Egyptian Parnell, committed to giving Egyptians greater control over their own country.

Augusta went to Egypt ready for adventure. The birth of her son had given her greater assurance. The frustration of her maternal instincts had given her a great store of unused energy. Subconsciously, she was annoyed with Sir William as a father; perhaps, half aroused, she was also annoyed with him as a lover. It is even possible that, having produced an heir, they were now concentrating on what they did best together—which was social, not sexual, activity.

The Gregorys arrived in Cairo in November, took up residence at Shepheard's Hotel, and immediately became part of the close-knit British community. Their friend Lord Houghton was in Egypt visiting his daughter and son-in-law, controller for the Anglo-French Control representing the bondholders. They met other British officials, among them Auckland Colvin, financial advisor to the British. Described by an enemy as "strong, self-reliant, hard," he was also a charmer and a philanderer. Augusta found him attractive; he was her type. But she was soon to meet a man who was the quintessence of her type.

Wilfrid Scawen Blunt and his wife, Lady Anne, also arrived in Cairo in November, delayed by an accident on their way to Arabia, a delay that turned into a three-month stay at the Hôtel du Nile. Augusta met them soon afterward. Wilfrid Blunt, then forty-one, was tall, bearded, imperious, and considered one of the handsomest men in Europe. He was a great English landlord. He was the owner of a famous Arabian stud. He was a poet. His *Sonnets and Songs by Proteus* had been published six years earlier, his *The Love Sonnets of Proteus* had been published that summer. They recorded his passionate two-year love affair with an English courtesan in Paris. (She was Catherine Walters, nicknamed "Skittles," well known to the English upper class, a former mistress of Lord Hartington, who sent her to Paris when he was married.) After several years of unimportant diplomatic service in Frankfurt, Paris, Lisbon, and Buenos Aires, Blunt had married the wealthy Lady Anne King-Noel, Byron's granddaughter. Shortly afterward he had inherited his family's great estate in Sussex. The Blunts had a nine-year-old daughter, who was, like the Gregorys' child, safely out of the way at home.

When they first met, Sir William told Blunt he had seen him years before in the bull ring in Spain, challenging the bull as amateurs were permitted to do, and had learned that he was attaché of the British Embassy. Leaning across the table, Sir William asked if Blunt had not been afraid, to which Blunt replied, "I was very much afraid indeed, but I would not give in."

Blunt's travels in the Middle East had led to the unexpected suspicion that British rule was not always the best. His arrival in Egypt just as nationalist aspirations were coming to the surface turned him, for the first time in his life, to political action. Blunt convinced the Gregorys that Arabi Pasha was right. He and Sir William wrote letters about him to the *Times*. Augusta and Lady Anne visited Arabi's wife, with Lady Anne, who spoke Arabic, acting as translator. Blunt and Auckland Colvin had a shouting match which ended with Blunt declaring, "I defy you to bring about English annexation or intervention!" It was not their bond interest that was going to be reduced, and the Blunts and Gregorys enjoyed themselves very much. Augusta forgot what was left of her shyness and talked so intelligently and wittily that Sir William, who had been watching her though he said he hadn't, made her "very happy by saying he was content."

Augusta was watching Blunt. She admired poets, liked horsemen, felt safe with wealth and power. And she believed, as she had been taught to believe, that beautiful people deserved to be loved.

The years of her marriage and those immediately after were the only time of her life during which her closest and most constant companions were not wild men. Her brothers, with their pranks, their sexual adventures, even their drinking, gave her a sense of vicarious freedom, a sense of going beyond bounds, that she later got from the strange men of the Irish Renaissance. Wilfrid with his challenge to British influence in Egypt was exhibiting the same exhilarating defiance of authority. He began to shimmer around the edges. Wilfrid, for his part, saw her as "a quiet little woman of perhaps five and twenty, rather plain than pretty, but still attractive, with much good sense, and a fair share of Irish wit."

Augusta's everyday relationship with him developed into the same deeply sympathetic, bantering, controlling, cool-headed management she had exercised—as she grew older—over her brothers. When Wilfrid appeared in the full white robes of the Bedouin (which he occasionally wore on his English estate), Augusta commented in her diary, "He is becoming impracticable, says . . . if England intervenes there will be a bloody war but that liberty was never gained without blood. In the middle of this Mr. Villiers Stuart came in & began to talk of mummies & the covering of the sacred ark. Wilfrid sat looking unutterably disgusted. I gave him the Arabian Nights and some bonbons to console him."

As Egyptian nationalist strength increased and Arabi was appointed Minister of War in a new cabinet with liberty to institute many reforms, the English began to fear they could not continue to dominate Egypt. When it became a question of whether the English and French or the Egyptians would control Egypt, what had been a titillating social excitement turned into serious business. Only the Blunts and the Gregorys remained faithful to Arabi, and Blunt decided he could do more good by arousing public opinion in England. (Before he and Lady Anne left, they bought a beautiful forty-acre garden in the desert near Heliopolis that became, as they grew progressively estranged, home for whichever of them was not in England.)

The Gregorys, not feeling the same pressure, took a side trip to Luxor, which Sir William described to Sir Henry with the wonderful assurance of ease and pleasure that accompanied him everywhere: "Nothing could have been pleasanter, in spite of the coldness of the weather. Fancy cold at Luxor! But so it was, and a deal of sneezing and coughing was the result. On the other hand, the extreme coolness permitted all kinds of long excursions to be constantly performed without fear of fatigue. We had agreeable society in the evening, for there were a number of learned men, such as Professor Sayce, M. Maspero, M. Rhone, M. de Naville, Mr. Villiers Stuart, and, last but not least, a young German, Dr. Wiederman, a perfect prodigy of learning, who charmed everyone by his modesty, gaiety, and good looks. . . . I think you would have been amused, and if Lady L—— had taken to the purchase of blue beads with the avidity of Lady G—— and her friend Mrs. Lee Childe (*née* De Triqueti), she would have had plenty of occupation. . . . I have picked up two very curious objects, both from Karnak, Greek glass heads, very well done, one of Pan and one of Serapis. . . ."

Back in Cairo, there were other distractions in their small social circle. Augusta wrote Enid Layard that a "young Englishman struck

Datzel [another Englishman] in the face without any provocation and refused to give him any reparation. Datzel appealed for a jury de honneur to pronounce in the case and after several sittings they gave him (Datzel) a certificate of honourable conduct." She added that Sir William was on the jury, and she ended with her constant cry when away from home, "In a little more than a month I hope to see baby!" She also confided that she was "looking about for two treasures, a nursemaid and a cook."

On their way back to England the Gregorys stopped for nearly a month on the coast of Sicily and arrived in London at the beginning of May. Sir William went on to Coole, and Augusta, instead of going first to their London house, apparently found herself not as anxious to see Baby as she imagined and went on to Crabbet, the Blunts' Sussex estate, for a day and a night.

Crabbet Park, set in the beautiful oak woods of Sussex, was much grander than Roxborough—though not larger. The house itself was as handsome and distinguished-looking as Wilfrid. There were fifteen house servants, including a little black boy to run errands. The stables and outbuildings were better kept, the horses in them of much finer lineage. But all in all it was a style of life Augusta undersood thoroughly.

There was one unusual aspect: Wilfrid was a Catholic. His father had died when he was two; his mother, free to follow her inclination, had become a Catholic. Though her three children at first regarded her conversion as a tragedy, they had followed her. Augusta found his Catholicism only added to Wilfrid's distinction; besides, he kept believing and not believing, and had even seriously considered becoming a Mohammedan. (Augusta's brother Frank, who had done everything out of the way, had done one more thing and, the year Augusta married Sir William, had himself married a Catholic.)

Augusta was back in London in time for her son's first birthday on May 20. She did find a nursemaid, a cook, and, most interesting, a servant she did not know she was looking for, a French maid for herself. Revol, recommended by Wilfrid, had worked for Madeline Wyndham, Wilfrid's cousin and one of his many former lovers.

In England, where hardly anyone was interested in Egyptian nationalism, most of the news was about Ireland. The new chief secretary, Lord Frederick Cavendish, and his under-secretary, T. H. Burke, had been murdered in Phoenix Park several hours after his arrival in Ireland. The Irish members of Parliament, led by Parnell (now out of jail), were obstructing nearly every piece of legislation brought before it. Wilfrid came to see the Gregorys, practically his only allies in the Egyptian cause, for lunch, afternoon tea, dinner, and sometimes for breakfast. Augusta dropped by 3 James Street, his *pied à terre* in London, to give him news. When Sir William realized that England might intervene militarily in Egypt, he withdrew his public support. Wilfrid wrote in his diary, "Gregory has failed us." And Sir William wrote Wilfrid, "I must talk the matter over with you when you return to London, though perhaps we may have a few words tomorrow before or after the Derby." Sir William, a pillar of his class, had gone far enough in a matter that separated him from that class.

In Egypt, Arabi's forces held the forts of Alexandria. On July 10 Augusta wrote in her diary, "They say Alexandria is to be bombarded tomorrow. Wilfrid does not mind, says there must be bloodshed before things come right." At the Queen's annual garden party at Marlborough House on July 13, Augusta noted "the Queen very grey, the Princess not so pretty as usual in blue and white. The news of the massacre and burning of Alexandria cast rather a gloom over the party." Wilfrid attended the same party and wrote, "Her Majesty was looking beaming—I suppose elated at her bombardment."

The next week Augusta, all by herself, suddenly left for Ireland to visit her bothers at Roxborough. She and Wilfrid exchanged tender notes about each other's health. Mr. Blunt to Lady Gregory: "You looked so wretched when I saw you last that I have not been able to get it out of my head that you are seriously ill. Colds like yours are not to be trifled with and I shall not be happy till I hear that your native air has done you good." Lady Gregory to Mr. Blunt: "I hope your toothache has disappeared. It spoiled my pleasant evening a little to see you suffer so much."

In the first of her twelve sonnets about her affair with Wilfrid, Augusta wrote:

> Could I find heart those happy hours to miss,
> When love began unthought of and unspoke
> That first strange day when by a sudden kiss
> We knew each other's secret and awoke?
> Ah, no! not even to escape the smart
> Of that fell agony I underwent,
> Flying from thee and my own traitor heart,
> Till doubts and dreads and battlings overspent,
> I knew at last that thou or love or fate
> Had conquered and repentance was too late.

Though she first realized her love for Wilfrid and fled to Roxborough in July—returning to London in August—she then went off to Europe with her husband in September, returned to London in October, and held off the consummation of the affair until December.

Arriving in Ireland in July 1882 during the worst disturbances of the Land War, more or less in an agony of conscience about her love for Wilfrid, Augusta, nevertheless, had a very good time. At Roxborough she found "seven soldiers in the harness room drinking whiskey out of tea cups"—the bodyguard supplied by the British army for her brother Algernon, who, in addition to his ordinarily dangerous occupation as land agent trying to collect rents from tenants who did not intend to pay, was then serving in the even more dangerous capacity of High Sheriff for County Galway, Augusta wrote Wilfrid that she drove about with her brother Gerald, "who being landless presents no mark . . . and I don't think they would hit me if they tried!" When she was not driving about sympathizing with the neighbors, or watching the soldiers eat gooseberries in the garden ("gooseberry patrol," she called it), she stayed home and wrote about her visit to Arabi in Cairo.

She enjoyed the turmoil, particularly as it coincided so well with her interior conflict, but her later descriptions of it do not convey the rawness and brutality of the time. The Persses' acquaintance Robert Martin of Ross had returned to Ireland to recruit "emergency men" to work for families boycotted by the Land League. A neighboring Catholic landlord asked for his help. The ladies of the family were harvesting their cabbages, tending their cattle, and feeding their pigs on peaches from the garden. The men were working in the fields. Augusta wrote that when the strikebreakers from the north of Ireland arrived, "one of them celebrated his arrival by drinking too much, and having divested himself of all his clothing, he seized a hatchet and rushed about the yard, his employer fleeing before him."

Two weeks later, having enough of Irish diversions, Augusta was back in England, finding "Baby hopping about in his nightdress and blue shawl." A week later she "went down to Crabbet and stayed to dinner and talked treason. Wilfrid hopes the English will be beaten." She and Wilfrid were not yet lovers; they were fellow conspirators against authority. Sir William then took her off to Belgium, Germany, and Italy to look at more pictures in more museums. She did not protest, but commented ruefully in her diary, "I used to say that if ever I need to take a trade, I would be found fitted at least for that of a courier."

In Ireland, tenants were being evicted. In Egypt, British troops were advancing on the army under Arabi. From Berlin, Augusta sent her article on Arabi to Wilfrid, who replied that he thought it was excellent and should be published under her own name "to do any good." Excusing herself for her writing, she quoted a male friend who had told her, "A lady may say what she likes, but a man is called unpatriotic who ventures to say a word that is good of the man England is determined to crush." She understood well the uses of powerlessness.

She asked Sir William's permission to publish, and wrote Wilfrid, "Rather to my surprise Sir William said he saw no objection to my publishing my article in my own name if one of the magazines will take it." Then, on September 12, 1882, the Egyptian army under Arabi was completely defeated by the British at Tel-el-Kebir. Sir William changed his mind. Augusta wrote Wilfrid in distraction: "What will you say to me. Will you be angry with me. . . . I feel like a coward withdrawing it just after the defeat. I quite broke down today but having cried like a baby all morning and stayed quiet all afternoon I begin to think there may be a bright side. Has it not been a dreadful week."

It became more dreadful when it appeared that Arabi would be tried by the English and perhaps hanged. Sir William changed his mind again and gave her permission to publish. Wilfrid took "Arabi and His Household" to the editor of the *Times*, in which it appeared on September 23, 1882—Augusta's first published work—though she was not paid for it.

In it Augusta presents herself as a sympathetic and powerless woman. She does not try to justify Arabi politically. Rather she tries to arouse sympathy for him by showing the warmth of his family life. She tells of being served a huge meal by Arabi's wife: "I was in despair until I found that one of the children, my little bright-eyed Hassan, was quite ready to sit by me, and be fed from my plate, and so I disposed of my share to his great satisfaction. . . . By the time dessert arrived he said he liked me but hated other ladies and would like to come and see me in England, but did not know if he could manage it, as his father wanted the carriage every day." (She wrote Wilfrid that she purposely did not mention Arabi's having been divorced twice and his wife once.) She wrote of Arabi's concern for *her* child: "I showed him a picture of my little boy; he raised it to his lips and kissed it, hoping he would someday come to Egypt and be a friend of his children. Perhaps I have not been a fair judge of his case since then." She concluded by presenting the question posed by Arabi's wife, who asked, "puzzled and troubled, 'Why should the Christian powers want to harm my husband?' " On her return to London, a friend told her that she had "made every woman in England Arabi's friend."

From Germany the Gregorys traveled to Venice to visit the Layards at Ca Capello, their palazzo on the Grand Canal. When they finally got home in October, Sir William found he was pleased with his wife's success. All his friends at the Athenaeum complimented him on "Arabi"; some of them said it was so good people would think he wrote it, and one, equally pleasing, said, "I know you didn't write it because I know you couldn't."

At his own expense, Wilfrid had sent lawyers to Egypt to defend Arabi. He collected contributions for a defense fund—as much to arouse sympathy for Arabi as to raise money. Augusta threw herself into the work. She translated a passage from her beloved Dante that neither aroused sympathy for the prisoner nor appealed to the generosity of possible contributors but described the similar good deed of an Italian nobleman:

> 'Twas when, he said, I lived in high estate
> I did not shrink and I did not disdain
> To stand a beggar at Siena's gate
> That freedom for my friend I thus might gain.
> To rescue him who lay in prison sore
> The pangs of wounded pride I gladly bore.

She rushed off to the University Club early one morning—before anyone was alert enough to enforce the "No Women" rule—to check its newspaper files "some sleepy and astonished waiters watching me" and gather facts for a statement Wilfrid wanted to make.

Only £200 was contributed to the defense fund. Augusta contributed £5, Sir William £10. The lawyers' bill from Egypt was already £3,000, and Wilfrid's supporters urged compromise. The battle for Arabi was over by December, when he agreed to plead guilty to treason and be exiled instead of executed. The place of exile was to be Ceylon, where Sir William's influence could make him more comfortable. Wilfrid deplored the admission of guilt where there was none, but he could not go on paying lawyers forever. When a friend complimented him on his expensive espousal of justice, he put the expense in perspective, replying lightheartedly, "And have I eaten a chop the less?"

Wilfrid wrote of his affair with Augusta that "at the climax of the tragedy [the Egyptian debacle] by a spontaneous impulse we found comfort in each other's arms. It was a consummation neither of us,

64

I think foresaw. . . ." Augusta, however, had certainly foreseen it for quite some time, though, as she wrote:

> . . . I denied thee, vexed thee with delay,
> Sought my soul's coward shelter, not thy peace,
> And having won thee still awhile said nay.

But, finally, having saved Arabi, Augusta was ready to succumb. On December 9 Sir William went to Ireland to check on his agent's rent collection and shoot at his birds. That same day Augusta went with Wilfrid to Madame Tussaud's to see the new wax model of the man of the hour: Arabi. The next day she went to Crabbet for two days and stayed in her usual room over the bow window. Her diary entry: an elaborate curlicue, a cross between an X and a W, and "Wilfrid in the evening." At last she experienced, as she wrote in a sonnet, "the joys I was so late to understand." Wilfrid wrote that their lovemaking was "quite a new experience in her quiet life. It harmonized not ill with mine in its new phase of political idealism and did not in any way disturb or displace it." In a sonnet to Wilfrid, Augusta wrote:

> I kiss the ground
> On which the feet of him I love have trod,
> And bow before his voice whose least sweet sound
> Speaks louder to me than the voice of God.

Outside the bedroom and the sonnet form, Augusta's relationship to Wilfrid was as bright, cool-headed, and self-possessed as ever, very like her relationship to her brothers. Being paid attention to, being petted—as Wilfrid did pet his lovers—was a delightful sensation on which she could not focus. Being involved directly with another person was a skill she did not have. Her sonnets show her conducting the affair in almost total isolation, loving Wilfrid first, vexing him with delay, soothing him in his "most troubled hour." Even in her affair she was, as George Moore later said of her, "*sans attaché*." The larger context in which she and Wilfrid met was, most specifically, the common cause of Egyptian nationalism, and, more broadly, their decorous resistance to established authority. In the same way, her bond with her brothers was not direct and personal but founded on their mutual relationship to "the Authorities." Wilfrid too liked a family feeling in his affairs, many of which were with near or distant relations—his "grand passion" yet to come would be with his second cousin, daughter of an also beloved first cousin.

The day after Augusta's visit to Crabbet, she had Wilfrid, Lady

Anne, and her brother William to lunch at St. George's Place. On the 19th Sir William returned from Ireland. He and Augusta had their usual boring Christmas dinner with Lady Molesworth. On the 27th Augusta decorated a huge fir tree sent by Wilfrid from Crabbet to the poor parish of St. George the Martyr and entertained the children with Lady Anne's doll collection. Her diary entry for January 16 is an "X" and the one word "Wilfrid."

In the spring of 1883, four months into the affair, she and Sir William went to Portugal. Wilfrid went home to Crabbet and his beautiful young daughter Judith, who adored him, and wrote Augusta gently complaining letters about his bad cold. "Also I feel very sorry for myself. . . . Write me something to make me feel happier." He wrote about his own unhappy time in Portugal—to which he had been sent by a compassionate Foreign Office to recover from his love for Skittles. Augusta responded that she was having "a cork stick cut for you in the woods, but it is such a club you will never be able to use it but might hang it up as a trophy." He wrote her from Knebworth House, the estate of his friend Robert Lytton, former Viceroy of India (as it seemed that every third acquaintance of his and the Gregorys' was a former Viceroy of India), "I like being here although the bric-a-brac nearly drives me wild." Arriving at the same time as this letter, the news of the death of her half-sister Maria, widowed for many years and living in England, came as news from another world.

In her sonnets Augusta adopted the conventional suicide-for-shame attitude toward the discovery of their affair: "So, when it comes, with one last suppliant cry / For pardon from my wronged ones, I must die." She does not show the same concern in her letters. When she got back to London, she wrote Wilfrid, "I expect to see you walking in to lunch very soon and tell me all your news, the sooner the better for baby has not come back yet and I require all the attention my friends can bestow on me to make up for his absence!" When Wilfrid did come strolling in, her friend Frederic Burton was there. She wrote Wilfrid afterward, "You saw F. Burton here yesterday. Was I civil to him? Did I talk to him about Gran Vassio and the fine arts? Did I even mention Arabi and the Khedive. . . . He was here 2 hours by clock, meets Sir Wm afterwards at the Athenaeum and says, 'I went to see Lady Gregory, but didn't stay as I found I was de trop!' I am furious!"

In her sonnets she wrote:

> Behold me here to-day
> Leading a double life, at shifts with lies,
> And trembling lest each shadow should betray.

Though she said she trembled, it is very possible that Sir William, a man of the world if ever there was one, knew of her affair and accepted it. He knew Augusta well enough to know she would not let it endanger his comfort. Augusta did not tremble about Lady Anne, though she should have understood her position perfectly, for she was already preparing herself for the time she would

> See a strange woman put into my place
> And happy in thy love, as I was loved:
> This were too much. Ah, let me not yet see
> The love-light in thine eyes, and not for me.

The Blunts came to dinner and lunch at St. George's Place frequently; the Gregorys often went to Crabbet. They met at all the places—Covent Garden, the British Academy, Mansion House—where everybody went to meet each other. Augusta wrote that on June 1 Lady Anne came by after lunch "complaining of headache and looking overworked." She and Sir William had a small dinner party, including Lady Anne, and when they left their guests to go outside and look up at the new flowerboxes at the windows, they met Wilfrid arriving late from the debates in the House of Commons. Augusta felt, as she wrote in her sonnets, the "mad throbbing of my foolish heart."

She badgered both Wilfrid and Lady Anne about getting photographs taken, even sending instructions to Wilfrid, "she in her riding habit . . . you with a light coloured coat, full or three-quarters to choose from. Make a fuss about it. It is a pity unflattering portraits go down to posterity." She did not like the results and finally took matters into her own hands: "Took Wilfrid and Lady Anne to Nault to be photographed, she made a great fight against it."

The conduct of her affair shows Augusta in a new light. Like her father, she could be ruthless, limited not in her ability to get what she wanted, but only in what she was able to want. And like her father, who believed he would be "washed in the blood of the lamb," she too believed she would be forgiven if she were contrite enough.

As a cover for her sexual excitement, she took up Louie Edgar, a beautiful Irish girl with an unreliable mother, whom she had first befriended in Cairo. She took her to Lady Jersey's, "where she made a sensation." She collected compliments for her, one from James Russell Lowell, who said he liked Irish girls, "They had so much go!" And had a laugh at John Ruskin, who told her "he had seen a much prettier beauty than mine, Miss Louie Edgar!" She oversaw the marriage of her cousin—her mother's brother's daughter—decorating the church with flowers from Crabbet. She squired her sister Arabella, who had come from Dublin for the wedding, all over London to look for a husband.

Wilfrid was overflowing with poetry, writing "The Wind and the Whirlwind," his indictment of Europeans in Africa and Asia, and "The Idler's Calendar," a month-by-month account of aristocratic pleasures: cover shooting, trout fishing, the London season, a jaunt to Paris. He asked Augusta's opinion, as he considered her a better judge of poetry than he. Augusta was her usual cool-headed self: "Wilfrid getting on with his verses, but the Arabi part is weak." She deprecated herself as a poet, though at the time she was writing a sonnet sequence as good as any of his. "*I* wrote a sonnet once and a song and a prologue and several translations . . . and am prompt at rhyming (though not quite as prompt as my cousin R. O'Hara who the other day when a whole crowd were puzzled for a rhyme to 'Arabi' said promptly 'where can O'Hara be') so you had better apply to me when you stick fast."

They enjoyed themselves through the spring and summer. Then August arrived and the Gregorys prepared to go to Coole to save money. Wilfrid was planning to go to India. His poem on Egypt was finished, and so were her sonnets, in which she prepared herself for the end of their affair:

> Wild words I write, and lettered in deep pain,
> To lay in your loved hand as love's farewell.
> It is the thought we shall not meet again
> Nerves me to write and my whole secret tell.

In the last sonnet she writes to him, "Go forth, dear, thou hast much to do on earth." She writes about herself:

> For me the daylight of my years is dim.
> I seek not gladness, yet shall find content
> In such small duties as are learned of Him
> Who bore all sorrows, till my youth is spent.
> Yet come what may to me of weal or woe,
> I love thee, bless thee, dear, where'er thou go.

Augusta went to Crabbet on August 6. She and Wilfrid spent the night together in the room over the bow window, and in the morning she handed him her sonnets. Her diary for August 7 reads, "Back to town in great crush, shopping and packing." On the 8th Wilfrid came to lunch in a flurry of excitement about a minor political event. The day is marked with two small X's. In the evening she left for Ireland. Sir William stayed in town for a wedding.

At almost the same time Augusta gave Wilfrid her sonnets, Lady Anne handed him a long statement about her grief and loneliness. Though she did not mention Augusta, she had finally realized that he had been unfaithful to her with many women over many years. Lady Anne described her own grief: "A wound years ago remains a wound for ever to me, poor worm of the earth, as long as I live." Augusta was never so faithful to her hurts and disappointments—though it is possible that at thirty-one, after three and a half years of marriage and one affair lasting eight months, her sex life was over.

Augusta was in Ireland from August 1883 until May 1884, but if it was a punishment, she never let on. She arrived at her mother's house in Merrion Square, saw her brother Edward and three of his boys, and then went on to Coole, feeling she had arrived east of the sun and west of the moon. A letter from Wilfrid was waiting for her, and she replied immediately: "It was very good of you to write me, your letter has brightened my first morning here, a very wet and dull one. Our journey was without accident and baby is delighted with the cows and chickens and country sights and sounds. It seems strange we are coming back to this extreme quiet and seclusion and I am ashamed at not taking more interest in the affairs of the neighbourhood but all things come with patience. Egypt and Arabi and the House of Commons and Crabbet seem a long way off." Sir William arrived from London and caught cold. The new servants were quarreling. But "Baby" was enjoying himself. She sent Wilfrid iris bulbs: "Plant deeply and next year please think of me when they come into flower." William never buried himself in the country long enough to feel buried, and after three weeks he dashed over to London "to see how the grass is growing in Piccadilly and pay some visits—to Lady Molesworth and others. I stay here with Baby."

Wilfrid left for India, writing in farewell, "You have not written for a long time or as often as I had thought you would, I want to hear about the politics of Ireland and so goodby and god bless you." In December, Sir William left for Ceylon. Sir Edgar Boehm had made a statue of him, at the expense of the residents of Ceylon, to stand in front of the natural-history museum he had established in Colombo. (The statue was so impressive that the sculptor cast the legs again and put on them the torso of Sir Francis Drake, who did not look impressive enough on his own legs.) Sir William had been invited to Colombo for the unveiling.

Augusta was at last going to have enough time with her son: "I am glad of the silence. I may find three months of it too much!" She stopped writing in her diary. She did not write to know herself, but to record how well she was doing her duty; with Sir William away, she was off duty. She wrote several articles about her travels with Sir William. When the *Fortnightly Review* paid her £5 for her article about Portugal, she was delighted with her "first *earned* money." She saved the money from her articles until she had enough to buy red William Morris wallpaper for the drawing room—"his most beautiful I think, the red and gold poppy pattern."

She visited the country people without enthusiasm. Leaving one cottage, she was mistaken for the priest's sister, but the country woman, recovering quickly, exclaimed, "Aren't we happy to have such a plain lady." Finally, she gave up and took Baby, now nearly three, to spend the last month with her brothers Dudley, Algernon, and Gerald at Roxborough.

Meanwhile, Sir William was having a wonderful time in Ceylon, writing Sir Henry: "My head is so turned by the fuss the good people of this island are making about me, both the English and the natives, especially the latter, that if I write conceitedly and egotistically, you will understand that it is only a temporary aberration, and that I shall subside very soon into my habitual humility on returning to England."

Unlike his tenure in Parliament, his account of which is filled with satisfied comments about good bills proposed that came to nothing, his position as Governor of Ceylon, with the power of the British Empire behind it, had been exactly suited to the carrying out of his good intentions.

In Ceylon he had greatly increased the prosperity and health of the island, on which whole districts had been dying of malnutrition, by having built a great system of water tanks and irrigation channels. He had begun the breakwater in the harbor at Colombo, which had increased government revenue by port charges and private economy by increased trade. Unlike even the most successful governors elsewhere, he had interested himself in preserving the monuments of the ancient civilization of the country. He was not good, however, at persevering in the face of discouragement, and the death of his first wife so demoralized him that he resigned before his term was up: "I made up my mind that I could not recover my spirits if I remained in Ceylon."

On his return visit Sir William was still pleased with his work. "On my arrival at Colombo the first thing I saw was fourteen large steamers, all riding undisturbed within the magnificent breakwater, over four thousand feet in length, which I began, and which is now finished." The inland districts were flourishing. But he wrote Augusta, "There is not an hour of my stay at Anaradhapura in which I was not longing for you."

Sir William returned to Coole on the 1st of May; he and Augusta, with Baby (now called Robert in Augusta's diary), proceeded to London. Augusta was planting the flowerboxes with primroses when Wilfrid walked in, full of new observations about British rule in India. Sir William was growing indulgent toward Augusta and Wilfrid's political enthusiasms: "You and Wilfrid talk more nonsense than any two people—settling the affairs of the world. As old Mrs. Harris said of the two commissioners sent to investigate the potato disease, 'There's isn't a ha'porth o' sense in both your blocks.' " The Blunts and Gregorys resumed their frequent lunches and dinners, but there are no more X's in Augusta's diary.

Disapproval of the British Empire at least provided a long view, a spaciousness in Augusta's London life, which was otherwise full of constant motion but no very great purpose. She and Sir William went to the Zoo to see the animals "with Professor [Thomas] Huxley doing the honours," to the British Museum to see the new bronzes, to Christie's to see whatever was for sale, to Crabbet to help the Blunts entertain Frederic Harrison and John Morley, to the House of Commons to hear Gladstone denounce women's suffrage. (During the speech proposing it, Augusta "began to think it might be a useful measure," but after Gladstone spoke against it, she "found myself thinking, 'What a very wicked person Mr. Woodall must be to have thought of doing such a dreadful thing!' ") They went to see *Nana*—a play based on Zola's novel. She called it an "indecent picture" and said it made her think she "had more sympathy with women's emancipation than women's franchise." Again they had Christmas dinner at Lady Molesworth's. Sir William began writing his memoirs and she copied them. They went to see the painter George Watts at his studio; she took her brother Algernon to see pictures at the Academy. She went to the dentist, who pulled four teeth with laughing gas and put her out of circulation for several days. William went "to suffer at the Roseberys' and to meet the Prince." On June 13 she wrote in her diary that "A. Clark talked to me of the troubles of married life." She went by James Street to see Wilfrid, had lunch there to meet Mohammed Abdu, and suddenly summer struck, economizing became paramount, and the Gregorys left for Coole.

After four years of marriage, life had settled into a routine of summers at Coole, winter and spring in London, the rest of the time elsewhere—Paris, Rome, wherever everyone else was. The summer at Coole was always the least pleasant part of the year, a shock to Augusta's fast-paced nervous system. "What did I do? What did I care for when I was here before? How did I fill my days?" Then she would remember: "Patsy Reilly wanting a plaster, Mrs. Quirke with flannel. May Brennan wanting a trousseau for America. . . . Old Brennan, for whose funeral I gave £1 last year is walking about as lively as ever but thinks he is going blind. . . . Assault case between Farrell and Mrs. M. By lecturing the Farrells and Howleys and writing to Father Fahy, I think a peace is patched up." She always left with relief: "Summer is over! I was very good, visited the poor, bought flannel. . . ." One summer she bought so much homespun flannel that she had it all dyed red and made into petticoats which she retailed to her London friends Enid Layard, Countess Fingall, and Lady Anne.

In November 1885 there was a break in the routine—the Gregorys left for India and Ceylon, stopping to visit the Layards at Ca Capello in Venice. While there Sir Henry told her, and she wrote Wilfrid, that Wilfrid "was the only man in England, except me, who has the courage of his opinions." Augusta again met Enid's mother, the former Charlotte Guest, widowed and remarried, no longer interested in Welsh legends but collecting porcelain and antique playing cards with an almost sexual avidity. She used Augusta to translate passages from an old German book on playing cards. Augusta was not impressed, and never made a connection between what her friend's mother had done for the Welsh legends and what she herself later did for the Irish ones. If she learned anything from Enid's mother, it was that the successful practice of literature does not, in itself, inoculate against triviality; a wider context is required. Near the end of the visit Enid called the doctor and put Augusta to bed, suffering from "severe nettle rash."

Sir William and Augusta boarded the *Nizam* at Brindisi, where she bought some yarn "to learn to knit a 'straight jacket.' The passengers don't look interesting." She was in the same happy, eager frame of mind in which she had gone to Egypt four years before. What remained from her affair with Wilfrid was an attitude about the British Empire that set her apart from her own class without really damaging her position in it. She wrote him that her chief occupation was loaning his book *Ideas on India*, very critical of English rule, to the Anglo-Indians on board and "waiting for the explosion."

She discovered she was not a knitter and immediately found someone to look after, a Mr. Trevelyan, who had recently lost both wife and child and who was now returning to his post in India. When he read Wilfrid's book, "at first his indignation and wrath seemed to overcome his melancholy: 'A most improper book, a pack of misstatements—a book that should be burned by the common hangman, yet there is much truth in it.' " They sat together one night waiting for the moon to rise, "and it was so long in coming he went to whist and I stayed and stayed, looking where I had always looked and *nothing* but darkness, and at last I thought I saw a light in front of the ship and it was the moon which had been up for some time, and I had forgotten we had changed course and are now going directly eastward." A few weeks later she wrote a poem turning her comedy of errors into a romantic situation.

She was the center of social life on the ship, which contained mostly Anglo-Indian officials and a British regiment on its way to a border war in Burma. After a day of sports—three-legged races, tug-of-war, etc.—she gave out the prizes, reciting a poem before each award. In conclusion, Judge Brandt, a shipboard admirer, rose and recited a poem to her:

> Thank patrons, judges, donors.
> Also let all thank the lady fair
> Who last bestowed the honours
> Whose speech enhanced each modest prize
> With quips and graceful fancies
> Of native wit, in whose clear eyes
> Fun flashes, humour dances.

She organized an evening of charades, writing, directing, acting in them, and finding a good cause to sanction their fun: "I made wigs and gowns and invented scenes and did my best. The word: Cat-ass-trophy. 1st scene, Mr. Scales, young lady at the window interrupted by a cat . . . 2nd scene, court room dispute over ass grazing on someone else's grass. Mrs. Hart and I counsel for defense and prosecution. I had to write Mrs. Hart's speech as well as my own which was much applauded. 3rd scene, someone being awarded a trophy. The whole represented by the shutting of the bar just as the Blue Ribbons [the group of officers on board] arrived to make a night of it.

"I thought it would be a good opportunity of getting a little money for the poor sick stewardess, so I announced on the programme, 'an address on Bimetalism' and between two scenes I came forward and recited:

> "There's a lonely woman below, friends,
> Who lies on a fevered bed.
> She had come far over the sea, friends,

73

To work for her children's bread.
. . .

What you give a sister in want, friends,
I promise, will never be missed.
So put your hands in your pockets,
And let's see who will head the list!

"And with that I hopped over the footlights (amidst much applause) with a pencil in one hand and a paper marked 'Bimetalism Illustrated' in the other . . . Mr. Trevelyan following with the lid of my workbasket to collect the money. . . . We collected over £25. The poor woman had no idea anything was being done. 'Oh, my goodness,' she said when she heard the amount." After it was over the Gregorys were invited to "a select supper given by the Blue Ribbon boys on stage"—a practice she later introduced at the Abbey. And at the end of her diary entry for the day, "William so pleased with my verses and the compliments paid me." The scene was a microcosm of her later connection with the Abbey Theatre: finding a good cause in which to put herself centerstage.

The Gregorys' status rose even higher once they set foot in India. They were not tourists, they were members of the ruling class, Sir William a former ruler himself. They were received with elephants, lancers, striped tents, banquets, and tours of the monuments of British administration, the jails and hospitals. She wrote about the elephants, "The getting up of the elephant is very disagreeable, but I liked the noiseless footfall and being at such a height—even camels looked small." At one jail she rescued a little boy. The prison was "a dreadful sight, the prisoners crammed together and a little boy, about 12, came crying bitterly and begging them to take him out. He had done nothing wrong but had been locked up there in the famine year and kept ever since. They don't like giving up their children to missionaries and there is only one small asylum in Hyderabad. . . . I have written to the Subar if he would board him out, in some decent family, and I would pay for him."

Everyone was delighted to see them. Everyone, from the Viceroy to the district administrators, felt bored and isolated. M. E. Grant Duff, Governor of Madras and Sir William's former colleague in the House of Commons, worked at his Latin translations when not occupied with government business, and collected specimens of Indian flora for the sake of their Latin names. After a month in India, Augusta wrote in her diary, "I have not met one single English officer or official with the sole exception of Cordery who has the least idea or takes the smallest interest in the history of the country, in its races or religion, and the women, with very few exceptions, are coarse and common in manner and appearance."

Gossip was an important occupation for the Anglo-Indians. As Augusta was idly listening to talk about divorces and affairs, she suddenly heard the name of Auckland Colvin, her old friend turned enemy over the question of Arabi, who "began life by getting his commander-in-chief's wife into a scrape, and after 3 or 4 other cases was brought with descriptions of an undefended writ into the District Court in which the wife of a Colonel Grogin was divorced for him and people thought Colvin would marry her, but he didn't but went to Egypt." He was now in Calcutta as financial advisor to the Viceroy.

The Gregorys went through Bombay and the Native States to Calcutta, where they were entertained by their fellow Irishman, Lord Dufferin. A party in their honor was fairyland to Augusta, but she did not forget the statistics: "There were 83 to dinner and 32 servants (I counted) and 250 people afterward." Lord Dufferin asked her for the first quadrille; she refused, because there had been no dancing lessons at Roxborough, and had the satisfaction of telling her mother afterward. As she watched the dancers from an easy chair, Colvin, now Sir Auckland Colvin, wearing his Alexandria medals won during the English bombardment of Arabi's army, bowed before her, delighted to see her again. Augusta was ready for friendship: "We have quite made peace. I think I was unjust to him." He went on to criticize Lord Dufferin, "In fact he talked as I should have expected Wilfrid to do." One of his chief criticisms was, "No wonder he knows so little, when he never talks to a *man*, watch him and you will never see him do so."

In fact, Lord Dufferin was very interested in all Augusta had to tell him about his kingdom: "At dinner I was next to His Excellency and as usual introduced serious talk, first about Cashmere and I gave him a good dose of the atrocities there . . . he wanted to know why I cared so much for these Mohammedans." She urged him to use his influence to raise Arabi's allowance. Dufferin checked everything she told him with Sir William, and before they left, he asked Sir William if he would allow him to propose him to Gladstone for the governorship of Madras, "as he should feel it such a boon and comfort to have him within call to consult and lean upon." Sir William was doubtful, but Augusta was enthusiastic: "He has so much good work in him and is so well in India, and we could have Robert here for 3 or 4 years at all events, but I daresay it will be given to some more active supporter at home after all"—as it was.

75

Mr. Trevelyan from the *Nizam*, who was also in Calcutta, had been at the state ball. Augusta went to the park next day, where "deer were chasing peacock over the green grass," and met him there. He told how popular Dufferin was, "especially amongst the old ladies," and that "Colvin was the only man worth tuppence."

On leaving for Ceylon, they "sent into council for his Excellency who came out quite shocked having forgotten or not taken in that we were leaving before him. 'They won't miss me in there, they're all fighting!' He seemed really sorry to part with us and said taking my hand and putting his arm around me at the same time, 'I won't forget your friend Arabi.' "

Augusta, with her husband safely beside her, was not sure whom she was in love with: Colvin, Trevelyan, even Dufferin. She wrote a poem about the moonrise, telling how her friend went in to play whist instead of waiting outside with her for the moonrise:

> Oh! fling your painted cards away
> And see beyond this mimic strife.
> The ace of hearts that there today
> With honours waits to crown your life!

She wrote:

> I think we just a step above
> That mystic laboratory stand
> Where friendship is transfused to love
> By the chance contact of a hand.
>
> I think the sparks that flash and fly
> From our four eyes, were we alone,
> Would fire the mine now guarded by
> The non-conductive looker on.

(The non-conductor apparently being her husband.)

In Ceylon she saw Sir William's statue, "very imposing," in front of the museum. She visited Arabi, who told her, "I know all you have done for me these four years. I speak as to a mother." She promised to send the women in his family each a dress. They all asked for pink. She had a letter from Robert, now nearly five, "written quite *alone*," and one from Wilfrid, who told her the political news and ended, "I have got quite cheerful while writing as I might have done sitting in an armchair in St. George's Place and drinking tea with you." She met an old friend of her brother Frank who told her, "Oh I was awfully fond of him—such a good fellow. I've seen him on a frosty night

76

in Grafton Square knock down three policemen of the B division one after another—with one blow!" She asked an English official about the chances of her brother Harry getting a post, but was told, "Nothing can be done for him unless he passes the examination"—which he never did. She admired the birds and butterflies, suffered from the heat and mosquities, saw the sacred bo tree, also saw "some fish walking across the road to reach some water on the other side 5 or 10 yards away. They were standing on their fins and getting on very well." She began wearing out on March 16, the day after her thirty-fourth birthday. Sir William went out visiting, and "I lay on the sofa and watched lizards catching flies on the ceiling." The day they sailed was so hot, "I grew faint and could hardly get through it." On shipboard she adopted another widower:: "I like Mr. Sanders best, he also has lost his wife and is taking his two little children home, one not a month old!" They arrived in Venice in the middle of April 1886, going to the Grand Hotel because the Layards were back in England. "It is just 6 months since we sailed away from here and all our journey has been most pleasant and full of delight."

She wrote a poem in the back cover of her Indian diary asking what awaited her in England. Robert awaited her:

> But then I know a bright haired child
> Stands waiting in the open door
> And when he is in my arms again,
> My heart is home—I ask no more!

She wrote that Wilfrid was not waiting for her:

> Ah me! I would it were not so,
> But there within the silent door,
> Naught greets you but the vacant shrine
> Of one gone forth forever more.

Another poem begins, "Alas! a woman may not love!" and describes love for brothers and sons who grow up to think nothing of her love, love for a husband that "Fades in the dull tints of common life / With misty cares and clouds of strife," and of a lover, "Found by her too late, too late." The poem ends with her most direct criticism of the social scheme as she saw it: "Perchance not so in heaven above / But here, a *woman* may not love."

All the suppressed sexual excitement had done her a world of good, even improved her appearance. Robert said to her, with the elegant diction that was the birthright of every upper-class five-year-old: "I should not have known you had I met you on the street." And when

77

they got back to Coole, a countryman said to her, as the country people were always commenting openly though always flatteringly on the appearance of the gentry, that "I had grown very good looking since I went to India and hadn't I great courage to face the ocean."

Several new developments awaited them. First was Gladstone's proposal for Home Rule for Ireland and the purchase of Irish estates by the tenants. She quoted with derision Gladstone's comment: "No doubt the educated classes are against me, but if the opinion of the men who can't read or write was taken against them they would be found nearest to the counsels of God!"—an opinion she herself would adopt in her final Irish phase.

Her brother Algernon, now forty-one, was engaged to Nora Gough, daughter of one of the great land-owning families near Roxborough, an engagement to which her father had consented "in spite of the dark prospect of the country." And her friend Mrs. Lee Childe had died, leaving her orphan nephew Paul Harvey without a home. He would be another in the long list of homeless young men Augusta looked after.

But as soon as Augusta and Sir William's feet touched English soil, even though they were not yet in their own house, which was still rented, they were running—"Private view at the Grosvenor"—to the Colonial Exhibition: "The Prince and the Crown Princess and Prince Edward arrived and Lady D. and I had to hide as no ladies were to be admitted." A few days later they moved from the hotel back to their house: "I had to spend 3 hours at the Co-op and look after Reilly's men with the inventory and Craces with the decorations and see Laby [her dentist], and finally, for a rest, I went to the St. Ormond Street mothers meeting and was asked to give a talk on India," which she did.

Grant Duff's daughter described the Gregorys as they appeared in society, "he funnily enough in those days considered the more important of the two, whereas he actually was merely a charming old gentleman and a good raconteur. . . . Lady Gregory was then a witty and friendly person, immensely fond of society with a highly developed social consciousness. . . . At that point she detested the idea of Home Rule."

She was entertaining frequently, writers and duchesses as well as old neighbors from Ireland—George Moore, Edward Martyn from Tulira Castle near Coole, and Count de Basterot whose summer home, Duras, was on the Burren coast.

Wilfrid, back in London after toying with the idea of entering a monastery in Rome (Lady Anne notwithstanding), was applying the principles of nationalism learned in Egypt to Ireland and finding they fit exactly. The Gregorys had seen him briefly on their way through London to Venice in October, when he "scandalized William by his views on home rule." She was not pleased either, writing him, "I must send you 'United Ireland' some day, Parnell's paper, to show you how vulgar and virulent it is—so unlike the Irish people, the poor who are so courteous and full of tact even in their discontent." Even Robert—at five years old—had unexpectedly developed firm political opinions, and refused to greet Wilfrid when he came to call. Augusta described the meeting in her diary. She asked him, "Don't you know Mr. Blunt?"

"No," said Robert. "He has gone in for Home Rule."

"But I was always a Home Ruler," said Wilfrid.

"Well, when you get it, perhaps you won't like it as much as you think," said Robert.

Wilfrid had been to Ireland in March to observe evictions, which he described as "a brutal and absurd spectacle, 250 armed men, soldiers in all but name, storming the cottages one after the other of half starved tenants, and faced by less than half their number of women and boys. . . . The houses were ransacked, the furniture thrown out, the fires quenched, and a bit of thatch was taken possession of as a token in each case that the landlord had reentered his rights. Then the inhabitants were turned adrift in the world. . . . The sight made me so angry that I was positively ill, my heart hurting me." Augusta, who had never seen an eviction, preferred to take a less serious view, writing in her diary of a reported eviction at which a bedridden old man was found to have his "boots on and was shamming." She was also annoyed because the Roxborough tenants had collected money for "a very handsome salver" as a wedding present for Algernon but asked that "it might not be mentioned in the list of presents as they were afraid of the Land League and the Tuam news." These were the same tenants from whom seven soldiers had been protecting Algernon a few years earlier.

Gladstone's Home Rule bill was defeated in Parliament. Augusta wrote a friend, "Gladstone beaten by thirty, isn't it delightful!" A few days later Wilfrid came by after breakfast rather subdued, "but thinking of standing for an English constituency." He himself wrote more ominously about his visit: "Called on Lady Gregory (in London), who is growing very bitter against my politics, if not against me. It is curious that she, who could see so clearly in Egypt, when it was a case between the Circassian Pashas and the Arab fellahin, should be blind now that the case is between English landlords and

Irish tenants in Galway. But property blinds all eyes, and it is easier for a camel to pass through the eye of a needle, than for an Irish landlord to enter the kingdom of home rule." While in India, Augusta had written a poem about helping an Irish vagrant, washing his feet, giving him food and wine:

> But as he left in the evening cool
> He mockingly looked back and smiled
> For while I tended him, poor fool,
> His hand had stripped my sleeping child.

The coolness between Wilfrid and Augusta ended with Augusta's writing him to come say goodbye to her before she left for Ireland, which he did. She thought that he had given up Ireland and again taken up Egypt. However, he wrote from Scotland, "I would like to attend Lord Clanricarde's eviction as it would give me a chance of seeing you. We are hunting the Stag." Like Sir William, Wilfrid never questioned the rightness of his aristocratic pleasures—even while working to undermine the system that made them possible.

But he went to Paris and then to Rome with Lady Anne, and Augusta did good works in Ireland, where she felt "at the back of the North Wind, reading exciting Irish news in the papers and living such a still, peaceful life. We are yet on most cordial terms with our people—but we mustn't boast too much till rent day comes." There was no trouble on rent day at Coole, but there was trouble at other estates, and Augusta twitted Wilfrid, prophetically as it turned out, "I must condole with you on not being in Ireland just now, you would have such a good chance of imprisonment."

She filled the house with men and boys—Robert, Paul Harvey, her own brothers Harry and Gerald. They went shooting. Evictions were going on all around them. She had a party for 180 workhouse children. She took her guests to a tennis party at Castle Taylor. Her brothers and Paul left and some female relations arrived—"A fine day, but the girls don't make up for the boys!" William was uncomfortable with eczema over his lips and "angry and unjust about Robert." At seventy, he was finding it difficult to be patient with his six-year-old.

Occasionally Augusta saw and felt the rawness of Irish life:

In the afternoon drove Louise Frank to see Widow Burke's little girls, the eldest 17, getting the same look her sister had before she died and from the same cause, and I try to get their mother's consent to her going to Dublin for better advice. The little one, 9 years old, is dying . . . and lay almost in a stupor with dilated pupils and tiny shrunken arms. Poor little thing, she said the other day, "Mother, don't fret. I'll soon be in heaven praying for you with me own Biddy"— the sister that died. I had been upset by Frank telling me a dreadful story (a true) about a child who died in the Fort Fear Hospital and the father going to have a last look found the coffin had been too small and the men had broken the legs to fit her in. It, and the sight of this other poor little dying skinny creature half in the grave already, and I fainted on the earthen floor.

In 1887 the tenants demanded a twenty-eight percent reduction in rents. Algernon—not a practiced negotiator—got them to accept twenty-five percent—which is what they intended in the first place. That year Augusta and Sir William stayed on at Coole past their usual time, and when they left in October, it was not for the London season but for Italy, where the living was cheaper.

Augusta did not want to leave Robert, who was going to spend the winter with his Aunt Eliza. When she saw him off, "He was bright enough, thinking of his drive to Castle Taylor with Gip, he does not know the pain of parting, but I think he will miss me, poor little man."

Their first stop was at the Layards' in Venice. On October 26, just as they were getting into a gondola to look at pictures at the Academy, Sir Henry told her "of the news in today's Times of the row at Woodford and the arrest of Wilfrid Blunt." And so began one of the most conflicted periods in her life.

Wilfrid had finally gone to Ireland to be present at evictions on the estate of her neighbor Clanricarde. A tenant meeting Wilfrid was scheduled to address was proscribed. It was held and he spoke anyway. He and Lady Anne were pushed off the platform by police. He struggled back and began his speech again. He was pushed off again by seven or eight policemen. Lady Anne, as loyal and valiant as ever, clung to him and was pulled off by one of the policemen, who grabbed her by the throat from behind. Wilfrid was arrested and spent the night in Loughrea jail.

Augusta wrote him immediately: "How bad of you to get into such a commotion. The first accounts in the papers were horrible and I did not know whether you and poor Lady Anne had been hurt in the scuffle, and if you were already in jail and I was more anxious than you deserve your friends should be—and to try if I could have been of any help to Lady Anne to whom please give my love. I suppose you are rather enjoying the trial now taking up so much of the paper. I hope you will somehow escape being locked up, for these cold nights and dark evenings are not the time to try imprisonment with complacency and you have been in for one night which is enough for you. You will have to write a poem to yourself in prison, none of the Irish leaders have got the gift.—Oh! I can jest about it in writing but the whole troublous time is very near my heart."

Wilfrid was tried, found guilty of speaking at a proscribed meeting, and sentenced to two months' hard labor in Galway jail. Hard labor was not terribly hard—his job was to pick tar out of old ropes—but the jail was very cold, and the nights were long and dark.

Augusta, far away in Rome, was bored and cross. She missed her son. She was tired of economizing. She fell back in love with Wilfrid—an emotional complication suffered by most of his women friends. She tried to make him more comfortable. Most of the people she needed were already in Rome, among them her friend Sir Michael Morris, Chief Justice of Ireland, who was not much help: "delighted to tell me of Wilfrid Blunt's imprisonment, hopes he will be 'sha-a-ved' as then he can't pose as an Oriental for a long time to come." The Bishop of Galway, also in Rome, told her Wilfrid could not receive letters, but promised to visit him when he got back to Galway. Sir William told his steward at Coole to send Wilfrid game and vegetables. Augusta wrote one of her relatives who was a visiting magistrate. Wilfrid's accommodations did not improve, but the jailors were impressed by his connections.

In Rome, Augusta wore a white-and-gold dress to the Christmas party at the Embassy and "received compliments on my youthful appearance!" She had a tea party at the hotel that was "a great success and not an 'abominable orgy' as William had prophesied." She wrote Wilfrid in cold Galway jail, "I had a brilliant party yesterday. How I hate Christmas away from home and my child." She too was cold, then tired, then headachy, then vomiting. This was the beginning of the migraines that were to torment her for many years. When she was well, she was writing love poems to Wilfrid. (She did not mention them in her diary, but they were found in Blunt's papers marked, "Written to me while in prison by Lady Gregory.")

She wrote in "A Lament":

> My heart is in a prison cell,
> My own true love beside,

> Where more of worth and beauty dwell
> Than in the whole world wide.

She wrote "Without and Within," contrasting the ordinary life outside the prison with the prisoner's life inside, and ending:

> Without the gate, without the gate
> I early come, I linger late,
> I wait the blessed hour when he
> Shall come and cross the bridge with me
> Without the gate, without the gate.

Eighteen years later she would write *The Gaol Gate*, one of her most moving plays, about two Irish country women, a mother and a wife, waiting outside Galway jail for news of their man. She knew the gate well.

At last, in April 1888, to Augusta's great relief, she and Sir William left Rome. In addition to her worry about Wilfrid and fretfulness about being away from Robert, she found the all-encompassing Catholicism distasteful. She wrote about the Pope's mass on January 1, "a mummery as usual, the rites looking altogether pagan, and His Holiness drinking all the wine that had been consecrated had a ludicrous look." After another mass she wrote, "Feel more indignantly Protestant than ever."

Back in London, William gave her a beautiful ivory-handled umbrella that lived on into her other life as theater manager and playwright, constantly being lost, always being found. And she at last saw Wilfrid, one month out of jail, "looking none the worse for his imprisonment."

But the Gregorys were still economizing, and left London immediately for Coole. Augusta visited her mother, who, giving up on the Dublin marriage market, had returned to Galway with Arabella. With great difficulty Augusta got herself admitted to Galway jail, where she sketched the two empty cells in which Wilfrid had been imprisoned. She sent them to him and he thanked her for "two very interesting drawings of localities in Galway" and sent her his picture in prison clothes. Sometime that summer she sent him another poem, "The Eviction," using the metaphor of an Irish eviction to describe her attempt to put him out of her heart:

> Unruly tenant of my heart,
> Full fain would I be quit of thee.

> I've played too long a losing part.
> Thou bringest me neither gold nor fee.

After describing her attempt to evict him, she concludes:

> For lo, in stillness of the night,
> O'erturning stone and guard and door,
> Thou art come with thy lost tenant right
> And hast possession as before.

Wilfrid was already in love with several other women, but he was impressed by the poetry.

Wilfrid and Lady Anne were back in Galway in June for the trial of another Irish patriot, and even paid a call on Augusta's mother, "a fine old lady who talked to us of Jesuit intrigues and popery generally." Augusta did not invite them to Coole; Sir William was away and she was not sure he would approve. While he may not have minded Blunt's having an affair with his wife, she was fairly sure he was angry with Wilfrid for contributing to the decline in his rents.

When Sir William got back, she entertained so many uninteresting guests so well that he remarked, "Augusta deserves to have good company, she is so splendid at entertaining bores." And she felt, she said, "like a hotel-keeper without the emolument." When her guests were gone, she visited her new sister-in-law, Algernon's wife, Nora, and her sister Eliza at Castle Taylor. She disapproved of her brother Harry's marriage to Miss Ada Beadon, remarking with unusual unkindness on her return to Coole that "Harry and Ada drove over from Castle Taylor. She is very plain, but quite subdued now. Her spirit must have been broken at Castle Taylor." It was another dull summer: "The trivial round, the daily task."

By now Augusta realized that Coole was mortgaged to her husband's cousin and that Sir William was doing nothing to pay it off. The money they saved living at Coole or Rome went to pay the interest (at 4.5 percent) and to maintain their life in London. While she felt it was important that Sir William continue to live in the style he thought appropriate, she also felt the strain of wanting something different for her son.

When she got back to St. George's Place in October, she spent the week reclaiming it so vigorously, "cleaning, painting, washing and slave driving," that when she went out on Friday night, she fainted at dinner.

Her brother Frank, now the father of several children, was in London working for an architect. He was, wrote Augusta, "very diligent, makes his own tea, buying presents for wife and children his only luxury. One should despair of no one after this."

In November 1888 Wilfrid, on his way to Greece and Egypt, asked her to see his prison poems, *In Vinculis*, through the press, which she did between violent headaches, and was rewarded by Wilfrid's sending her a piece of tarred rope.

She finally saw a doctor about her headaches and vomiting. He said they were caused by a "nerve connecting the stomach and brain and that the brain has been taking the nourishment the stomach ought to have." He promised to cure her. She continued to be sick. Her life was beginning to involve too much duty and too little reward.

The following year Wilfrid brought out another volume of poems, *A New Pilgrimage*. She and William read the book in turns, taking it out of each other's hands. She immediately defined the lack in all his poems: "I feel that one is rather led in them to expect a revelation of your very inmost soul and they stop just before that comes"—a complaint she would not have about W. B. Yeats, her next poet. She herself was suffering from lack of exposure to the "inmost soul," her own as well as that of anyone else.

When she was much older, she would write, in a rare moment of recognition of the isolation in which she lived, "Are we not but as prisoners in adjoining cells, scratching a signal on the wall with a rusty nail, trying to wear away the stone." At the time, however, dizzy from the years in London society, Augusta would have found it hard to say exactly what she was living for or what she wanted. Still hungry for compliments after a childhood in which any kind of approval was rare, she was beginning to lose her sense of the self to which they were directed. After the death of her friend Alexander Kinglake, whom she had visited daily, she wrote in her diary: "Kinglake's nurse came to lunch. I am to be sent two small favourite swords of his, as he wished me to have a souvenir. She says he often spoke of me as beautiful in my charity and writing the best letters, and having the clearest political head of any woman he knew—and said, that . . . the servants and all in the house liked me better than any of his other visitors. Please God, I may not grow bad, but earn a good opinion from others." She had reached the same point in her marriage that she had reached in her spinsterhood just before she married Sir William: the activities and duties of her life, instead of rewarding her, were beginning to exasperate her.

She wrote in her diary, summarizing 1890, "Most thankful that my own dear husband and child are strong and well and my own health is restored and no grief in my family." But a week later, after a hard day of charitable work, she was "not able to keep down the vegetables and soup I took, and twice awoke with headache."

January, February, and March of 1891 were darkened by her dread of Robert's departure for boarding school. She was diverted only by family problems. The agent who replaced Algernon at Roxborough died; her brother Frank, happy to give up his drudgery in London, took over the job. And her sister Arabella, now forty-two, finally got married—to a widower from Galway, Wainwright Waithman, unpleasant, unstable, and miserly. Augusta wrote in her diary on the day Arabella announced her engagement, "She lost her chance of Sir E. Bunbury who was sitting with me when she came home." After an unpleasant day going over finances with her fiancé, Augusta asked Arabella, "How do you like the prospect of an engagement for life with him?" Augusta wrote, "Poor A. I think the shopping and being made a center of interest made up for a great deal."

On the day in April 1891 before Robert, now nearly ten, left for boarding school, he put his arms around her and said, "Mamma, I'm not so ready to go to school so much now." When she and William saw him off at Victoria Station, she "could not take a last look at my child as the train went off." She had a raging headache, but that same day took twenty poor boys to the Natural History Museum, said she could not go to dinner, and in the evening went to the opera, relieved to sit at the back of the box where her tear-stained face would not be noticed. The next day she had such a terrible headache that, in the long tradition of migraine sufferers, "I felt a sympathy for those who commit suicide." The next month she went to see Robert at school. "He is very full of cricket and kept explaining terms to me. He would rather be at home, but at all events not unhappy." She felt much better, but not really happy until he came home to Coole in July. "We wept all around, he talked cricket. And then he went to bed, sleepy and happy, but no one can know how happy I was!"

The summer of 1891 was her last happy time at Coole for many years. She had a story published in *Argosy* in June, "A Philanthropist" (by "Angus Grey"), about a young Englishwoman who becomes so attached to the Irish country people she becomes engaged to the local doctor so she can stay in the district. Insofar as Augusta intended to become a writer—"the occupation for which [as a child] I had the most reverence, perhaps because of some unconscious aspiration"— she already knew her material was in Ireland. And she already sensed that she had a problem with self-revelation, even in this veiled, innocuous account of herself trying to find her appropriate relationship to the country people. She was aware that, unless one is a genius, intimate revelations tend to undercut one's social position and embarrass one's husband. She would later see a way to recast at least some of her emotions as those of the country people themselves.

She tried again to learn Gaelic with an old gardener who was "languid, suspecting it may be some hidden mockery, for those were the days before Irish became the fashion."

And she was still struggling with the literary form, writing Wilfrid, "I am trying to write a local story, but don't think it will come to much. It is easy to write 'situations' or conversation, but the trivial parts are the difficulty, getting people up and down stairs, or in and out of the house gracefully." She would later discover that most efficient means of moving people about: the stage direction.

In October, Wilfrid, who was preparing his poems for an edition by William Morris's Kelmscott Press and having an affair with Morris's wife, Janey, asked Augusta if she would correct the proofs and if he could include her sonnets. She replied collectedly, "I shall be very glad if I can be of any use to you in correcting. I see no reason why those 12 sonnets should not be published if you think them worth it—merely call them 'Sonnets by a Woman.' " But she wrote him another sonnet:

> —To-day you take it from me, my poor rhyme,
> And lightly ask me, "Why these foolish tears?"
> You give the world my secret—"it was time.
> What can it matter after all these years?"
> Ay. What in truth? Yet herein lies the smart,
> That grief for you no longer grieves my heart.

Charles Stewart Parnell, who had led the Irish party for eleven years, died in October 1891 after a year of bitter turmoil, involvement in a spectacular divorce trial arising out of his affair with the wife of another Irish member of Parliament, dismissal as head of the Irish party, and a frantic attempt to regain his former power. Augusta wrote, in the same letter that gave Wilfrid permission to publish her sonnets, "Parnell's death and funeral impress the imagination," and added, "We may see 'a dead man win a fight.' " She too was captivated by the appeal of "the lost leader," so prevalent in Irish mythology, who at the last pointed a way to a vaguer and more glorious nationalism. The immediate result of the violent passions aroused by the dispute over Parnell's leadership was a widespread disgust with all politics. People began to search for an Irish national identity apart from politics and turned to Gaelic studies, folklore, poetry, and drama. . . .

For Augusta too, the life she had lived for the last eleven years was nearly over. The Gregorys went to London in November, where "poor Robert rather got into trouble, letting off explosions which marked the ceiling." Then he went back to school: "I felt stunned when he left, the place so silent and vacant. . . . And William came in to dine tired and what he used not to be, peevish and irritable—and my head still so bad that I cried a little on my dark side of the library—I had not looked forward to London, but it is worse than I expected."

Before he came down to dinner, Sir William had written Sir Henry: "I must tell you, as my closest friend, the whole truth—I am extremely ill. As you are aware, I suffered from what seemed to be palpitation of the heart when I was with you in the summer, and I also had a severe, almost dangerous, attack of bronchitis. Both of these ailments have disappeared, but they have been succeeded, ever since my return to England, by a constantly increasing diarrhea. I am getting weaker and weaker, thinner and thinner. . . . I have very little care for life, but I should like a few years more, to help poor Augusta and Robert, for these are critical times for them."

Augusta thought he was getting better and wrote Wilfrid, "Sir William keeps gaining ground," but he wasn't. The doctor sent him away from the raw cold of London to Bournemouth. When Robert went to say goodbye before he left for school, Augusta had overheard his father say, "Goodbye, my little man, mind you take care of your Mommy now, for I'm not able to do it any longer." Back in London in February, he insisted on going to a meeting of the directors of the National Gallery. Then he went home to die. He was delirious for nineteen days, and Augusta sat by him, going without sleep for nineteen nights. On the evening he died, "He opened his eyes for the first time with full consciousness, took my hand and said, 'The tie that has bound us is going to be loosened at last—I have loved you very much and grieve very much at leaving you. I hope Robert will grow up a good man. I know you will be a good mother to him.' I said, 'Who knows but we may meet again?' 'Oh,' he said, 'and who knows but we may not,' and then taking my hand in both of his and laying it on his heart, he said, 'Remember I die, believing in God, not an unjust God, but a God of Mercy. We are all God's children.' "

He died on March 6, two days after their twelfth wedding anniversary. A year later, when she started keeping her diary again, she recalled, "And I sat there all night alone, writing to Robert and my mother and Layard." She slept all the next day, then "A telegram of sympathy from Eliza made me cry for the first time. Oh, my husband! Do you know how little I have forgotten you!"

She received a long, gossipy letter from Wilfrid in Egypt telling her, "For the first time in my life, I think, this winter I have been absolutely and entirely happy," and advising her, "Sir W. might do worse than buy a few acres here for his winter residence." Then came the letters of condolence from him and Lady Anne.

She had a memorial service for Sir William at St. George's, Hanover Square. "I have never seen so many *men* with tears in their eyes." Her brothers Frank and Gerald came from Ireland to take the body back to Coole for burial. The next Sunday she went to Southampton to meet Robert. He was ten. She had her fortieth birthday nine days after William's death. The sheltered years were over.

III

The Rediscovery of Ireland

WIDOWHOOD: 1892–1897

Then felt I like some watcher of the skies
When a new planet swims into his ken.
JOHN KEATS, "On First Looking into Chapman's Homer"

AUGUSTA stayed in London for a month after Sir William's death. Her friend Sir Arthur Birch helped her with estate business. Sir William's doctor took her driving in the evenings. She gave away Sir William's clothes and her own. She never again wore her gold-and-white gown; her black dress with red roses that had seen such valiant service in India ended its days as upholstery on a drawing-room chair. Though she had dressed to please Sir William during his life, once he was gone she disregarded his specific instructions: "I trust that nothing will induce you to wear funeral trappings in coif or crape"—and wore mourning for the rest of her life.

For forty years, when she looked in the mirror, she saw black. Her mourning costume cast a darkness around her, causing people who did not know her to misjudge her. She did not, however, look often at herself, and if people misjudged her, it was partly her intention they do so. Her mourning made it appear that she was not a participant in Vanity Fair; yet, in reality, her heart was as hungry as any of theirs. Her demanding, crippled, uncertain ego could not plunge naked into the struggle for love and glory. Being Sir William's wife had protected—and limited—her. With his death, the limitations fell away; she kept the protection.

Her mourning did make one thing clear. Though she had collected compliments eagerly for twelve years, she never wished for the great compliment of another marriage proposal. She had done that duty. For the first time in her life, no one was determining for her how she would live, where she would live, what she would live for. It took her five years to translate her freedom, which she could not use, into duties, which she could.

She saw her first care as the maintenance of Coole Park debt-free for Robert. Like many of her duties, it turned out well for her. Robert was never, in fact, master of Coole, but Coole became for her a temple, a second self that was not in mourning, to which she could invite those with whom she wished to share her life. Sir William's will appointed her trustee of Coole until Robert came of age—with the right to live there rent-free throughout her life. She was also left the household and contents of the London house. She had Sir William's desk (the "great ormolu table" of Yeats's poem "Beautiful Lofty Things") shipped back to Coole. She sold the leasehold of the house immediately, along with the silver, and the receipts went directly to Sir William's cousin, Charles Gregory, who was rather startled, preferring his high interest to his principal. Augusta leased Coole to a Welsh tenant for the summer; again the receipts went to Charles Gregory.

After taking Robert to Coole for one day to visit his father's grave, she sent him back to school in England and stayed there alone until the summer tenant took possession. It was very quiet: "I sometimes read aloud to myself for the sake of hearing a human voice." She spent days driving along the wild west coast: "The rocks that shattered the Armada are splendid." The last weeks she sent her two maids away, remaining completely alone: "The house is very empty. The grave is not so silent, for I listened there today and could hear the rush of the river."

Next door, at Roxborough, everything was in turmoil. A week after Sir William's death, her half-brother, Dudley, finally succeeded in drinking himself to death. Her brother William, who lived in England, inherited. He put Frank out of the agency and Algernon back in. Then he came over to visit and liked being "Master" so much he took over himself. Augusta was sent for. She found William "as I had found Dudley before, killing himself with drink." Once she got him sober, he and his wife, Rose, returned to London. Her brother Gerald took over as agent and began suffering from "nervous depression," not letting Augusta out of his sight. She wrote, "I am glad to be wanted anywhere but would wish myself less isolated."

She was actually running the estate, as she had years earlier. Except for Robert, who joined her at Roxborough when school was out, she might have wondered whether her marriage and the bright life in London had ever really happened. William, who remained drunk once he got back to London, got the idea she wanted to have him committed to an asylum and take over Roxborough herself. He telegraphed orders for her to go. The shock of being put out made Augusta start writing her diary again, no longer to note her successes but to record her sorrows: "And on the last night of the saddest year of my life, in bitter cold, Robert and I left my old home and took refuge at The Croft [her mother's home in Galway]. Here I am wanted and likely to stay at present. But there is a terrible difference in my life." Her brother's telegram was followed by "a *brutal* letter . . . insulting my husband's memory."

Six weeks after William put her out of Roxborough, in February 1893 he too succeeded in drinking himself to death. Now her diary recorded her goodness: "It is best so! He could not resist and the mind was going, and he would have brought shame and trouble on us all. Yet I did not think I could feel so sorry, and thank God, I can forgive him and have no bad feeling."

At Roxborough her brother William's thirty-year-old son Arthur took possession, and his mother, Rose, returned as dowager of Roxborough. She and her daughters were delighted to slight Augusta, who moved in much higher social circles than they in London but who had come down in the world: "Rose and the girls full of cuts at the family . . . and after the good, the high-minded society I had enjoyed in London, they seemed so empty, narrow, trivial and common, Rose's swagger so vulgar and blatant." When her brother Gerald became engaged, she wrote, "Gerald accepted by Ethel Rockford, and as Eliza says, we shall be glad of a real lady as sister-in-law after Rose!" Though Gerald, who was drinking heavily, never married his real lady, the magic circle of wild brothers was broken. Nor could she feel any longer her childhood sense of romance in the sweep of Roxborough hills—they were no longer hers.

Life at the Croft was unpleasant. Her mother, who had presided over the massive order of Roxborough, was now surrounded by quarreling and inefficient servants who did not keep the house clean, who barely cooked the meals, and who occasionally stole. Rats coursed through the walls of the house, and though they did not get into Augusta's room, they left an earthy smell and kept her awake at night.

Going to church in Galway, she was startled—after her long exposure to religious tolerance—to hear the minister declare that he was sure every person in the congregation believed literally in every word of the Bible. The narrowness of her old life was rising up around her on every side.

She took refuge in thoughts of her London life and wrote a pamphlet against Home Rule, which was again under consideration, entitled *A Phantom's Pilgrimage: or Home Ruin*, in which Gladstone comes back from the grave and sees the devastation brought by the change he so desired. But Augusta knew that, devastating or not, the change was coming—and the land was going.

At last she escaped back to London and her friends, staying with the Layards, "and the pleasant talk and being made welcome helped to restore my self-respect which had really been shaken." She was lavishly complimented on her pamphlet: "Lecky, Billy Russell, Sir H. Layard, Sir F. Burton particularly commended it. . . . Successful day, Lord Selborne and Lady Sophia came to dinner especially to meet me."

Even in London, however, her family needed her help. Her beautiful worn-out sister Adelaide was finally separating from the husband it had cost her so much to marry. The Reverend John Lane had a mistress, and though Augusta felt that "a more worldly wise woman would have for the children's sake kept the home unbroken," Adelaide could tolerate no more. Adelaide had her husband's love letters to his "woman"; Augusta got her to give them up and passed them on to the lawyer to be burned. She oversaw the details of the legal separation. She got Adelaide's son Hugh a job at Colnaghi's (an art dealer), and she paid Adelaide's debts, for, as she wrote in her diary, "I could not say 'depart in peace, be warmed and filled' and do nothing for her."

Wilfrid Blunt came to see Augusta at the Layard's and "found her sad in her widow's weeds." He suggested she become the political writer for a new magazine his friend Margot Tennant was bringing out, to be called "Tomorrow: A Woman's Journal for Men." (Wilfrid had recently spent a night making love to Margot Tennant in her "little virginal bed" in her parents' home in Scotland. She never asked him back, but the next year she asked him whom she should marry, ignored his advice, and married Herbert Asquith, the future Prime Minister.) Augusta turned down the chance to write for her magazine—which was to have Oscar Wilde as another contributor—but it did not materialize anyway. Still stunned by the great changes in her life, she explained her refusal: "I can only drift, not taking much interest in anything but Robert, and he is quite lost to me at school." She spent Whitsuntide of 1893 at Crabbet with Wilfrid, "very happy in the beauty of scenery and weather," all the time steeling herself for her return to Ireland and to Coole, for which she had not found a tenant for the summer: "My heart rather fails me at the idea of six weeks alone before Robert comes."

On her return to Coole, as she wrote Enid, "many things seem unpleasant and wrong." Her most trusted housemaid was "odd in her manner" and after a few days collapsed completely, out of her mind with drink. Augusta sent her away, but soon realized if she fired every servant who drank, she would be alone indeed.

Waiting for Robert to return, she preserved gooseberries, visited Lord and Lady Morris at Spiddal on the west coast, and—in October 1893, before anyone else in the Irish Renaissance—went to the Aran Isles, the three islands twenty miles off the coast of Galway where the Gaelic language and an isolated, archaic way of life made visitor after visitor more keenly aware of the tensions, triviality, and materialism of life on the mainland. She was stormbound there for five days, living on potatoes in a cottage with people who hardly spoke English. "I was quite happy."

Back at Coole, she read *Lavengro*, George Borrow's story of a wondering philologist—an occupation she would take up in a few years. She read *Beside the Fire* by Douglas Hyde, a retelling of Irish folktales in which he appeals to the public of Ireland for more collectors to preserve this vanishing tradition, using as his epigraph: "They are like a mist on the coming of night / That is scattered away by a light breath of wind." She read *Irish Idyls* by Jane Barlow, about a miserably poor Irish village in which the cold, hunger, and dirt are compensated for by the kindness and uncomplaining resignation of the people who must endure them. The author, another upper-class Irishwoman, the daughter of an earl, was, like other writers of the time, using her observation of the Irish people as a vehicle for her self-expression. Augusta sent *Irish Idyls* to Enid Layard, telling her, "It really gives me sympathy with the people. It is one of my sermon books." But Augusta, who was not much motivated by sympathy, had not yet found any attitude toward the Irish people that would provide a vehicle for her own self-expression.

Devoting herself to old duties, Augusta spent the summer preparing Sir William's memoirs for publication, so that, as she wrote in her preface, "his name, which was known, and kindly known, in many counties besides his own, may be kept alive a little longer, and that for his sake a friendly hand may sometimes in the future be held out to his boy." The book was accepted by the publisher John Murray, who suggested that Sir Henry Layard, as her husband's old friend and someone "more in the world" than she, go over the manuscript with her. As she saw it, their task was to leave out anything that might have "vexed the living or slighted the memory of the dead." Augusta never had the modern passion for "the truth." For her, a narrative was an act of complicity between author and audience, which, while not necessarily a useful approach to nonfiction, suited her well for writing drama. (Years later, when Wilfrid consulted her about publishing his diaries and ignored her advice, he found the people he criticized were nearly as pleased as the people he praised.)

Augusta stayed on at the Layards' flat through the fall of 1893 when they went to Venice, using Sir Henry's typewriter to produce a new draft of the memoirs, using their housemaid as cook for a "little tea party." She had Henry James and four other men and Emily Lawless (another daughter of an Irish earl writing about Irish subjects) and three other women, writing Enid, "I had been to tea with Miss Lawless the day before and she had only one man, so I felt proud of my superiority!"

She decided she needed a flat in London for Robert's sake because without it, "I might possibly become dull in society, whereas now I have the name of brightness and agreeability. I should lose sight of William's friends by staying away and they may in 8 or 9 years be of great use to Robert as I see from Paul and others the difference made to a lad of a good start and influential friends."

She rented rooms in Queen Anne's Mansions near the Layards. The help her friends gave her in furnishing indicates how well she had kept her friendships in repair. Sir Henry gave her a print of his portrait. Enid gave her a Florentine carved chair and a tea service. Paul Harvey, now twenty-four and a secretary in the War Office, gave her a Chippendale chair, Sir Frederic Burton a large drawing, Lady Lindsay three beautiful rugs and a cabinet.

She hung the Burmese silk curtains from St. George's Place and began entertaining furiously, taking her guests to the restaurant in Queen Anne's Mansions for dinner. Sir Auckland Colvin came to visit. She invited Sir Frederic Burton and the Layards; she and Enid "teased Sir F. to say which of us he liked best." She entertained Wilfrid and a "horsey" set. (Wilfrid's annual sale of Arabians at Crabbet had become an event of the London social season.) She again took up her mothers' meetings, writing in her diary, "These parties cost me more than I could well afford, having my poor Coole as first charge, but they gave great pleasure." It was a test of courage going alone to the restaurant, and if she did not have company, she usually, as she wrote in her diary, "had a sandwich at the station."

Fortunately, she was invited out frequently. Her diary has long lists of people she dined with, among them a note that in the early spring of 1894 "at Lord Morris' met Yates [sic] looking every inch a poet, though I think his prose 'Celtic Twilight' is the best thing he has done." Yeats, then twenty-nine, was very poor, looked starved, and dressed completely in seedy black with a flowing black tie around his long, naked throat. He constantly ran his hands through his black hair and "murmured ends of verse to himself with a wild eye." An admirer later declared that he was one of the three "handsomest and most romantic-looking men" she had ever seen in her life—the other two being Wilfrid Blunt and Roger Casement, who was executed by the British in 1916 as a traitor for trying to create an Irish brigade to fight for Germany against England. The tall, thin, dark, romantic-looking man in his black poet's costume, bowing in dark silence over the hand of the small, bright, agreeable woman in her widow's black, was a prefiguration of things to come—the meeting of the characters in front of the curtain before their drama begins. Some elements of Augusta's past life would have to fall away, some aspects of her love for Ireland would have to come into focus before Yeats would become for her liberation and inspiration, and she would become for him "mother, friend, sister and brother."

One pillar of her old life fell away in July of 1894 with the death of Sir Henry Layard, who, as her husband's closest friend, had seemed his continuing representative. Enid sent for her on the night he died. When she arrived, Enid's bewilderment reminded her so much of her own two years before that she broke into passionate sobbing. Enid comforted her. They sat together through the night. At five in the morning Enid asked what time it was, and when Augusta told her, she said, "Then morning has come," and burst into sobs. They now had in common their widowhood. Augusta wrote of their long friendship, "Childless and with sufficient wealth, she had no anxieties such as mine, and her interests did not widen as mine did. Yet she was the nearest of my women friends, and our affectionate friendship was never broken."

The summer of 1894 at Coole was more pleasant than usual. Sir Arthur Birch, whose wife had recently died, came with his sons—slightly older than Robert—his daughter, footman, housemaid, and lady's maid. He and Augusta shared expenses, a pleasant and familial arrangement that allowed her to test, as it were, the advantages of re-marriage—which she could easily have justified as being for Robert's good. She could see that Robert might well be better off with a fuller family life, with brothers, sisters, and a stepfather, with a mother hovering about looking after her men. She felt the strain of raising a child alone—but she was not tempted. Safely encased in black, filling the house with cousins, nephews, friends, and tutors, she kept herself to herself.

Augusta, who had once sympathized with Wilfrid Blunt's claim that his beautiful young daughter, Judith, was the one person in the world he feared, now felt the fear of losing Robert's love. He was the one person whose relationship to her she—who felt safe only with managed relationships—had no ability to manipulate. Raising him was the one duty whose successful performance would not be noted in heaven alone; taking care of Robert, she was thoroughly aware, as she was not in the performance of her other duties, that someone depended on her.

Robert was proud and shy, easily embarrassed but not easily cowed, passionate about sports, and still—at twelve, thirteen, and fourteen—opinionated about the benefits of the British Empire. Augusta held before him the success of his father and grandfather and great-uncles at Harrow—which was the next step in his education—and hoped for the best.

All in all, it was a "grand and happy summer," but in September Sir Arthur and his daughter returned to London. Then, when the boys left for school a few weeks later, Augusta was completely alone. Anxious to get back to London before the publication of Sir William's autobiography, she nevertheless stayed at Coole until nearly the last minute to save money. After the solitude, the wide spaces, the cold and damp of Coole, her London rooms looked wonderful, "clean and cozy, with fires and a new Belgian housemaid." Starved for company, and anxious to promote Sir William's book, she entertained every night.

Three days after she arrived, on October 18, 1894, the book was out. She had sent copies to a long list of influential friends. The book was reviewed everywhere, and most of the reviews were enthusiastic. She was complimented by her publishers, not only on her literary success, but on her promotional activity, "as many authors left all the trouble to them." Arthur Birch asked if "I did not feel three inches taller at the success of the book. I said no, but ten years younger, which is true." Sir Arthur had his copy from Mudie's, the lending library, which notified him, "This book being *in great demand* is to be returned as soon as possible."

Wilfrid Blunt, as an author who understood these matters, had written her earlier that "I shall look forward to the publication of your book of memoirs and *shall buy it*." After he did, he wrote, "It is the

97

very best book of its kind that I ever read. Your few lines at the end brought tears to my eyes . . . I hardly know why, for you effaced yourself throughout the book and what you at last say is very little and very simple." He concluded, "I hope you will write to me sometimes, even now that you are a literary celebrity. You do not know how proud I feel of your success."

Her few words are indeed simple and moving. The book is entirely in Sir William's words up to his return from Ceylon three years before he remarried. Augusta tells the story of the last years of his life with extracts from his letters to Sir Henry, introducing them with a five-page summary of his views and accomplishments, saying, "He has written so frankly and candidly of the errors of his youth, that it is only just that his great success of later days should be dwelt on." She described his accomplishments in Ceylon; she gave his solution to the Irish problem (which was that eventually adopted: tenant land purchase); she recognized the "genius for kindness" that made him popular with all classes; and she concluded, listing the wreaths that were sent to his funeral, "These went with him to Coole, where his people laid him beside his mother, who had devoted her life to him, and his father, who had died in their service in the Famine years."

The publishers wanted a second edition within a month. Augusta sped around to her friends getting their lists of corrections. She left out a few passages that, in spite of all precautions, had annoyed a few people, and she and Paul Harvey spent several late nights organizing the changes for the printers. Charity was not nearly so much fun: "An urgent invitation—this was to ask me to help in their bazaar! I nearly cried but consented."

And even in London she was busy looking after her trivial, common, beloved relatives, whose world was coming down around them. Her brother Gerald came to visit with their nephew Jocelyn Persse (brother of the new heir of Roxborough and soon to become a friend and literary inspiration to Henry James). Gerald had his arm in a sling, "having had his wrist cut from a piece of glass brought down on it by a falling brick as he sat in the Club."

Her nephew Hugh Lane was fired from the job she had got him at the art dealer's and had taken to dealing in pictures on his own. He came to lunch; she wrote afterward, "His second rate fashionable talk and the vulgarity of mind irritate me." But later she described with approval his first brilliant transactions in picture dealing by which he made a fortune—much of which he would dedicate to Ireland.

Augusta spent the years immediately after her husband's death crossing and recrossing the Irish sea, keeping her English friendships in repair, testing out a literary career in London, looking for something to do in Ireland, looking really for an appropriate outlet for her great energy and her great ambition.

By 1894 Augusta had begun to change her opinion of the Irish country people. "A Gentleman," a story she published that year in *Argosy* (again as "Angus Grey"), is a charming illustration of her conversion from a feeling of superiority to one of reverence. The chief character is a young English lady married to an older Irish landlord and living on an estate like Coole. The title character is O'Loughlin, her Irish gardener, who scandalizes her by his drinking, fighting, and slightly different moral code (his answer when asked how to start a clutch of eggs: borrow a hen and steal some eggs), and who finally wins her entire respect by his good sense and kindness. After his death, the lady goes to visit his grave in an ancient ruin and sees nearby

> a recumbent figure carved roughly in the grey limestone. The features were almost worn away, but there was something of dignity in the stone pillowed head and the tunic-clad figure lying undisturbed in that silent rock-bound wilderness. The words underneath were legible, "O'Loughlin, King of Barren." She stood and mused for a time beside it, an irritating flash of memory bringing before her a richly decorated monument at Putney to a late eminent owner of silver mines.
>
> "So this is 'the best man of his family,'" she murmured to herself, "I had found out long ago that he was one of Nature's gentlemen, but I think they might have told me that he was descended from a king."

Like the English lady in the story who recalled with irritation her father's ostentatious grave, Augusta too was beginning to feel the triviality of her own class, and to realize the inevitability of its eventual demise. She wrote of the new land bill before Parliament, "It is necessary that as democracy gains power, our power should go. . . ." Her response, however, was not to abandon Ireland for England, but to see more value in the people who were going to displace her.

All by herself she had come to the conclusion other people all over Ireland were coming to: that the Irish people were more valuable, that they had a greater heritage, than previously realized. In 1892 her second cousin Standish Hayes O'Grady had published *Silva Gadelica*, his translation of old Gaelic texts: tales of saints, folklore, history. Her third cousin Standish James O'Grady had since 1878 been publishing at his own expense his history of Ireland, when in the early 1890's he suddenly found himself one of many with the same sense of Ire-

99

Influence

land's past value. In 1893 Douglas Hyde, the author of *Beside the Fire*, who cycled about Ireland collecting folklore and songs, founded, with several others, the Gaelic League for the purpose of preserving and reviving the Gaelic language, the old customs, the old sports and song fests. Also in 1893 W. B. Yeats published *The Celtic Twilight*, his retelling of folktales collected around his mother's old home in County Sligo.

By 1895 Augusta had begun to enjoy her contact with the Irish people. When she returned to Coole in early April after her winter in London—and a brief visit with her mother at the Croft, where she suffered from "the perpetual talk of food and servants . . . the dirt and disorder"—she was "delighted to be home and free again." She hired Mike John as groundskeeper and gamekeeper and another Mike as his helper—positions they would hold to the end of her life. She hired Frank as her agent. One tenant owed rent for a year and a half:

> Frank had his jennet seized. He wanted it back, on grounds the debt was his mother's, but Frank had spared the mother's cow, and would not give in, and it was put up for auction and the only bid 11/- for it, so Mike brought it back here, shut it up in the stable and then he and Mike John had to sit up nights with it lest there should be a rescue. Hanbury now says mother is going to give up the land. I let him take the jennet on promise of ½ year's rent in May.

Though the country people had not changed individually, as a class they were on the rise, and she felt a tension and vibrancy in her relationship with them that had never been there before. Now her dealings with the country people did not give her the old, dull satisfaction of doing her duty she had got when their relationship was unalterably that of superior to inferior. Now she felt somewhat as if she were playing with a young, tame tiger. And as she was still mistress of Coole Park, and more and more a master of negotiation, she usually won.

She was back in England by the end of April. Robert, much to her delight, won a classical scholarship at Harrow. When she went with him to help furnish his room, she put his father's autobiography to the use for which it was intended, taking his headmaster a copy. She stayed on in London through May and June of 1895 to attend Harrow Speechday in July. She then returned to Ireland, writing on the day she left, "Very hot, my poor little room was boiling and the struggle to dress and get on without maid or carriage rather trying. But it is better to keep going and not drop out until Robert's start in life."

Coole was a liberation. She entertained Robert's friends. She rented a typewriter and began typing up her notes on Sir William's grand-father, who had been Under-Secretary of Ireland in the early part of the century. She made a narrative out of the letters he received during his long term in office. As Under-Secretary he had sympathized completely with English rule, but Augusta's reading of history led her to sympathize with the Irish. She called Catholic Emancipation (granting Catholics the right to hold office, which finally occurred in 1829) "the dramatic idea of his tenure." She wrote, "The stars in their courses fought for it." When a friend later thought he detected in her book a tendency toward Home Rule, she denied it, but added, "I defy anyone to study Irish history without getting a dislike and distrust of the English." In the book she wrote of a newly appointed Lord Lieutenant of Ireland who was supposed to be very intolerant, "But even in crossing the Channel he seems to have drunk of that mystic love-compelling draught, of which Ireland since the days of Iseult has held the secret."

The balance had shifted; her return to England in the fall of 1895 was unpleasant. When she got to her little flat in September, "I not at all well, only fit to lie on the floor and cry, but revived by degrees." She helped Enid Layard move out of her large house into her brother's house in Savile Row. When Enid had asked advice about moving, Augusta told her, "You will find it an immense comfort to have a *man* in the house," and added, "I think you ought to be much comforted by finding that your brother wants you and that you can be of use to him." Yeats, the man Augusta would find such a comfort to have in her house, had just moved to town from his parents' house in Bedford Park to begin—while very much in love with Maud Gonne, a woman who would not have him—his hesitant love affair with Olivia Shakespear, a young married woman who would.

Augusta, like Yeats, was living in rooms without cooking facilities, and, like him, often went without eating. She developed a rash, cried easily, and dreaded eating alone in restaurants. After seeing her doctor, who ordered her "to pay more attention to my meals—and more money for them! which I always grudge," she went up to the Queen Anne's Mansions restaurant, but was already so sick she could not eat. Another day she was "very low and tired and cried from weakness, bread and butter for breakfast." She bought some knives, forks, and plates so she could dine better at home, especially when Paul Harvey, who also lived alone and dreaded eating in restaurants, came to see her. When he did come, she stayed up until midnight washing up after he left.

Paul was drifting into an engagement with, as Augusta called her, "a second-rate self-satisfied little woman who is trying to run him down." She dithered and hesitated about speaking to him, but Henry James, who had been fond of Paul's dead aunt, came to the rescue and told him with uncharacteristic directness to put the woman out of his mind, which he did. It was clear to Augusta that Paul needed a wife. Augusta, like so many people who feel wounded by the social system, was one of its staunchest supporters, and though she had no intention of marrying again, she was an enthusiastic and formidable match-maker.

When she and Robert returned to Coole for Christmas of 1895, she planted thousands of seedlings that she tended with great maternal energy—for this she had gone without food in London. She found she had much to be thankful for. She wrote about her sister Eliza's financial difficulties: "but Castle Taylor has always had a crooked name." Her sister Arabella had been shut up all winter with her miserly husband, "with bronchitis, no money, no interests or power of helping anyone outside—just skinning the rats for the Waithmans' benefit." Adelaide was separated from her husband and living in England. Gerald was drinking. Alfred, married to the daughter of a local landlord, was over £1,500 in debt at the bank. Algernon was a farmer, Frank was a land agent. Harry was doing nothing. She had the most interesting life. She moved in the highest social circles, and though no one in Ireland cared, she had a small measure of literary success.

During the next few months, before she met Yeats again and her life changed dramatically, everything fell into place to facilitate that change. She was a little disappointed in Robert. After winning his scholarship, he relaxed completely and his masters wrote that he was careless and inattentive. (She had described his appearance as he left for school, "in his little tail coat and flat straw hat—an absurd little object enough for he keeps his baby face.") He did not write often, which saddened her.

Augusta's mother died in March of 1896. On Augusta's last visit she had looked back at her mother sitting in her carriage, "and the thought flashed across me that I would not see her again, and I went back and opened the carriage door to say goodbye and said I would bring Robert to see her, which she did not seem to notice at the time, but everyone says she spoke of it and clung to his coming." (Dying on March 22, her mother added another date to Augusta's month of anniversaries, which already contained her birthday, her wedding day, and the day of Sir William's death.) In August her oldest sister, Eliza, died at Castle Taylor. Augusta felt more changed than grieved, writing that their deaths made "a strange blank, having known them all through my life and suddenly finding they are gone give a sort of sense of my foundations having slipped away."

Her brother Edward's daughter, Ethel, who had been Augusta's mother's companion at the Croft, came to Coole after Eliza's funeral. Augusta had written earlier that Ethel seemed "half-asleep, probably the effect of the Croft life," and decided she needed a husband. Paul Harvey was at Coole, and "within 48 hours they were engaged and head over heels in love, a very good engagement. And I am so glad to have at last helped to make my dear Paul really happy."

One way or another, Robert and Paul, her mother and her sister were out of her care and off her mind. She had more room in her head for other loves and other loyalties.

At Easter 1896 she accompanied Enid Layard, who was afraid to travel alone, to her palazzo in Venice. While there they visited an Italian countess who managed her own estate, and who was "also full of enthusiasm for art and literature." Augusta wrote, "A talk with her opens the windows of the mind. Yet I think love is lacking, she has no good word to say of the people she lives amongst. We are happier at Kiltartan [the name of the barony in which Coole was located]."

Back at Coole in that summer, Augusta learned that W. B. Yeats and Arthur Symons—minor poet, critic, and Yeats's friend—were visiting her neighbor Edward Martyn at Tulira Castle. Edward Martyn had not only not married her sister Arabella as her brothers, in a flight of fancy, had wished so they could "shoot the whole county," he had steadfastly refused to marry anyone, much to his mother's distress. He spent his time studying and writing in a plain, bare room in the old tower of the magnificently and expensively refurbished castle and slept in an equally plain room over the stables. Though a Deputy Lieutenant of the county and a Justice of the Peace—even a member of the Kildare Street Club in Dublin—he was finding the rewards and duties of his class insufficient for his intellect, limited as it was by his submission to the Catholic Church, and his aspirations.

He had burned his Greek verse, written a tedious anti-Voltairian satiric novel (on which Sir William had congratulated him: "You have written a clever book not one in a hundred will read and not one in a thousand will understand"), and was now writing plays—a curious form of expression for so isolated a man. His closest friend was his distant cousin and fellow landlord George Moore, with whom he had gone on the Grand Tour of Europe, and with whom he now maintained a symbiotic relationship—with Martyn the ascetic glorying in

103

and deploring Moore's worldliness, his sexual conquests, his loose language, and his tangible success as a realistic novelist. George Moore, who was becoming an enthusiastic admirer of Yeats's poetry, had introduced Yeats to Martyn in London.

Augusta was aware that Yeats was at the center of a new movement emphasizing Irish literature rather than Irish politics. From his writings she knew him to be Irish with family connections to County Sligo. She was vaguely aware that his father was an unsuccessful portrait painter. Yeats, the leader of the Irish Renaissance, was in fact the one participant who had already fallen so far out of his class that his activity was not an effort to reach beyond it but eventually came to look like an effort to clamber back into its narrowness and arrogant stability. His father came from a line of Church of Ireland rectors and small landowners, his mother from a Sligo merchant family. Yeats was cut off from his roots by his father, who, qualifying as a barrister, turned artist and atheist, and by his mother, who, having married the barrister and watched him turn into an individual, had several minor strokes that left her barely aware of her surroundings. Before the strokes, she had had five children in seven years, one of whom died. Though her husband had inherited a small property in County Kildare, his improvidence and lack of success as a painter and her lack of domestic ability kept them, as they moved from Sligo to Dublin to London, at the very edge of gentility, with a maid, but occasionally without food in the house. Growing up in these surroundings, Yeats's only real identity was with himself as a poet. His love for Ireland did not spring from deprivation but from an excess of individuality.

He had been brought to the love of Ireland by the old patriot John O'Leary, who had survived three years in prison and seventeen years of exile for Fenian activity, and who taught him that there is no literature without nationality. Yeats set out to create around him a national literature so that he might be a national poet. He had founded Irish Literary Societies in Dublin and London and was busy promoting existing Irish literature and encouraging others to write more of it.

Looking everywhere for ground to put under his feet and a sky to put over his head, he was also deep into astrology and mysticism. For many days during his visit to Tulira he made invocations to "the lunar power, which was, I believed, the chief source of my inspiration." After nine nights he saw between sleeping and waking "a galloping centaur, and a moment later a naked woman of incredible beauty, standing upon a pedestal and shooting an arrow at a star." He remembered ever after "the tint of that marvelous flesh which makes all human flesh seem unhealthy." The next day Augusta arrived and asked Edward Martyn and his guests to lunch. Later, when she had become so important to him, Yeats "believed or half-believed" that she came in response to his evocation.

The literary group from Tulira, consisting of Martyn, Symons, and Yeats, joined the family party at Coole consisting of Augusta, Robert, and Augusta's three nieces, daughters of her dead sister Gertrude, "wild, merry girls" of twenty-one, twenty-two, and twenty-three. (Augusta wrote, "It touches me very much having them, as if poor Gertrude herself had come back from the grave.")

Yeats loved big houses, recalling his grandmother's house in Sligo and the houses of the Sligo county lords whose beautiful daughters he had admired from afar. He was impressed by Edward Martyn's Tulira, a large and even stately mansion. He was not as impressed by Coole, which was clearly a house and not a castle. But he was impressed by the mementoes of service, thought, and adventure he saw in the pictures and books, the bowls and knickknacks, the swords and shields that were all there for some reason. However, when Yeats entered the drawing room after lunch and Augusta asked him what she could do for the movement, he replied, not knowing her and expecting a momentary enthusiasm, "If you get our books and watch what we are doing, you will soon find your work." Augusta wrote in her diary, "Yeats is full of charm and the Irish revival and I have been collecting fairy lore since his visit."

A few days later Yeats and Symons left for a family gathering in Sligo. When Yeats returned to Coole for a few days before going back to London, she already had collected a few stories told her by people on the estate. She wrote up one of them and published it anonymously in an English magazine. But she soon realized that Yeats needed money more than she, so after that he wrote up the stories from the notes she gave him and they were published by the editors to whom Augusta introduced him.

Yeats and folklore changed her life. As she began to collect Irish lore for Yeats, as she entered the cabins and got the people to talk to her, she found a world view that reinforced her own and added emotional richness to it. She found people who lived like her, not from their center, but from the circumference. She found people who had a great capacity for attachment, but who, like her, did not look fully and directly at other human beings, so they loved what could not look back at them. She wrote, "Love of country . . . is, I think, the real

105

passion; and bound up with it are love of home, of family, love of God. Constancy and affection in marriage are the rule, but marriage 'for love' is all but unknown."

These people too lived in a spiritual world that was alive and observant. She wrote that "if by an impossible miracle every trace of Christianity could be swept out of the world, it would not shake or destroy at all the belief of the people of Ireland in the invisible world, the cloud of witnesses, in immortality and the life to come."

She found people who, like her, did not rail against existing powers; like her, they accepted. She did not have enough self-knowledge to realize that, like her, they also shifted those powers about considerably and, while always submissive to God, were submissive to landlords at one time, to priests at another, and most recently to the Land League. Like children, they did not stand up and protest against the evil that hurt them because the hurt came from their parents, on whom they were dependent. There is a remarkable amount of death, sickness, and sorrow in the folklore she collected, and a remarkable lack of passion, terror, or even resentment. A mother tells of the death of her little boy, who was, she believed, taken by "them":

> He was always pining, but I didn't think he'd go so soon. At the end of the bed he was lying with the others, and he called to me and put up his arms. But I didn't want to take too much notice of him or to have him always after me, so I only put down my foot to where he was. And he began to pick straws out of the bed and to throw them over the little sister beside him, till he had thrown as much as would thatch a goose. And when I got up, there he was dead, and the little sister asleep beside him all covered with straws.

Whatever evil was on the earth, Augusta and the Irish people could continue to feel safe so long as it came from those in power over them.

There was also a political canniness at the heart of Augusta's devotion to the country people. She knew they were going to get the land she loved, so emotionally at least, when the change came, she would not be dispossessed. With such inducements, she overlooked and even accepted their craven changes of loyalty, their plain ignorance, their occasional brutality. These faults, along with her position as mistress of Coole, were part of her superiority to them. She entered her new world as a great lady—greater than she could ever be in London society, no matter how many biographies she edited.

The social ramifications of serving the Irish people by collecting their folklore and glorifying their past were also pleasant. In her youth, her devotion to Ireland seemed to require that she be associated with Manchester hooligans who got themselves hanged. Now she was in the company of her cousins O'Grady and O'Grady. Douglas Hyde, another Protestant gentleman and landlord's son, was leading the movement for the Gaelic language. And W. B. Yeats, the brilliant, charming poet with the wild eye, was at the center of it all.

She wrote: "This discovery, this disclosure of the folk learning, the folk poetry, the ancient tradition, was the small beginning of a weighty change. It was the upsetting of the table of values, an astonishing excitement." With a sudden intake of breath she sensed the great, vibrant spaces expanding around her. She had at last found her people, her tribe, to whom she was at once both equal, superior, and inferior, giving her great security, great satisfaction in serving them, and great freedom to rise above them.

In her devotion to the Irish people Augusta achieved the double-think that lies at the heart of many great plans for living. By becoming part of the great family of the Irish people, she felt both valuable and secure. She felt relieved of all need to achieve more value. She sensed that with this protection, and with this excuse, she would be capable of a dramatic expansion of her abilities that would lift her above the group. What did she want? What the "little-welcomed girl" at Roxborough had learned to want without daring to think it: to be lifted above the brothers and sisters. Under cover of service, she aimed for personal glory, and she added another layer to her emotional camouflage, the primary layer of which was her widow's black, worn when she was anything but mourning.

Even at this turning point, family troubles intruded. After Eliza's death in August 1896, her brother-in-law Walter became irrational and eventually had to be put in an asylum. Her dear Paul, in a pretty house, furnished chiefly with her things, was rude to her; she does not say how, only noting "Paul's little aberrations from good manners." There was trouble at Roxborough. Arthur, the new heir, felt that Gerald was incapable of doing his job as agent and asked Augusta to tell him so. Frank was put in his place. "A sad business," Augusta wrote, "but it might have been worse, had a stranger been put in." And she herself was spending too much money, her chief expenses being the mortgage on Coole and Robert's tuition at Harrow, where he continued not to distinguish himself. She figured that £500 per year would pay the mortgage in six years, but she wanted it paid in five so that the estate would be clear when Robert came of age.

When she went to London for the winter of 1896, she became confused by all the possibilities of service to Ireland. A royal commission had reported that Ireland had been overtaxed for years. Augusta, still protesting that she was against Home Rule, thought she saw a way to unite all elements of Irish opinion, writing, "It is not getting the money that is the important thing—it is getting all Ireland into line." She had Yeats to dinner, as representative of the literary movement, along with Barry O'Brien, a member of the Irish parliamentary delegation, and Horace Plunkett, who had been working for years to establish cooperative farming in Ireland. She was going to help them all. She herself had written a report on the taxation report, which she gave to Mr. Plunkett, who was attending the financial debates. She gave Mr. Plunkett's pamphlet on agricultural cooperation to Mr. O'Brien, hoping to get the parliamentary delegation interested in establishing a government department to encourage it. And she gave Yeats the folklore she had collected during the fall in Ireland. The party lasted until midnight, and when it was over, she wrote, "I think I did my best for them all."

She saw Lady Fingall about the Gort Industries, her project to teach the nuns in the convent near Coole to make clothes acceptable to the tastes of London society. She introduced Yeats and his poetry to her London friends. Sir Alfred Lyall liked Yeats, "taken with his simple enthusiastic way." Sir Frederic Burton liked the poetry, but refused to meet the poet, saying he was "afraid of breaking the spell if he comes and that he would rather keep his poet ideal." She went with Yeats to her first meeting of the Irish Literary Society to hear a lecture on James Clarence Mangan, whom Yeats called the only poetic genius of the Young Irelanders, which ended with Yeats disagreeing with everybody. Augusta was busy stirring the pot, herself along with it, not yet sure what brew was being concocted.

For her forty-fifth birthday on March 15, 1897, Enid Layard gave her Sir Henry's typewriter. In April she and Robert returned to a very rainy Ireland. She wrote, "Even with Robert I feel a little chill coming back to the grey silence and the small cares. But that will pass away in service for others. And I feel very much for the people not able to sow their crops." This was the summer she would sow her most abundant crop, begin her long collaboration with Yeats, and with him and others found the Irish Literary Theatre.

IV

Hitching Her Wagon to a Star

YEATS COMES TO COOLE: 1897–1898

> *May God be praised for woman*
> *That gives up all her mind,*
> *A man may find in no man*
> *A friendship of her kind . . .*
>   W. B. YEATS, "On Woman"

AUGUSTA rarely looked at herself. When she did, she saw a
woman in black. When she looked at Coole in April of 1897,
she saw that it was beautiful. Narcissus, tulips, phlox, wallflowers,
anemones, and columbines were in bloom. Tree peonies were bud-
ding. The sunflower bushes and the yellow berberis were gold. The
white clematis was just opening. Bluebells were breaking through the
soil in the fields of Shanwalla beyond the garden.

With her left hand, without thinking about it, she had transformed
the walled garden into a replica of the magic efflorescence of Roxborough. Neither Sir William nor his mother had had the happy
patience, the alert watchfulness of real gardeners. Augusta did. She
attempted no feats of feudal gardening like those of her second cousin
William O'Grady, archdeacon of the little Killinane church in her
youth, who had pits dug nine feet deep and filled them with peat so
his red-blossomed rhododendrons could flourish in that limestone soil.
Even Augusta's small ventures out of the ordinary failed, as when
she found the begonia tubers she had ordered from an English nursery

109

in a huge pot in the kitchen, where they had been "experimentally cooked" before she could give her instructions. She planted all the ordinary flowers: roses, lilies, iris, carnations, sweet william, sweet herbs; and they bloomed abundantly. Inside the garden was a large, spreading copper beech, its beautiful gray-green, lichen-spotted bark reminiscent of the stone of plaques and gravestones—waiting for inscriptions. Augusta would use it as her guest book, a living record of the remarkable people she would bring to Coole.

Augusta did not spend money on herself. Even when she could barely afford them, she bought and planted trees at Coole. She did not plant them for eventual harvesting, but in a kind of deep and fruitful rebellion against her father, who had destroyed his land and his son's inheritance, she planted as an embellishment to the land and a gift to her descendants. She did not attempt the feats of Sir William, who, during his short phase as a self-proclaimed Coniferomaniac, had planted and replanted exotic specimens in the nut wood behind the garden—so that it was sometimes called the Rich Wood, not because the towering blue-green pyramids looked rich, but because one should have been very rich to attempt the planting at all. Augusta planted trees that grew well—the silver-stemmed fir, the larch with its "rosy blossoms and delicate green branches."

She worked with the gardener who had held the post since old Mrs. Gregory's days, and who invariably wore a frieze-tail coat, corduroy breeches, gray woolen stockings, "a high hat, brown and fluffy" (as Augusta described it), and tied around his head a red handkerchief which "was never put to the use for which it was manufactured." They went out together in the wet and cold of winter to coat the young stems with tar to keep the rabbits from nibbling them, and with slasher and spud in summer to clear away vines and brambles.

When she and Robert arrived, the lake was full. During their marriage Sir William had installed a pump worked by a horse that walked round in circles, and an underground pipe that brought water from the lake to the house. Bathrooms installed some years before became workable without many servants in attendance—though not reliably so. The housemaid often had to rush outside and clang the workmen's bell three times to tell the worker who lounged by the pump, lost in thought and tobacco smoke, to stop the horse—the tank on the third floor was overflowing. Even the water at Coole was "racy of the soil"— the Young Irelanders' criterion for poetry subsequently adopted by Yeats—containing bits of weed, small snails, and even, occasionally, a leech.

Yeats had been invited for July. Augusta worked through May on her narrative from Mr. Gregory's letters. Robert, who became a fine fast-break bowler and who eventually bowled for Ireland, organized cricket matches on the pitch under the huge ilex on the front lawn. Other players were shopkeepers from Gort, tenants, workmen. They played against teams from nearby towns and estates where there were cricket enthusiasts to organize them. For many years the Gort team remained unbeaten.

Augusta took out the old phaeton, hitched up the pony named Shamrock, and followed the stories about a witch named Biddy Early. She stopped first at her family's hunting lodge, Chevy Chase, on Slieve Echtge. The next day she drove "eight strong miles over the mountain. It was a wild road, and the pony had to splash his way through two unbridged rivers, swollen with summer rains." The road was deep in red mud. She drove through the magic landscape of her childhood, the brown bogs, the purple heather and foxglove, into the green pastureland of Clare on the other side of the mountain. She put up her pony at a little inn and walked to the cabin where the witch and healer had died twenty years before. The woman living in the little cottage showed her the shed where Biddy Early had practiced her cures. (Someone had already given Augusta a bottle of her medicine, which remained, unopened, on the storeroom shelf at Coole.) Augusta called the country people together and got all their stories of Biddy Early. Though she would eventually write them up herself, coming home over the mountain she felt like a cat bringing a mouse to lay at the feet of its beloved.

In June at Coole the white thorn trees in the park bloomed. Sir William used to come over from London especially to see them. The lilacs and laburnums were in bloom, as were the white horse chestnuts and smaller crimson chestnuts. The paths were covered with the brown blossoms of the beech trees. Coole looked like a bride, "so radiant, so decorated." In the long light of the Irish summer evenings Augusta stayed out until nine and ten o'clock: "One must stand and look at blossoming tree after tree."

Although not in love, Augusta could not keep away from Yeats. Hearing he would be arriving at Tulira, she went over. Someone had given her some trout, and though her Catholic maids and workmen needed them as much as Edward Martyn, she decided that since the next day was Friday he should have them. She arrived to find Yeats "just arrived from Dublin, white, haggard, voiceless, fresh from the Jubilee riots."

The day before in Dublin, Yeats's beloved Maud Gonne, whose power over him Augusta was just beginning to realize, had been a principal speaker at a rival demonstration to the celebrations of Victoria's Jubilee. Maud and Yeats had then walked in a procession she helped organize bearing a huge coffin inscribed "THE BRITISH EMPIRE," draped with flags embroidered with the names of those hanged by the British and the death tolls of the Irish famines. As the crowd grew wilder and windows began to break, Maud, as Yeats described her, walked "with a joyous face; she had taken all those people into her heart." Yeats, who had already lost his voice from too much shouting at a disorderly debate, knew he could not stop her or the crowd: "I too resigned myself and felt the excitement of the moment, that joyous irresponsibility and sense of power." Finally he got Maud away, and when the crowd grew wilder yet, Yeats locked the door of the room where they were having tea to prevent her from rejoining them. Two hundred people were injured and one woman killed. Maud told him he had made her do the only cowardly thing of her life by keeping her from the crowd—though when he had asked her what she would do if he let her out, she replied, "How do I know till I get out?"

Maud Gonne was unique. Her mother, a wealthy Englishwoman, had died when she was four. Her father, an English army officer stationed in Dublin, had died when she was eighteen. Her pleasant, privileged life at the viceregal court in Dublin contrasted with some especially cruel evictions which she and some friends had ridden out to see as a lark; her brief experience with a detested English guardian who severely rationed her liberty and her money had made her hate England and, like Augusta as a child, love the Ireland that was oppressed. When she came of age, she took over her own life, living in lodgings in Dublin and an apartment in Paris. With her extraordinary beauty, her wealth, and her great courage, she flouted the conventions of Victorian England. She had a streak of the strange rigidity of the terrorist. She was willing to lie, and she was willing to incite other people to kill.

Yeats had been in love with her for eight years, since she had arrived at his father's house in London with an introduction from the Irish patriot John O'Leary, told him she liked his poem "Mosada," and had him to dinner at her lodgings every night for the remainder of her short stay in London. His first vision of her remained with him throughout his life: "I never thought to see in a living woman so great beauty. It belonged to famous pictures, to poetry, to some legendary past." She had a beauty, wrote another observer, "that surprises one—like the sun when it leaps above the horizon." Along with great natural kindness and gentleness, Yeats sensed her love of excitement and her confused hatred of all restraint. He was so in love with her that it completely "broke up his life" for several years. Then he felt he had grown stronger and "while still cherishing her did not feel it in the same way." But after the riots in Dublin he felt once more overwhelmed by his desire for her and was suffering "tortures of hope and fear." All this he would soon tell Augusta.

Augusta herself was in some disgrace in the neighborhood because of the Queen's Jubilee. Her neighbor George Gough at Lough Cutra, anxious to demonstrate the loyalty of the gentry, had urged his fellow landlords to light bonfires. She refused "on the grounds of the Queen's neglect of the country." The next Sunday at church Gough's wife asked if she had not received a "dreadful letter" from him, but she replied cheerfully, "No, it was only a wail over a lost soul."

A few days after her brief visit to Tulira and her glimpse of Yeats, Augusta went to stay at Duras, the seacoast home of her husband's friend Count de Basterot, whom she had seen most frequently in London and Rome. (Like her father, the Count was paralyzed from the waist down from the excesses of his youth.) While she was there, Edward Martyn arrived with Yeats to spend the day. After lunch, as Augusta wrote, "I thought the Count wanted to talk to Mr. Martyn alone; so I took Mr. Yeats to the office where the steward used to come to talk." There they had tea and sat together through a rainy afternoon, and, as it says on the plaque now on the wall of the main room, "began between them the conversations which led to the founding of the Abbey Theatre."

Augusta had just read *Maeve*, a play by Edward Martyn that he had loaned to the Count, who had passed it on to her for an opinion. (It was about an Irish girl who dies the night before her wedding to an Englishman after having a vision of her ideal fairy bridegroom.) Augusta thought it a fine play. *Maeve*, along with Martyn's other play, *The Heather Field*, a realistic drama imitative of Ibsen, had been offered to London producers without success. Martyn thought of trying to have them produced in Germany. Yeats said he had written two plays also, one of which had actually been produced in 1894 as a curtain raiser to Shaw's *Arms and the Man*. Yeats had already told Augusta about the play he was then writing and had startled her by saying about half his characters had hawks' faces. Yeats too thought of trying to get his plays produced in London. As she wrote, "We went on talking about it, and things seemed to grow possible as we talked, and before the end of the afternoon, we had made our plan."

A few days later Yeats came over to Coole for the day. They began the first of their many sessions with Augusta at her typewriter in the drawing-room window—typing holes in the ribbon as she in her excitement forgot to reverse the cartridge—Yeats striding up and down in front of her. Together they composed the prospectus for an Irish literary theater, which read in part:

> We propose to have performed in Dublin, in the spring of every year certain Celtic and Irish plays. . . . We hope to find in Ireland an uncorrupted and imaginative audience. . . . We will show that Ireland is not the home of buffoonery and of easy sentiment, as it has been represented, but the home of an ancient idealism. We are confident of the support of all Irish people, who are weary of misrepresentation, in carrying out a work that is outside all the political questions that divide us.

They stated that they planned to make the experiment for three years only. The prospectus was signed by W. B. Yeats, Edward Martyn, and Lady Gregory. Not only does the heart have its reasons, the mind has its reasons the mind knows not of. Augusta had found her life's work, and a properly subsidiary position from which to manage the whole enterprise.

Augusta thought she had had very little to do with drama in her life, but she had raised money. She and Yeats hoped to obtain guarantees to cover those costs of production not covered by admissions. Augusta pledged the first £25. When Yeats left to visit his uncles in Sligo, she kept typing up their proposal and sending it out to her friends. Though she would later protest—not very vigorously—about the "donkey work" that was left to the woman, at the time it was the most interesting work she had.

She was delightfully good at influencing people. She sent the proposal to Aubrey de Vere, an old, respected Irish poet of the Lake School, a Catholic convert, friend of Tennyson and Browning, who responded enthusiastically. She enclosed a copy of his letter in the proposal sent to several other friends. When William Lecky pledged £5 instead of the £1 for which she asked, she mentioned his enthusiasm to Lord Dufferin. Not everyone was enthusiastic. Her friend Emily Lawless pledged £1, but appended a long and sensible list of reasons why the project would fail. All in all, the list of guarantors was very satisfactory. Yeats was responsible for some: Maud Gonne, John O'Leary, John Eglington, Edward Dowden, the Irish members of Parliament. Augusta was responsible for the rest.

When Edward Martyn let it be known that he would pay the costs for the first production of his play *The Heather Field*, and for Yeats's *Countess Cathleen*, the whole process of asking for guarantees became merely a means of stirring up enthusiasm. But it was also emotionally useful to Augusta who, in effect, was asking her friends for their approval of her transfer of allegiance from England to Ireland.

Toward the end of July, Yeats wrote that he would be arriving shortly with his friend George Russell. Yeats thoughtfully outlined his friend's career so Augusta would know whom she was entertaining. Russell had begun his education as an art student, but had given it up because he believed that "the will is the only thing given us in this life as absolutely our own, and that we should allow no weakening of it, and that Art, which he cared for so much, would he believed weaken his will." He became a bookkeeper in a drygoods store, devoting his evenings to editing a magazine on theosophy, writing poetry, painting visionary beings on the walls of his lodging, and encouraging a small group of theosophists who depended on him for leadership and inspiration.

He was the one leading participant of the Irish Renaissance who had no family connections with the landlord class. He was from a middle-class Presbyterian family from the north of Ireland. His father was also a bookkeeper. Not feeling the threat of the impending loss of his social or financial position, he was looking forward to the eventual loss of his earthly body—hence the title of his first book of poems, which had just been published: *Homeward Songs by the Way*. They were signed AE, that name symbolizing his more spiritual self. He was the only participant in the Irish Renaissance who put spiritual values ahead of artistic values. But, for all that, he would occasionally cause Augusta and Yeats as much trouble as any ordinarily mischievous troublemaker.

Yeats wrote that Russell was his model for the character Michael Robartes in "Rosa Alchemica." Accordingly, Augusta got down her recently received copy of *The Secret Rose* and read "with his wild red hair, fierce eyes and sensitive lips and rough clothes, Michael Robartes looks something between a peasant, a saint and a debauchee."

With some trepidation Augusta met the two at the Gort station, finding Yeats as exhausted as ever and Russell tall, bearded, and mild-mannered. She wrote Enid that, after her alarm, she was relieved to find him "a very quiet and harmless person, visionary, gentle, and, as Mrs. Quirke says of her meeting with a seraphim, 'He was more in dread of me than I of him.' "

Though George Russell was in some ways as wild as she could wish, Augusta had no special use for him. She wrote, "His chief virtue is that he draws Yeats, who is full of fire and brilliancy." But the talk during their visit was not exclusively literary. Sitting up late at night in the library, Yeats made them laugh until they cried with stories of his London friends—Lionel Johnson, when drunk, gravely recounting an imaginary conversation with Gladstone, and Mr. Emory, Florence Farr's alcoholic husband, removing coins to buy liquor from the coats of his guests as they hung in the hall.

George Russell was facile at seeing visions and reported that fairies were thick on the ground at Coole. One afternoon the three rowed across the lake to a cromlech—a prehistoric stone monument—where they all waited expectantly until he saw a "purple clad druid." As a result, Robert reported one morning at breakfast that he dreamed he would be given the power to see visions, but, thinking it might spoil his eyesight for cricket, he had refused. Though Augusta was closely associated with these unusual events and sometimes outrageous imaginings, she took care never to be caught with the goods on her person, saying she could not see visions because "I am like Martha, much cumbered with serving."

It was obvious to Augusta that Yeats was on the verge of a breakdown. (His friend Katherine Tynan wrote, "He never had the slightest idea of looking after himself.") Always an able nurse, Augusta was now an enthusiastic one. She put him in the best bedroom on the third floor—a privilege maintained, even after Robert's coming of age, during the lifetime of the hostess. She sent him beef broth when he was called in the morning to get his strength up for breakfast. She kept him in the open air, driving him from cottage to cottage collecting folklore. The country people were used to Lady Gregory, but when they saw her driving about with the thin, strange young man in black, one went to his priest in a panic telling him, "Lady Gregory is bringing a missioner to convert us." Father Fahy told him shortly not to be a fool. Augusta, at Yeats's request, treated him like a schoolboy, sending him to his room mornings and evenings to work.

After George Russell left, Yeats told Augusta about his love for Maud Gonne, his first meeting with her, his long devotion, and the revival of his hope and desire, now stronger than ever. When old he wrote:

> I have not lost desire
> But the heart that I had;
> I thought 'twould burn my body
> Laid on the death-bed.

All this he told Lady Gregory, with her long experience in drawing men out, and Augusta, safely encased in black, heard him.

Yeats wrote that his first meeting with Maud Gonne was like "a sound as of a Burmese gong, an overpowering tumult that had yet many pleasant secondary notes." Yeats and his love for Maud had something of the same effect on Augusta. Her association with him gave her what she, in her isolation, greatly needed. She got from Yeats what any admirer of his poetry got, only with more immediacy and power: the sense of another soul. "Pride, shyness, humility," which held her back from making contact with others, did not exist for Yeats writing his poetry. Yet, in spite of his freedom of expression, the soul he expressed in his poetry was in basic harmony with her own sense of limitation and deprivation. He and she were together outside the satisfactions, entanglements, and maturities of satisfied love.

Augusta, signaling her access to and sympathy with his secrets, began to call him "Willie." He, recognizing the distance at which she kept him, continued to call her "Lady Gregory." He called her Lady Gregory until she died. Preserving the chastity of their souls, neither looked directly at the other. And they had so many subjects between them that there was always something else to look to. It is evidence of the great accuracy of Augusta's instincts that in balancing her need for achievement against her need for emotional protection, she chose a man to whom she was superior in order to maintain her freedom of action, and to whom she was inferior in order for him to be of any use to her.

Of Willie on his first long visit from July to September, Augusta wrote in her diary, "A most brilliant, charming, loveable companion, never out of humour, simple, gentle, interested in all that went on." She later crossed out "loveable" and "simple." She described their easy relationship: "Then if I was typing in the drawing-room [Willie] suddenly bursting in with some great new idea, and when it was expounded laughing and saying: 'I treat you, as my father says, as an anvil to beat out my ideas on.' "

Another friend described Yeats at the time as "beautiful to look at with his dark face, its touch of vivid colouring, the night-black hair, the eager dark eyes." But he always wore the slight pouting air of the rejected lover. Willie described Augusta at that time as "a plainly dressed woman of forty-five without obvious good looks, except the charm that comes from strength, intelligence and kindness." Augusta was still slim and quick-moving. She held herself very straight and smiled frequently. Willie told her she had only one fault, her enmity toward the squirrels that damaged her young trees.

Augusta offered him care, comfort, order, and stability. She offered him Coole, house and lands, lake and garden, and he took them into his soul as if it had been a photographic plate waiting to receive their

117

imprint. Augusta vicariously shared his homelessness, his freedom, and the huge, empty sky over his head that he frantically strove to fill with deities. He gratefully shared the privileges and traditions of her social class, accepting for stability what was already in precipitous decline.

He wrote beautifully of Coole: "This house has enriched my soul out of measure because here life moves without restraint through spacious forms. Here there has been no compelled labour, no poverty-thwarted impulse." In fact, had he been less self-absorbed, he would have seen that there had been much forced labor, many restraints, some poverty-thwarted impulses. But for him Coole was food and drink, beds made, friends entertained, letters typed, garden paths swept before him. And he and Augusta did, successfully and intentionally, perform at Coole the ancient feat of making time stand still for art: "Where we wrought that shall break the teeth of Time."

There was, however, an emptiness at the heart of their union; they were using each other. Augusta kept him at arm's length with her superior social position. She encouraged him to impose upon her. Yet their association had many of the qualities of a happy, exciting and fruitful marriage. Yeats wrote of Augusta that "she / So changed me that I live / Labouring in ecstasy." And Augusta, through her union with Willie, found the only freedom she was to know as a playwright, the most fun she was ever to have as a theater manager, and the most exhilarating acclaim she was ever to have as both.

Not everyone was pleased. Arthur Symons, Yeats's companion on his first visit to Coole, called her "La Strega"—the witch—and declared he knew by the look in her "terrible eye" that she would "get Willie." And after Yeats won the Nobel Prize for Literature in 1923, she wrote a friend: "In the years [Yeats] came here my friends and family in the neighborhood never realized he had genius, but knew or thought he was a revolutionist, and lamented my folly and obstinacy in having him and other writers in the house instead of ordinary 'country house parties.' "

Augusta began to invite to Coole all those who might be useful to the cause of Irish development, both spiritual and practical. Standish James O'Grady came for a day, but was called away immediately on business. Horace Plunkett came for a few days. Augusta did her best to give him an audience for his talk on agricultural cooperation. "We had asked the farmers to meet him, but it was a fine day after long rain, and very few came. We had to call our workmen and even F.'s driver to fill the background, but he came and talked to them, explaining the methods with so much courtesy and earnestness, that he won their hearts." (When Augusta wrote, "*We* asked all the farmers" and "*We* had to call our workmen," she was writing of no one but herself. She used her commitment to Yeats and their common goals to rid herself of a great burden of isolation and to diminish her appearance of independence. She never knew which she liked least: dependent women or independent women.)

Edward Martyn, finding his poet taken away, came over during Yeats's visit. He walked around Coole with his thick body, his balding head, and his air of intelligent, stubborn timidity and confessed to Augusta that he thought the country people "a horrid lot." He told her it made him "ill to see a country man come into the yard to talk to him." The people, in turn, had complained to Augusta about his treatment of them, with "a sixpenny or maybe a threepenny thrust out at you through the window." Over the years he became more at ease with them, and Augusta was given credit for the change, a countryman telling her, "I have it in my heart and in my conscience that it is the woman of this house that has been the cause."

Later, when Augusta had taken all his guests and she and Willie had squeezed him out of the theater he helped start, he wrote, "Lady Gregory, though not intellectually profound, is intellectually acute and has a social tact and mastery amounting almost to genius." Augusta did not use her tact on him, and when she heard he was going to act as chairman at a political meeting, she gasped, "You? Chairman?" and only apologized in her diary, "I'm afraid I was not too polite—but it was really too absurd." When the Kildare Street Club expelled him for his nationalist activities, he sued the club committee and got himself readmitted. After he left the Irish Literary Theatre, he supported the Theatre of Ireland, which performed Irish plays and European classics from 1905 until 1916. He refurbished the parish church of Ardrahan near Tulira with stained glass from the famous Tower of Glass workshop in Dublin. He endowed a Palestrina Choir, permitted to sing baroque music only, for the Dublin Pro-Cathedral. But, unlike most of the people pell-melling over one another to serve Ireland, he experienced no dramatic expansion of his abilities, and—Ireland not particularly wanting to be served—he got little respect or gratitude for his generosity.

At the end of Yeats's visit, Martyn invited Yeats and Augusta to Tulira for a "Celtic Party" along with Douglas Hyde, founder of the Gaelic League, who came pushing his bicycle up the drive after they had gone to meet him at the station. Hyde, in his late thirties, was a cheerful, round-faced man with walrus mustaches, who had been collecting Irish folklore since his undergraduate days at Trinity College. He himself wrote Gaelic poetry almost indistinguishable in tone and feeling from the original poems he translated into English. He signed his poetry, in Irish, "The Delightful Little Branch." He was immensely popular. At festivals where Irish was recited and sung, country girls wore hats with his pen name embroidered on the headband. (As Yeats was quick to point out to George Moore—always jealous of everybody—"No woman has ever done that for you.") When the Republic of Ireland created the largely ceremonial office of president in 1938, Hyde, who had avoided politics and resigned from the Gaelic League when he saw it was working for political goals, was the agreed choice of all parties. He served until 1945 and died in Dublin in 1949 at the age of eighty-nine. He, like Augusta, Yeats, Martyn, even Maud Gonne, found his life's work in the idea of Ireland, but, unlike most of the others, he remained fairly ordinary and conventional.

Another guest at the "Celtic Party" was William Sharp, a strange Scotsman who convinced everyone he had a friend named Fiona MacLeod, an even stranger Scotswoman who wrote strange stories on Celtic subjects—which William Sharp actually wrote himself. Augusta was not taken with him: "an absurd object, making himself ridiculous, talking to the men of his love affairs and entanglements, seeing visions (imitative of Yeats). The apparition clasped him to an elm tree from which he had to be released." Willie, always more tolerant of visionaries, explained to her that William Sharp's soul had flowed into the sap of the tree.

The last member of this interesting group, Moritz Bonn, an economist specializing in the economies of colonies, was no more successful with Augusta, who described him as "an odious German." Augusta in her widow's black was the only woman, but, like Joan of Arc in her soldier's costume, no one seemed to notice.

This party was the last of the holiday gaieties. Willie went back to Dublin to accompany Maud Gonne on a rabble-rousing tour of England, writing Augusta, "She is very kind and friendly but whether more I cannot tell." Robert went back to Harrow. Augusta settled down to finish her manuscript of *Mr. Gregory's Letter-Box*.

Before leaving Ireland she spent ten days at Spiddal on the coast with Lord and Lady Morris and their other guests, William Lecky and his wife. She had a spirited argument with them all over the importance of Gaelic, Lecky sneering at her for calling it a modern language, to which she replied, "Yes, just in the same way as modern Greek." Lady Morris had to intervene to tell them it was spoken all around Spiddal.

Augusta had finally started to learn Gaelic herself. According to her story, Robert wanted to learn, and she was learning to help him. That summer he had ridden over to Edward Martyn, who didn't know Gaelic either, for help and advice and had come back with a fine Irish Bible. He and Augusta went over the grammar, translating bits out of the Bible and running out to Mike John, the groundskeeper, to get the pronunciation right. When the Birch boys arrived for the shooting, Robert abandoned Gaelic. Augusta kept working at it, as she said, "by Robert's wish."

Back in London in November 1897, she had more projects than usual, most of them now related to Ireland. She immediately checked out Willie's lodging in the Woburn Buildings and bought him blue curtains and a large armchair. (She had done the same for Paul Harvey.) She sent him tinned fruit and wine, a fountain pen. Willie thanked her: "How extraordinarily good you are . . . nobody has ever shown me such kindness. Everybody tells me how well I am looking, and I am better than I have been for years in truth. The days at Coole passed like a dream, a dream of peace."

When Augusta realized that Willie still had hardly any money, even with the £10 or £15 he received for each folklore article, she began leaving money behind the clock on the mantel. Willie wrote her in perplexity, "Ought I to let you do all these kind things for me? . . . I have reasoned myself out of the instincts and rules by which one mostly surrounds oneself. I have nothing but reason to trust to, and so am in continual doubt about simple things." She, who always played by the rules but was willing to make up a few of her own, told him, "You must take this money. You should give up journalism. The only wrong act is not doing one's best work."

She descended on the Yeats family home on Blenheim Road to see what good she could do there. She arrived on a particularly artistic evening. Yeats's father, John Butler Yeats, was sketching Edward Martyn while Martyn himself was being entertained by the singing of Susan Mitchell, a young woman from Dublin who boarded with the family and subsequently became one of the wits of the Irish Renaissance.

One of Augusta's talents was her accurate assessment of the uses to which people could be put, and she quickly realized that the elder

121

Yeats did his best work in pencil, in one sitting and unretouched. (He worked on a self-portrait in oils for the last eleven years of his life.) She forthwith commissioned him to do pencil sketches of Willie, George Russell, Horace Plunkett, and Douglas Hyde—the payment for which formed a significant portion of his income for the year. (She later performed the unlikely feat of getting her sister-in-law Nora, Algernon's wife, to commission a portrait of herself.) Yeats senior also did a picture of Augusta, which she described as "sort of a Mother of Sorrows with tearful eyes." Though she was grinning on the inside, and smiling a good deal on the outside, when it came time to make a record, Augusta adopted the mood indicated by her mourning.

Because her parents had been unperceptive and the country people were accepting, Augusta thought most people could be easily fooled by whatever manner she chose to adopt. But as she left the friends of her class, who were polite and who at heart really did not care, she encountered more and more people who were offended by her clumsy attempts at graciousness. Because she too, at heart, really did not care about most people except as objects of service, her manner with them was an unpleasant mixture of humility and autocracy.

Yeats senior, who possessed an inexhaustible fund of good cheer, hopefulness, and canny intelligence, gave her credit where credit was due, writing his daughter, "On the whole I am very glad that Lady Gregory 'got Willie' . . . though it is not easy personally to like her." He told her, "You have the courage that comes from absolute disinterestedness," and added to his daughter, "That is one of the reasons why she is so infernally haughty to lesser mortals—or whom she thinks lesser mortals."

Being disliked, even covertly, was a new experience for Augusta. She did not often realize it, but when she did, she found a difference of politics or policy to account for it. As a child she had felt her conversion protected her, as an adult her husband had protected her, and now she felt her mourning protected her. She could not believe that anyone disliked her for herself. In any case, the discomfort of dealing with people who were not charmed by her was far outweighed by the pleasures of her new life.

In her 1898 New Year's letter to Wilfrid Blunt she wrote, "My own life is happy now, and I *almost* say to the passing moment stay." She also wrote about her new friend, "who is a genius and will go far." In the new year she took Willie to meet her old lover, "but the visit did not go off very well though Yeats did a vision for him and succeeded in making him see a flower." Wilfrid wrote about Yeats's incantation, "The performance was very imperfect, not to say null." But he was otherwise impressed, describing Yeats as "an Irish mystic of an interesting type . . . tall, lean, dark, good looking."

Willie was spending as much time with Maud Gonne as she would permit, attending meetings and trying to see visions. All in all, Yeats understood her very well, but he did not realize, though he heard persistent rumors of it, that she was the mistress of a French journalist, Lucien Millevoye. Her first illegitimate child by Millevoye, born the year after she met Willie, had died of meningitis. (At the time she told Willie in distraction about a little child she had adopted who had died.) Her second child, a girl who was now three, was cared for by servants at her Paris apartment. Willie sensed her confused unrest. He knew she could lie, but he did not think she would lie to him.

In February, Maud upset Augusta completely with her plan, relayed to Augusta by Willie, to go to the famine districts of Kerry, where she intended to incite the people to steal and slaughter sheep to relieve their hunger. Maud hoped this would cause the English soldiers to fire on the people "and so draw attention to their case." Augusta was horrified. Talking with Willie, she tried to reason away the need to do anything, "telling him the famine is problematic, and that if it exists there are other ways of meeting it, but we who are above the people in means and education ought, were it a real famine, to be sharing all we have with them but that even if suffering starvation was before them, it would be for us to teach them to die in courage than to live by robbing—that the attempt would end in arrests."

Augusta never had much sympathy with either starvation or evictions—the most brutal forms of distress visited on Ireland by its system of government under England. Unlike Maud, she could not put herself in clear-cut opposition to the English power structure, and since such opposition was the appropriate reaction, Augusta reasoned herself out of reacting at all.

Augusta saw Willie off at the station "to Ireland where I hope he won't get into mischief." Meeting him in Dublin, Maud did not want him to go with her to Kerry either, saying "she didn't think it was in his line." She herself went and did succeed in getting public relief for the hungry people of Kerry, where there was indeed a famine.

Augusta had something else to worry about, and on March 6, 1898, the sixth anniversary of her husband's death, she wrote in her diary, "My book comes out tomorrow and I am getting anxious about it. Smith says it has been fairly well subscribed, but much will depend on the reviews." She was particularly anxious because she was

123

paying the cost of publishing. The reviews, as it turned out, were good. Her friend William Lecky wrote that it was "so full of interest, so brightly written, the narrative so skillfully interwoven with the letters." He also prophesied to her privately that she would go on writing because it is "like drink." The *Athenaeum* applauded the "brilliant unorthodoxy" of her editing. Frank Lawley wrote what she called "a gushing notice" in the *Telegraph*. At the Morrises' she complained, "I say the worst of the *World* review is that people will expect me when I dine out to be as amusing as Lord Morris," to which Lady Morris replied, "So you are."

Mr. Gregory's Letter-Box is charming and interesting. As in the case of her husband's autobiography, she insists she is doing proper women's work, done for the benefit of her family and with their approval. She notes that "Old Mr. Gregory's bust looks benevolently on my labours." The writing is confident and witty—a sharp contrast to the style she was developing for her folklore. She includes homey details, telling of an English official in Ireland who had given a lady a lesson in salad making; when the lady then wrote a book in favor of Catholic Emancipation, he burned it, saying regretfully, "I wish I had not given her the secret of my salad!" Augusta also mentions having been puzzled by the statement in a letter that "Young Gee says he has shot a Caravat" and wondering what kind of bird it was until she discovered that Caravat, like Ribbonman and White-boy, was the name of a secret society.

The book is well done and historically accurate, but Augusta could not present herself simply as an author. The last letter she quotes, having nothing to do with the politics of Ireland, is from her own husband, written when he was an eighteen-year-old schoolboy at Harrow. She concludes, "To-day it is Mr. Gregory's great-grandson who is a Harrow boy, whose mother hopes he may put into the work he has to do as much good will as she has brought to this self-imposed task of hers."

She was immediately and cruelly disappointed in this. A week after the publication of her book, on her birthday, she received a letter from Robert's tutor telling her he had been "formally rebuked for idleness and turned to the bottom of the class." She wrote Robert and his tutor, had an Irish lesson, had lunch with Enid Layard, and went home to grieve:: "A splendid review of me and my book in the *World*, and I sit—but my heart is hurting all the time. I would rather my book had failed and my boy had done well."

A worse grief was to come, adding another dismal day to her month of anniversaries. On March 26 she received a telegram from her sister-in-law Rose at Roxborough: "GERALD DIED IN MY ARMS THIS MORNING AFTER BRIEF ILLNESS." He had drunk himself to death, the third of her nine brothers to do so. He had been her favorite, and the favorite of the people around Roxborough, who reported they saw him several times after his death crossing the countryside in a carriage from which came sounds of merrymaking and laughter. His death made Robert's failure more frightening. She wrote, "Poor child, poor boy, he is gone, and what is saddest is one couldn't wish him back again. A life of great possibilities spoiled by some weakness of will or defect in bringing up." Returning to Ireland in April, she went to his grave, "which upset me very much." She thought of the Aran Isles, "where I could learn Irish for WRG [Robert] and collect folklore for WBY." She went the next day and stayed for several weeks, cut off from her grief and somehow more connected with herself: "I find it fascinating here. . . . When a sea fog comes and masks all landmarks, you begin to feel that you have slipped anchor and have drifted in very truth into mid ocean."

While she was there, she saw from a distance another visitor: "I first saw Synge in the north island of Aran. I was staying there, gathering folklore, talking to the people, and felt quite angry when I passed another outsider walking here and there, talking also to the people. I was jealous of not being alone on the island." With the solid unconsciousness of men about the most obvious accomplishments of women, Synge, who was setting himself up to be observant, wrote in his journal that, as regards staying on the island, "it would be hardly possible perhaps for a lady for more than a few days."

Shortly after Augusta's return to Coole, Willie arrived for the summer with news of the other outsider. He was John Millington Synge, a young Irishman of an old Protestant family. Yeats had met him several years before in Paris, where he was living on a tiny income from his mother and attempting to become a critic and writer. Yeats, who had just returned from a visit to the Aran Isles, advised him to go there himself, thinking he would find, as he did, an Irish subject to write about instead of foreign and literary subjects.

Seeing him as a possible beneficiary instead of a rival, Augusta had Willie invite him to Coole. Several weeks after they had exchanged considering glances across the ridge of Inishmaan, Synge arrived— another historic arrival—at Coole.

John Synge was then only twenty-seven and had done very little with his life except to work stubbornly at difficult and unrewarding tasks. He had studied languages, including Irish, at Trinity College, and music at the Royal Irish Academy. But he did not have the talent to be a musician, and exercised his literary ambitions writing essays on obscure topics.

His father, who died when he was very young, came from a long line of distinguished Church of Ireland clergymen, one of whom had been Archbishop of Tuam, a contemporary of Jonathan Swift and George Berkeley, and one of the great churchmen of his day. One of Synge's uncles had been the first Protestant missionary on the Aran Isles. The family had had large land holdings in County Wicklow, with the family seat at Glanmore Castle. His mother was the daughter of a Protestant clergyman from the north of Ireland; the twin objectives of her life were salvation and respectability. She never ceased to love her youngest son, but his lack of belief and his interest in a literary career, especially when it turned to playwriting, distressed her greatly. Synge's brothers were lawyers and colonial administrators. His sisters were properly and smugly married. In later years not one of his family ever attended a performance of his plays.

Synge was reserved. He watched people with detachment, but behind his reserve he was as starved in almost every way as it is possible for a human being to be: emotionally, financially, socially, sexually. Like Augusta, he harbored, as yet unknown even to himself, a fantastic vitality waiting for an outlet, which, when he found it, showed itself as an exuberant and observant humor, a yearning for love and beauty, a wonder at and submission to the tragedy of life as he saw it.

Augusta, Willie, Edward Martyn, and George Russell were busy collecting guarantees and considering possible locations for *The Heather Field* and *The Countess Cathleen*, finally scheduled for the following spring. Synge, not then a playwright, was never as impressed with Coole as was Yeats, and he did not enjoy being part of a movement as did Augusta. Yet, as his visit to Aran had given him the subject matter for his writing, so his arrival at Coole, his alliance with Yeats and Augusta, gave him the practical framework, the emotional support and encouragement to make use of his subject matter.

Yeats later wrote of the men Augusta brought to Coole:

> They came like swallows and like swallows went,
> And yet a woman's powerful character
> Could keep a swallow to its first intent;
> And half a dozen in formation there,
> That seemed to whirl upon a compass-point,
> Found certainty upon the dreaming air,
> The intellectual sweetness of those lines
> That cut through time or cross it withershins.

126

Synge was one of those half-dozen whose lives were dramatically modified by their contact with Yeats and Augusta at Coole. Augusta's childhood friend and fellow writer Violet Martin, who was not indebted to Coole for her inspiration, yet wrote Augusta after a visit, "There was a curious enchantment over all. . . . I think the constant output of spirit and mind at Coole creates a very special atmosphere."

Augusta was finding she did have a genius for inspiration. And it was not only that she had a beautiful estate to which to invite people or that the foremost writer in Ireland was there to stir them up. She inspired people not only because of her "powerful character"—Willie was the only beneficiary who felt its full weight—but because she was excited. Because she did not become involved with people personally, her excitement was conveyed as a generalized vitalization. Running one's race before a cloud of witnesses has its uses: it makes others feel they too are in extraordinary company. Often they rise to the occasion.

Synge, with the same evangelical influences from his mother that Augusta had from hers, whose grandfather's body had been seized for debt while lying in state on what had been a much grander estate than Coole, had a truer appreciation of the insecurities, both emotional and financial, of the landlord class. And while Yeats would describe Coole as an earthly paradise, "a life of order and of labour, where all outward things were the image of an inward life," Synge saw it differently. He had written in his journal after visiting the ruins of his grandfather's estate: "Everyone is used in Ireland to the tragedy that is bound up with the lives of farmers and fishing people; but in this garden one seemed to feel the tragedy of the landlord class also." He carried this pessimism about his class to Coole and remained indifferent to its charms.

He knew in his bones, in the cancer that killed him at thirty-six, that he belonged to a dying class. That Augusta and Willie belonged to it too and were full of hope and energy was a further reproach to his despair, but also a source of vicarious energy for him. Augusta wrote Yeats after Synge's death, "I think he got vitality from us, as he did from those wild people in the Blaskets." The three of them, along with all the other Irish gentlemen who were invited to Coole to do something for literary nationalism, were joining hands to leap out of their dying class into literary glory.

Sometime during the summer Augusta took Willie to the garden, handed him a knife, and told him to carve his initials on the trunk of her copper beech. Each summer she added more initials. Her fan, on which she would continue to accumulate signatures through the

127

1920's, was not appropriate to commemorate the junction of person with living place now occurring at Coole.

At the end of her summer of guests, Augusta left Coole with relief. "I am so tired of housekeeping I dreamed I was being served up for my guests and awoke only when the knife was at my throat." The beautiful order of Coole, however, rested finally on the maids and cook, the workmen who watched the pump and cleared the paths. It was a shaky foundation. Augusta once went to the station in Gort to meet a maid, hired sight unseen, who arrived "looking like a converted Maori dressed in a missionary's cast off clothing with a fuzzy head, a white shirt front and black cravat, and who got a fainting fit as a result of tight lacing!" Augusta sent her back on the next train. (Her letters and diaries contain many of these fleeting glimpses of women's tragedies—which she never saw.) Another time she reported on her interview with a cook: "I asked did she understand making kedgeree, with fish, rice and eggs. 'To be sure I do!' she says, 'to be throwing them to and fro.' But I think we shall get on all right."

The misdeeds of the Irish servants were numerous, from the gardener who—no other holder being handy—stuck his lighted candle in the buttonhole of a guest's coat left hanging in the harness room to the kitchenmaids who polished silver with the damask napkins.

Augusta joined Enid in London and the two traveled together to Ca Capello, where Enid could look after the housekeeping, and where the guests were much grander and more forgettable than those at Coole. Among others, the Emperor and Empress of Germany came to dinner with the King and Queen of Italy. But even among kings and empresses, Augusta thought of Ireland. She began a play (everyone else was writing one) in verse, called *Colman and Guaire*, about Saint Colman and King Guaire, the two most important people in the semi-historical mythology of her little part of Galway.

Though it contains some lovely lines and touching situations, the play is overburdened by her desire to do and be good. It concludes with a direct injunction to the audience to be mindful of the great services performed by Saint Colman:

> Oughtmana, Kilmacduagh, hold his traces,
>> So when you tread the fields his footsteps trod,
> Or pass by any of those hallowed places
>> For him and all the Saints give thanks to God.

Colman and Guaire is a parable about the demands of religion on everyday life, and in it Augusta was glorifying Coole and indirectly herself—as Yeats was to do so much better. In her play Coole is holy ground, the birthplace of a saint, the site of a healing well.

Augusta was trying to reconcile religion and art, writing that she "did not aspire to a stage production, but I thought a little play in rhyme might perhaps be learned and acted by Kiltartan school children." As she had asked her English friends to approve of her connection with the Irish theater by asking them for pledges, so she took her play around to the local religious authorities—both the Church of Ireland archdeacon and the Catholic priest of her neighborhood—and got their approval.

She was recalled from Venice by such confused and desperately unhappy letters from Willie that she hurried back to Dublin to see him. Along with much else, Willie had written, "My nerves are still feeling the effects; and a restless night has given me a rather bad cold and a little asthma so that I feel like a battered ship with the masts broken off at the stumps." What had happened was that Maud Gonne had changed the terms of their friendship. For the first time in Yeats's nine-year adoration of her, she had kissed him with, as he said, "the bodily mouth," and then proceeded to tell him "with every circumstance of deep emotion that she had loved me for years, that my love is the only beautiful thing in her life, but that for certain reasons which I cannot tell you, reasons of a generous kind, and of a tragic origin, she can never marry. She is full of remorse because she thinks that she has in the same breath bound me to her and taken away all hope of marriage."

Maud's reasons for her inability to marry were very vague; she had not yet told Willie of her French lover or her two children. But she was ready for a "spiritual marriage." They sat together seeing visions. Once Maud heard a voice saying, "You are about to receive the initiation of the spear." They sat silently while "a double vision unfolded. . . . She thought herself a great stone statue through which passed flame, and I felt myself becoming flame and mounting up through and looking out of the eyes of a great stone Minerva."

Augusta, arriving in Dublin and going to her favorite hotel, found Maud also staying at the Nassau. The next day Maud came to call on her friend's friend. The six-foot-tall, very beautiful, exquisitely dressed Maud Gonne looked down on the short, plain widow in black, and Augusta was shocked by her appearance. Instead of what she expected, "a vision of beauty, I saw a death's head [Maud had been sick], and what to say to her I knew not. She does not know I know anything so it was constrained. However, we got on amicably." Maud reported of this meeting that Augusta had asked her intentions in

129

regard to Willie, and that she had replied rather shortly, "I have more important things to think of than marriage and so has he."

Augusta, in fact, believed Willie and Maud to be closer to marriage than ever, writing Enid, with whom she apparently had discussed Yeats's distracted letters as they arrived in Venice, "Poet better than could have been expected. I think all will come right for him, at least that marriage will come, but whether that will be for good is another question." She concluded her letter, full of news of Wilfrid Blunt and his daughter's marriage, with the kind of information reserved only for one's dear women friends: "I bought a jacket in London, cloth without fur, and had no time for a hat. I wonder how you are getting on. It is so strange to be without you. I keep thinking of things to tell you."

Maud continued to be very affectionate to Willie, "and would kiss me very tenderly, but when I spoke of marriage on the eve of her leaving said, 'No, it seems to me impossible.' And then, with clenched hands, 'I have a horror and terror of physical love.' " She left for France. Augusta offered Willie money to follow her, told him not to leave her until she had promised to marry him, but he replied, "No, I am too exhausted; I can do no more."

However, Willie did follow Maud to France, and there she told him what she had been concealing for years, that she had been someone else's mistress, that she had had two children, one living, and though she no longer loved her former lover, she felt "she was necessary to him. She did not know what would happen to him if her influence was not there." Augusta's need to comfort Willie outweighed any need to condemn Maud, but she wrote Enid, "I am afraid she is only playing with him, from selfishness and vanity," and quoted an Irish saying, "I don't wish her any harm, but God is unjust if she dies a quiet death."

Christmas of 1898 was a Gaelic and family affair at Coole. In fact, she had some difficulty managing the family, writing Enid that "I am rather discouraged about nieces at present, for Frances, who I thought uninteresting but a quiet creature, quite lost her head at the sight of the Birch gang of men, and on the second time of finding them landed in the smoking room, I had to speak with severity, and she has taken the air of a martyr since then, but I never did set up to be able to manage girls." Aside from family and the Birch boys, who were practically family, the only other guests were Douglas Hyde, who thoroughly enjoyed the shooting, and Augusta's Gaelic teacher from London, Miss Norma Borthwick.

Miss Borthwick held classes for the country people every afternoon in the gate lodge, attended, on alternate days, by eight young women and forty young men. At Augusta's Christmas party for workhouse children, her niece Frances had the pleasure of playing Judy to one of the Birch boys' Punch, the performance in English, followed by Miss Borthwick and Douglas Hyde acting in Gaelic to the great delight of the children. Augusta wrote in her autobiography years later, "I sometimes think with a little pride that when Michael Collins and Eamonn de Valera were in their short jackets going to school or marching from it, I was spending time and money and energy bringing back the Irish among my own people."

She herself filled twenty-four little school exercise books with Gaelic exercises, stories taken down in Gaelic, a few stories composed by her in Gaelic. At night, after her guests went to bed, she sat up writing out the folklore collected at every opportunity from the country people around Coole. She once wrote that the requisites for a good folklore collector were patience, leisure, reverence, and a good memory. The leisure she no longer had, but her energy was prodigious.

Writing part of the time in English, part of the time in Gaelic, continually listening to the country people with their distinctive rhythm and vocabulary, she developed her own rendition of Irish speech. She called her style "Kiltartan." (Her use of it in coming years, coupled with its use by imitators, led Ezra Pound to remark that the Irish Renaissance had three phases: dove gray, shamrock, and Kiltartan.)

"Kiltartan," like the language of the Book of Common Prayer, which she read daily, is the speech of the group, not the individual. It expressed the feeling of community she got through her association with the Irish people. And this feeling became the new circumference of her life, a new cloud of witnesses.

She could therefore dispense cheerfully with the approval of her other neighbors, the Unionist gentry who began to look on her with more and more disapproval. That Christmas, a neighbor, on hearing that one of her gentleman guests spoke Irish, responded immediately, "He can't be a gentleman if he speaks Irish." At a later house party of Irish enthusiasts, Hugh Lane, finally a successful art dealer in London and not yet an Irish enthusiast, told one of the women that his Aunt Augusta had "lost her position in the county by entertaining people like your husband." Augusta, however, knew the gentry were on the losing side.

As the Irish people were the circumference of her new world, Yeats was the center. But she was also beginning to find her own center. Toward the end of 1898 and the beginning of 1899 she went through the menopause. She wrote Enid with her usual lack of clarity about per-

131

sonal matters, "I have suffered a good deal from the worrying sickness, but will soon get all right, for I can take things easy now." Though she was obviously not thinking about having a child, as the certainty that she would never again be called upon to have one slowly seeped into her mind, she felt a lightening, a slow but growing flood of energy that made possible the final flowering of her creativity.

She is one of those remarkable half-life artists who take half a lifetime to come through the demands made on them by society, biology, and their own temperament to arrive at the free use of their talents.

V

Living off the Land

THE IRISH EPICS AND *CATHLEEN NI HOULIHAN*: 1899–1902

John Synge, I and Augusta Gregory, thought
All that we did, all that we said or sang
Must come from contact with the soil, from that
Contact everything Antaeus-like grew strong.
W. B. YEATS, "The Municipal Gallery Re-visited"

AUGUSTA spent the next few years paying her debts to the Irish people and to Yeats. She moved toward playwriting like a soldier across hostile country, taking cover behind every rock and bush and broken wall.

During the production of the first plays of the Irish Literary Theatre, Augusta learned more about what producing plays does to people than she learned about playwriting. She learned that it attracts people; it makes them excited and importunate. She had already gone around to her friends asking for their support. Then, when Willie and Edward Martyn went to Dublin to rent a theater, they found that the licensed theaters were too large, too expensive, and booked too far in advance. It was illegal to give performances for money in an unlicensed hall. Augusta decided to get the law changed. She asked William Lecky, then a Unionist member of Parliament for Ireland, to attach a proviso the Local Government Bill for Ireland then going through Parliament, which he did.

The Local Government Bill of 1898, to which the rider was attached, effectively transferred control of local affairs from the landlords to the middle and lower classes. No longer would generations of Persses, Gregorys, and Blakeneys automatically become High Sheriffs, Justices of the Peace, and Deputy Lieutenants. By her own contrivance, the same law that drove one more nail in the landlords' coffin broke open one more way for Augusta to get out.

Willie and Martyn then rented the Antient Concert Rooms in Dublin for the week of May 8, 1899. They assembled a cast in London with Florence Farr as director. Augusta was in residence at her London flat. George Moore looked in at rehearsals and discovered that Willie's play, *The Countess Cathleen*, was going very well and Martyn's, *The Heather Field*, very badly. Willie was in Paris seeing Maud Gonne. George Moore took over, arranged for other actors for Martyn's play, and directed it himself.

In Yeats's play, a wealthy and compassionate woman, modeled on Maud Gonne, sells her soul for money to save the people from famine and prevent them from selling their souls for food. A Catholic priest declared publicly that it was heretical. Martyn was frightened and wrote Yeats on the verge of hysteria, "I do not wish to be mixed up in the concern any more. I have had too much trouble in various ways and cannot stand any more." Augusta, just beginning to draw on the undreamed-of reserves of pacification she was to employ on nervous and irate theater people for the next thirty-four years, made Martyn promise not to make a public statement. Yeats then submitted the play to a learned Jesuit, who found it non-heretical as well as beautiful. Martyn was satisfied. Only George Moore was disappointed, saying he would have written an article on " 'Edward Martyn and His Soul' . . . It was the best opportunity I ever had. . . . Nobody has ever written that way about his most intimate friend." (Twelve years later he wrote "that way" in detail about Martyn as well as Willie and Augusta in *Hail and Farewell*, his account of his temporary infatuation with the Irish Renaissance.)

Then, just before the plays were to be produced in Dublin, another passionate Catholic attacked the play, quoting speeches of the demons as Yeats's own beliefs. A popular disturbance was feared, and, like several other famous Irish plays, *The Countess Cathleen* opened with policemen—policemen in the employ of England—waiting outside should they be needed. There was some booing but no real disturbance. From the first, the Protestant founders of the Irish theater underestimated the strength of Catholic opposition. Augusta and Synge, accustomed to the personal Protestant narrowness of their mothers—which

was partly a reaction to their sense of social and political powerlessness—did not anticipate that such narrowness in a majority of the
population would, in the end, bring the theater they were to create
into the doldrums of mediocrity.

In 1899, however, the Irish Literary Theatre was the most public
expression of the new national sense of cultural worth. Except for the
few who came expressly to make a disturbance, the first-night capacity
audience—of over two hundred—was enthusiastic. The plays were
well attended throughout the week. Though some reviews criticized
specifics of the plays themselves or the method of acting, there was
widespread enthusiasm for the idea of an Irish theater. The plays gave
reviewers a chance to express, as English plays did not, their ideas
about the direction of Irish culture. They provided a focal point and
gave people somewhere to go to express their Irishness. Mary Maguire—then a college student in Dublin, later Mary Colum and a well-
known literary critic—wrote of attending the plays wearing "a white
garment with blue and green embroidery, a blue brath [cape], copper
broaches, and other archaeological adornments." A friend of hers wore
"gorgeous purple and gold, a torc [metal circlet] on her forehead, a
Tara broach fastening her brath, and various other accouterments of
the ancient Irish." The audience sang patriotic songs during inter-
missions.

Greatly encouraged, Yeats and Augusta, Moore and Martyn began
planning for the next season. They booked the Gaiety Theatre in Dublin, which seated over a thousand, for the week of February 19, 1900.
They planned to give Martyn's *Maeve*, his new play, *A Tale of a
Town*, and a brief play by Alice Milligan, an acquaintance of Yeats,
called *The Last Feast of the Fianna*. Yeats and Moore then decided
that *A Tale of a Town* was unacceptably amateurish. They decided
to rewrite it and, in the summer of 1899, went to Martyn's castle to
do so. Augusta, sure Edward could not stand the sight of two opinionated men revising his play before his own eyes, asked them to come
to Coole instead.

Augusta and George Moore did not like each other. She wrote in
her diary that one of the actresses said he looked like "a boiled ghost."
Moore, writing for the public, described Augusta as "a middle-aged
woman, agreeable to look upon, perhaps for her broad, handsome, intellectual brow enframed in iron-grey air. The brown, wide-open eyes
are often lifted in looks of appeal and inquiry, and a natural wish to
sympathize softens her voice till it whines." He was jealous of her
influence over Yeats, describing Willie entering the drawing room at
Coole, where Moore was talking with Augusta, "somewhat diffi-

dently, I thought, with an invitation to me to go for a walk. Lady Gregory was appeased with the news that he had written five-and-a-half lines that morning, and a promise that he would be back at six, and would do a little more writing before dinner." Augusta, in turn, was jealous of Moore's influence. Moore wrote of her commenting on their collaboration: "something about a man of genius and a man of talent coming together, speaking quickly under her breath, so that her scratch would escape notice at the time." And Moore was jealous of her care for Yeats. When Augusta had to leave Coole for a few days and sent Yeats back to Tulira, Augusta supposedly told Moore that "I must be careful not to overwork him, and that it would be well not to let him go more than two hours without food—a glass of milk, or, better still, a cup of beef tea in the forenoon, and half an hour after lunch he was to have a glass of sherry and a biscuit." Moore, who was Augusta's equal in rank, intelligence, and talent—if not in good temper and modesty—momentarily regretted that he himself was not the chosen one. He wrote that, "thinking of how happy their lives must be at Coole, implicated in literary partnership, my heart went out towards her in sudden sympathy. 'She has been wise all her life through,' I said, 'she knew him to be her need at once, and she never hesitated . . . yet she knew me before she knew him.' "

Through the fall of 1899 Willie and Moore sat under the huge catalpa tree in the garden at Coole working on their joint projects with Augusta as referee between them. Writing about it later, George Moore called the tree a weeping ash, and though he was to insult her far more grievously, at the end of her life she chose to forgive all, including "his slander in miscalling my catalpa tree a weeping ash . . . among all trees the one for which I have least affection, even a slight feeling of dislike."

In the New Year they all moved over to London to supervise the casting and rehearsal of the second year's plays. Martyn's *A Tale of a Town*, rewritten chiefly by Moore and renamed by him *The Bending of the Bough*, was also signed by him since Martyn refused to accept it. Augusta, Willie, and George Moore then traveled back to Ireland together in February of 1900 for the performance of the plays. Edward Martyn, exaggerating his humiliation, acted as baggage man and traveled ahead with the actors. On the train Moore read them his speech for the Irish Literary Society in praise of the Irish language. Though he had no intention of learning it, he threatened to disinherit his nephew unless he did.

The evening they arrived in Dublin, Yeats and Moore attended a dinner given by the Irish Literary Society in honor of the plays. Augusta, a woman, was not invited, but a few days later she and the actresses were invited to a lunch meeting of the literary society at which Moore delivered his fighting speech about the language.

During the week of performances at the Gaiety Theatre, Augusta invited reporters to tea at her hotel to ask why the plays had not got better reviews and to get promises of better reviews the next time. (She had just met Mark Twain in London and, regarding this arrangement, told his joke about a man incorrectly reported dead—for which the newspaper editor refused to apologize, but offered cheerfully "to put you free of charge among the births to-morrow morning.") As before, specifics of the plays were criticized, but the overall reaction was favorable.

After her dose of Dublin, a town she never really liked, Augusta took Robert to London and then to Italy for Easter. London was full of enthusiasm for the Boer War and full of temporary enthusiasm for Ireland as its ally against the Boers. Augusta found both emotions repellent. St. Patrick's Day was celebrated with shamrocks everywhere. She walked to lunch with Enid across St. James's Park, "the whole place like Birnam Wood marching—shamrock bunches as big as cabbage heads tied with Union Jack ribbons on every ragamuffin!" She herself wore an ivy leaf, Parnell's emblem.

Augusta was a little afraid to face Enid because her new ally George Moore had written to the papers denouncing the Queen's proposed visit to Ireland. Fortunately, Enid had not read the letter and spent their visit telling Augusta enthusiastically about her plans for an officers' hospital in Madeira, for which, as Augusta wrote, she was having "safety pins made with little Union Jacks on for Tommy to fasten his bandage with." Deferring to friendship, Augusta "put my ivy leaf under my cloak, pinned with my diamond wheatear, thinking it really distressed Enid."

In Rome she received the May 1900 issue of the *Cornhill Magazine* containing her article "Felons of Our Land," in which she glorified the Irish tradition of rebellion. Count de Basterot, also in Rome, read it and "gave me a talking to." He scolded her for "going so far from the opinions of my husband and son." She told him that "I am convinced my husband would have been with me in all I have done so far"—which sounded as if she intended to go much farther—but added in her diary, "I had already determined not to go so far towards political nationality in anything I write again, because I wish to keep out of politics and work only for literature; and partly because if

Robert is Imperialist, I don't want to separate myself from him."
Thereafter her formula was: not working for Home Rule but preparing for it.

In Rome she and Robert were entertained, as she and Sir William
had been entertained so often, at the British Embassy: "I felt like a
revenant, but very proud of my fair-haired son." She was forty-eight.
Robert was nineteen and a student at Oxford, having passed safely
through Harrow. (Augusta had written in her diary, "A little disappointed he has not left more of a mark on Harrow.") Robert was
indeed Imperialist, very opposed to Home Rule for Ireland. But though
Augusta would feel until the day he died a great fear of losing his
love, they did not quarrel. He continued to disappoint her scholas-
tically, however, and after only a few months at Oxford was "sent
down" temporarily for failing an exam. He wanted to spend the time
at Coole, but she wired him not to come because "he would be idle
and there would be much talk, people would think it was for bad
conduct."

During the summer of 1900 at Coole, Augusta entertained the usual
group of Robert's friends and her literary house guests. She was enjoying herself, especially in contrast to the early days of her widowhood. She was still writing out her folklore—uncritical, completely
accepting retellings of the stories she collected—and beginning in
1903 she would publish a book of folklore every few years for the
rest of her life.

Her folklore was to her playwriting as her mourning was to her
personality. She used both folklore and mourning to present the
façade of a good woman permanently fixed in the attitude of reverence and remembrance. Indeed, her folklore was widow's work, commemorating what had gone. After finding Biddy Early's cottage, her
achievement for 1900 was to locate the grave of Raftery, a poet dead
since 1835, whose songs in Irish were still sung everywhere Irish was
spoken. She paid for a gravestone and, with Douglas Hyde and the
local Catholic priests, established an annual *feis* at the grave for the
singing and reciting of Irish. But, like the charities of her youth, folklore made no demands on her intelligence, nor did it bring her much
acclaim. She found in the retelling of the ancient Irish epics a task
that expressed the same reverence for Ireland but also demanded a
good deal more from her.

In February 1900, Dr. Robert Atkinson, Professor of Romance Lan-
guages and Sanskrit at Trinity College, had, under pressure from the
Gaelic League to introduce Gaelic in the schools, made a report on
Gaelic literature that stated: "It has scarcely been touched by the

movements of the great literatures; it is the untrained popular feeling. . . . My astonishment is that through the whole range of Irish literature that I have read (and I have read an enormous range of it), the smallness of the element of idealism is most noticeable. . . . And as there is very little idealism there is very little imagination. . . . The Irish tales are devoid of it fundamentally." These were fighting words to a woman committed to showing, as she and Yeats had written in the prospectus for the Irish Literary Theatre, that Ireland was "the home of an ancient idealism." Always a good girl, when Augusta described this denigration of Irish literature by the professors at Trinity College, she added, "and I was quite sorry when Profeseor Atkinson died."

The Irish epics are an episodic series of adventures similar in structure to the Arthurian legends and the Welsh *Mabinogion*. Malory's *Morte d'Arthur* was the favorite book of her childhood. Her best friend's mother had retold the Welsh epics. In the summer of 1900 Yeats told her an English publisher had suggested he retell the Irish epics but he had refused because he didn't have the time. A few days later she asked if he would object if she tried it herself. As Augusta wrote, "After a short hesitation, he thinks the idea very good, so I will try and carry it out, and am provided with work for the rest of my life."

In fact, Augusta flew through the work. It took her only two and a half years, from October 1900 to June 1903. The stories existed in many variations and in many different styles. Augusta set out to weave them into a coherent and interesting tale, using the Kiltartan style she had developed for her folklore.

Returning to London in the winter of 1900, she found most of the manuscripts she needed in the British Museum. She told the clerk she would be working on " 'The Cuchulain Saga' and as that did not seem to convey much, I said, 'Ancient Irish History.' He asked how long I expected to be at it. I said I didn't know, perhaps two years, at which he jumped, having expected me I think to say two hours. Then he said I must make formal application and have a reference." She asked if Sidney Colvin (head of the museum print department) would be satisfactory. "His respect increased and he said if I would go to him I could get my order at once. . . . Then Sir Edward Thompson, the Librarian, came in, an old acquaintance, and gave me a reading order which made all the clerks bow before me like Joseph's sheaves."

For weeks she worked at the museum all day, eating alone at the Austrian Restaurant nearby and returning to the museum to work until nine or ten. She read Dickens avidly afterward at her flat, finding in *Bleak House* "an immense relief, a sort of warmth and refreshment in its humour, its humanity; a reaction no doubt from those hours in the ancient world of heroism and dreams." She still dined out frequently, but found she no longer enjoyed society as she had. The Boer War was still the chief topic of conversation. Queen Victoria had just died and been succeeded by her son, whom the society ladies referred to as "Edward the Caresser." Wilfrid Blunt was always in Egypt during the winter when she was in London. For many reasons English society seemed less important.

Back in Ireland for the summer of 1901, she found some of the books she needed at the Royal Irish Academy, some at the National Library in Dublin, some at the Archeological Society. When the stories she heard from the country people seemed better than the published versions, she used them. She was instinctively aware of the needs and interests of her readers, and with a rapid courage she combined, left out, decided upon chronology, and pieced together. (Again doing real women's work, making a quilt from the ragbag of Irish epic manuscripts.)

As with the Irish folklore, she found much in the epics to reinforce her own attitudes. The most important virtue is loyalty—though there is the average amount of treachery. The most important relationship is with the group. Augusta too lived chiefly through her relationship to the group, and since she had joined those doing battle for Irish literary nationalism, she felt as if she were one of a band of gallant warriors. After all her exciting summer guests left, she wrote:

> It is a long day without the sons of Usnach. . . . The place so still that I felt as if sudden gaiety had begun one day because the sheep had been put in the back lawn and I could see them from the windows; the old black sheep that always seems so friendly because William knew it, and the cuckoo lamb in its absurd last year's coat.

Life at Coole without the warriors dwindled down to trees and servant problems: "Patrick very boozy, holding silvers [fir trees] very sideways while Maurteen planted them." But she herself was a warrior: "I got some more of the rabbit mixture and stayed out till 5:00 in the snow seeing it put on, and came home soaking."

The epic heroes' attitude toward achievement was also similar to the attitude she attempted to maintain in regard to herself. The heroes, while very much interested in competition, are more interested in proving their worthiness in regard to some high standard. They do not have the ability to change or grow. Their attributes—Cuchulain's strength,

Deirdre's beauty—are gifts from birth. Thus their achievements do not represent additions to or changes in their basic capabilities, but are simply an acting out of their already existing potentialities. Cuchulain's victories are like dream battles with no preparation and no aftermath:

> Cuchulain stood up to him, and took his iron ball in his hand, and hurled it at his head, and it went through the forehead and out at the back of his head, and his brains along with it, so that the air could pass through the hole it made. And then Cuchulain struck off his head.

Like the heroes, Augusta attempted to make herself believe that her activities did not involve competing with others to raise her status, but were simply services performed in the course of doing her duty to the Irish people.

The epics also reinforced her fear of appearing a powerful woman. Women in the Irish epics are powerful—they own property, they lead armies, they win battles. It looks bad:

> When he died Macha asked for the kingship, but the sons of Dithorba said they would not give kingship to a woman. So she fought against them and routed them, and they went as exiles to the wild places of Connaught. And after a time she went in search of them, and she took them by treachery, and brought them all in one chain to Ulster.

It is obvious the power of women is resented. When Queen Maeve's army is defeated, one of her captains knows why: "And it is following the lead of a woman . . . has brought it to this distress."

In her dedication to *Cuchulain*, Augusta states that she has been diverted from her housewifely duties only because the men who should have retold the epics are neglectful:

> And indeed if there was more respect for Irish things among the learned men that live in the college at Dublin, where so many of these old writings are stored, this work would not have been left to a woman of the house, that has to be minding the place, and listening to complaints, and dividing her share of food.

Augusta dedicated *Cuchulain* to the country people around Coole, telling them with heavy-handed condescension, that

> When I began to gather these stories together, it is of you I was thinking. . . . When I went looking for the stories in the old writings, I found that the Irish in them is too hard for any person to

read that had not made a long study of it. . . . I have told the whole story in plain and simple words, the same way my old nurse Mary Sheridan used to be telling stories from the Irish long ago, and I a child at Roxborough. . . . And I am very glad to have something that is worth offering to you, for you have been very kind to me ever since I came over to you from Kilchriest, two-and-twenty years ago.

This sheep's clothing obscures but does not hide the shape of the hungry woman stalking fame and acclaim.

The summer of 1901, when this preface was written, was the turning point in Augusta's development as a dramatist. Willie and George Moore had decided they would write a play based on the Diarmuid-and-Grania love story from the Finn cycle for the third season of the Irish Literary Theatre. This they proceeded to do amid continual disagreement, with Augusta dropping in a speech here, a turn of action there. They decided they wanted a play in Irish to accompany *Diarmuid and Grania,* so Augusta sat down and wrote a scenario which Douglas Hyde obligingly rewrote in Irish. (*The Twisting of the Rope* is about a mother's trick to get a lover out of the house so her daughter can make the proper marriage arranged for her.)

Synge came to Coole that summer with a partially completed manuscript of a book on the Aran Isles. George Russell, then working for Horace Plunkett as an agricultural organizer, left his wife and son at home and came to Coole for the literary talk and the visions. Douglas Hyde came for the shooting and the company. Violet Martin, never converted to nationalism or playwriting, came for a short visit and was invited to carve her name on the autograph tree: "I smoked, and literary conversation raged."

During that summer, as Yeats wrote, he and Augusta wrote so many plays "in so few weeks that if I were to say how few, I do not think anybody would believe me." Willie, Augusta, and Douglas Hyde quickly whipped up the long, involved *Where There Is Nothing* primarily to keep George Moore, who was quarreling with everyone, from using the idea. The idea and outline were Willie's; Augusta and Douglas Hyde helped write the dialogue, as if the play were a jigsaw puzzle laid out on a table.

One morning during these miraculous "few weeks" Willie came down to breakfast and told Augusta about a dream "almost as distinct as a vision, of a cottage where there was well-being and firelight and talk of a marriage, and into the midst of that cottage there came an old woman in a long cloak." Willie had a feeling the woman was "Ireland herself, that Cathleen ni Houlihan for whom so many songs have been sung, and about whom so many stories have been told and for whose sake so many have gone to their death." The old woman in the long cloak was also Maud Gonne—who inspired the central character in most of Willie's early plays and who, like Cathleen, was disrupting for him the ordinary good of life, denying him marriage while she devoted herself to, and involved him in, the struggle for Irish freedom.

Willie went back up to his room to turn his dream into a play, but found he could not do it. He thought the language was the problem. He had dreamed of peasant characters and could not reproduce the peasant speech. What really happened was that he had seen a sliver of vision that, while it corresponded perfectly to his actual situation in regard to Maud, did not lend itself to reshaping closer to his heart's desire. The cottage where there was firelight and well-being and talk of a marriage was the good he was not going to get.

Willie asked Augusta if she, with her facility for the folk dialect, would make a play of his dream. Augusta took the germ of his idea and changed it to fit her experience of oppression and release. The cottage with the firelight and talk of a marriage becomes the oppression from which one must escape. Ireland might be oppressed by England, but oppression as Augusta knew it came from her family and the narrowness of the life they offered her. She knew from her own life, and from the futile, wasted lives of her brothers, that the real tragedy of Ireland was not specifically the oppression of Ireland by England but the lack of opportunities for growth and grandeur, for activity and success, in daily life. Resistance to this oppression, for her and for many of the Irish people, had found its outlet in resistance to the oppression of England. So when she sat down to write a play about Cathleen ni Houlihan, who was "Ireland herself," she re-created all the passion of her cramped girlhood finding release in the love of rebel Ireland.

She reached back to the brightest emotion of her youth and grasped the flash of excitement when Mary Sheridan told of the cheering when the French landed at Killala. (She set the scene: "Interior of a cottage close to Killala, in 1798.") That cheering is heard off stage at the beginning and throughout the play. It was an exciting, uplifting commotion, but, as Augusta and her audience well knew, the landing changed nothing. The cheering is not for freedom but only for resistance.

The play opens with mother, father, and son discussing the son's approaching marriage. When Willie later complained to her about

143

the delighted laughter at the beginning, which, he thought, detracted from the drama of Cathleen's entrance, she replied, "I hope you won't alter Kathleen [she always wrote "Kathleen"; Yeats always wrote "Cathleen"]. I am sure the simple enjoyment of a comfortable life without any mention of what is to happen is the best opening." Yet were it not for the kindness with which the family is presented, it would be immediately obvious that the life they offer is stifling. With the warmth and firelight and talk of a marriage, all the emphasis is on money, the fortune the bride is bringing, the money value of a son. The old father boasts:

> Yes, I made the bargain well for you, Michael. Old John Cahel would sooner have kept a share of this a while longer. "Let me keep the half of it until the first boy is born," says he. "You will not," says I. "Whether there is or is not a boy, the whole hundred pound must be in Michael's hands before he brings your daughter to this house."

There is a slight, soon-mended quarrel about the old wife's lack of a fortune:

> Peter: Indeed, I wish I had the luck to get a hundred pound, or twenty pounds itself, with the wife I married.
> Bridget: Well, if I didn't bring much I didn't get much. What had you the day I married you but a flock of hens and you feeding them, and a few lambs and you driving them to the market at Balina? (*She is vexed and bangs a jug on the dresser.*) If I brought no fortune I worked it out in my bones, laying down the baby, Michael that is standing there now, on a stook of straw, while I dug the potatoes, and never asked big dresses or anything but to be working.

The old father has great plans for the dowry money: "We can take the ten acres of land we have the chance of since Jamsie Dempsey died, and stock it." And the old mother has great plans for her younger son: "I do be thinking sometimes, now things are going so well with us, and the Cahels such a good back to us in the district, and Delia's own uncle a priest, we might be put in the way of making Patrick a priest some day, and he so good at his books."

This is the life Michael, the bridegroom, can look forward to until a strange old woman in a long cloak comes in. She says she is grieving for the loss of her "four beautiful green fields." The family members comment back and forth to each other, trying to place her. "Is she the Widow Casey that was put out of her holding at Kilgrass a while ago?" "Is she right, do you think, or is she a woman from beyond the world?" Michael sits down beside her.

Michael: Are you lonely going the roads, ma'am?
Old Woman: I have my thoughts and I have my hopes.
Michael: What hopes have you to hold to?
Old Woman: The hope of getting my beautiful fields back again;
the hope of putting the strangers out of my house.

She says the cheering they hear is for her friends coming to help her. With this Michael says, "I will go with you." His mother quickly sketches out his obligations at home: "You have plenty to do. It is food and drink you have to bring to the house. The woman that is coming home is not coming with empty hands; you would not have an empty house before her." (One of the great attractions of dying for one's country is, as everyone knows, the opportunity to get out of just such obligations.)

The old woman makes it clear that Michael is going to nothing but defeat and death:

It is a hard service they take that help me. Many that are red-cheeked now will be pale-cheeked; many that have been free to walk the hills and bogs and rushes will be sent to walk hard streets in far countries; many a good plan will be broken; many that have gathered money will not stay to spend it; many a child will be born and there will be no father at its christening to give it a name. They that have red cheeks will have pale cheeks for my sake, and for all that, they will think they are well paid.

Though this play has been described as "an expression of the worship of liberty in a subject race," it in fact has nothing to do with liberty—which involves decisions, responsibility, uncertainty. The play is about escaping from emptiness to emotion and getting an extra charge of emotion by paying for the escape with death.

The play up to this point would have been an accurate representation of a particular attitude, but Augusta had one more twist. The last line, said in response to the question "Did you see an old woman going down the path?" is "I did not, but I saw a young girl, and she had the walk of a queen." Though Michael has already rushed out to die for Cathleen, this line captures the emotions and approval of the audience, who are convinced by it that Michael is on the most powerful side, along with them. A drama scholar wrote, "I can remember as if it were yesterday the swing of sympathy, more sudden and complete than any other play I have seen, the releasing of exultation and vision. . . ." But in reality, except for the sudden expansion of emotion, this swing of sympathy is no different from the chronic Irish shifting of loyalty to whomever is perceived to be the strongest.

The play is enormously revealing, both of Augusta and of the Irish people who made it into a classic of Irish patriotism. While giving only the faintest hope of liberty, it depicts a spirit so completely oppressed that the only improvement comes from a change in the terms of the oppression—and that change is paid for by defeat and death. Augusta, however, like all artists who can embody their vision completely, had escaped from its power. She was not going to die a rebel, she was going to found a theater and write more plays. In *Cathleen ni Houlihan*, Augusta and Willie were Judas goats, making death for the cause appear attractive while they themselves had the wit to slip out a side door before the police arrived.

Augusta wrote the play in one of the little school exercise books she used for her folklore. Willie put in Cathleen's chants. Augusta typed the whole thing and handed it to Willie. He took it. After all, it was his dream.

Then, to brush away the last shreds of emotion and end the tension of *Cathleen*, Willie and Augusta wrote a short comedy depicting Irish peasants as lovable fools. *The Pot of Broth* is based on a folktale current in many cultures of a tramp who makes people believe that a stone will make broth when put in the pot and whiskey when put in a jar. In their play a tramp comes to a poor cottage while its owners, Sibby and John, are outside killing the old rooster for the priest's dinner. The tramp goes through his pockets to see what he has to offer and finds nothing: an empty pipe, a handkerchief, a knife handle, and a stone he had picked up to throw at a dog.

When the woman comes in and sees him, she is brief: "Then you may quit this house if you please. We have nothing for you." He replies, "It is a mistake you are making, ma'am, it is not asking anything I am. It is giving I am more used to." He holds up the stone and tells her it is magic. "All I'll ask of you now, ma'am, is the loan of a pot with a drop of boiling water in it." Distracting her and her husband by a tale of magic, telling how he got the stone from a little man in a hairskin coat, the tramp puts in handfuls of cabbage, onions, and meal and stirs the pot with a hambone. He uses their superstition against them, telling them that the stone, having come into Catholic hands, would if put in the pot with a bit of meat on a Friday, turn it black as black. He takes the chicken the woman has just plucked to demonstrate how on other days "it would do it no harm, but good." He uses flattery to keep the chicken in the pot:

Sibby (*getting up*): Let me take the chicken out now.

Tramp: Stop till I'll help you, ma'am, you might scald your
hand. I'll show it to you in a minute as white as your own
skin, where the lily and the rose are fighting for the mastery.
Did you ever hear that the boys in your own parish were singing after you being married from them—such of them that had
any voice at all and not choked with crying, or senseless with
the drop of drink they took to comfort them and to keep their
wits from going, with the loss of you? (*Sibby sits down com-
placently.*)

He sings to her of their love:

I was standing by the man that made the song, and he writing
it with an old bit of a carpenter's pencil, and the tears running
down—

> My Pastin Finn is my sole desire,
> And I am shrunken to skin and bone,
> For all my heart has had for its hire
> Is what I can whistle alone and alone.
> Oro, oro!
> Tomorrow night I will break down the door.

He keeps the chicken in the pot while he sings three verses and re-
peats the last, Sibby singing along with him, after which she says to
her husband, "I always knew I was too good for you!" Then she suddenly comes to her senses: "Did you take the chicken out yet?"
which he does, giving it a good squeeze. He gives the man and woman
a taste of the broth and drinks the rest himself. The woman declares
she has to have the stone, and so he gives it to her in return for (1) the
chicken and (2) their bottle of whiskey, which they won't begrudge
him, "when you can make plenty for yourself from this out." The
husband follows the tramp out to shake his hand and returns with the
news that "the priest's at the top of the boreen coming for his dinner.
Maybe you'd best put the stone in the pot again."

Augusta and Willie show the Irish peasants giving up their everyday nourishment for a stone, which in a way is the same thing they
had shown in *Cathleen*.

Augusta let Willie put his name on this play too. After all, she
never rode a horse after her father ordered her off one. She never
fired a gun. She never lit a fire in her fireplace (though she lit one in
Robert's) until the dahlias had been cut down by frost. Archdeacon
Burkett had prevented her and her brothers and sisters from giving

plays, not because he saw any harm in *Cinderella*, but because "you can't tell where it might lead to!"

On October 21, 1901, the third season of the Irish Literary Theatre got under way at the Gaiety Theatre in Dublin with *Diarmuid and Grania*, which Augusta had written bits of, and *The Twisting of the Rope* in Gaelic, which she had written first in English. She never missed a performance except when she held a reception for Yeats's brother Jack's picture exhibition, "Sketches of Life in the West of Ireland." She wrote an appreciation of the exhibition for the *Dublin Express*, "hoping it may be an advertisement," which when reprinted in an American paper, brought the artist to the attention of John Quinn, an American lawyer in New York reaching out for his Irish roots, who bought several pictures from Jack Yeats and his father, and who, within the year, would be at Coole carving his initials on Augusta's autograph tree.

The three-year trial period Yeats, Augusta, and Martyn had set for the Irish Literary Theatre—begun because Martyn and Yeats each had two unproduced plays on their hands—was over. They had more plays; they had an audience interested in seeing them; and they found Irish actors who could perform them. In the summer of 1901 Yeats began corresponding with the brothers Frank and Willie Fay, who were producing and acting in short Irish comedies in coffee houses. Frank Fay had been a shorthand writer, Willie Fay an electrician. Other actors worked during the day as shopgirls and railway clerks. They were but another manifestation of the extraordinary enthusiasm for Irish culture that inspired young men and women around Coole to walk miles for an Irish lesson that could do them no practical good.

Yeats agreed to let the brothers produce *Cathleen ni Houlihan*. George Russell gave them *Deirdre*, his play based on the love story in the Cuchulain cycle. The plays were to be produced under the auspices of a women's nationalist organization, the Daughters of Erin, founded by Maud Gonne, to which most of the actresses belonged. Maud agreed to play the lead in *Cathleen*, seeing it as a love letter to her and the perfect vehicle for her call-to-arms nationalism.

The union of playwrights with actors marked a sudden heightening of the excitement and a real step in the development of the machinery of the renaissance. Now added to the vital communication among playwrights was added the communication between playwrights and actors. Now that they no longer had to go to London for actors, the playwrights felt they were contributing more directly and powerfully to the cause of Ireland.

Augusta was in Dublin on her fiftieth birthday, March 15, 1902, for rehearsals of *Cathleen* at St. Teresa's Total Abstinence Hall, which was actually half a hall, divided from a billiard parlor by a partition. Augusta sat quietly listening to Maud recite her words while George Moore, George Russell, John Butler Yeats, William Butler Yeats, and the Fay brothers told Maud how to say them. Maud ignored them all, going off to the Wicklow hills to chant her lines alone. Just before the first performance Augusta slipped out of town to Venice for her customary Easter visit with Enid Layard.

Safely in Venice, she encouraged Willie: "I hope Kathleen ni Houlihan will be a success, I am sure it must be. Mind you keep all the notices for the theatre book." When he wrote that it was a success, she replied, "A great many thanks for your letter. I was *longing* to hear about the plays."

Her first book of Irish epics, *Cuchulain of Muirthemne*, was published in London in April 1902 as she was en route home to Ireland from Italy. She was kept busy collecting compliments. John Synge wrote her, "I had no idea it would be so great," and later, "*Cuchulain* is still part of my daily bread." From America she got admiring letters from Mark Twain and President Theodore Roosevelt—thereafter remarking casually, "I see Roosevelt is puffing my books again." George Russell wrote, "I never expect to read a more beautiful book . . . indeed the whole book made my heart beat with a half painful pleasure. . . . You have acted the fairy godmother to me and to many Irish people by bringing the good gift our hearts desired."

The book contains a preface by Yeats beginning, "I think this book is the best that has come out of Ireland in my time. Perhaps I should say that it is the best book that has ever come out of Ireland, for the stories it tells are a chief part of Ireland's gift to the imagination of the world—and it tells them perfectly for the first time." (Augusta had asked Willie for the preface, saying, "The chief thing is to show that you, representing the literary movement, accept this book and that it is not rubbishy amateur work.")

The epics presented by her in *Cuchulain* and *Gods and Fighting Men*, published in 1904, offered the Irish people an expansion of emotion. As Yeats wrote in regard to other Irish stories, "When our narrow rooms, our short lives, our soon ended passions and emotions put us out of conceit with sooty and finite reality, here at last is a universe where all is large and intense enough to almost satisfy the emotions of man." The epics gave the Irish people a great feeling of pride in themselves. Long accustomed to feel subordinate and inferior to England, they were surprised, they felt ennobled, to discover that

Ireland had had a heroic culture while England was still in the Dark Ages. The Irish epics, presented in popular form just when freedom from England was becoming a possibility, made the Irish people feel bigger and braver.

Augusta wrote that her books made it impossible for England to "scoff at our literature and its 'want of idealism.' " But the extremely limited set of ideals—heroic fighting and loyalty to the warrior band—presented to the Irish people without any accompanying critique of their failures and deficiencies, encouraged a kind of mindless loyalty and heroism in a people already—after centuries of oppression—severely deficient in political realism, flexibility, and a sense of social responsibility. The epics made the Irish people more willing to fight for freedom, but contributed to making them less fit to govern.

Like many other writers on Ireland, Augusta used and was nourished by the passion and comedy of Ireland, but the material she gave back to the Irish people was not basically useful to them. In fact, she did the Irish people a disservice while seeming to confer a benefit.

After reading the reviews of *Cuchulain*, Augusta sat down and read the notices for *Cathleen ni Houlihan*. Stephen Gwynn, drama critic, had left the performance wondering whether "such plays should be produced unless one was prepared for people to go out to shoot and be shot." The *Irish Times*, not in favor of Ireland's freedom from England, commented coldly that the play was merely Maud Gonne, the well-known Irish nationalist, playing herself. Bernard Shaw told Augusta after a later performance that play "might lead a man to do something foolish"—which, coming from that deflater of emotion, surprised her, she said, as much as if one of the stone lions in Trafalgar Square had scratched itself.

Drama is the adult activity most resembling child's play because, like play, it is a means of exploring attitudes and emotions without changing one's life. *Cathleen*, presented at that particular moment in Irish history, crossed the line from drama to propaganda because it did influence people to change their lives. Lennox Robinson, later a director of the Abbey Theatre, wrote several years afterward that *Cathleen* and *The Rising of the Moon* (also by Augusta) "made more rebels in Ireland than a thousand political speeches or a hundred reasoned books." So much so that after the 1916 rising, Yeats, who had long suppressed awareness of Augusta's contribution, wondered in his ponderous way, "Did that play of mine send out/ Certain men the English shot?" It turned out that the overcautious comment on playwriting made by Archdeacon Burkett in her youth—that you never could tell "where it might lead to"—was correct. Playwriting could be dangerous.

Augusta never claimed *Cathleen*. In later years, when her family protested, she would shake her head with a smile and say she could not take from Willie what was after all his only popular success. She did, however, within a month of her return from Italy, give to the Fay brothers for production a play written all by herself under her name alone.

VI

Laughing at Last

FIRST PLAYS: 1902–1904

Eternal Spirit of the chainless Mind!
Brightest in dungeons, Liberty! thou art,
For here thy habitation is the heart—
    Lord Byron, "Sonnet on Chillon"

Augusta had been preparing all her life to be a playwright. There are two fields of force operating in a drama, the forward force of the action driving toward a conclusion and the alternating current vibrating back and forth between audience and characters. Augusta's childhood, surrounded by the crowd of brothers and sisters with the Master and Mistress watching over all, gave her a continuous sensitivity to the shifting responses of the group. The forward force of her drama came from the lifelong conflict between what she wanted and what she felt to be her duty.

Out of that conflict came all the creative acts of her life. With her husband's death, the pace of the creative changes had accelerated— the reasons for these changes always just below the level of consciousness. Her desires were simple: love and liberty. She was under strict orders: she must serve. Her adoption of the Irish people and her acquisition of Yeats were both creative acts by which she brought duty and desire closer together.

Having gone so far, at fifty Augusta could go no farther. She could not take off her mourning and interact more normally and intimately with her fellow human beings. She could not cast off duty and be a writer for herself alone. She had, however, arranged things extraordinarily well. If she could not have freedom in her love and in her soul be free, she could at least write plays for Yeats and for Ireland.

Playwriting was the form of creative activity most suited to her personality and past experience. Her opportunity to write plays came just at the time in her life when she most needed it and when her release from the continual, wearing demand that she do her duty was most possible. She had never, until her widowhood, been alone. She had never had time to be deeply aware of her own emotions. Augusta wrote of the first years of her widowhood, "Loneliness made me rich—'full' as Bacon says." She was aware of the build-up of emotions—the longing for love, the longing for liberty—which she would not permit herself to express fully in her life.

She felt thwarted in her full expression or even exploration of her emotions by her cloud of witnesses, her super-ego always watching to see she was doing her duty. Playwriting gave her the opportunity to use and explore these emotions before a more benevolent audience. The conviction that in writing plays she was serving Yeats and Ireland permitted her to feel that playwriting was an acceptable activity. That conviction cleared the ground for her and took her mind off the cloud of witnesses. If the whole activity was permissible, she need not watch every speech, every turn of action.

The use of peasant characters and peasant speech permitted a further liberation of her emotions. Rich playwrights are different from you and me because they sometimes own the ground on which their characters live. That social and financial superiority—combined with many points of real similarity—allowed Augusta to use her characters to convey her own emotions. The fact that they were inferior to her and used a different idiom set her at a distance from them, made her feel less responsible for the emotions she expressed through them.

The expression of ideas through dialogue was particularly congenial to her. In playwriting, wrote Augusta, not quite accurately, "the talk is all." She had had long practice at "the talk." She had been conversing all her life with the Irish people, who were—as her fellow writer Violet Martin expressed it—"the very divil to talk and jackact." The talk in London society was equally vital. The little dinners at which conversation was "quick-firing, cut to the bone" taught her "the quick enrichment of sentences that one gets in conversation." They gave her "swiftness in putting thought into a word, a sentence."

Playwriting had the additional advantage that it, more than any other literary form, lends itself to collaboration. She wrote, "It is wonderful in playwriting especially how one mind seems to supplement another." She could approach playwriting cautiously, apparently unselfishly, writing dialogue for Willie and George Moore, even writing entire scenarios for Douglas Hyde to translate into Irish. She said of her collaboration with Willie: " 'He who loseth himself findeth himself' for I had no thought of any personal benefit to myself when I helped in his work."

What she lost was her self-consciousness; what she found was her creativity—a vitality freed from the necessity of being one of God's good children. Even while she was protected from the disapproving scrutiny of the cloud of witnesses, the conflicts she dealt with and the limitations that bound her did not change—they were, after all, the only real issues of her life—but they presented themselves in a more kindly and intimate form. She was better able to deal with them.

In writing her first play for the Irish actors, however, she made a mistake. In *A Losing Game* she depicted more love and freedom than she in her heart felt was permissible. As a result, though her small play has some exciting moments and touching situations, she was so thrown off balance by her attempt to slip a little love past the cloud of witnesses that the emotion and structure of the play do not mesh.

The play is as much a dialogue between Augusta and her cloud of witnesses as a dialogue between her characters. Augusta tried to protect herself immediately with her title, which was taken from a line from her sonnets about her affair with Wilfrid Blunt: "I staked my all upon a losing game." Perhaps, as in her affair, she could come in contact with love if it was eventually rejected. The play opens in a cottage where a young wife, Kate, having married an older man "to get a roof over my head," is accepting her fate. Christie, Kate's old sweetheart, returns from America and, finding her married, laments: "I thought we would have the one house between us, and you coaxing my child on your knee." Kate will have none of him. When asked if she likes her husband better than she likes him, she replies, "I must like him. Amn't I married to him?" But couldn't love do anything for her? Christie has brought £100 with him for their marriage, and she needs it. Though Kate has married for security, her husband is going to bankrupt and they are going to have to leave their cottage and go to Manchester, which "will be death to me to be there, and it will be death to Michael [her husband] too." Wouldn't it be permissible for love to give her security? And though Kate protests frantically, Christie sits down and loses his £100 to her husband at cards. Then Augusta gives Christie his freedom. When the neighbors comment, after he loses his money without seeming to care, "It must be a grand thing to be rich!" he replies, "It's grand, indeed. It's a grand thing to be free in the world, and not to be tied to your little bit of ground, in dread of the drought in the spring-time and rain in harvest. It's a grand thing not to be shut up in a narrow little house. . . ." He takes a dance with Kate and a kiss and is gone.

Christie is shining with passion and vitality; Augusta knew men could be like that. Kate is a poor, spineless, frightened girl; Augusta thought perhaps women should be like that. But the combination of what they achieve as a result of the action of the play is a fairly accurate picture of what Augusta herself had achieved: a secure position in the social structure and freedom to go out in the world—as well as her brief experience of passion in the losing game of her affair with Wilfrid.

As far as Augusta was concerned, she had gone too far. Having kept all her tricky bargaining with the cloud of witnesses just below the level of consciousness, in her own mind she had maintained the fiction that she was a completely dutiful person, interested in neither love nor freedom, but only in serving. She called the play "rather sentimental and weak in construction." Over the years she reworked the plot several times to eliminate the love.

The Fay brothers disapproved of the play also, on the equally unliterary grounds of the immorality of money being won at cards and the encouragement to emigration provided by the portrayal of a workingman returning from America after three years with £100. Augusta took the play home to Coole for the summer, reduced the amount Christie brings to £50, changed the name to *Twenty-Five* (the name of the card game), made a few other minor changes, and concentrated on finishing her book on the Finn cycle so she could repeat the splendid success of her book on Cuchulain.

On May 20, 1902, Robert Gregory came of age. Augusta had succeeded in paying off the mortgage. She had even bought a few acres across the lake—in Robert's name, not her own. She was feeling so rich she gave him a horse "to keep his spirits up." When he returned from Oxford to Coole in June, the tenants and townspeople greeted him with "bonefires," speeches, and presentations. They had asked Augusta to ask him to come on the evening train so the fires would make a better show. Augusta wrote Willie to be sure to be there, "for this should be picturesque."

Robert's coming of age made little difference in Augusta's management of estate or household. If he had any plans different from her own, he was not psychologically equipped to impose them on her. He had lived with her long enough to know that, though much of what she did was for him, she would not do anything she did not want to do. Augusta wrote about him to Wilfrid: "Robert is as good as gold."

As usual, Augusta filled the house with his friends and her friends. In August she and Willie, Edward Martyn, Douglas Hyde, and his wife went to the *feis* at Raftery's grave. There they met Jack Yeats and John Quinn, who had first heard of Jack Yeats from the notice Augusta had written about his pictures and who returned with them to Coole for a long visit.

John Quinn's biographer described him wonderfully as "a bachelor of thirty-two, of impressive aspect, whose bald crown saved him from being intolerably good looking. He was tall and commanding, an inch over six feet, a slender, strong, well-made figure, of erect bearing, carrying a finely molded head on a longish neck. His features were classically cut and proportioned, the face marked by lively blue eyes and a mobile, risible mouth." A successful lawyer, he was making his first visit to the home of his parents, who were Irish Catholic immigrants to Fostoria, Ohio, where he had been born and raised. Before he was old enough to vote, he had managed the campaign of a friend for the United States Senate. When his friend was appointed to the Cabinet by President Harrison, Quinn went to Washington as his secretary. He attended Georgetown University law school at night. He took a second degree at Harvard. At twenty-three he joined a prestigious New York law firm specializing in banking and insurance. At thirty-six he would establish his own firm. His biographer summarized his character: "At once an authentic original, very much himself, self-made, and the representative of a species, perhaps a peculiarly American species: the driving, pragmatical, 'successful' man of affairs who finds that not enough, yearns for 'culture,' but finds that not enough, yearns to make 'art' but has to content himself with a lesser order of usefulness, with knowing and having rather than making—the artist *manqué*." Quinn described the conflict in his character almost comically, writing Augusta, "Personally, I am a Morris socialist, although I have the misfortune to be a lawyer." Quinn, though shy of marriage, had a wide appreciation of many different kinds of women and a long string of conquests to indicate that he was appreciated in return.

He was delighted with Coole, describing the intellectual life, both cozy and unfettered, that Augusta had created: "There seemed to be magic in the air, enchantment in the woods and the beauty of the place, and the best talk and stories I ever found anywhere. . . . During the whole time of our visit the sparkle and brilliancy of the conversation never failed. Lady Gregory's interest in the people about her was untiring. . . . She had the faculty of laying aside her work and making all her guests enjoy to the full the pleasant side of life. . . . The mornings were devoted to work, the afternoons to out-of-doors, and the evenings to the reading of scenarios for plays, the reading of short plays. . . . I carried away two vivid impressions: first, the realization of a unique literary friendship between the chatelaine and the poet Yeats; and, second, of the gentleness and energy of this woman. . . ." Like George Moore, he envied Augusta and Willie their happy relationship.

During his visit, Augusta asked John Quinn to initial her autograph tree, but she had no idea of the energy and good will about to be unleashed in the service of Irish culture. Quinn gave the Fay brothers' acting company £50 to be administered by Lady Gregory and Yeats. He bought paintings from both John Butler Yeats and Jack Yeats. He set himself up as American agent for the Irish playwrights, and as each new play was published in Ireland, a copy was sent to him in America from which he had thirty to fifty copies printed to secure the American copyright. He suggested American lecture tours for Yeats and Hyde. Certainly, from Augusta's association with him came her belief that America was a place from which good things flowed. She later wrote that she felt she had been entertaining "an angel unawares" and told him she needed writing paper engraved, "Grateful thanks to John Quinn for——"

John Quinn was her type, and she knew it. After he left, she put her bookplate in the penny copy-book that contained her final handwritten draft of *Twenty-Five*. She filled in the blanks on the cover: "Name: Augusta P. Gregory. School: School of Loneliness." She added a typed draft of the play, wrapped them all in brown paper, tied them with string, sealed the crossings of the string with red wax, and sent them off to Quinn in New York.

In the fall Augusta received the now famous, very nervy letter from James Joyce—advised to apply to her by George Russell—in which he asked for help to leave Ireland and live in Paris:

I am going alone and friendless. . . . I shall try myself against the powers of the world. All things are inconsistent except the faith in the soul, which changes all things and fills their inconstancy with light and though I seem to have been driven out of my country here as a misbeliever I have found no man yet with a faith like mine.

Joyce, one year younger than Robert, was getting out of "the little narrow house." Augusta sent him £5 and got him a job with the Dublin

Daily Express reviewing books from Paris. Her help earned her his everlasting contempt and a long string of unflattering epithets in his work, such as "that old hake Gregory" and "the mother" with "them bagses of trash" (her folklore collections). Before he left Dublin, he went to a reception of hers to which she had not invited him. One of her guests wrote, "I can still see Joyce, with his air of half-timid effrontery, advancing toward his unwilling hostess and turning away from her to watch the company." From Paris he wrote a friend, who circulated the letter, that "W.B.Y. ought to hurry up and marry Lady Gregory—to kill talk."

His contempt for her folklore collections was not completely unmerited. In *Portrait of the Artist* his hero, Stephen Daedalus, describes an old Gaelic-speaking man in the west of Ireland with a short pipe and red eyes who, when he hears a discussion about the universe and stars, spits and says, "Ah, there must be terrible queer creatures at the latter end of the world," to which Stephen reacts, "I fear him. I fear his redrimmed horny eyes. It is with him I must struggle all through this night till day come, till he or I lie dead, gripping him by the sinewy throat"—which in many ways was an appropriate reaction to the ignorance and superstition exhibited in much of the folklore Augusta was so reverently collecting and retelling.

In October 1902 John Synge arrived at Coole on the way to his fifth and last visit to the Aran Isles, bringing with him the manuscripts of *Riders to the Sea* and *In the Shadow of the Glen*, both small masterpieces, and both in startling contrast to the one mediocre play he had written before his visits to Aran. Like Augusta, he had found in his experience of the more primitive Irish culture a world view that harmonized with his own, broadened it, and give it vitality. The fact that there were now Irish players looking for Irish plays was an additional impetus to playwriting.

In August the Fay brothers and their actors, now calling themselves the Irish National Theatre Society, had made a mistake fatal to their future independence but vital to their artistic development by electing Yeats president. They wanted the more gentle, democratic George Russell, who, already taking time from his disciples to be an agricultural organizer, could take no more time to be a theatrical producer. Russell was elected vice-president, along with Douglas Hyde as head of the language movement, and Maud Gonne as head of the Daughters of Erin. Though Augusta gave money, found props, and brought her famous barmbrack, a fruitcake heavily laced with rum, to rehearsal suppers, she was still officially on the outside, as was John

Synge. But within a few years the actors would find themselves taken over by Yeats and his playwriting friends.

Yeats immediately got Augusta's *Twenty-Five* into rehearsal. Augusta, beating the bushes for plays, had asked Wilfrid Blunt for one on an Irish subject. He responded with *Fand*, based on an episode in the Cuchulain cycle in which Cuchulain gets away with having a fairy lover and a fiercely possessive wife. (Wilfrid himself was now completely estranged from Lady Anne by his numerous infidelities.) Augusta sent Wilfrid's play off with Willie to the actors with instructions: "Don't let the Dublin youngsters be silly about Blunt's play. They can make a rule that any Englishmen that have been in prison for Ireland are eligible to write." The players accepted *Fand*, but did not get around to producing it for five years. And when it was produced, everyone was so busy that no one, not even Augusta, thought to tell Wilfrid—which miffed him.

When *Cathleen ni Houlihan* was produced for the second time in December 1902, at the Camden Street Hall at the back of a lane reached by maneuvering past the hanging carcasses and stacked egg crates of the adjoining grocer, Augusta was there. Mary Walker, the beautiful actress who played Cathleen, described her as "a short figure in rusty black with a long Victorian veil." She sat in the dark, protected by Yeats's name on the program, and saw Michael make his escape to a wider world. Though he faced death for it, nothing happened to her.

Her next play after *Twenty-Five* is about being a rebel for Ireland and getting away with it—though she did not know how it would turn out when she began writing it. The scene is a moonlit quay where policemen are putting up wanted posters offering a £100 reward for an Irish rebel escaped from jail. (In her childhood Augusta had been thrilled by the story of Hamilton Rowan's escape in a boat, and the boatman saying, "We know you very well, Mr. Rowan, and the reward that's on your head and there is no fear that we will betray you.") Though Augusta never mentions the jailbreak by James Stephens (the founder of the Fenians) that occurred when she was fourteen—and about which "All witnesses reported that in surprise, excitement, and popular identification with the object of a hue and cry . . . [it] was one of the high emotional peaks of Irish history"—it is most likely she did hear of it and that—not knowing whether she should be elated—it was one of the events that turned her away from her love of rebel Ireland and toward her religious conversion.

In *The Rising of the Moon* she plays the escape over again and lets the rebel go. A police sergeant stands guarding the steps to the water. A ragged ballad singer tries to slip past and the sergeant stops him. The ballad singer tries to frighten the sergeant, saying that he knows the wanted man, that he has killed several people. He says he is willing to stay and help keep watch. They sit together on a barrel, looking in different directions. The singer begins a song about "Granuaile" (another incarnation of Ireland in her troubles) and misses a line, which the sergeant supplies. The ballad singer says:

> Now, I daresay, sergeant, in your youth, you used to be sitting up on a wall, the way you are sitting up on this barrel now, and the other lads beside you, and you singing "Granuaile"? . . . Maybe it's one of the boys you used to be singing with that time you will be arresting to-day or to-morrow, and sending into the dock. . . .

He makes the sergeant change places with the rebel in his mind:

> Man: It's a queer world, sergeant, and it's little any mother knows when she sees her child creeping on the floor what might happen to it before it has gone through its life, or who will be who in the end.

> Sergeant: That's a queer thought now, and a true thought. Wait now till I think it out. . . . If it wasn't for the sense I have, and for my wife and family, and for me joining the force the time I did, it might be myself now would be after breaking gaol and hiding in the dark, and it might be him that's hiding in the dark and that got out of gaol would be sitting up here where I am on this barrel. . . . And it might be myself would be creeping up trying to make my escape from himself, and it might be himself would be keeping the law, and myself would be breaking it, and myself would be trying to put a bullet in his head, or to take up a lump of stone the way you said he did . . . no, that myself did . . . Oh! What's that?

The sergeant hears a boat arriving to pick up the rebel, who sings as a signal "The Rising of the Moon" (from the rebel songbook Augusta Persse treasured as a child):

> O, then, tell me, Shawn O'Farrell,
>   Where the gathering is to be.
> In the old spot by the river
>   Right well known to you and me!

The sergeant recognizes him:

> Sergeant: You are the man I am looking for.
> Man (*Takes off hat and wig. Sergeant seizes them*): I am. There's a hundred pounds on my head. There is a friend of mine below in a boat.

The two sides of Augusta's nature, the policeman and the rebel, face each other. The sergeant says to the rebel, "I am in the force. I will not let you pass." As they confront each other, two other policemen approach. The sergeant instinctively hides the rebel's hat and wig behind his back. The rebel hides behind the barrel. The policemen want to stay and watch the sergeant. He sends them off. They want to leave their lantern. He does not want it.

> Policeman: Well, I thought it might be a comfort to you. I often think when I have it in my hand and can be flashing it about into every dark corner (*doing so*) that it's the same as being beside the fire at home, and the bits of bogwood blazing up now and again.
> Sergeant (*furious*): Be off the two of you, yourselves and your lantern! (*They go out. Man comes from behind barrel. He and Sergeant stand looking at one another.*)
> Sergeant: What are you waiting for?
> Man: For my hat, of course, and my wig. You wouldn't wish me to get my death of cold?
> (*Sergeant gives them.*)
> Man (*going toward steps*): Well, good-night, comrade, and thank you. You did me a good turn to-night, and I'm obliged to you. Maybe I'll be able to do as much for you when the small rise up and the big fall down . . . when we all change places at the Rising (*waves his hand and disappears*) of the Moon.

The two sides of Augusta's nature have made peace, recognizing their essential unity, and their essential lack of responsibility in the face of chance and circumstance. Augusta's excitement at finding a formula that makes rebellion acceptable underlies every speech of the play. The fact that it "made more rebels in Ireland than a thousand political speeches or a hundred reasoned books" does not, however, speak well for the political realism or the self-respect of those so influenced, since the sum total of what the play shows about being a rebel is that it is exciting, acceptable, and more or less a matter of chance.

161

Toward the end of February 1903, just as Augusta was preparing to read John Synge's *Riders to the Sea* to a group of London literary people at her flat, she received word from Coole that the "Big Wind," a hurricane that had devastating effects all over the British Isles, had also done severe damage at Coole. She went on with her reading, the weird mournfulness of Synge's play masking her own agitation.

The Big Wind of February 1903 became the symbol for a severe shock in Willie's life which, because he was so close to her, had reverberations in Augusta's own. On February 21 Maud Gonne married Major John MacBride, the hero of the Irish Brigade in the Transvaal, a committed Irish rebel, a Catholic, and a limited and narrow-minded man. She later told Willie she had married him "in a sudden impulse of anger" because Lucien Millevoye, her former lover, had brought his new mistress to see their daughter and she felt she had to show she no longer cared for him. (Willie wondered forlornly why she could not have produced the same effect by marrying *him*.) Augusta, almost always proper, was one of the first to congratulate Maud on her marriage.

Willie, receiving Maud's telegram just as he was about to give a lecture in Dublin, delivered his talk with a roaring in his ears and total obliviousness to his surroundings. For some hours afterward he wandered about Dublin and, as soon as possible, went to Coole to recover. Seeing the devastation there, he wrote of his shock in terms of the storm that "blew down so many trees, and troubled the wild creatures, and changed the look of things." (Other observers reported that the storm marked a change in feeling all over Ireland: "Something has happened in the elemental world . . . the faery-folk are no longer there. . . . It is strange what a difference it makes. The heather is still rose-coloured, the sphagnum moss marvellously green, the reeds are silver, but the magic is gone!")

Augusta, staying assiduously away from the first performance of her first acknowledged play, remained in London, neglecting Willie and Coole, until after *Twenty-Five* had been performed in Dublin on March 14, 1903—the day before her fifty-first birthday. It was accompanied by Yeats's *The Hour-Glass*. Robert Gregory, wanting a share of the action, had done sketches for the scenery of Yeats's play. (The year before, he and his friends had written and performed a play at Coole—prophetically called "The Risen Wind"—and as Augusta was anxious to promote anything that was promotable, this was evidently not good enough, or not Irish enough.)

When Augusta got back to Coole in April, she found "the place sadly changed . . . ten lime trees down between house and stables, and the big lime to the left (greatest loss of all) and the big evergreen oak on front lawn, and some parts of the woods laid flat. Many thousands of spruce and larch down." Augusta ordered and planted 2,500 seedlings. The huge ilex on the front lawn could never be replaced, and without it shading the cricket pitch, the Gort team suffered its first losses ever. Augusta set up a sawmill to make use of the fallen timber.

She and Robert spent Easter alone together at Coole. Robert told his mother he wanted to be an artist, and though she would have preferred a career leading to a more formalized success (she'd hoped he would take an offered clerkship in the House of Commons), she accepted his decision. She had written Wilfrid, "If he were a rich man, I should be afraid of his being a dilettante, but as he will only have bread without butter if he doesn't work, I hope he will turn his hand to something." After his decision, still hoping for a formula, she again turned to Wilfrid, whose son-in-law, Neville Lytton, was an artist (and a dilettante), asking "would he give me some information as to an artist's best way of beginning life. . . . Robert will have a break between exams and thinks of going over to Paris to look about him, but I am anxious for some more definite information." Robert did go over to Paris to look about him, but decided on the Slade School of Art in London.

The end of the landlord class in Ireland came yet nearer in that year of 1903 with the passage of the Land Purchase Act. George Wyndham, the Irish Secretary (and Wilfrid Blunt's second cousin), had in 1902 presented a land-purchase bill that was rejected. Several landlords and churchmen proposed a conference with tenant representatives to work out a new bill, but nothing happened until John Shawe-Taylor, Augusta's nephew, wrote to several specific landlords and tenant representatives inviting them to a conference—the action later earning him a place, along with another of Augusta's nephews, in Yeats's "Coole Park, 1929" as "Impetuous men, Shawe-Taylor and Hugh Lane." The act resulting from his conference provided favorable terms for tenants to buy and inducements to landlords to sell. The difference between asking and offering price would be borne by the British government; the tenants could pay over a period of sixty-two and one half years; the British government would also buy up the tenants' installment debt from the landlord, thus allowing them to have all their money immediately. The huge cost of this measure was considered an acceptable price to pay for what it was hoped would be an alternative to Home Rule. Eventually, all of Coole would be sold under the terms of this act and its successors.

In May of 1903 Augusta stayed home at Coole while the Irish players performed in London. The young actors took time off from their
jobs, traveled all Friday night, arrived in London Saturday morning,
and played in the afternoon and evening at Queen's Gate Hall. They
performed Yeats's *Hour-Glass*, Augusta's *Twenty-Five*, Augusta and
Yeats's *Cathleen ni Houlihan* and *Pot of Broth*, and *The Laying of the
Foundations* by Fred Ryan of the acting company. Henry James and
James M. Barrie were in the Saturday-night audience. Wilfrid Blunt,
just recovering from influenza, sat through Yeats's *Hour-Glass*—"a
terrible infliction"—to see Augusta's *Twenty-Five*, which he called
"the most perfect work of art and the most touching play I have ever
seen acted." The players returned to Dublin delighted and surprised
to find they were the cultural and dramatic phenomenon Yeats had
been telling them they were, bringing back, as he said, poetry and
beauty to the English stage.

John Quinn in New York had prompted a reporter to write asking
Augusta for a picture of herself to accompany a story. She sent Quinn
the picture for him to keep and the reporter to use: "I rather grudge
giving the photograph, which is really charming in itself, and rather
expensive, to a newspaper, and it has struck me perhaps you would
like to have it to add to your Irish collection. I don't think there is
any sin in sending a picture done when one was younger, as the date
is marked. Imagination can add the ten years." Quinn wrote thanking
her for "your beautiful picture, which I prize more than I can tell
you. . . . It reminds me of how my mother looked when I was a boy,
and hers was a beautiful face. . . . I shall always keep it, and when it
is reproduced, I will see to it that the date shan't be marked because
I don't think it flatters you today." Quinn's sister had died six months
earlier, and mourning clothes made him so depressed and angry that
he would get off a subway if a woman in mourning entered. Augusta's
mourning, apparently, did not have that effect on him.

Augusta sent him a presentation copy of *Poets and Dreamers*, her
collection of Irish folklore, which was published that year. She wanted
to dedicate to him the second volume of the Irish epics, *Gods and
Fighting Men*, which would come out the following year. Quinn,
knowing the shifting passions of the Irish-American community with
which he was then in favor (and preferring to keep feminine admiration of him more private), asked her to dedicate it instead to the Irish
Literary Society of New York, which he had just founded.

During the summer of 1903 at Coole, Augusta helped Willie rewrite *The Stories of Red Hanrahan*, published the following year by
his sisters at the Dun Emir Press, which they founded. When Yeats

sent Quinn a copy, he inscribed it, "Lady Gregory has helped me and I think the stories have the emotion of folklore. They are but half mine now, and often her beautiful idiom is the better half." Augusta added to the inscription, "I was very glad and proud to help in the re-writing of these stories, and for any trouble I had I repaid myself by bringing Hanrahan back to Galway from Sligo where W. Yeats had first set him wandering." Augusta had at first written cheerfully of her help to Yeats, "My own [work] is just straw with which to bake your bricks," but later, getting tired of the donkey work, she made a slight, veiled complaint: "I think I must have been a very useful secretary to you when you were going for your first American tour. I remember . . . re-writing *Hanrahan* with one hand and typing your letters with the other. But I have to gather my own straw."

That summer Augusta also wrote the scenario of *The Poorhouse* for Douglas Hyde to write in Irish, as the previous year she had written the scenario of *The Marriage*. Both were so complete that Hyde had only to translate them. (She then translated them back into English.) She was, at the same time, working with Willie on a "little miracle play" that eventually, in 1909, became *The Travelling Man*. She helped Willie with his interminable tinkering with *The Shadowy Waters* (about his love for Maud Gonne). She wrote the dialogue between the fool and the blind man in his *On Baile's Strand*. She went over dialogue for his *The King's Threshold*.

The production of *The King's Threshold* in October 1903 brought a new participant into the development of the Irish theater. Miss Annie E. F. Horniman, who paid for the staging and designed the costumes, had been in the wings for a long time. She had paid for the staging of Shaw's *Arms and the Man* with Yeats's *The Land of Heart's Desire* as curtain raiser in 1894. In April 1902, after the success of *Cathleen ni Houlihan*, she told Yeats she might do something for the Irish players.

When Augusta was not in London, Miss Horniman sometimes served as Yeats's secretary. He had been her sponsor for the Order of the Golden Dawn, the mystic group to which he had also introduced Maud Gonne. In her letters she called him "Dear Demon," and of her part in *The King's Threshold* she wrote, "Do you realize that you have given me the right to call myself 'artist'? How I do thank you!" Her satisfaction, however, was brief. Combining diplomacy with intransigence in his treatment of her, Yeats reduced her nearly to tears on the stage of the theater by criticizing her costumes. (They were stiff, ornate brocade. Lennox Robinson later called them "incredibly graceless and ugly.")

Miss Horniman, then in her early forties, was herself neither graceless nor ugly, but often appeared so. She was from a wealthy Manchester manufacturing family from whom she was estranged by her devotion to drama and the cause of women's suffrage. She suffered, even more than Augusta, from being carried by her artistic aspirations into situations in which she was not at ease. G. B. Shaw described her ordinary tone of conversation as that of "a woman pursuing a quarrel with a person she violently dislikes."

More important than the involvement of Miss Horniman, however, was the Irish National Theatre Society's introduction, in October 1903, of the one great dramatist of the early Irish Renaissance. John Synge's *In the Shadow of the Glen* was produced to mixed reactions and mixed reviews. In it a young Irishwoman, married to an older man, and about to go off with a younger man, leaves both behind to go out on the roads with a tramp: "You've got a fine bit of talk, stranger, and it's with yourself I'll go." In a way the play is simply another version of Michael rushing out of his little, narrow life to follow Cathleen to an uncertain future. It also fits exactly Yeats's description of all Irish plays as "a cry for a more abundant and a more intense life." (Maud Gonne MacBride walked out of the play and later resigned from the theater society because she could not tolerate a play showing an Irishwoman doing something so immoral.)

In November 1903 Yeats left for a lecture tour in America arranged by John Quinn. Augusta typed his lectures and helped choose his wardrobe. Quinn, as good at nurturing and hectoring as Augusta, looked after him in America, writing him at one point: "The first thing you want to do Monday morning after reading this letter—the very first thing—is to call the porter and have your laundry attended to. . . . If you should happen to run short of money telegraph me from any point where you may be a day and I will send you more money *by telegraph*."

Back at Coole, with someone else worrying about Willie, Augusta "began with the daring and light-heartedness of a schoolboy to write a tragedy in three acts upon a great personality, Brian the High King. . . . I made many bad beginnings, and if I had listened to Mr. Yeats's advice I should have given up." At Christmas she wrote Willie in America, "I am giving myself a little Xmas present by writing to you instead of to people I ought to be writing to," and reported, "I am at work on Brian Boru; I can see your face when you think of it, profound distrust and some alarm."

Augusta wrote at "her great ormolu table" in the library at Coole. She wrote in penny copybooks and on the backs of business correspondence. She drew sketches in colored pencil to show the position of characters on stage or used little paper figures to plan their entrances and exits. (One of her letters to John Synge contains, perhaps by accident, two paper dolls.) The act of writing itself became delightful to her—a new way of relating to herself.

She wrote of her first attempt at a three-act historical drama: "Desire for experiment is like fire in the blood." Experiment implies freedom—the absence of compulsion to get one result or another. And though Augusta had quickly come to the end of her freedom in dealing with her few limited themes, she found another way to escape the sense of compulsion by creating new forms: "One has to go on with experiment or interest in creation fades, at least so it is with me."

Kincora, named for Brian's palace, is about the conflict between service, embodied in Brian Boru, the first great king to unite Ireland and drive out the Danes, and freedom, as represented by his wife, Queen Gormleith, who loves conflict and disorder. They both have dignity, vitality, and power, and neither changes in the course of the play.

Brian serves Ireland, first by fighting and then, when he has conquered all his enemies, by serving the church and men of learning. Brian's greatest hindrance to bringing peace is Gormleith, who came to him when he was winning battles but who becomes dissatisfied as soon as he stops fighting. She is eventually unable to tolerate the dullness and security: "Let them make much of the linnet in the cage; the hawk will leave them for the free air!"

As Gormleith is leaving Brian to join with the invading Danes, she insists that her betrayal of him is not her own fault: "You were asleep; I tried to waken you. . . . You have chosen it; not I, not I." Brian accepts the entire responsibility, saying, "It is myself have betrayed my people. The blame is on me." As in *The Rising of the Moon*, Augusta shows that the rebel is not responsible for her rebellion. Only the super-ego could have final responsibility. Augusta got her own feeling of freedom from presenting the two characters and from the fun of writing a three-act play.

John Synge's second small masterpiece, *Riders to the Sea*, was produced by the Fay brothers in Dublin in February 1904. It was the only one of his plays produced during his life to give no offense to anyone.

In March, Willie came home from America with £646 in his pocket—"the first money I ever earned beyond the need of the moment." His father wanted to borrow £20. His sisters wanted money for their Dun Emir Press. Willie wanted to repay Augusta for her many small loans, but was staggered to find that they had added up to £500. She refused repayment: "Not until I think you have enough money to feel independent."

The players went to London again in March. In April, Miss Horniman wrote Yeats, with copies to other members of the acting society, informing them of her intention to buy and renovate a Dublin hall for the free use of the players because of her "great sympathy with the artistic and dramatic aims of the Irish National Theatre as publicly explained by you on various occasions." (She made the money in the stock market on the rise of her shares in the Hudson's Bay Company; her astrologer approved the gift.)

Augusta resented and minimized Miss Horniman's involvement. Years later, when Lennox Robinson sent her his notes for a history of the early Abbey, Augusta used them to light the fire, writing angrily in her diary, "Quite untrue about the founding of the theatre, Miss Horniman made the *building*, not the theatre." However, the delightful and ironic aspect of Augusta's reaction to Miss Horniman's magnificent gift was that she was reassured by any kind of structure, no matter where it came from. The fact that the players now had a home (and would have a subsidy) made Augusta feel that they were more appropriate recipients of her service. Because Miss Horniman was not a legal resident of Ireland, Augusta, the most socially prominent and financially secure Irish member of the theater group, would hold the patent, or license, for the theater.

The Rising of the Moon was accepted by the players, but production was delayed—delayed eventually four years—because some of the ultra-nationalistic actors objected to the sympathetic portrayal of an Irish policeman. But they also accepted *Kincora*, and this they put into rehearsal immediately. Augusta began to suffer from the delightful feeling of being exposed.

She felt like hiding—and running and shouting at the same time. In *Spreading the News* she does both. In a play that takes less than twenty-five minutes to perform, she took all her fears, all the dearest wishes of her heart, and set them chasing each other around in a circle until they are all meaningless and the only appropriate reaction is delighted laughter. Love and liberty are the motives for a non-existent crime at the center of the whirlwind; punishment is swift, sure, and completely mistaken.

Bartley Fallon, her hero, is a poor, spiritless countryman who characterizes himself, "If there's ever any misfortune coming to this world, it's on myself it pitches, like a flock of crows on seed potatoes." In an elegant, intricate series of speeches and stage business, Jack Smith, a local farmer, forgets his hayfork, and Bartley picks it up to return, upsets his wife's basket, and convinces everyone left behind that he is pursuing Jack Smith in a rage.

> Tim Casey: Following Jack Smith with a hayfork! Did ever any-one hear the like of that. (*Shouts*) Did you hear the news, Mrs. Tarpey?
>
> Mrs. Tarpey: I heard no news at all.
>
> Tim Casey: Some dispute I suppose it was that rose between Jack Smith and Bartley Fallon, and it seems Jack made off, and Bartley is following with a hayfork!

They both go off to spread the news. Next Mrs. Tarpey hears that Jack Smith's wife is drying her washing on the hedge and announces Jack Smith's murder: "Laying out a sheet for the dead! Lord have mercy on us. Jack Smith dead, and his wife laying out a sheet for his burying!"

> Mrs. Tully: What was it rose the dispute at all, Mrs. Tarpey?
>
> Mrs. Tarpey: Not a one of me knows. The last I saw of them, Jack Smith was standing there, and Bartley Fallon was standing there, quiet and easy—and he listening to "The Red-Haired Man's Wife."
>
> Mrs. Tully: Do you hear that, Tim Casey? Do you hear that, Shawn Early and James Ryan? Bartley Fallon was here this morning listening to red Jack Smith's wife, Kitty Keary that was! Listening to her and whispering with her! It was she started the fight so!

Bartley's wife returns and defends her man. She goes out. (Frank Fay wrote about a successful performance, "We got a tremendous pace into it, the pace of a hard football match"—this in a play by a woman whose most vigorous exercise was walking fast.) Bartley comes back with the fork and is greeted with the news that Jack Smith is dead.

> Mrs. Tarpey (*rocking to and fro*): I wonder now who will take the expense of the wake for poor Jack Smith?
>
> Bartley: The wake for Jack Smith!
>
> Tim Casey: Why wouldn't he get a wake as well as another? Would you begrudge him that much?
>
> Bartley: Red Jack Smith dead? Who was telling you?
>
> Shawn Early: The whole town knows of it by this.
>
> Bartley: Do they say what way did he die?
>
> James Ryan: You don't know that yourself, I suppose, Bartley

Fallon? You don't know that he was followed and that he was laid dead with the stab of a hayfork?

Bartley: The stab of a hayfork!

Shawn Early: You don't know, I suppose, that the body was found in the Five Acre Meadow?

Bartley: The Five Acre Meadow!

Tim Casey: It is likely you don't know that the police are after the man that did it?

Bartley: The man that did it!

Mrs. Tully: You don't know, maybe, that he was made away with for the sake of Kitty Keary, his wife?

Bartley: Kitty Keary, his wife. (*Sits down bewildered.*)

Mrs. Tully: And what have you to say now, Bartley Fallon?

Bartley (*crossing himself*): I to bring that fork here, and to find that news before me! It is much if I can ever stir from this place at all, or reach as far as the road!

A magistrate and a policeman enter; the villagers scatter.

Magistrate (*sternly*): Tell me this truly. What was the motive of the crime?

Bartley: The motive, is it?

Magistrate: Yes; the motive; the cause.

Bartley: I'd sooner not say that.

Magistrate: You had better tell me truly. Was it money?

Bartley: Not at all! What did poor Jack Smith ever have in his pockets unless it might be his hands that would be in them?

Magistrate: Any dispute about land?

Bartley (*indignantly*): Not at all! He never was a grabber or grabbed from anyone!

Magistrate: You will find it better for you if you will tell me at once.

Bartley: I tell you I wouldn't for the whole world wish to say what it was—it is a thing I would not like to be talking about.

Magistrate: There is no use in hiding it. It will be discovered in the end.

Bartley: Well, I suppose it will, seeing that almost everybody knows it before. Whisper now. I will tell no lie; where would be the use? (*Puts his hand to his mouth, and Magistrate stoops.*) Don't be putting the blame on the parish, for such a thing was never done in the parish before—it was done for the sake of Kitty Keary, Jack Smith's wife.

Magistrate (*to policeman*): Put on the handcuffs. We have been saved some trouble. I knew he would confess if taken in the right way. (*Policeman puts on handcuffs.*)

Bartley: Handcuffs now! Glory be! I always said, if there was ever any misfortune coming to this place it was on myself it would fall. I to be in handcuffs! There's no wonder at all in that.

Jack Smith enters, completely alive and singing. When he hears he has been killed and Bartley Fallon was going to elope with his wife, he threatens to "break the head of any man that says that." They all tell him Bartley said it.

Jack Smith: Let me at him! Isn't he the pleasant sort of scarecrow for any woman to be crossing the ocean with! It's back from the docks of New York he'd be turned (*trying to rush at him again*), with a lie in his mouth and treachery in his heart, and another man's wife by his side, and he passing her off as his own! Let me at him, can't you.

The magistrate solves the problem by throwing them both in jail: "I see it all now. A case of false impersonation, a conspiracy to defeat the ends of justice." As they are led off, justice has indeed been defeated. Watching the play, the cloud of witnesses has gone cross-eyed. Augusta felt freer and safer than she had ever felt before.

Playwriting brought round to her, in a slightly different form, all she had missed in her life. She even felt for her characters the cherishing, forgiving, delighted love she never felt for her son—an admirer describing her attitude toward them as "the last secret of maternity."

Playwriting gave her great success with "the talk" with which she enjoyed only middling success in her life. Because she did not give and receive feelings directly, she overvalued the importance of words in her relationships with people. As Mary Colum, an astute young theater-watcher described her, "She did not care enough about people to have a native friendliness to them and so was by nature tactless. But with discipline and cultivation she had acquired a perfectly fearsome artificial tact." Tact, of course, is diplomatic talk without the feeling. Augusta used it as protection in an uncomfortable world; it did not serve her perfectly. But the transfer of her belief in and long practice of "the talk" to playwriting, where it fused with feeling and became extremely effective, was a continual excitement and delight. While in her life she was hacking away with a dull knife at influencing people, the dialogue in her drama became elegant swordplay.

Her playwriting brought round to her also the resolution of her lack of ease with people. Though she could not deal with people individually, she understood the group. And while she had been baffled and thwarted by her audience in the sky all her life, playwriting let her sit in the midst of an audience who loved her.

Once she was absolutely sure it was safe (which took a while), Augusta loved to attend her plays. She sat in the dark, bathed in the warm and vital exchange between actors and audience: "There is no excitement like it, the words going direct to the audience, and the applause coming back!" Mary Colum—like most people who thought they did not like her—also loved to attend her plays: "Some rich emotions not visible on the surface of her relations with people went into her plays . . . and went right to the hearts of her audience in the theatre."

Augusta's creativity brought her love, liberty, and success. But, unlike the creativity of more complete artists, it did not continually lead her on to new questions. Many admirers, among them Sean O'Casey, have fumed at the miscellaneous activities that took her from playwriting, "doing too many things, linking herself up with too many people to allow perfection in the work that she could do so splendidly herself." But she was wiser than they. She never asked more of her creativity than it could give her. Her many activities, her beautiful home, her beloved son, Yeats, the theater were, for her, as necessary as playwriting. Yeats wrote, "The intellect of man is forced to choose / Perfection of the life, or of the work." The subconscious balancing of woman obviated the choice. Her plays were the crowning luxury of her life, the final explosion and release of her great housekeeping energy that put a fire in the fireplace and lit up all the windows.

VII

Prolific at the Abbey

THEATER MANAGER AND
PLAYWRIGHT: 1904–1908

I grant sometime that of glory the fire
Doth touch my heart.
SIR THOMAS WYATT, "To John Poynz"

YEATS described a rehearsal:

The kid Benson [an actor] is to carry in his arms was wandering in and out among the artificial ivy. I was saying to myself "Here we are a lot of intelligent people, who might have been doing some sort of work that leads to some fun. Yet here we are going through all sorts of trouble and annoyance for a mob that knows neither literature nor art. I might have been away in the country, in Italy, perhaps writing poems for my equals and my betters. That kid is the only sensible creature on the stage. He knows his business and keeps to it." At that very moment one of the actors called out "Look at the goat eating the property ivy."

They were all stage-struck, Augusta, Willie, Synge, the Fay brothers, the actors who worked long hours in dingy halls after their day's work for bread. Like the enterprising goat, they found nourishment in illusion. What they created was not illusory.

While other people were seeing visions, learning Gaelic, and plotting the downfall of England, the playwrights and actors were doing what Ireland most needed, creating a structure that would use the energies and develop the talents of some of their fellow citizens while entertaining others. They were creating—in the midst of "the little narrow house"—a wider world, providing another outlet for the hunger for excitement and achievement that had previously been satisfied primarily through emigration or rebellion. And a study of their survival—their use of compromise, flexibility, and good sense in the service of an ideal—would have been far more useful to those working for Irish freedom than the study of ancient myths. Padraic Pearse, who was shot by the English for his part in the Easter Rebellion of 1916, had carved in the hall of his school the epic hero Cuchulain's boast on the day he took arms: "Though I live but a year and a day, I will live so that my name goes sounding down the ages." The Abbey Theatre lives yet, had over twenty-five years of glory, left a great name, and made a lasting contribution to world literature.

The participants in the theater project all believed that "a Spirit from beyond the world" was breathing on them. Yeats in 1904: "It may be coming upon us now, for it is certain that we have more writers who are thinking, as men of letters understand thought, than we have had for a century, and he who wilfully makes their work harder may be setting himself against the purpose of that Spirit." Looking back to the past greatness of Ireland, and forward to future freedom, they felt a light shining on their particular moment. Their creative thought and excitement changed the atmosphere, so that scholars and tourists are still thick on the ground, trying to get a whiff of the ozone still in the air from the electrical discharges, the squibs, crackers, backarappers, sparklers, torches, dwarf candles, elf fountains, goblin barkers, and thunderclaps that lit up the Dublin sky seventy and eighty years ago.

Actress Sara Allgood described the excitement of the time: "It seemed to me as though a new province was being added to Ireland." Wordsworth had described the feeling in connection with another revolution: "Bliss it was in that dawn to be alive. / But to be young was very heaven!" Augusta was fifty-two, and happier than she had ever been.

She also had more than one world in which to live, and during the summer of 1904 she remained at Coole. During July her guests were Willie, AE, and Synge. Willie wrote, of the other two, "Though they have come to their task from the opposite sides of the heavens they are both stirring the same pot—something of a witches' cauldron, I think."

174

In Dublin, Miss Horniman bought and remodeled into a vestibule and auditorium seating five hundred the old Mechanics Institute and an adjoining building that had once been the city morgue. The buildings were in Lower Abbey Street, a block off O'Connell Street (then Sackville Street) on the unfashionable north side of the River Liffey. Miss Horniman commissioned stained glass from Sarah Purser and pictures of the actors and actresses from John Butler Yeats.

Yeats, going briefly to Dublin for the hearing on the theater license, reported on its favorable outcome, with praise for Miss Horniman, who "gave her evidence first and was entirely admirable. She was complimented by the Solicitor General and is proud as punch. Excitement always seems to give her the simplicity which she sometimes lacks."

In September, John Quinn came to town on his third pilgrimage. Finally, Augusta left Coole. Early in the morning, she was driven to the station in Gort, took the local train nine miles to Athenry, changed trains, rode 120 miles and three hours across Ireland, and arrived in Dublin ready to take part in the action. It was a journey that was to become part of the rhythm of her life, tying together the private excitement of Coole and the public excitement of theater management in Dublin.

In his account of this visit John Quinn wrote, "Lady G. Came in very fresh and fine" with news that she had finished a three-act tragedy (*Kincora*) and a one-act comedy (*Spreading the News*). She gave a reception for him as a contributor to the theater, with chicken salad, grapes, peaches, cake, and even flowers, all brought on the train from Coole. The beautiful Mary Walker recited verse. Another actress sang. The party lasted until one.

The next evening Quinn dined with Augusta and Yeats and then attended a rehearsal of *The Pot of Broth* and *Kincora*. Researsals were still at the ramshackle Camden Street Hall, which now had a stove and a teapot. Joseph Holloway, attending in his semi-official capacity as architect of the new theater, wrote about Yeats that "a more irritating play producer never directed a rehearsal. He's ever flitting about and interrupting the players in the middle of their speeches, showing them by illustration how he wishes it done, droningly reading this passage and that in monotonous preachy singsong, or climbing the ladder on to the stage and pacing the boards as he would have the players do." And Augusta, wrote Holloway, "was the very opposite to W.B.Y. in sitting quietly and giving directions in quiet, almost apologetic tones." After rehearsal, according to Quinn, the whole crowd "marched along together" to Lady Gregory's hotel, where they continued their discussion until one in the morning. When Quinn went on to London, Augusta went back to Coole.

A week before the opening of the Abbey, Miss Horniman gave a tea party at the theater for her friends and proudly showed them over the building. Augusta was sick at Coole. On December 27, 1904, the Abbey opened with performances of Yeats's *On Baile's Strand,* Augusta's *Spreading the News,* and their *Cathleen ni Houlihan.* Augusta was so sick that she felt she learned "how easy death may be when it comes for I felt I could not stay in this suffering ailing body," but she recovered in time to see the plays later in the week, and wrote Wilfrid Blunt that "the audience would laugh so much at 'Spreading the News' that they lost about half the dialogue. I mustn't be so amusing again!"

On opening night the spotlight belonged to Yeats and to Miss Horniman, who behaved as if it were natural for her. A gossip writer described her appearance at a performance: "tall and dark . . . an interesting and artistic figure in a rich robe of crimson clasped with a buckle, on which was enamelled a cluster of peacock's feathers." (She was also famous for wearing around her neck an opal-studded dragon five inches in diameter.) But though Mary Walker described Augusta as "a pleasant if at times rather condescending person" and Miss Horniman as "an extremely likeable person," Miss Horniman was the outsider. Her association with the Irish theater was, from the first, a process of being made use of and squeezed out. When she realized how deeply both players and playwrights were committed to Ireland, she wrote Willie in dismay that she wanted nothing to do with "hole and corner Irish ideas."

Her outrage over Irish nationalism was, however, muddled by her general outrage over a number of subjects. Shortly after the Abbey opening she wrote Willie about an article by George Moore, whom she particularly disliked, in which he seemed to be speaking for the Abbey management. "I shall look upon it as a public insult offered to me by the whole Society severally and collectively unless those writings are publicly repudiated." Augusta later commented on Miss Horniman's unreasonable and illogical demands, saying that she was "not quite in her right mind." Augusta also described her to Willie as "a shilling in a tub of electrified water." She habitually referred to her as "Saxon shilling." (Willie Fay referred to her as "Tabby"— which she encouraged by purring when she was pleased, extending her fingers like claws and growling when she was angry.) Yet the Abbey needed her shillings; she was pacified, she was invited to Coole, where she was, as Augusta wrote, "a rather trying guest." The

The castellated entrance to Roxborough, the Persse family estate

Augusta Gregory, as she appeared
at the time of her wedding

(ABOVE) Sir William Gregory caricatured in *Vanity Fair* and as he actually appeared

The dashing Wilfred Scawen Blunt

Robert Gregory, at the age of twenty-one

William Butler Yeats, the
young poet, at the time
he met Lady Gregory

Sean O'Casey

A drawing of John M. Synge
done by John Butler Yeats

Lady Gregory, on the frontispiece for *Our Irish Theatre*

Robert Gregory in RFC uniform

The library at Coole

Coole Park, photographed by George Bernard Shaw

Lady Gregory at the height
of her career

John Quinn at the age of fifty-one

Augusta sitting under the Catalpa tree at Coole

Abbey cleaning woman described Augusta's receptions at which Miss Horniman "would smoke a cigar and enjoy a glass of claret-cup made by Lady Gregory's own hands."

Augusta herself was not completely comfortable in her new milieu. She did not know how to behave with people she did not need. Wrote Mary Colum, "Lady Gregory behaved as if she were a grand duchess, and as if the people of Dublin were somehow her subjects." She did not know how to act toward people whom she needed but who were not her servants, the Abbey handyman commenting, "Lady Gregory never forgot to show appreciation of any effort, even when it was not successful. In fact, she was, at times, so lavish in praise that one was inclined to suspect her sincerity."

Augusta found that in serving Ireland through literature she offended both those against Ireland's freedom and those who were for it but who saw literature only as propaganda. She was convinced her cause was right, and, though as a battle tactic she would declare herself "a lover of peace," she loved a fight. She loved the commotion, the telegrams and conferences, the crises with which she was to be so generously supplied for the rest of her life.

Some of the alarms had nothing to do with the Abbey and were in consequence much less enjoyable. Two months after the opening, Maud Gonne MacBride gave a cry from Paris asking Willie for his help. Her husband, drinking heavily for some time, had committed the unpardonable offense—assaulting her half-sister. Yeats hurried to Paris and then, back in London, wrote Augusta, "I feel as if I had been through a circle of Hell, with no peaceful Virgil by my side." Augusta sympathized, gave him advice about starting divorce proceedings for Maud, and sent him instructions about the props for *Kincora*: "So I want you, please to go to Clarkson's as early as you can tomorrow and pay him 30/– and get the wig to bring over."

Kincora was produced on March 25, 1905. Robert designed the scenery. Augusta—following Stendhal's advice that if a woman *must* write, she should say she is doing it for her son—told everyone "it was her son's part in the production that pleased her most." Violet Martin went to the opening, liked the play, but did not think much of Augusta's entertainment afterward: "Augusta swept me and others to tea *on the stage*. A stranger thing I have seldom done, and oh! the discomfort of the sloping stage floor! . . . A. (who swept me about as if I were blind and drunk), also introduced Lord M— . . . Then W. B. Yeats, and *very* high-class conversation, inspired by sips of black tea and a cheese-cake."

Back at Coole, Augusta kept peace and managed her sawmill: "Estate business has settled down, but I have had a very bad fortnight and could not have left home for a day. I just prevented war with the grass farmers, and I am very much in want of sleep." Tenants were going to the land courts demanding reductions in rent and in some case offering to buy their holdings under the provisions of the Wyndham Land Purchase Act.

Willie stayed most of the summer. Though he still looked twenty-five, he turned forty on June 13. Augusta collected £40 from his friends and bought him a copy of the rare and beautiful Kelmscott Chaucer. She herself gave him a stand to put it on. She wrote John Quinn, thanking him for his contribution to Willie's present and listing the others: "You see we have begun with good names, and now I don't mind who comes in."

Augusta gave appropriate gifts, and never had qualms about setting people to their appropriate work. As she wrote Willie once when he was arriving at Coole later than expected: "I don't like losing any of your visit, the summer slips away so quickly and oh! you have so much work to do . . ."; or, as Willie wrote Florence Farr (with whom he was trying to be in love), "I was about to write to you to-day, when I was sent off to catch perch for some Catholics who are to dine here to-night."

During the summer of 1905 Augusta wrote *The White Cockade*, produced at the Abbey in December, based on the story that King James II had tried to escape from Ireland in a barrel after being defeated at the Battle of the Boyne by William of Orange. The hero, Patrick Sarsfield, James's Irish general, speaks movingly of the rewards of service to one's country:

> If she is in trouble or under sorrow, this sweetheart who trusts him, that trouble, God forgive him, brings him a sort of joy! To go out, to call his men, to give out shouts because the time has come to show what her strong lover can do for her—to go hungry that she may be fed; to go tired that her dear feet may tread safely; to die, it may be, at the last for her with such glory that the name he leaves with her is better than any living love, because he has been faithful, faithful, faithful!

(Yeats later described people of Augusta's type: "Though they can stand utterly alone, indifferent though all the world condemn, it is not that they have found themselves, but that they have been found faithful.")

King James, however, is unfaithful and tries to escape to France. His soldiers throw away the white cockades symbolizing their loyalty.

Sarsfield himself pulls out the feathers in his, one by one. But when bystanders call attention to the feathers scattered at his feet, he takes up another cockade and puts it in his hat, "his hand still trembling." When asked, "Why would you go spending yourself for the like of *that* of a king?" he replies, "Why? Why? Who can say? What is holding me? Habit, custom. What is it the priests say?—the cloud of witnesses. Maybe the call of some old angry father of mine, that fought two thousand years ago for a bad master!"

Maud Gonne MacBride, in the midst of getting a divorce, wrote Willie from France about the play: "Lady Gregory knows the soul of our people and expresses it as no one else does. Through the surface of triviality, of selfish avarice, of folly which often jars on one, she never ceases to see and to express in her writing that deep passion which only heroic action or thought is able to arouse in them." Miss Horniman too approved: "I am proud of Lady Gregory because she makes people laugh in a witty way."

Augusta then wrote a short comedy completely turning around the theme of *The White Cockade*—making fun of service and dwelling on the silliness and folly of those for whom it is performed. *Hyacinth Halvey*, produced at the Abbey in February 1906, is a commentary on Sarsfield's—and her own—desire to have one's name "set in clean letters in the book of the people." In her note to the play Augusta commented on the inability of the Irish people to form an accurate judgment: "He [Hyacinth] found himself in Cloon, where, as in other parts of our country, 'character' is built up or destroyed by a password or an emotion, rather than by experience and deliberation." Everyone is taken in by Hyacinth's glowing references, the accuracy of which can be judged by his comment on one of the writers: "It was very kind of him indeed, and he not knowing me at all."

Hyacinth arrives in Cloon with his bundle of wonderful references to take up his job as sub-sanitary inspector. The police sergeant, who is organizing a lecture on character building, decides to have Hyacinth stand on the platform during his lecture wearing a temperance button. The priest's housekeeper runs to rent him a lodging opposite the priest's house and behind the police barracks, which the two previous occupants had left, one "because he dared not pass the police coming in, as he used, with a rabbit he was after snaring in his hand," and the other because he played cards and was asked to leave.

Hyacinth realizes he will have no fun, put on a platform "with every person praising me." He mourns for his former freedom: "To have left Carrow, if it was a poor place, where I had my comrades, and an odd spree, and a game of cards—and a coursing match coming on, and I promised a new greyhound from the city of Cork. I'll die in this place, the way I am. I'll be too much closed in." He tries to get rid of his "character," steals a sheep and robs a church, but each crime is turned to his credit, and he exits on the arms of a cheering crowd. Amid a cloud of laughter, he is taken captive by the sergeant and the priest, church and state, forced to assume a respectability he would prefer to avoid. (In sympathy with Hyacinth, Augusta once wrote Willie from Enid Layard's in Venice that she had met only one person "who knows I have ever done anything at all. Very good for me, and indeed a rest, no character to keep up!")

In September 1905 Miss Horniman offered to guarantee the salaries of the actors. Yeats, Synge, and Augusta had been looking for an opportunity to reorganize the company, which had, they felt, too much control over the choice of plays. The letters exchanged by the three at this time show how completely Yeats's previous control had been based on personal dominance and his joint action with Augusta and Synge—and how the three worked together to obtain formal control. Yeats, in what could be a manifesto for all new enterprises, wrote, "Instead of merely deducing ones actions from existing circumstances, one has to act so as to create new circumstances by which one is to be judged. It is all faith." He rounded up Synge, who was traveling somewhere in the south of Ireland, writing, "Where are you? It is really of great importance for you that you can be at the General Meeting of Soc. [the acting society] Friday 22nd. You must weigh this importance against your other occupations . . . it may be necessary for you and I and Lady Gregory and the Fays to stand in together, having come to a previous agreement." Soon Synge was writing Yeats, "This is the sort of case in which the *three of us* should be of one mind *before* a definite line of action is taken up."

In the midst of the reorganization Augusta had a splendid Christmas at Roxborough, reporting to Willie on the holiday ball—a great departure from the non-dancing days of her mother's reign: "no chaperones or non-dancers. I meant to be the exception but my nephew Arthur dragged me out three times. It was the merriest dance I ever saw. (My experience has not been great. Buckingham Palace and Viceregal and Embassy balls chiefly.)" To Synge she confided, "Our dance went splendidly. I think it has sent me up several degrees in the estimation of my neighbours."

Returning to the theater problem after the holidays, she, Yeats, and Synge created—with Miss Horniman's money—a limited liability company with themselves serving as directors without pay and with the Fays and the actors reduced to employees. Their best and most beautiful actress, Mary Walker, her brother Frank, actor and playwright Padraic Colum, and actor George Roberts left the Abbey in protest and formed the Theatre of Ireland, financed by Edward Martyn. (Augusta regularly referred to it in private as "the enemy," and made uncharitable remarks such as "I hope that literary society will depart this life.") The seceding actors left because they regarded their work as a patriotic service to Ireland. Augusta felt the same way, but, fortunately, no one was offering her a salary.

Mary Walker also left because she objected to the better parts being given to Sara Allgood. As Mary was staying with Yeats's sisters and trying to bring them into the quarrel, Augusta wrote them, telling Willie that in her letter she took "no notice at all of the attacks on you, but trying to show what a perfect idiot Maire has been." She also wrote Synge, telling him, "I have written old Yeats a long letter this morning, explaining our position for he talks so much, and so many of our enemies bring their complaints to him in order that they may come round, that he might as well be kept posted." Frank Fay wrote Augusta about his discussions with Padraic Colum: "I fear if some of the directors don't come to my rescue, I shall be found some fine morning knocking loudly on the door of the Richmond Asylum asking, What is Nationality? What is a Nationalist? and do two Nationalists make one Nationality? It's the straight road to lunacy trying to talk to these people." Augusta wrote Colum in the mildly hectoring tone at which she was adept, "You are thoughtlessly committing a folly which you will probably afterwards be sorry for." To Synge she wrote, "What a poor creature he is!" (He was also Robert's age, had written one good play, and seemed likely to write many more—which he did.)

At this point George Russell, to whom the actors brought all their complaints, completely lost control of his goodness and wrote Willie a long, acrimonious letter saying, among other things, that the players had wanted him, instead of Yeats, as their president, that "There is probably not one of the younger people of whom you have not said some stinging and contemptuous remark," and that "the Irish people will only be led by their affections." Willie and Augusta were undeterred.

Though they lost some of their actors, Augusta, Willie, and Synge were left in control. Augusta quoted a saying of the country people that three yew trees planted in a row "will wear out the world from its beginning to its latter end."

Taken together, the three of them form a fine Freudian triangle: Synge, sick, unhappy, inhibited, mildly sado-masochistic, and extravagantly sexually frustrated; Yeats, full of poetry, vitality, and

181

unsatisfied desire; and Augusta, who, believing in the incompatibility of love and the social structure, had long ago written, "Perchance not so in heaven above, / But here, a *woman* may not love." They were all defeated lovers.

But they had each other. Yeats wrote about Synge, "Often for months together he and I and Lady Gregory would see no one outside the Abbey Theatre." Augusta wrote "of the theatre years in Dublin when none of us saw anyone from the outside. We just moved from the Abbey to the Nassau and back again, we three always. . . ." They formed a surrogate family with Augusta as devoted wife and mother and Synge as wayward child. Because the three of them were Ango-Irish Protestants, because the three of them were creators, they gave each other the kind of non-practical, non-verbal support that exists in families and that frequently enabled them to carry their point against less unified opposition.

Like a child, Synge was interested only in his own projects. After his death Augusta wrote Yeats: "He was ungracious to his fellow workers, authors and actors, ready in accepting praise, grudging in giving it. . . . On tour he thought of his own plays only, gave no help to ours, and if he repeated compliments they were his own." Commenting wryly on his self-absorption, she wrote Willie, "I daresay a week's rehearsal will do you well enough if the music works all right. Synge ought to be judge of that, if he will attend to anything but *Shadow of the Glen*."

Willie and Augusta assumed the prerogatives of parents. When the American impresario Charles Frohman came to inspect the Abbey's wares for a possible American tour, he was shown six plays by Yeats, four by Augusta, and one by Synge.

Synge lived with his mother off and on all of his life. Though he loved her—and though she was probably the only person in the world who genuinely loved him—his own inability to establish himself in a life of his own made him feel she loomed too large in his life. At Coole he tended to ally himself with Robert Gregory; his constant wishes in his letters to Augusta to be remembered to Robert are faint calls for the sympathy of a fellow sufferer. In 1906, when he was thirty-five, he became engaged to the nineteen-year-old actress Molly Allgood (stage name: Maire O'Neill). She was working-class, Catholic, unintellectual, and uneducated. Both Molly and Synge feared telling Lady Gregory of the engagement as much as they feared telling Synge's mother. Both women accepted the engagement, with many mental reservations but no reproaches.

Augusta's letters to Synge have a vitality that is both businesslike and playful. Synge protected himself from his many limitations by isolating himself and regarding others with detachment. Though the amoral view of people this detachment produced gave Augusta no credit for her goodness, it also released her from her need to pose. She described to him the discomfiting of a possibly unfriendly London critic:

> I thought the stars had not exhausted themselves last night when I arrived at the Abbey to meet William Archer who came in with Lawrence!!! But some good star had made him so sea sick on the journey that he had to go out in the middle of the Workhouse, came in again for the end, and had to leave before Cockade! I was so thankful!

After Synge's death she wrote, "I sometimes wondered whether much of my liking for him did not come from his being an appreciative listener—he would take out his cigarette and have a long comfortable laugh, and then put it back again." And, most important, "One never had to rearrange one's mind to talk to him."

While she was busy rearranging her mind to talk to most people, she had the great pleasure of being effective—a quality annoying to those who did not reap its benefits but appreciated by those who did. Sara Allgood described Augusta's management of her mother, who became so angry on learning Sara intended to become an actress that she chased her to the theater. Whoever admitted her had the presence of mind to take her to Augusta, who

> took command, invited my mother to sit and watch the rehearsal. . . . Lady Gregory enlarged upon my ability as an actress, said she would look after me as though I was her own daughter. Finally, Mother was brought back into the vestibule (we had no Green Room in those days) and given tea and cake. . . . Apparently Lady Gregory had enlarged to my Mother on how good an actress Maire Walker was, for, as we walked home, my mother made a complete about face, saying to me that it was ridiculous to call Maire Walker a good actress, that she could see what a much better actress I was.

When an actor came to Augusta for remission of a fine for being late to rehearsal with the time-honored Irish excuse that he was at mass, she refused, "saying he could claim compensation in the next world, which he agreed to!" Occasionally her famous tact was not necessary. Lennox Robinson described her firing an actress:

> Once she was induced to bring a new actress into the theatre to

183

play a small part in *Workhouse Ward*. The unfortunate creature so suffered from stage fright that she was unable to speak a line— somehow Arthur Sinclair and Fred O'Donovan pulled the little play through. Coming off stage the girl was confronted by Lady Gregory. "I suppose I needn't come tomorrow night?" she asked tremblingly. "You needn't," was the uncompromising answer.

She described, with enjoyment and vexation, the trials of a theater manager:

> I came round before mealtime. M. wanted to speak to me "to tender his resignation" in consequence of Miss N. having insulted him during *Cross Roads* last night, before the stagehands, asked him what the devil he meant because he had missed his cue. . . . Also he was knocked down in *Cross Roads* by O. instead of being choked sitting in a chair, and this he seems to think was revenge, because he had at some previous time hit O. with the pipe he throws him in *Workhouse Ward*. I spoke to Miss N. who accuses him of a variety of small offenses connected with cues. . . . P. had been up a few minutes ago asking for a rise of wages. On my way back to the auditorium I met Miss Q. and asked her about the quarrel. She says M. is desperately in love with N. He has been much worse since Mr. Yeats did her horoscope saying she was to marry a fair man. He walked up and down saying, "I am that fair man." She went to him the other day and told him he was foolish and ought to put N. out of his head, but at the end he said, "I know very well that you are in love with me yourself!"

Augusta was in love with them all. And with the audience. John B. Yeats said of her, "Is she not a born leader? I am certain that she must love these people that gather on the benches of the Abbey Theatre."

She did everything in her power to make them gather there. When audiences were small, she would leave the theater by the stage door, go around to the front, and re-enter, "hoping that in the dimness I might pass for a new arrival and so encourage the few scattered people in the stalls." When newspapers did not send a critic, "often near midnight, after the theater had closed, I have gone round to the newspaper offices asking as a favour that notices might be put in, for we could pay for but few advertisements." (Neither the little girl at Roxborough nor the proper married woman in London could have imagined that she, in her fifties, would be joyfully walking the streets of Dublin at midnight, protected by her good cause.)

Augusta's most important contribution to her good cause was the writing of her plays. During the eight years from the opening of the Abbey in 1904 through 1912 she wrote nineteen plays (thirteen one-act tragedies or comedies, one two-act comedy, and five three-act tragedies or comedies) as well as seven translations. Her plays were very popular. From 1904 to 1912 there were 600 performances of her plays at the Abbey or on tour, compared with 245 performances of Yeats's plays, 182 of Synge's, 125 by William Boyle, 78 by W. F. Casey, 65 by Lennox Robinson, 47 by Norreys Connel, and 44 by G. B. Shaw.

But the Abbey still needed more plays than the Abbey playwrights were writing. Willie Fay suggested that he and Synge work up a play by Molière. Then, according to Fay, "up rose Lady Gregory and said, 'I will go home to Gort this day and I will make a translation in the Galway dialect that I have used in my own plays, and then it will be sure to suit our people.' And so she did." During her career Augusta translated four of Molière's plays, *The Doctor in Spite of Himself*, *The Rogueries of Scapin*, *The Miser*, and—in her seventies—*The Would-Be Gentleman*. Willie Fay called them "a revelation of what can be done in colloquial dialect." He described his performance as the hero in her translation of *The Doctor in Spite of Himself* when "some of the audience laughed in a way which nearly made me forget my lines . . . it was genuinely disconcerting, simply because it was so delightful."

Molière was congenial to Augusta, though her own plays are full of condescending love or exalted feeling and Molière's are full of an intellectual understanding of the faults of his characters. Molière understood thoroughly Augusta's chief methods for getting along in this world: self-deceit and manipulation. But even in protected moments of creativity Augusta was unable to face or examine these traits in her own plays. Molière took her farther into herself than she was able to go alone.

On May 5, 1906, she wrote John Quinn, who was overseeing Douglas Hyde's lecture tour in America, that "I have another comedy all but ready and should be ashamed of producing work so quickly but it had to be done by somebody, Synge and Yeats having been silent for so long." The play was *The Jackdaw*, another of her short, elegant peasant comedies. But it was not performed at the Abbey until February 1907 because she wrote two more plays that year that got in ahead of it.

The Jackdaw is her first attempt to take the love element out of the plot of *Twenty-Five*. The heroine is Mrs. Broderick, a middle-aged widow about to be declared bankrupt because "Haven't I the mean, begrudging creditors now that would put me into the Court?" She is rescued by her stingy brother, who brings £10 to save her but who does not want her to know for fear she will ask for more. He gives the money to Joseph Nestor, Mrs. Broderick's crony, who buys her pet jackdaw for £10, telling her a friend from South Africa wants it as a companion in a dark mine. Immediately the whole town, including her brother and the magistrates on the bench, start catching jackdaws to sell to the non-existent buyer.

When Mr. Nestor tries to tell the brother that there is no buyer, the brother, looking at everyone rushing after jackdaws, refuses to be convinced and shows that he too, like so many of Augusta's characters, can recycle the past to conform to his interpretation of the present: "There is surely some root for all this. There must be some buyer after all. It's to keep him to themselves they are wanting."

The activity of the play swirls around the non-existent buyer, just as the activity of *Spreading the News* radiated from the non-existent murder. The minds of the characters slide around the empty space, fastening only on the story they want to believe. Mrs. Broderick's brother insists that Mr. Nestor stole his money instead of giving it to his sister:

Cooney: No, but listen to myself. I brought the money to you.
  (*Pointing to Mrs. Broderick*)
Nestor: If he did, he wouldn't trust you with it, ma'am.
Cooney: I intended it for your relief.
Nestor: In dread he was you would go follow him to Limerick.
Mrs. Broderick: It is not likely I would be following the like of
  him to Limerick, a man that left me to the charity of strangers
  from Africa!
Cooney: I gave the money to him. . . .
Nestor: And I gave it to yourself paying for the jackdaw. Are you
  satisfied now, Mary Broderick.
Mrs. Broderick: Satisfied, is it? It would be a queer thing indeed
  I to be satisfied. My brother to be spending money on birds,
  and his sister with a summons on her head.

The play ends with the magistrates coming to Mrs. Broderick's looking for the buyer from Africa. A bystander reports:

He could not be found in any place. They are informed he was
never seen leaving this house. They are coming to make an investigation. . . . The police along with them. It is what they are
thinking, that the stranger was made away with for his gold. . . .
If he is not found they will arrest all they see upon the premises.

There are "sounds of feet and talking and knocks at the door." Mrs. Broderick, her brother, and Mr. Nestor all hide. As in *Spreading the News*, Augusta's characters are about to be in trouble for a crime they didn't commit.

The play was a great success. Augusta wrote with her complex modesty and pride:

> We were astonished at the success of *The Jackdaw*! It was splendidly acted. . . . There was great laughter, especially towards the end, then great applause and actors applauded once or twice; then cries of "Author!" till I bowed from the stalls, but they would not be satisfied, went on applauding and shouting "Lady Gregory" till at last I had to go round to the stage and had a great reception.

It is a charming picture, Augusta in her satin tea jacket, her lace mantilla and pearls, her long black dress, bowing, smiling, to a crowd of nobodies—as she would have considered them anywhere but in the seats of the Abbey.

About this time her portrait was painted by the Italian artist Antonio Mancini, who had been brought to Dublin by her nephew Hugh Lane. Mancini had an unusual technique. He put a grid of strings in front of his sitter, and a grid of strings in front of his canvas; then, as Augusta described it,

> he would go to the very end of the long room, look at me through my net, then begin a hurried walk which turned to a quick trot, his brush aimed at some feature, eye or eyebrow, the last steps would be a rush, then I needed courage to sit still. But the hand holding the brush always swerved at the last moment to the canvas, and there in its appropriate place, between the threads, the paint would be laid on and the retreat would begin.

Augusta liked the result: "His portrait of a woman growing old, and a dusty black dress, and a faded brown curtain would have lighted up a prison cell." She sent John Quinn a photograph of the painting, telling him, "It is a wonderful picture, luminous, radiant and triumphant."

Augusta spent the spring and summer of 1906 at Coole and on the Burren coast, while Synge accompanied the Abbey players on tour— and enraged Miss Horniman by holding his sweetheart, Molly, on his knee in a public room where passers-by could see them. Miss Horniman was generally enraged by the rowdy conduct of the players. Yeats investigated and found that one of the actresses did actually blow a tin horn out of the train window, and that "The Miss O'Dempsey who was engaged for small parts is obviously impossible, loud, irresponsible. . . . Her sister has naturally few opportunities for flirtation, but she is noisy."

In July, Synge, Yeats, and Augusta met at Coole with Willie Fay. (Miss Horniman wrote Willie that if she had been there, "I would establish myself on a sofa in curling pins & an old dressing-gown & refuse to move, only moan and drop ashes on the carpet.") The only definite conclusion they reached was to hire a secretary to relieve Willie Fay of business matters. With somewhat less unanimity they also agreed to hire a new actress, Miss Florence Darragh, promoted by Miss Horniman and felt necessary by Yeats to play in his poetic plays.

Augusta, with her house full of company and her head full of theater problems, wrote the first drafts of two plays that became *The Gaol Gate* and the three-act *The Canavans*. *The Gaol Gate* was written in August, typed in September, and produced in October. It is the most moving tragedy she ever wrote.

In *The Gaol Gate* a man gives his life for the ideals of his country and his class. Two peasant women from the mountains beyond Coole come to Galway jail to see the son and husband they believe has informed on his friends. When they arrive in the early morning darkness, they are told the man is dead. They grieve for his bad name as an informer. His wife keens:

> I would not begrudge you, Denis, and you leaving praises after you. The neighbours keening along with me would be better to me than an estate.
>
> But my grief your name to be blackened in the time of the blackening of the rushes! Your name never to rise up again in the growing time of the year!

The gatekeeper returns with Denis's clothes. When the women ask if they can bury him or follow him to the grave, they are told he was buried the previous morning: "A long rope and a short burying, that is the order for a man that is hanged." When the women realize that if he was hanged he could have given no evidence against his two friends who actually committed the crime, they are triumphant:

> Are there any people in the streets at all till I call on them to come hither? Did they ever hear in Galway such a thing to be done, a man to die for his neighbour? . . . Gather up, Mary Cushin, the clothes for your child; they'll be wanted by this one and that one. The boys crossing the sea in the springtime will be craving a thread for a memory. . . . I will go through Gort and Kilbecanty

and Druimdarod and Daroda; I will call to the people and the singers at the fairs to make a great praise for Denis!

The child he left in the house that is shook, it is great will be his boast in his father! All Ireland will have a welcome before him, and all the people in Boston.

I to stoop on a stick through half a hundred years, I will never be tired with praising! Come hither, Mary Cushin, till we'll shout it through the roads, Denis Cahel died for his neighbour!

The play goes deep into one of the central events of community life: the willing self-sacrifice of one individual for the good of the group. This was Augusta's idea of the ultimate in service. And though the person making the sacrifice is transformed into a hero, it also shows the great disadvantage of such service in that it allows one nothing of one's own, not even life, not even identity. The play also shows, though not intentionally, the perversion of the instinct for group loyalty by the long oppression of one people by another. The group becomes unable to evaluate what is actually for its own good. In Augusta's play the self-sacrifice of a simple man protecting two murderers is looked upon as a great good simply because it is done in defiance of an alien law. After this play Augusta drew back for a time from her emphasis on service.

In October 1906 Willie Fay eloped with Bridget O'Dempsey, whose family disapproved of the match. Augusta had been his confidante during their difficult courtship, and he had written her in September, "I want to thank your kindness to me and I think you will understand me when I say my own mother could not have helped me more than you have done." (From another world comes the voice of Arabi in exile in Ceylon saying to Augusta, "I know all you have done for me. I speak to you as I would to a mother.")

In November, Miss Darragh appeared in Yeats's *Deirdre*. (He later told a friend that "Lady Gregory wrote the end of *Deirdre* on my fundamental mass." In the end, the lovers die.) Augusta, in great distress about Miss Darragh's unsuitability, had written him:

This is the difficulty, ought I through personal friendship and affection for you . . . accept an actress . . . to the deterioration of all our work and our ideals, on the other hand, ought I to thwart you and have you always believe you had lost a great opportunity? I often think in these struggles of the story of Paul, "The love of God is a very terrible thing!"

Another time she wrote to correct a misunderstanding caused by her illegible handwriting: "It was 'piffle' Miss Darragh called your work, not 'miffle.' " Even Yeats then had to admit that Miss Darragh was not suitable.

In *The Canavans*, begun in August and produced in December 1906, Augusta balanced the compulsion to serve the strongest against the attainment of personal courage. The hero, Peter Canavan, a miller, begins by saying, "Now, where there is a course of action put before any man, there is but the one question to put and the one to answer; and that question is 'Is it safe?' "

The play is set in Ireland during the time of Queen Elizabeth. Peter Canavan cannot decide whether to accept the position of Mayor of Scarltana offered him by Elizabeth's soldiers. It is a difficult decision for a cautious man when power is constantly changing sides. He defends his timidity with great vigor:

> Oh, there is certain assurance of quiet and great good in settling yourself to the strongest. There is very great peace and immunity in surrendering our will to their commands. . . . Would you be buzzing about at your own will the same as a heap of flies? I tell you thousands have been damned through no other thing than following their own will and fancy.

When his brother Antony deserts from Elizabeth's army and takes refuge with him, they are both arrested as traitors. To escape from prison, Antony, who is always brave, dresses in women's clothes and impersonates Queen Elizabeth. Headley, the officer in charge of the garrison, who is already infatuated with the idea of the Queen and who has been sending her poems, is completely taken in:

Headley (*sinking to his knees*): The Queen! The excellent and glorious person of her Majesty!
Antony: You are before your sovereign.
Headley: Oh, angelic face! Where the red rose has meddled with the white.
Antony: This is the man of whose beauty I have heard—who sent me sonnets. . . .
Headley: Oh, the fourth of the Graces has read my sonnets!
Antony: That is prose. I expect a poet to talk poetry.
Headley: Oh, that I had a pen—a pen—a pen.
Antony: Go on. Essex would do better than that.
Headley: I'd say: God save the Queen—Amen, Amen—
Antony: That is getting on.
Headley: Oh, Crown of Lilies, say that you forgive!
Antony: Do as I bid you and you yet may live.
Headley: Lay orders, dearest dread, trust me again!

Antony: Then go at once and send away your men! Look here, young Apollo, you must have the gates left clear for me to go out. There must be no blemish upon the name of Defendore Fides!

The brothers escape back to the mill, Peter Canavan believing he has seen the Queen and completely infatuated: "Taller than any woman ever stood upon a floor she was! She stood up over me the same as an elephant! A great grand voice she had, pitched someway squeally like a woman's, but strong and high as if used to giving out orders." He energetically assumes the position as mayor and loyal Queen's man, but when asked if he has turned Protestant in the Queen's service, he replies, "No hurry, no hurry, till I will know is the new faith safest in *both* worlds. I'm not one to say Her Majesty to be the *real* head of the Church. But it's greatly in her favour she being such a success."

When the clothes his brother Antony wore impersonating the Queen are found stuffed up the chimney, Antony is accused of killing her. Peter's loyalty changes immediately: "A great man, a great man, there can be no doubt at all of that! . . . Why wouldn't I make a boast and he my own brother? Oh, he will leave a great name after him in history! 'Queen Elizabeth was very strong,' they will say, 'she killed lords and priests and bishops; but poor Antony Canavan was stronger; it was he killed Queen Elizabeth!' " Antony creeps to a bench and sits down "trembling, as weak as water and as pale" . . . because it has been prophesied that he will die when his "name goes up." The miller, seeing his brother so timid, is suddenly brave himself and exclaims triumphantly in the last speech of the play:

Let you not be daunted! It is I will protect the whole of ye! Where is fear? It is banished from the world this day. The strongest! Isn't it the fool I was wasting time—wasting the years—looking here and there for the strongest? I give you my word, it was not till this present minute that I knew the strongest to be myself!

In a reversal of the ending of *Spreading the News*, the hero is suddenly brave and free, but, as in *Spreading the News*, only because of ridiculous misunderstandings. (But Augusta herself, with her success and her ceaseless productive activity, was beginning to feel a great deal stronger and braver herself.) She disassociated herself from the conclusion of her play, writing in her note, "The play seems (to me now) somewhat remote, inexplicable, as if written less by logical plan than in one of those moments of light-heartedness that come, as I

191

think, as an inheritance from my French great-grandmother, Frances Algoin. . . ." (Actually, the play was rewritten over the period of a year, with a second version produced in October 1907.)

Augusta frequently used the notes to her plays to correct some impression of strength or power of which she did not consciously approve. (A critic called them "Irish nanny notes.") They are rambling, disjointed, occasionally very revelatory but never giving the impression they had been organized in any way. Unlike her hero Peter Canavan, she did not feel strong enough to stand alone proclaiming her strength and went out of her way to conceal the independence and power she had gained through creativity.

Willie wanted a new manager at the Abbey to direct his verse plays. Ben Iden Payne was suggested by Miss Horniman. Augusta and Synge objected vigorously because he was English and would not do justice to their work. Willie was not above using his manipulative skills on Augusta, and in their discussions it came out that he had once promised Miss Horniman the right to produce his plays if anything happened to the Abbey. Augusta felt betrayed: "Those plays were our children, I was so proud of them, and loved them, and now I cannot think of them without the greatest pain." Though neither he nor she believed he was really serious, he made Augusta feel obligated to him when he went to Miss Horniman and retracted his promise. Augusta wrote Synge about her reluctant decision to side with Yeats in the hiring of Ben Payne.

> I would not for a moment think of accepting this "fancy man" but I think Yeats wants a new excitement, a new impetus, or will tire of the theatre, and I feel myself very much bound to him, besides personal friendship, because we are the only survivors of the beginning of the movement. I think his work more important than any other (you must not be offended at this) and I think it our chief distinction.

Synge was as offended as it was possible to be while remaining aware of the great benefits he received through his association with Lady Gregory and Yeats. He wrote Molly: "I am tied to the company now by your own good self, otherwise I would be inclined to clear away to Paris and let them make it a Yeats-Gregory show in name as well as in deed. However, it is best not to do anything rash. They have both been very kind to me at times and I owe them a great deal." In fact, Synge had just presented the Abbey with one of the great plays of world literature. During December 1906 *The Playboy of the West-*

192

ern World was being rehearsed behind closed doors, and on opening night, January 26, 1907, it caused a riot.

Synge was not personally disliked by the Dublin public. Mary Colum explained with fine Irish logic when she criticized Augusta for not going to Dublin literary evenings, "Synge seldom did either, but we knew he preferred the company of country people." She added, "Though shy, he was always affable and courteous." Neither was he a happy man, and the envious Dublin public was perspicacious enough to realize they did not have this to envy. Yet his plays, except for *Riders to the Sea*, almost always caused trouble. *In the Shadow of the Glen* had offended nationalists who refused to admit there was such a thing as a loveless marriage in Ireland. The Abbey wisely refrained from producing his *Tinker's Wedding*, which shows a priest being beaten by tinkers, and left it to find first production in London. His *Well of the Saints*, produced in February 1905, merely played to empty houses. *The Playboy* caused the most serious and lasting trouble. Yeats, ever a fighter, said of him, "Synge is invaluable to us because he has that kind of intense, narrow personality which necessarily raises the whole issue."

The Playboy is about a young man who thinks he has killed his father. He is transformed into a hero and a lover by the admiration of the villagers, who, in traditional Irish fashion, accept and glorify any act of lawlessness because the laws were made by England. Synge writes of his characters with an amazed delight and a complete understanding of their hypocrisy, their narrowness, and their vitality.

Augusta never liked the play, a minor reason being her jealousy for Willie, whom she wrote, after a rehearsal, "It did make me a little sad as I watched Playboy to think how easily that sort of work comes to our players, and how long it will be before your plays can go as well all round. . . . You have never looked like a tiger with its cub as Synge did last night with Playboy." She was never explicit about her major reason for disliking the play, but most likely it was because of its amorality, its sexuality, and its "bad language," much of which was omitted from the Abbey production.

The first-night audience, which came expecting to be outraged, took some time to find anything at which to be offended. After the first act Augusta wired Willie, who was giving a lecture in Scotland: "PLAY GREAT SUCCESS." After the third act she wired, "AUDIENCE BROKE UP IN DISORDER AT THE WORD SHIFT." In the play Christy says: "It's Pegeen I'm seeking only, and what'd I care if you brought me a drift of chosen females, standing in their shifts itself, maybe, from this place to the Eastern World." Finally, public opinion settled on the idea that the villagers' glorification of Christy for supposedly killing his father was a slander on the Irish race.

The directors refused to withdraw *The Playboy*. On succeeding nights the uproar was so great the actors occasionally went through their parts in dumb show to save their voices. Once or twice during each performance the curtain was rung down while the police put out troublemakers. The Dublin public, showing the same dislike of law that caused the villagers to make a hero of Christy for breaking it, was further incensed. One night some undergraduates of Trinity College who had been given tickets to clap *for* the play were drunk. According to Joseph Holloway, "one of their number . . . made himself objectionable and was forcibly removed by Synge and others [including the actor playing Christy's dead father] after a free fight amongst the instruments of the orchestra." Hugh Lane, dressed impeccably in black tie and tails, led out disturbers while Augusta and Willie (returned from Scotland) conferred in the stalls. One of the actors described Augusta after such a performance: "Lady Gregory stood at the door of the Green Room as calm and collected as Queen Victoria about to open a charity bazaar. Seeing Paddy Tobin and myself, she beckoned us over and handed each of us a piece of the huge barmbrack which she had baked at Coole and brought up to Dublin for the Abbey cast."

Each morning Yeats went down to the police station to testify against the disturbers, who were fined ten shillings each. Augusta— unwittingly following Oscar Wilde's advice to "Love your enemies, nothing annoys them more"—offered to pay the fine for Padraic Colum's father, arrested by mistake. Her offer was refused.

The play went on every night for which it had been announced. As Augusta wrote, "It was a definite fight for freedom from mob censorship," and she emphasized that "In art the many count less than the few." Augusta, who had set out to serve Ireland and literature, suffered and continued to suffer from the apparent split between the two, but she unhesitatingly chose literature.

The Monday following the opening the directors held a public debate on the play that was also nearly a riot. Yeats responded to those calling him anti-Irish with his famous and flamboyant "The author of *Cathleen ni Houlihan* addresses you!" (which prompted Joseph Holloway to comment in his diary, "The odd thing is that Fay told me Lady Gregory wrote the whole of it except the part of 'Cathleen' "). Mary Colum said of Yeats that evening, "I never witnessed a human being fight as Yeats fought that night, nor ever knew another with so many weapons in his armory. He was then in his forties, but he looked under thirty, a fearless, dominating man in spite of, or perhaps because of, all his dreams and visions and esoteric philosophies." Augusta wrote Synge, who was too sick to come, "I was sorry while there that we had ever let such a set inside the theatre, but I am glad today, and I think it was spirited and showed we were not repenting or apologizing."

A few weeks later when her *Jackdaw* was wildly applauded, she modestly wrote about her curtain call, "I daresay it was partly to show we were forgiven for Playboy." That they would not be for many years. *The Playboy* was denounced from the pulpit by priests who had never read or seen it; district councils passed resolutions against it. Augusta herself was forbidden by the local council to visit the workhouse or entertain the schoolchildren. And Father Fahy, the local Catholic priest, replied smoothly but unhelpfully to her letter requesting his intercession with the local council. Referring to an earlier party she had given the children, he said: "You will I am sure be able to remember that I never objected to the feast you kindly provided for the children. The request coming from you shall have all the more weight when forwarded to the board by yourself." Five years later, when Augusta was greeted with coldness and suspicion in the little village on the Burren coast where she had bought a cottage, she realized again the permanence of the harm caused by her association with *The Playboy*: "when an idea gets into these remote places, it stays there."

The reaction to *The Playboy* was a disheartening, frightening illustration of the limitations and narrowness of the Irish people, even of the Irish country people, whom Augusta tended to exempt from the criticisms she made of the Irish middle class. John Quinn, who watched from afar and saw his share of the battle when the Abbey players brought *The Playboy* to America, wrote angrily that the Irish would never be open to new ideas and new ways of expression until they were "freed from the leading-strings of parish priests and parochial ignorance, and released from terror for their damned little immortal souls."

In addition to the trouble with *The Playboy*, there was trouble, or at least uneasiness, at Coole. Robert was engaged to be married. His fiancée was Margaret Graham Parry, a fellow art student at the Slade. Augusta described her as "a very charming girl . . . clever, pretty and very bright and good. She is Welsh, with a Spanish grandmother and a French great-grandmother and has no English blood, and that I am just as glad of." Augusta gave Robert a sapphire for Margaret's engagement ring and settled on her some shares of Ceylon tea stock. Since Robert was legal owner of Coole Park, his wife might expect to be mistress—though Augusta still had the right to live there rent-free throughout her life. She wrote John Quinn, "I shall for the present stay here to look after things for them but will fade away by degrees as they can be more here, for young people should have their own chance." But to Willie she confided that she felt "a slight nervousness about the advent of Margaret, happy as I am about her, it must make a difference. I had been so free and unquestioned."

In the spring of 1907 she, Willie, and Robert got away from it all on a leisurely tour of the Italian hill towns. Augusta read Castiglione's *Courtier* to Willie, and it especially appealed to him after his own fight with "the rabble" over *The Playboy*. His inaccurate glorification of the aristocracy in his poetry was one of his methods for isolating himself from the antagonism he felt all around him in Ireland. Trying for a more secure place in it, when he got back to Ireland he told George Russell that, as a result of his genealogical researches, he had discovered that "if he had his rights, he would be Duke of Ormonde." George Russell took it calmly and replied, "In any case, Willie, you're overlooking your father."

When Augusta got back to London in May, she visited Wilfrid Blunt, who reported to his diary that she was "in terrible trouble about her plays." He and she both saw that "the worst of it is that she is already boycotted personally on account of it at Coole, the Local Council forbidding the schoolchildren to go to her house, or even to accept cakes or presents of any kind from her."

Her next play, *Dervorgilla*, in typescript by July 1907, produced at the Abbey in October, was written out of guilt. The heroine is Dervorgilla, wife of O'Rourke, King of Breffney, who eloped with Diarmuid, King of Leinster, in the year 1152. Her husband invaded Leinster in retaliation, and Diarmuid appealed to Henry II of England for help in driving him out of his domain. Henry sent him an army under Strongbow, which was the beginning of the English domination of Ireland. (Augusta's Barry ancestors probably came to Ireland with this expedition.)

Augusta said she wrote *Dervorgilla* out of remorse for accepting an English director at the Abbey: "I felt as if I should be spoken of some day as one who had betrayed her country's trust." Though her Dervorgilla is certainly remorseful at having been the cause of the English coming to Ireland, it is hard to believe that the depth of her remorse and her awareness of her explicitly sexual crime—and anything sexual is unusual in Augusta's writing—were fueled solely by the author's remorse at accepting Ben Payne as manager at the Abbey, particularly since she also referred to his hiring as "the path of expediency, which I now think was the wise one."

She assumed that because she was suffering she was guilty. She was being boycotted by the local schoolchildren. Her position at Coole was threatened by Robert's marriage. Now that she was about to lose him, she felt guilty about the diversion of so much energy from Robert to Willie and the theater. And while she was feeling guilty, her psyche dredged up guilt from as far back as her affair with Wilfrid Blunt. (Dervorgilla described her lover: "It was he cast down the great, it was the dumb poor he served!"—which description of a medieval war lord owes less to historical accuracy than it does to Wilfrid Blunt's crusades for the underprivileged and unrepresented subjects of Britain's colonies. Dervorgilla's claim to primacy in the relationship, "It was I myself led you astray!" is an echo of Augusta's claim in her sonnets to Blunt that "One sin, most certainly, I need to atone: / The sin of loving thee while yet unwooed. / Mine only was this wrong, this guilt alone." Dervorgilla described her husband's death in an image that Augusta had used to describe Blunt's flirting with official disapproval. Dervorgilla says, "The head I made bow with shame was struck off and sent to the English King." Augusta had quoted a political enemy who said of Blunt, "The fellow knows he has a handsome head and he wants it to be seen on Temple bar.")

In *Dervorgilla* Augusta showed someone like herself accepting responsibility for a crime, suffering for it, even cursed for it; on the other hand, she herself went ahead and did what she wanted. In the play Dervorgilla, now an old woman, has been living at an abbey for more than half her life, "no one knowing her name or race," praying to be forgiven. Like Augusta, she is known throughout the neighborhood for her charity and her goodness. On the day of the play she is awarding prizes to the children for their games—which Augusta was no longer permitted to do. Dervorgilla thinks perhaps she has not caused so much harm: "It is many years since we had a day like this of sport and mirth-making. It seems as if those were wrong who said the English would always bring trouble on us; there may be a good end to the story after all." But one of the children runs in with a dead crane just shot by an English bowman. A wandering minstrel appears and sings about the country's troubles, the quarrels that brought in the English, ending: "If't was Diarmuid's call that brought in the Gall, / Let the weight of it fall upon Dervorgilla!" He goes out to sing for the English soldiers, and Dervorgilla sends her servant after him to pay him to go away. The soldiers shoot her servant, and his wife in her grief lets slip the name "Dervorgilla." The children turn to stare at her and slowly give back their prizes. She accepts their judgment, telling a little girl who hangs back:

Do not be afraid to give back my gifts, do not separate yourself from your companions for my sake. For there is little of my life but is spent, and there has come upon me this day all the pain of the world and its anguish, seeing and knowing that deed once done has no undoing, and the lasting trouble my unfaithfulness has brought upon you and your children for ever. There is kindness in your unkindness, not leaving me to go and face Michael and the Scales of Judgment wrapped in comfortable words, and the praises of the poor, and the lulling of psalms, but from the swift, unflinching, terrible judgment of the young!

Having disposed of her guilt, Augusta picked herself up and went on with her life. In fact, she sent on to John Quinn a copy of Wilfrid Blunt's play *Fand*, writing in it: "Given by W. S. Blunt to A. Gregory and by her to John Quinn, 1907"—a startlingly clear-cut example of the oft-occurring transfer of the gift of the old lover to the new, or prospective, lover.

In the middle of September 1907 Synge had an operation on the glands in his neck and seemed to recover rapidly. The doctors, however, knew he was suffering from Hodgkin's disease and would soon be dead. He was not told.

On September 26, 1907, Augusta saw Robert and Margaret married in London. (The painter Augustus John was best man.) Augusta was, she wrote, "glad for Robert, for he had only me and would have been very lonely in time if he hadn't married." In October her *Dervorgilla* was produced at the Abbey. In November her reworking of *Where There Is Nothing*, written with Willie in 1902, was produced as *Unicorn from the Stars*. When Augusta and Willie began rewriting, he found that "since I had last worked with her, her mastery of the stage and her knowledge of dialect had so increased that my imagination could not go neck and neck with hers . . . and so after an attempt to work alone I gave up my scheme to her."

Robert and Margaret rented an apartment in Paris, but were with Augusta at Coole on Christmas Day, when she boldly defied the ban on her visits to the workhouse in Gort. She was, she wrote, "received with great glee by the inmates. The sister told me that the old men had refused to decorate the rooms until they were assured I would not be kept out. A very old woman asked Margaret if she knew me, and when she said yes, the woman said, 'If you know Lady Gregory, God is with you.' "

The Abbey company was in disorder. During the tour of November 1907 Willie Fay had been unable to keep discipline. He singled out Molly Allgood, Synge's fiancée, for being late to rehearsals. (Synge defended her on the ground that she had an artistic temperament and was always late to everything. Augusta wrote to Willie that "we all have 'artistic temperaments'—if we choose to flaunt them.") Fortunately, the other actors were also up in arms against Willie Fay, which was a relief because the directors had earlier feared that if they broke with him most of the actors would leave too. Willie Fay demanded that he be given power to hire and fire actresses. Augusta met with him early in January 1908 and told him the directors were not disposed to make any changes. Willie Fay, his brother, and his wife resigned from the Abbey company, which they had done so much to create.

Yeats had written of him at one point, "I have seen him telling the truth and known by the look on his face that he did not know it was the truth." Augusta had written Yeats in reference to Fay, "There is no getting over the class distinctions in the way of friendship." And Yeats had written Augusta about the prospect of their managing the Abbey without the Fays: "I can see Synge is very terrified at the thought of being left to manage."

Synge's terror was justified. After fourteen months as a theater manager, he would be dead—though that occupation was only the final stress of a lifetime. Thirteen months after the Fays left, Augusta would nearly die of a "very dangerous seizure"—though their departure was only one stress among many. Just before Augusta's seizure Willie would have a "curious breakdown of some sort," briefly unable to "use my mind on any serious subject." He raged against the loss of energy and time taken from his poetry by the theater, believing that the Fays should have been kept on, blaming and forgiving Augusta for their departure: "If Lady Gregory, who has done so much for me, made, as I believe, this one mistake, I must endure the results with patience and good will."

Their easiest problem was the replacement of their major actors. Either one or both of the Fays had appeared in nearly every play produced at the Abbey from the beginning. Yet within a year new actors, Arthur Sinclair and Fred O'Donovan, had filled their place.

Augusta, Willie, Synge, and the actress Sara Allgood directed plays. Augusta translated *Teja* by Hermann Sudermann, which Synge directed. She translated *The Rogueries of Scapin* by Molière, which

Willie directed. They had a succession of business managers. (Though Willie was quite capable of understanding the overall financial operation of the Abbey, he was so ignorant of business practices he signed the Abbey checks "Yours sincerely, W. B. Yeats.") Two new dramatists, W. F. Casey and Lennox Robinson—beginning his lifelong association with the Abbey at twenty-one—contributed plays. Synge struggled with *Deirdre of the Sorrows*, his last play. Willie struggled with *The Player Queen*, another verse play that eventually became a prose play. Augusta wrote a new peasant comedy, rewrote *Kincora*, translated another play by Molière, and started or tinkered with several more. Robert Gregory, newly married and in Paris, did not produce scenery designs for the production of Synge's *Well of the Saints* as promised. Augusta gave up and told Synge a letter from him would have more effect than a letter from her.

Meanwhile the Fays, with the élan, hardihood, and everlasting hopefulness typical of actors, were off to conquer new worlds, performing Abbey plays in America. Their producer Charles Frohman, was billing them as the National Theater Society of Ireland—the name they had first given their acting company and which now belonged to the Abbey. John Quinn, American guardian of the Abbey, wrote them several angry letters and threatened to sue; they changed the name to The Irish Players from Dublin. They were not a great success in America, but they did pay royalties on the plays used, which were especially welcome to Willie and Augusta, who received no royalties on their plays produced at the Abbey.

Augusta wrote a new comedy for them—and for the Abbey—turning *The Poorhouse*, which she had written in 1903 for Douglas Hyde to translate into Irish, into *The Workhouse Ward* with two equal parts for men, a very small part for a woman, and scenery consisting of two beds. As the play opens, two old men who have grown up together and always fighting are side by side in the workhouse infirmary, fighting still. Michael accuses Mike of pretending to be sick:

> If you have pains within your inside there is no one can see it or know of it the way they can see my own knees that are swelled up with the rheumatism, and my hands that are twisted in ridges the same as an old cabbage stalk. It is easy to be talking about soreness and about pains, and they maybe not to be in it at all.

They argue about their past:

> Mike: Little wonder you to have good nourishment the time we were both rising, and you bringing away my rabbits out of the snare.

200

Michael: And you didn't bring away my own eels, I suppose, I was after spearing in the Turlough? . . .

Mike: And what do you say to my garden that your two pigs had destroyed on me the year of the big tree being knocked, and they making gaps in the wall. . . .

Michael: And what happened to myself the fair day of Esserkelly, the time I was passing your door? Two brazen dogs that rushed out and took a piece of me. I never was the better of it or of the start I got, but wasting time from then till now!

They argue about their families:

Mike: Look at all my own generations that are buried at the Seven Churches. And how many generations of the Miskells are buried in it? Answer me that! . . .

Michael: I tell you but for the wheat that was to be sowed there would be more side cars and more common cars at my father's funeral than ever left your own door. . . .

Mike: And what do you say to the banshee? Isn't she apt to have knowledge of the ancient race? Was ever she heard to screech or to cry for the Miskells?

From there they go on to wishing for each other's death: "It is a pity the banshee not to be crying for yourself at this minute"; and then wishing to be separated forever: "I'd sooner than ten pound in my hand, I to know that my shadow and my ghost will not be knocking about with your shadow and your ghost, and the both of us waiting our time. I'd sooner be delayed in Purgatory! Now, have you anything to say?"

They have a chance to get their wish. Mike's sister comes to take him home. He is delighted; his crony is dismayed:

Ah, Mike, is it truth you are saying, you to go from me and leave me with rude people and with townspeople, and with people of every parish in the union, and they having no respect for me or no wish for me at all! . . . All that I am craving is the talk. There to be no one to say out to whatever thought might be rising in my innate mind! To be lying here and no conversible person in it would be the abomination of misery!

Mike realizes he cannot be parted from his friend. He asks his sister to take Michael also. She refuses angrily: "Let the two of you stop together, and the back of my hand to you." She goes out and the two start quarreling immediately.

Unlike many of Augusta's short comedies, which have an empty space at their center around which the action swirls, this play is about love, but love turned inside out, so that Augusta, in presenting it, felt quite safe.

During 1908 she rewrote *Kincora*, her play about the conflict between service and rebellion, and in the new version the rebellious Queen Gormleith accepts responsibility for her actions. When she is offered the traditional woman's excuse for aiding her husband's enemies, "You were maybe misled, made use of?" she replies: "No . . . I did my own part, I have no mind to deny or to hide my own share in it at all." Though her husband again takes responsibility for her actions, the play shows the change in Augusta brought about by four years of activity and success. She was more independent, she did not have to genuflect toward service every time she made a move.

Ireland, what is more, was becoming more difficult to serve. At the time of the outcry against *The Playboy* she wrote: "Poor Ireland is in rather a heartbreaking state, the flocks and packs in full cry, and a deadening of all individual life." Hugh Lane, under consideration for the position of curator of the Dublin National Gallery, had been passed over the previous year in favor of a "safe" government man— though, as it turned out, the appointee was not at all safe and took part in the Easter Rising of 1916 against England. Lane, who was also offering thirty-nine invaluable modern paintings to the city of Dublin on condition the city provide a proper museum, was being put off from year to year. It is, she wrote, "extraordinary the animosity against anyone who is doing anything." She was realizing she had to look beyond Ireland, to simpler, more universal, and yet more personal standards.

VIII

A New Lease on Life

CHANGING—A LITTLE: 1908–1911

> So, when spring comes
> With sunshine back again like an old smile,
> And the fresh waters and awakened birds
> And budding woods await us, I shall be
> Prepared.
>
> ROBERT BROWNING, "Pauline"

A UGUSTA went to Dublin in May 1908 to oversee the work of the Abbey while John Synge had a second operation—for the removal of an enlarged gland in his side. She then returned to Coole to greet Robert and Margaret, who were returning from Paris. She wrote Synge, who seemed to be recovering, "Margaret is still very unwell, but I think only from natural causes." Margaret was in fact in the first months of pregnancy with her first child, due in January 1909.

Robert and Margaret were treated as favored guests at Coole Park, but Willie was treated as the most favored guest. It was impossible for Augusta to refuse precedence to a man who had written, among many other beautiful things about Coole, "In the Seven Woods":

> I have heard the pigeons of the Seven Woods
> Make their faint thunder, and the garden bees

203

Hum in the lime-tree flowers; and put away
The unavailing outcries and the old bitterness
That empty the heart.

As she was planting trees in the ground, Yeats was sowing beauty in the language. Robert Gregory, however, had engendered a child who, Augusta feared, might displace them both at Coole.

But while she still had the power, Augusta treated Willie royally at Coole, as described by fellow guest Sir Ian Hamilton, a famous soldier and one of Augusta's O'Grady relations:

> No one even can have heard anyone play up to him like Lady Gregory. . . . All along the passage for some distance on either side of Yeats' door were laid thick rugs to prevent the slightest sound reaching the holy of holies—Yeats' bed. Down the passage every now and then would tiptoe a maid with a tray bearing (they told me) beef tea or arrowroot, though once I declare I distinctly smelt eggs and bacon. All suggestions that I could cheer him up a good deal if I went into his room and had a chat were met with horror. What I said about his groans and grumbles is hardly correct for they only came to me by hearsay through Lady Gregory and the servants. Actually I never once set eyes upon the aristocratic features of my friend Yeats on that occasion.

Robert Gregory was startled one evening when he called for a bottle of an especially fine vintage Torquey laid down by his father to find it was all gone, served bottle by bottle by his mother to Willie over the years while the rest of the guests were given more ordinary wine. Willie was not altogether pleased with Robert either, for he wrote, "I thought of this house, slowly perfecting itself and the life within it in ever-increasing intensity of labour, and then of its probably sinking away through courteous incompetence, or rather sheer weakness of will, for ability has not failed in young Gregory."

Augusta felt she should give up Coole to her son and daughter-in-law and the coming baby but she had no intention of doing so. This transgression was too great to be paid for with a play. Yet the issues in "the little miracle play" she and Willie had been working with for years suddenly became clear to her. In *The Travelling Man* a widow with a young son forgets her obligation to be continually thankful to Christ for her home and her son; she is not punished, but merely brought back to the proper state of mind by a miracle.

The play, set near Coole at Ballylee near the rising of the river, opens with a woman talking to her young son and making a cake to honor "the King of the World." She tells of being turned out of her job as a servant girl and having to "go walking the bare bog road, through the rough hills where there was no shelter to find, and the sharp winds going through me, and the red mud heavy on my shoes." She saw "a very tall man, the best I ever saw, bright and shining that you could see him through the darkness; and I knew him to be no common man." He led her to a house where the owner, who had been recently widowed, took her in and eventually married her. The woman continues, "I was kneeling to thank him, but he raised me up and he said, 'I will come to see you some other time. And do not shut up your heart in the things I give you,' he said, 'but have a welcome before me.'"

The woman goes out to borrow flour. A ragged traveling man holding a branch with both fruit and flowers comes in and talks with the child. Together, using the mother's dishes and bowls, they build a replica of the garden from which the wonderful branch came. The mother returns and is furious:

> Did ever anyone see the like of that! A common beggar, a travelling man off the roads, to be holding the child! To be leaving his ragged arms about him as if he was of his own sort! Get out of that, whoever you are, and quit this house or I'll call to some that will make you quit it.

He asks for shelter: "I walked the long bog road, the wind was going through me, there was no shelter to be got, the red mud of the road was heavy on my feet." (He is outside, as she had once been outside, and as Margaret was now, Augusta felt, outside asking to be taken into her place at Coole.) The woman refuses him shelter. Then she sees her best dishes on the floor; she slaps her son for getting them down. With humility but a great surge of underlying power, the traveling man tells her it was he who took them down. "I would not refuse these hands that were held out for them. If it was for the four winds of the world he had asked, I would have put their bridles into these innocent hands." She turns him out: "You are not fit to come into the house of any decent respectable person!" The room begins to darken as he leaves.

The child runs after him to return the branch. The mother is suddenly terrified the child might drown in the rising river, but he returns with the news that the man "is gone over the river."

> Mother: He couldn't do that. He couldn't go through the flood.
> Child: He did go over it. He was as if walking on water. There was a light before his feet.

She sees the branch with fruit and flowers and recognizes it as "a branch that is not of any earthly tree." She falls on her knees: "He is gone, he is gone, and I never knew him! He was the stranger that gave me all! He is the King of the world!"

Though the woman has proved herself unworthy of her safe home and her dear son, she gets to keep them. Augusta once again exhibits her creative capacity for bringing joy and safety out of threats and dangers. She continued the idea in her note to the play, quoting the folk story on which it was based, and which ended with the woman reproving Christ for her failure to share: "But why didn't you give me a heart that would like to divide it?" Christ grants her request: "From this out, whenever you have plenty in your hands, divide it freely for My sake." Augusta felt she had been granted—or had granted herself—permission to be better at her leisure.

Through the fall and winter of 1908 she worked at translating Molière's *Miser*, suffering from rheumatism for the first time in her life, so that her hands, like Michael's in *The Workhouse Ward*, were "twisted in ridges the same as an old cabbage stalk." Her one beautiful feature, of which she was so proud, was gone. (And the one feature in which she surpassed Maud Gonne, about whom Willie wrote, "You are more beautiful than any one, / And yet your body had a flaw: / Your small hands were not beautiful.") Augusta wrote Willie in late 1908, "I am very sorry, but I am afraid *The Miser* may not be ready in time. . . . I am ashamed, for I have never failed before to be up to time, but these last days I have gone to pieces, from want of sleep chiefly, and could do nothing."

On January 6, 1909, Richard Graham Gregory was born at Coole. Although Augusta did not admit it even to herself, her second reaction (after her first delighted woman's reaction to any birth) was consternation. The birth of her own son had greatly increased her own sense of importance and security. It had put her husband's relatives out of the hope of inhabiting Coole. She therefore felt that parenthood authorized Robert, and especially Margaret, to become Master and Mistress of Coole.

She went to Dublin in January to oversee rehearsals of *The Miser*—in which an old man is robbed of his wealth by his children, and which she had finished in time for the opening on January 21. She then returned to Coole. Margaret was up and about; the baby was well.

On February 2 Synge entered Elpis Nursing Home in Dublin, and by then everyone knew that he was going there to die.

The next day, February 3, Augusta had a sudden seizure and lay for a day and a night in her room, watched over by the bust of Dante

206

given her years ago by her husband, floating between life and death. When Yeats in Dublin got Robert's letter telling of her attack, he wrote:

> I did not recognize her son's writing at first, and my mind wandered, I suppose because I am not well. I thought my mother was ill and that my sister was asking me to come at once; then I remembered that my mother died years ago and that more than kin was at stake. She has been to me mother, friend, sister and brother. I cannot realize the world without her—she brought to my wavering thoughts steadfast nobility. All day the thought of losing her is like a conflagration in the rafters. Friendship is all the house I have.

Though the doctors later decided Augusta had had a cerebral hemorrhage, within two days she was able to write Yeats in pencil that she had "very nearly slipped away." Willie wrote and sent to her:

> Sickness brought me this
> Thought, in that scale of his:
> Why should I be dismayed
> Though flame had burned the whole
> World, as it were a coal
> Now I have seen it weighed
> Against a soul?

And added in his letter, "I mean by sickness and the scales that when one we love is ill we weigh them against a world without them." In his journal he wrote, "All Wednesday I heard Castiglione's phrase ringing in my memory, 'Never be it spoken without tears, the Duchess, too, is dead.' That slight phrase, which—coming where it did among the numbering of his dead—has often moved me till my eyes dimmed, and I felt all his sorrow as though one saw the worth of life fade for ever."

Augusta felt she was recovering very slowly, and wrote Willie, "I am still deeply depressed at the prospect of creative work and perhaps am off it altogether." In fact, if she had had a cerebral hemorrhage, her recovery was miraculously rapid and complete. At the end of the month Robert and Margaret, exhibiting no desire to take over Coole, went back to their artists' life in Paris, leaving their new son in her care. She, who had feared the loss of her position at Coole, was now indispensable. (She later said to Theodore Roosevelt about her grandchildren, "I looked upon the joy as one we had hardly a right to expect, a sort of bonus given at the end of life!") Her grandson became for her, like his father, part of the structure of her world, reinforcing her authorization to do what she wanted as long as it looked as if she were doing it for them.

Augusta was still recovering at Coole on March 24 when she got a letter from Willie which said: "In the early morning Synge said to the nurse, 'It is no use fighting death any longer,' and turned over and died." He was thirty-eight years old—like Augusta, a half-life artist, but one who did not survive the burdens of biology, temperament, or his membership in a narrow family and a dying class long enough to enjoy the full use of his talents.

Augusta wrote Willie, "This sudden silence is so awful. Yesterday you could have asked him his wishes & heard his thoughts—today, nothing." She wrote:

> You did more than any for him, you gave him his means of expression—You have given me mine, but I wld. have found something else to do, tho not anything coming near this, but I don't think Synge would have done anything but drift but for you & the theatre—I helped him far less—just feeding him when he was badly fed, & working for the staging of his plays, & in little other ways—& I am glad to think of it, for he got very little help from any other except you & myself—I wonder if he was ever offered a meal in Dublin except at the Nassau. . . . I am glad you were in Dublin as I couldn't be there, it seems a very lonely death indeed.

The next day she wrote him, "It is I who ought to have gone first—Death is a mysterious thing." And later to John Quinn, "I think I ought to have been taken in his place." She had, in fact, twenty-three more years to live.

Augusta was back in Dublin by April. With Synge's fiancée, Molly Allgood (who seemed more relieved than grieved), she and Willie put together and produced his last, unfinished play, *Deirdre of the Sorrows*, with Molly playing Deirdre. Augusta was better at dealing with Synge's executors, his brother-in-law and his lawyer, who were suspicious of poets and theater people. Willie wrote that "Lady Gregory who, unlike me (I always endow a stranger with much virtue) assumes that the man she has to deal with is more or less of a goose, within an hour got the will shown to Miss O'Neill [Molly Allgood, to whom Synge left an annuity] and Deirdre promised." Having access to but no control over Synge's papers, she copied out an angry poem he had written cursing the sister of a man who opposed *The Playboy*. It began, "Lord, confound this surly sister / Blight her brow with

208

blotch and blister." (Synge had told Willie that the woman was indeed overtaken with disasters, her husband contracting syphilis from a prostitute, which he passed on to her.) Augusta gave the copy of the poem to Willie, fearing Synge's family might destroy it.

Wealth and travel made Dublin battles easier to bear. In May she went for a restorative visit to Enid Layard in Venice:

> I am in my old state room, at the corner of the water floor, looking through four ivy trellised windows at the sunlight on the water, only hearing the splash of oars and a gondolier singing. The room is full of beautiful furniture, and when I came in last night, at midnight, from the long dusty journey and found the Italian housemaid who has welcomed me for twenty-five years on the steps to kiss my hand, and other servants bringing Chianti in a flask and soup in a silver bowl, it felt like fairyland!

Even fairyland, however, had its exertions, though of a different kind:

> ... as Lady L. and I came out from church, there was a sailor on the landing with a note from the Royal Yacht which had arrived, asking if the Queen, the Empress of Russia, Princess Victoria, a party of twelve altogether might come to lunch at 1.00 o'clock. Lady L. said, "Impossible." I said, "Possible." She said, "2.00 o'clock." I said, "1.30," and so it was. We came straight back and rushed to the kitchen, and the cook wasn't fussy and said it would be all right. Then I took the gondola and went to ask for the loan of the Curtis's servant, and sent to look for flowers. At 1.30 they arrived, the Queen looking younger than when I had seen her a year ago. . . .

Her energy returned. Within the month of her return to Coole in June of 1909, she had produced the typescript of a three-act play, *The Image*, in which she combines the idea of service to the community from her early tragedies with the comic bungling of her early comedies. The result, as she saw it, was "my chief play," though audiences and critics have been less enthusiastic. (George Moore called it "a bog slide!")

Her subtitle was "Secretum Meum Mehi" (My secret to myself). She explained in her note that exposing one's secret ideals leads to their destruction, that they crumble "at the touch of reality, like the wick that has escaped the flame and is touched by common air." In the play, two whales have been washed ashore and the priest decrees that the money from their oil is to "be laid out for the good and for the benefit of the whole headland." The three oldest men of the dis-

209

trict, who are chosen to oversee the plan, decide to spend the money on a statue to some great patriot. A "crazy mountainy man," Malachi Naughton, who has found a bit of board with the name Hugh O'Lorrha on it and who believes it is the name of a great hero he is meant to glorify, convinces them all to put up a statue to O'Lorrha. (The board is actually a plank from a wrecked fishing dinghy and "Hugh O'Lorrha" the name of an obscure fairy-tale character.) Each of the old men votes for O'Lorrha for his own private reasons. One—a stone-cutter who hopes to make the statue—votes for him because no one knows what he looks like, so people cannot "be coming and criticizing it, saying it would not resemble his features or his face." A very timid old man votes for O'Lorrha because he is afraid if he votes for either Dan O'Connell or Charles Stewart Parnell the supporters of the other will ever after be against him. And the third old man votes for O'Lorrha to make fools of the others who are taking the choice so seriously. Then, just as officials and townspeople arrive with a band and speeches to see the drawings for the statue, the three old men realize to their consternation that he is a fairy-tale hero and not the political patriot they thought. They also learn that one whale has been washed away and the other has been stolen. They were so busy planning how they were going to spend the money that no one bothered to make sure they really had it.

The characters all retreat into their small worlds, one saying, "But the time I'll go doing comfortable things again, it's within my own mind I'll go do them, the way I won't suffer in my skin." They are not really unhappy. Even Malachi Naughton is satisfied because the conventional designs for Hugh O'Lorrha's statue did not do him justice: "a thing the very spit of yourselves, and ugly out of measure. . . . Oh, my heart secret, wait till I'll hide you from them all, and they not able to understand a thing they are not fit to understand!"

The play is a parable about the disappointing state of Ireland, and of the Abbey in particular. Neither was turning out as Augusta and Yeats had visualized. When they started, there was a great feeling of excitement that, like the wealth from the whales in the play, created a great fund of energy to be devoted to the public good. Now, like the whales in the play, that feeling was gone. Instead, in its place there was, as she said about Hugh Lane's activities for Ireland, extraordinary animosity against anyone who was doing anything. Then there had been hope of great beauty; now she saw an uglier reality. In fact, Malachi Naughton's indignant rejection of the designs for Hugh O'Lorrha's statue—"the very spit of yourselves, and ugly out of measure"—is a paraphrase of her condemnation of the new realistic plays

210

she and Yeats were producing at the Abbey because they were the only plays forthcoming.

Yet, as she wrote in her note to the play, it is only by working for one's vision, even if it does not turn out as expected, that the world is made better:

> But if the dreamer had never tried to tell the dream that had come across him, even though to "betray his secret to the multitude" must shatter his own perfect vision, the world would grow clogged and dull with the weight of flesh and clay. And so we must say "God loves you" to the Image-makers, for do we not live by the shining of those scattered fragments of their dream?

She dedicated the play "to my nephews, Hugh Lane, and John Shawe-Taylor, image-makers." And she herself would have to be included in her salutation, "God love you," to the image-makers. The play and her note were an unusually straightforward attempt to explain and overcome her discouragement about the dispiriting state of Ireland.

She and Robert and Margaret were poorer at the end of July 1909 than they had been at the beginning. In that month fifteen tenants were granted rent reductions of approximately twenty percent by the Land Court. During the year two additional taxes, which fell chiefly on the landlord class, were imposed. Willie, who was staying at Coole when she received news of the rent reductions, wrote "Upon a House Shaken by the Land Agitation":

> How should the world be luckier if this house,
> Where passion and precision have been one
> Time out of mind, became too ruinous
> To breed the lidless eye that loves the sun?

Out of the fall of a class that had had few moments of greatness, Yeats was making great poetry. Augusta, however, gave no evidence of bathing in the beauty and emotion of these poems, which are really indirect (and often direct) praises of her, in the way she delighted in the audience response to her plays. She seemed to regard them more impersonally, as public testimonials to her goodness. A few years later, when she learned that Yeats's poem "To a Friend Whose Work Has Come to Nothing" was written to her and not to Hugh Lane as she had thought, she commented in her diary, "So I feel the richer for that!"

In August 1909 the Abbey accepted G. B. Shaw's *The Shewing-up of Blanco Posnet*. It had been banned in England by the censor, who, nevertheless, had no authority in Ireland. The proposed production led to one of the Abbey's many crises—episodes in the epic story of its survival. Augusta took over rehearsals, finding "an extraordinary interest and excitement in the work." She was then called upon to deal with the English officials at Dublin Castle, who threatened heavy fines and loss of the Abbey's patent if they gave the play. Augusta described her conference with the Lord Lieutenant:

> Mr. Yeats, until he joined the conference, being kept by the secretary, whether from poetical or political reasons, to the non-committal subject of Spring flowers; my grieved but necessary contumacy; our joint and immovable contumacy; the courtesy shown to us, and, I think, also by us; the kindly offers of a cup of tea; the consuming desire for that tea after the dust of the railway journey all across Ireland; our heroic refusal, lest its acceptance should in any way, even if it did not weaken our resolve, compromise our principles . . .

After the meeting she and Yeats consulted counsel and decided they could not afford the fines and would have to withdraw the play. But as a rehearsal was already scheduled, they went through with it. Afterward

> When we had left the Theatre and were walking through the lamp-lighted streets, we found that during those two or three hours our minds had come to the same decision, that we had given our word, that at all risks we must keep it or it would never be trusted again. . . .

(At the last dress rehearsal, according to Augusta's daughter-in-law, Margaret: "realising that all the English and Foreign critics had collected and that there was a stir, he [Yeats] asked her to let him take the rehearsal, saying he wished the reporters to think he had stage-managed it, and she is so used to giving way to him that she agreed.") The play was performed; there were no fines; the English officials had been bluffing. The immediate results was the enthusiastic approval of Nationalist groups, who usually disapproved of the Abbey. The most lasting result for Augusta, aside from the great satisfaction of having kept her word, was her pleasant friendship with G. B. Shaw and his wife (who were both, like herself, Anglo-Irish Protestants).

In 1909 her best plays were published in *Seven Short Plays*. Though individual plays had appeared in print before, this collection was her bid for a place in the literature of the world. And, indeed, on this small book and on these very short plays rests most of her claim to literary fame. There are no self-deprecatory notes. There is only a dedication: "to W. B. Yeats . . . one for every day of the week, because he likes them and because he has taught me my trade." She gives Yeats more of the credit, and more of the responsibility, than he deserved. And she exercises her unfailing skill as a promoter by noting that the plays are liked by the leading poet of the country. But, finally, she calls playwriting "my trade," a modest but, for her, an unusual assertion of importance. She took herself seriously as an artist. She said about playwriting, separating it from her feeling for Ireland: "Sein Finn—'we ourselves'—is well enough for the day's bread, but is not Mise Fein—'I myself' and the last word in Art?"

All the plays in the book, *Spreading the News, Hyacinth Halvey, The Jackdaw, The Travelling Man, The Gaol Gate, The Rising of the Moon*, and *The Workhouse Ward*, are masterpieces of abbreviated complexity. They all have the shimmer and solidity of tiny jewels. Being complete in themselves, they are separate from their author and do not refer to her. Yet they were powered by her deprivation, little explosions designed to allow her to let off steam and preserve the status quo. In 1909 such plays were behind her. She was moving into an emotional world that was more open, in which she felt less need to pose and hide. As a result, her plays are more straightforward, less complex, more descriptive.

Her next play, *Grania*, is a heroic attempt to explore her own personality. While writing it, she was working with Yeats and Molly Allgood on Synge's *Deirdre of the Sorrows*, which tells the most popular love story of the Irish epics: beautiful Deirdre choses Naisi for her lover, runs away from King Conchobar, to whom she is betrothed, and after Naisi is killed by him, kills herself rather than marry King Conchobar. Augusta's play is based on the other great love story of the epics, in which Grania choses Diarmuid for her lover, runs away from the great King Finn, to whom she is betrothed, and—when Diarmuid is brought to death by Finn's treachery—marries Finn. Augusta said she chose Grania rather than "lovely Deirdre, who when overtaken by sorrow made no good battle at the last," because Grania "had more power of will, and for good or evil twice took the shaping of her life into her own hands." Augusta also felt more affinity for Grania because Deirdre was a legendary beauty, and Grania was not.

As usual, even the plays Augusta chose to translate were part of the creative process of the plays she wrote, adding sidelights, presenting themes in another light, and while she was working on the two sad and weighty love stories from the epics, she translated *Mirandolina*, a comedy by Carlo Goldoni, the plot of which is a comic parallel to *Grania*. In it the charming innkeeper Mirandolina, in no hurry to marry the suitable man to whom her father betrothed her before he died, discovers a woman-hater lodging at her inn and sets out to conquer him. Her wooing is a comic version of the mysterious fated love Grania feels for Diarmuid, Mirandolina telling her woman-hater that she feels for him "this sympathy, this feeling for one another . . . sometimes found even between people who have never met. I myself felt for you what I have felt for no other." She succeeds so well with him that his attentions frighten her. She sends him away and gives her hand to Fabrizio, her father's choice, saying of her suitor: "He is gone and he will not return, and if the matter is over now I call myself lucky. Poor man, I succeeded only too well in making him care for me, and I ran an ugly risk. I don't want to do it again." She side-steps love, gives up her dangerous freedom, and makes the conventional marriage her father chose for her. Grania insists on having her love and gets into all sorts of trouble because of it, but in the end she too makes the conventional marriage her father chose for her.

Augusta's *Grania* begins with the heroine coming of her own free will to marry Finn, coming for his protection as a child comes to a father. But when Diarmuid, Finn's foster son and follower, appears, she recognizes him as the man she had seen and loved as a girl. She makes Diarmuid run away with her, but Diarmuid, who does not want to go, promises Finn he will not become her lover. ("The Authorities," as Augusta knew, were against sex.)

Grania and Diarmuid do become lovers after several years, and as soon as they do, Grania wants to go back to "some busy peopled place." She recognizes, as Augusta recognized, that love is not enough; one must have a place in the social structure; "for it is certain it is by the respect of others we partly judge even those we know through and through."

Diarmuid wants to go away to a mythical island.

Diarmuid: But beyond Aran, far out in the west, there is another island that is seen but once in every seven years.

Grania: Is that a real place at all? Or is it only in the nurses' tales?

Diarmuid: Who knows? There is no good lover but has seen it at some time through his sleep. It is hid under a light mist, away from the track of traders and kings and robbers. The harbour is well fenced to keep out loud creaking ships. Some fisherman to break through the mist at some time, he will bring back news of a place where there is a better life than in any lovely corner of the world that is known.

214

Grania: I am willing to go from this. We cannot stop always in
the darkness of the woods—but I am thinking it would be very
strange there and very lonesome.

Diarmuid wants to live in a fairy tale; Grania wants to live in the
world. What they are quarreling about is the reconciliation of love
with social power. To Grania's suggestion that they go to her father
and raise an army and make a truce with Finn, Diarmuid replies,
"There is no going back for us, Grania, and you know that well yourself." In the legend this is exactly what they do, but Augusta believed
there was no room in the social structure for lovers.

Grania accepts what she can get, and when Finn's messenger (who
is Finn in disguise) overtakes them, she proudly defies him: "Tell
Finn you saw a woman no way sad or afraid, but as airy and high-
minded as a mountain filly would be challenging the winds of March!"
She does not lose her courage when she loses her love.

Diarmuid is brought in dying of a wound he has received from the
King of Foreign. He regains consciousness before he dies, sees Finn
and thinks they are both dead. He tries to remember to ask pardon for
some offense he has given Finn. When Finn reminds him of Grania,
Diarmuid replies, "It would be a very foolish thing, any woman at all
to have leave to come between yourself and myself. I cannot but laugh
at that." As Augusta wrote long ago, "Perchance not so in heaven
above, / But here, a *woman* may not love." There were simply no men
free to love her.

Finn, realizing he loved Diarmuid far more than he loved Grania,
gives her up. Like the "little welcomed girl" at Roxborough, Grania
is left with no one who cares for her. She refuses to be rejected:

He [Diarmuid] will think to come whispering to you, and you
alone in the night time. But he will find me there before him! He
will shrink away lonesome and baffled! I will have my turn this
time. It is I will be between him and yourself, and will keep him
outside of that lodging forever!

Grania forces herself on Finn because she is jealous of Diarmuid,
jealous as if they were children competing for a parent's love.

Augusta wrote that "Love itself, with its shadow Jealousy, is the
true protagonist," but really the true protagonist is the little girl with
six sisters and nine brothers who had to break down the closed door
of heaven to find someone to love her. She reveals in *Grania* what she
gives no hint of elsewhere: that she was enormously jealous, that she
was seeking, through her religious conversion, through her devoted

215

service, through her goodness, "Not universal love, but to be loved alone."

The play is a hologram of her personality. Grania's marriage to Finn is like Augusta's submission to "the Authorities," whether represented by her parents or God and his cloud of witnesses. It was a submission for which explanations could be offered. But the effort to think in terms of cause and effect was difficult because, like the characters in her comedies, and like most people, Augusta thought backward and forward from the existing situation, allowing it to make its own past in her mind so that to her the most powerful reason for its happening was simply that it had happened. The attempt to explain and the attempts to free herself of the consequences were concurrent activities. No final explanation was possible until she had at last changed her situation. That never happened; Augusta was always married to Finn, but her writing of *Grania* marks her emotional coming of age. The play was written not by a good child, or even by a sneaky child, but by an adult trying to understand, explain, and take responsibility for her actions.

Grania reveals a mind-set and an emotional development very similar to that revealed by Synge in his *Playboy*. Just as Christy tries to kill his father and romances Pegeen, so Grania runs away from Finn and makes Diarmuid accept her as a lover. When Christy's father comes back, Pegeen turns on him just as, when Finn returns, Diarmuid confesses that he loves Finn more than he ever loved Grania. Both lovers prove unworthy, and as a result, both Christy and Grania turn back to the authority from which they had attempted to escape. Both have gained confidence and power, Christy telling his father, "I am master of all fights from now out." Grania has gained somewhat less, but she at least comes to Finn as an equal instead of a child.

The most fascinating and the saddest aspect of both plays is that when the main characters turn back to the authority from which they attempted to escape, it is not because of any weakness in themselves or any overwhelming strength in the authority—but because those they loved are unable to love and value them in return.

Augusta told more about herself in *Grania* than she wanted known. In July, August, and September of 1910 she wrote three one-act plays: *The Deliverer*, produced within a month; *The Full Moon*, produced in two months; and *Coats*, produced in three months. *Grania*, which was in final typescript by August of 1910, was not performed during her lifetime. She said she could not find the right actors. (Appropriately, considering her desire to keep it secret, since her death

216

it has been produced more frequently in Irish translation than in English.)

None of the three short plays that accompanied *Grania* into the world is particularly good, but they all refer to an emotional world that is healthier and more open. *The Deliverer*, her only play powered by spite and anger—emotions she had not heretofore permitted herself to exhibit in public—is about the Jews' rejection of Moses as their would-be deliverer. In her note Augusta says she was writing primarily about the Irish rejection of Charles Stewart Parnell, who was hounded from office in 1890 and died shortly after. In her play, as in the Bible, Moses learns he is a Jew and assumes leadership of his people's struggle to escape from bondage. At first the people, especially the women, praise him. Then they turn against him because of his religion: "He to have broke out of their creed, and not to have joined in our own, would not be a fitting leader for ourselves." They turn against him because of his attempt to cross class lines. When he appears in rags instead of his gorgeous Egyptian clothes, they say, "He has put on poor clothes like our own for a mockery." Finally, they turn against him because of his assumption of power over them. When he breaks up a quarrel between two Jews, they turn on him viciously, stone him, and throw him to the caterwauling Egyptian cats. Augusta departs so far from the Bible story that when the Jews see Moses passing slowly, with his clothes torn and bloodstained, they insist that he is dead and they are seeing a ghost. In a final allusion to the fickleness of the Irish people, one of the women says, "I wish I didn't turn against him. I am thinking he might be an angel."

The emotional charge Augusta had felt at Parnell's death twenty years earlier (when she was against his politics) could not have supplied the indignation and contempt for the people she expresses throughout this play. Like Moses in her play, she herself had been exposed to the contempt of the people for her class, her religion, and her success. (Mary Colum reported, "I remember once partly overhearing an argument between her and one of the Irish members of Parliament at the Abbey Theater, in which she must have gained the upper hand. On her leaving the seat beside him with her studied graciousness he pressed his fingers to his forehead and said in a very loud and harassed voice, 'Oh, God, oh, God, this Protestant tact! I can't bear it!' ") For the moment, Augusta—like Yeats, who cried out against "the daily spite of this unmannerly town"—was fed up with service.

The handwritten version of this play is dated July 10–15, and on

217

the 25th Augusta was insulted personally and directly for her service to Yeats. She, with Edmund Gosse and several others, had been working to get a Civil List pension for Yeats. After receiving a courteous letter from her about the matter, Gosse wrote unaccountably rudely in reply:

> I cannot express my surprise at the tone of your letter. If this is your attitude, I wish to have no more to do with the matter, and I am lost in wonder at what can have induced you to interfere in an affair when your opinion was not asked, and when you seemed to intend neither to give any help or take any trouble.

Augusta, insulted by Gosse, was more upset that Willie did not immediately come to her defense. A few days later, in an unrelated discussion, Yeats commented, "I am amused with Dumas's people. They do good and evil in obedience to a code. They never give a moment's thought to any moral question—all that is settled by their code. They must have been very dull to know. Never for a moment has anybody a modern mind." Augusta replied immediately, "A code is necessary; there is not time to reason things out." Yeats realized she was thinking of his failure to act in regard to Gosse's letter:

> I come to see that Lady Gregory and Robert expected me to act at once, on a code. Instead of asking, "Why has Gosse done this?" instead of being, what is worse really, interested in his character and motives, I should have been in a very simple state of mind. I should have spoken of him with contempt, or written to him with contempt—there was nothing else to do.

Yet Yeats was committed, and proudly committed, to a slower and more complicated method of judgment:

> Since I was fifteen and began to think, I have mocked at that way of looking at the world, as if it was a court of law where all wrong actions were judged according to their legal penalties. All my life I have, like every artist, been proud of belonging to a nobler world, of having chosen the slow, dangerous, laborious path of moral judgment.

But even the slow, laborious path did not lead him to defend his friend. He wrote several letters which, in the end, Augusta asked him not to send, and finally he judged himself: "I neither dealt with the matter like an artist, nor as a man of the world." (In the end, because of the efforts of Gosse, Yeats was awarded a Civil List pension of £150 per year.)

Coats, the first draft of which is dated September 14, 1910, is about a quarrel between two friendly editors of rival newspapers that, says Augusta in her note, "is so violent you think it can never be healed, but the ordinary circumstances of life force reconciliation. They are the most powerful of all." Willie and Augusta too were reconciled by "the ordinary circumstances of life." They needed each other too much to permit a quarrel, even about the most basic differences, to separate them.

The real-life quarrel was much more serious than the dramatic one. In Augusta's play the two editors, who eat together at the local hotel every week, accidentally exchange coats, and each one finds in the pocket his own obituary, providently written by the other to have on hand when needed. They are both outraged, but after a full and satisfying expression of their anger, they sit down and finish their dinner. One remarks to the waiter that there had been "some sort of battle," to which the waiter replies, "Ah, what signifies? There to be more of battles in the world, there would be less of wars."

The emotional impetus for *Coats* being her anger at the Gosse letter, the play was impoverished because she excluded from it the elements of the situation that would require her to look beyond her own personal code to a broader and more complex view of human nature. Unlike many of her earlier plays which give the impression of several streams of emotion coming together to find release, this play has only the one explosion of the code-bound quarrel.

Though *Coats* is not as good as her earlier comedies, it indicates a happier emotional situation. Written in response to an immediate emotional conflict, it indicates that after her huge effort with *Grania* she was caught up on her backlog of emotional conflicts and freer to live in the present moment. Also, it is her first play in which two fairly normal people care for each other without disaster. Until now she had been so shy, not only of love but even of affection, that she did not show these emotions existing except in people who were somehow hidden away and out of contact with ordinary standards, like the paupers in *The Workhouse Ward*.

Simultaneously with *Coats* she wrote *The Full Moon*, a sequel to *Hyacinth Halvey*, in which her young hero, confined to the little world of Cloon, succeeds in breaking out. The inhabitants of Cloon from her earlier peasant comedies, *The Jackdaw*, *Spreading the News*, and *Hyacinth*, have reassembled, as if for Hyacinth, and for her, to say goodbye to as he leaves.

When the play opens, Hyacinth has been living in Cloon for a year, "an example and a blessing to the whole of the town." He is still liv-

ing in lodgings opposite the police and next to the priest. He is about
to be engaged to the priest's housekeeper, "a fortied girl," to be made
Clerk of the Union, and to open a little shop to "be keeping the accounts, the way you would not spend any waste time."

He enjoys his authority and the respect with which he is treated,
but he is also sick of the confinement and desperate to get away. When
he hears that the next day is Fair Day in his old home of Carrow, he
timidly suggests he would like to go "for one night only—and see what
the lads are doing." The villagers will not let him get away:

> To go away from Cloon, is it? And why would you think to do
> that, and the whole town the same as a father and mother to you?
> Sure, the sergeant would live and die with you, and there are no
> two from this to Galway as great as yourself and the priest. To
> see you coming up the street, and your Dublin top-coat around
> you, there are some would give you a salute the same nearly as
> the Bishop.

Cracked Mary is the only one who recognizes his problem: "A fine
young man to be shut up and bound in a narrow little shed, and the
full moon rising." The villagers believe they themselves are going
mad with the light of the full moon. Cracked Mary suggests they let
the moon decide who is mad; she opens the door and the light falls on
Hyacinth. It takes all this for him to realize that "I made a great mistake coming into this place," and "it is foolishness kept me in it ever
since. It is too big a name was put upon me."

The villagers try to hold him, but he runs out and catches the evening train, declaring, "The wide ridge of the world before me, and to
have no one to look to for orders; that would be better than roast and
boiled and all the comforts of the day."

The power of "the ordinary circumstances of life" appeared so
strong to Augusta that the only way to escape them was, as she said
in her note, by the "call of some of those unruly ones who give in to no
limitations, and dance to the sound of music that is outside this world.
. . . Where he is now I do not know, but anyway he is free." Though
Hyacinth's freedom has no content, its achievement was nevertheless
a real accomplishment for Augusta. She too was feeling that she had
fewer people "to look to for orders."

One of the people she did not have was Miss Horniman. Miss Horniman, who had decided to put no more money into the Abbey aside
from her promised subsidy, had been harassing Willie and Augusta
for the past year over a series of trivial difficulties at the theater. (Her
letters to Willie were now addressed to "Dear Managing Director.")

Then on May 6, 1910, Edward VII died. Willie was in France visiting Maud Gonne. Augusta was at Coole. The twenty-three-year-old Lennox Robinson, in charge at the Abbey, wired Augusta asking what he should do. (Augusta had a favorite joke about the mindlessness of subordinates—the railway stationmaster in India who wired headquarters: "TIGER ON THE PLATFORM, PLEASE WIRE ORDERS!") Augusta's wire, "SHOULD CLOSE THROUGH COURTESY," arrived after the matinee had started. The damage being done, Robinson kept the theater open for the evening performance as well. Miss Horniman was infuriated and demanded an apology. Not satisfied with the explanation that the opening was accidental, which she took to be "a regret that it was not deliberate," she threatened withdrawal of her subsidy. Though arbitration awarded the remainder of the subsidy, due to lapse in six months anyway, to the theater, Augusta wrote Willie, "I have been thinking of Miss H's behavior through sleepless nights.... I have come to the conclusion we ought to give up the £400 subsidy still owing and be free of her." Miss Horniman, as irascible, generous, and unpredictable as ever, let them assume the lease to the Abbey buildings and contents for £1,400, a fraction of their value, then wrote them in January 1911, "Unless the £1000 due to me be paid before Jan 23rd . . . I must consult my lawyer as to taking proceedings against the Directors. They have possession of my property & have not paid for it."

Miss Horniman was paid. A tour in England netted £500. A further campaign in 1911, including London lectures by Yeats and G. B. Shaw, netted an endowment fund of £2,169 and an invitation from theatrical producers Liebler and Company to play in America with expenses guaranteed. Yeats and Augusta had outstayed their difficult patron, and both breathed a great sigh of relief. In *Our Irish Theatre* Augusta exercised her famous tact: "I feel sure Miss Horniman is well pleased that we have been able to show our gratitude by thus proving ourselves worthy of her great and generous gift." She had written Willie earlier what could be a valediction on their first ten years: "We have certainly seen a good deal of the seamy side of human nature since we began this theatre. E. Martyn's childishness, George Moore's pirating, the succeeders' vanity, Miss Horniman's malignant arrogance."

Augusta began to relax. Her next play, started in April 1911, is about freeing oneself from impossibly high standards. *The Bogie Men* involves two chimneysweeps who meet accidentally in a shed by the coach stop. Each has come to meet his cousin whom he believes to be rich and powerful. At first they are not pleased to see each other: "It is not one of my own trade I came looking to meet with." (Augusta's observation that she preferred to keep company with her superiors is relevant here.)

The two sweeps discuss the troubles their grand cousins have caused them:

Darby: I never had a comrade lad.

Taig: My mother that would hit me a crack if I made free with any of the chaps of the village, saying that would not serve me with Dermot, that had a good top-coat and was brought up to manners and behavior.

Darby: My own mother that drew down Timothy on me the time she'd catch me going with the lads that had their pleasure out of the world, slashing tops and pebbles, throwing and going on with games.

They eventually realize what the audience has known all along: they are the two cousins. Both are relieved to find the difficult example that had been held over them was only a bogie man, and the two go out together sharing their salted herring and porter. Darby declares: "It is great things I will be doing from this out, we two having nothing to cast up against one another. To be quit of Timothy the bogie and to get Taig for a comrade, I'm as proud as the Crown of France." Taig refuses to be swept away from reality: "Be easy now. We are maybe not clear of chimneys yet." They accept their lot in life, one declaring, "I am free from patterns of high up cousins from this out. I'll be a pattern to myself."

Augusta—who had lived and not died, whose position at Coole had been strengthened and not weakened by her grandson, who had published her *Seven Short Plays*—made a partial peace with herself. She felt relieved of the tremendous strain of trying to rise in the world. But, unlike the chimneysweeps, she was relieved not because she had discovered success was a bogie man but because she had actually risen.

IX

Triumph in America

TOURING WITH THE ABBEY: 1911–1913

I struck the board, and cry'd, No more:
I will abroad!
GEORGE HERBERT, "The Collar"

A U G U S T A thought she would not go to America with Willie and the Abbey company, which had been engaged for a three-month tour beginning in September 1911. She wrote John Quinn, "They wanted me to go also, but I have refused. Ireland holds me too close." Ireland held her too close in a number of ways. Margaret was pregnant with her second child. In May, Augusta's brother Algernon had died. Violet Martin wrote, greatly over-estimating his place in her life, that "the gap made by Algernon must be a great one. This must darken all your work for a time." In fact the death of her nephew John Shawe-Taylor, also in May of 1911, was a greater grief.

However, at the last minute a new actress was hired to play Pegeen Mike in Synge's *Playboy*. Willie insisted he needed Augusta to coach her in the required dialect. Augusta stayed on at Coole until the birth of her granddaughter Augusta Anne on September 11. Then she left a christening cake, borrowed a car because the trains were on strike, was driven southeast across Ireland to Queenstown, and sailed for America aboard the *Cymric*, arriving on September 29, 1911.

America was a liberation. Her real opinions on a variety of matters tumbled out effortlessly—though she continued to be circumspect

223

about *The Playboy*. She discovered she was a delightful public speaker. She discovered that rather than thinking she was older than she was, people thought she was younger—and she was only fifty-nine. Unlike the Dublin public, who regarded her with suspicion, the American public, she found, were delighted by her superior manner because they did not automatically infer from it their own inferiority. And she felt so securely isolated from the Irish-Americans who insisted on rioting against *The Playboy* that she enjoyed the excitement and her own calm handling of crisis after crisis. She, who liked to associate with her superiors, became friends with former President Theodore Roosevelt. She and John Quinn, who had long since established definite limits on their emotional lives, fell in love with each other.

She went to America expecting good things. She had her horoscope drawn in 1908 and 1910, and both astrologers predicted great things for 1912: "This year promises happiness and prosperity," and "About the end of 1911 and the beginning of 1912, a great benefit will come into the life." She mentioned these predictions to friends several times when 1912 did turn out to be a very good year.

Crossing the ocean toward John Quinn, she wrote a one-act play, *McDonough's Wife*, about a passionate man in love—but screened herself and her audience from the full impact of this love by having the woman to whom it is directed completely out of the picture. McDonough, the piper, returns from a sheep-shearing festival at Augusta's old home, Cregroostha, to find his wife dead of a miscarriage. He mourns because he has spent all his money and cannot give her a great funeral. He then realizes he himself has the power to honor her:

> But I am of the generation of Orpheus, and have in me the breed of his master! And of Raftery and Carolan and O'Daly and all that made sounds of music from this back to the foundation of the earth!

He plays a lament so moving that everyone at the fair outside wants to take part in the funeral. He goes out rejoicing:

> If you got no great honour from your birth up, and went barefoot through the first of your youth, you will get great respect now and will be remembered in the times to come.
>
> There is many a lady dragging silk skirts through the lawns and flower knots of Connacht, will get no such grand gathering of people at the last as you are getting on this day.
>
> It is the story of the burying of McDonough's wife will be written in the book of the people!

John Quinn would not be called upon to bury her, but he would fight valiantly for her. Augusta was preparing herself to accept his attention.

She later gave the manuscript of the play, including the ship's menu on which she wrote her first draft, to John Quinn with a note:

> . . . and being still new to me I think it worth offering to you, Dear John Quinn, but you shall have a better if a better one should come, tho' this will be all the more valuable if it should be my last. [She wrote fourteen more.] I don't suppose anyhow you will be able to read a word of it.

Augusta arrived in Boston to be met by Willie and the press. Willie then left the Abbey players, fifteen of them, all under thirty, in her care, gave a few lectures, and returned to Ireland. When Augusta discovered that the American producers expected her to have a maid, she wrote, "If I had known, I might have brought out someone for the spree!" Augusta was different in America—even her language was freer. Like many another fortunate emigrant, she left her cloud of witnesses at home.

An Abbey actress described Augusta in the early days of the theater "drawing up her short rather bulky figure, squaring her shoulders and smiling rather grimly in a thin-lipped manner in the face of opposition." Away from the constrictions of home, she blossomed. The Boston reporter who interviewed her on her arrival described her:

> Although she confesses to grandmotherhood, she seems scarcely beyond middle life, and there is youth in her smile which makes one forget the grey hair smoothed away from her forehead. Her eyes, keen and dark, light up with a quizzical expression as she talks. She gives the impression of one who has found and will find much that is pleasant in the things about her.

The reaction was the same everywhere. Another Boston reporter wrote:

> Lady Gregory is of stately figure, with the grace and beauty of a true gentlewoman. She dresses entirely in black, which emphasizes the rosiness of her complexion, for Lady Gregory is as fair as the bloom of a flower. Her head is crowned with a wealth of luxuriant hair that was once a deep velvety black, but which is now fast turning a silvery grey. Two very kind, very merry and indeed very young brown eyes look out at you and smile a cordiality which heightens your pleasure.

Augusta must have felt her mother's prayer that she grow in stature and in beauty had at last been answered. The third Boston reporter wrote:

> Under the shadow of her wide hat, her still-rounded cheeks bright with the earnestness of her subject, Lady Gregory talked to me of the new Irish drama and its playwrights. And although Lady Gregory is no longer a young woman, it was of Romney that I thought as I looked at her, and of how he would have painted her—the eagerness, the bloom, and the tantalizing shadow of the hat. Then she lifted her head and I saw her kind-shrewd eyes. "Franz Hals!" I exclaimed to myself. . . .

Augusta was delighted and sent the papers home: "It was my first experience of this way of giving news, and I was amused by it." She wrote that only one reporter was unkind, possibly because the reporter wanted to talk about *The Playboy* and she did not, "saying that I had no sense of humour and that my dress (Paris!) 'had no relation to the prevailing modes.'" This reporter, seeing some of the sternness that almost every artist who painted her over-emphasized, also said that "Lady Gregory's face is of the American Indian type of Irish face, to use an Irishism." Another reporter, however, thought it necessary to say, "Lady Gregory is quite unlike her published portraits."

In Boston there was a letter in one of the newspapers denouncing the plays but no organized opposition. On the night of her arrival "I went to the Plymouth Theatre and found a large audience, and a very enthusiastic one, listening to the plays. I could not but feel moved when I saw this, and remembered our small beginnings and the years of effort and discouragement."

She was invited to lecture at Harvard, Yale, and Bryn Mawr. In the early days in Dublin, Mary Colum remembered her chilling refusal to address a group of Irish college women, on which occasion "she rose to her feet and said with her elegant lisp, 'I never speak except through the beautiful voices of our players in our little theater.'" When, in America, she learned she was expected to "say a few words" at clubs and meetings, she was "quite miserable" and said she would prefer a regular lecture so people would know "what they were coming for instead of having a stranger let loose on them just as they were finishing their lunch." To Robert she wrote that her extemporaneous remarks were nevertheless quite successful. "Mrs. Jack Gardner who is the leader of fashion and has a large collection of pictures, came and seized my hands and said, 'You are a darling, a darling, a darling!' I told her I should like to try a reading or a little lecture of my own, and she offered her home." Augusta wrote that her lecture was a success; she kept to her time and referred to her notes only occasionally. She also enjoyed herself very much.

Her American lectures reveal how satisfactory playwriting must have been for someone who wanted to be reassured—as Augusta did—that she was on the path to heaven. One of her rules was that all irrelevancy must be eliminated: "In a play you must hurry to the gate of heaven or it will be shut before you." She explained the great advantage of the Abbey, "that unofficial school of playwriting," as the opportunity it gave to see one's plays acted. "An audience cannot tell a lie. Critics may lie from the best of motives, but if an audience is bored, it will cough, if it is amused, it will laugh. Immediately it rewards you, or convicts you of sin."

G. B. Shaw was quoted in a newspaper article about her: "If ever there was a person doomed from the cradle to write for the stage, to break through every social obstacle to get to the stage—nay, to invent and create a theatre if no theatre existed—that person is the author of 'Hyacinth Halvey,' of 'The Workhouse Ward' and of 'The Rising of the Moon.' " Augusta became so enthusiastic about herself as a dramatist that she declared, "Had I not become interested in the Gaelic movement . . . I should doubtless have turned my attention to the music halls of England." The article continued:

> Perhaps no other field of endeavor has ever seriously presented itself to her mind. "The music halls appeal to me because they reach such an enormous audience—all of the poorer members of society who are financially unable to patronize the first-class theatres. I have, for instance, seen the Tivoli Music Hall in London crowded with spectators who paid perhaps sixpence apiece for admission. See what a tremendous range that gives anybody who succeeds in pleasing their fancy."

This ambition is not mentioned in her published writings and makes a delightful contrast to Yeats's famous and exaggerated farewell to the Abbey, written in 1919, in which he tells her he is no longer interested in the Abbey because "I want to create for myself an unpopular theatre and an audience like a secret society where admission is by favour and never to many." Augusta and Willie's ambitions for their theater would diverge like those of parents with differing hopes for their child.

Augusta, going in a different direction, wanted, and found in America, an even larger audience. In the hope of giving that audience what it wanted, the Abbey players had brought over a large repertoire of plays by her, by Synge, T. C. Murray, St. John Ervine, and William Boyle—but only *Cathleen ni Houlihan* by Yeats—though Augusta was to declare on this tour, as she always declared, that her only hope in working for the Irish theater was to get his plays produced. To Maurice Browne and his group of actors in Chicago who were on the verge of establishing the Chicago Little Theater Society, she said, "We had one liability which you will not incur; we confused theatric with literary values." Augusta had chosen theatric values.

The entire visit to America was just the sort of drama she played best, with herself cast as national literary heroine defending Ireland and art against ignorant slanders. The opposition to *The Playboy* in America was a distillation of the confused but organized opposition at home. When it manifested itself in Ireland, it disrupted the never consolidated efforts of all those working for Ireland's freedom from England. It had to be lived with and suffered through. When it showed itself in America, it could be isolated, it could be attacked for the ignorance and slander it was.

Irish-Americans who saw *The Playboy* as an attack on the dignity of Ireland did not attempt to explain to the public how the play offended that dignity or to present their version of the truth. They attempted simply to prevent the play from being shown. Mary Colum several years later wrote that, though she had met "some of those who demonstrated against the play, I do not think I ever met anyone who was perfectly certain why he or she protested."

On October 28 the *Gaelic American* was rather mild in its denunciation of the Abbey players: "The company which insists on presenting that atrocity insults the whole Irish race and should be boycotted by every decent Irish man and woman in the cities where they go." By November 18 the attack had become more personal, and expanded from Synge and Yeats to Augusta: "When a woman chooses to put herself in the company of male blackguards she has no right to appeal for respect for her sex." From a denunciation of *The Playboy* the protests spread to attack almost all the plays, including Augusta's. A writer in the *National Hibernian* declared that, "Having seen them all, I have this to say, that, with one or two exceptions, they are the sloppiest, and in most cases the vilest, and the most character-assassinating things, in the shape of plays it has ever been my misfortune to see." In a way, the ignorance and misplaced vehemence were a comfort because they presented themselves so obviously. Augusta, smiling, would say to reporters about *The Playboy*, "I will admit that I have some sympathy for the honest objectors to it," but no one ever asked for her objections.

The players were denounced by some Catholic priests, who ordered their parishioners to keep away: "Nothing but hell-inspired ingenuity and a satanic hatred of the Irish people and their religion could suggest, construct, and influence the production of such plays." Augusta, well practiced in avoiding conflict with the Catholic Church, merely pointed out that, with two exceptions, all of the players were Catholic and found nothing objectionable in the plays. (When Theodore Roosevelt asked her if she were Catholic, she replied quickly, "All who do anything are Protestants.")

There was little organized opposition during the performances in Boston, but to be on the safe side Augusta gave tickets to a group of Harvard boys, who cheered "whenever there was a sign of coming disapproval." The players moved on, with one-night stands in Providence and New Haven, to Washington. Augusta described her lecturing and sightseeing along the way:

> and the roar of Niagara Falls, and the stillness of the power house that sends that great energy to create light and motion a hundred or two hundred miles away, and of many another widespreading, kindly city where strangers welcomed me, and I seemed to say good-bye to friends. Dozing in midnight trains, I would remember, as in a dream, "the flight of a bird through a lighted hall," the old parable of human life.

In Washington she was invited to the White House to meet President Taft. (She wrote Robert that she preferred her visit to Roosevelt at Oyster Bay.) When she was invited to address the Gaelic Society in Washington, a Jesuit newspaper declared that the invitation was forged and had been repudiated by the society. John Quinn, "in possession of the original invitation and printed programs bearing Lady Gregory's name, offered to donate a thousand dollars to charity if the charges were proven, the editor alternatively to make public apology. Nothing more was heard of the matter."

John Quinn and Augusta finally met in New York for the first time since 1904. He did not go to Boston to meet her because of a two-year-old quarrel with Yeats over Yeats's indiscreet remarks about Quinn's mistress, and he had missed her when she passed through New York on the way to Washington. He accompanied her to the theater for the first three nights of their run. The first night there was riotous opposition. The actress playing Pegeen Mike was hit by a potato. Rosaries and stink bombs rained on the stage. Men began booing and crying, "Shame! Shame!" Augusta left her box, went around to the fireplace opening in the set, and whispered to the players to keep playing but to spare their voices, as the scene would be repeated. Disturbers were removed by the police and the play continued. Afterward she made a short speech from the stage, which was described by John Butler Yeats (Willie's father had come to America in 1907 when he was sixty-eight and refused to go home): "so clever, witty, with the good nature of what the Americans call 'perfect poise.' . . . You gave the Giant Stupidity a mortal thrust with a courteous smile." John Quinn was "astonished at Lady Gregory's unshaken calm."

The second night the audience was chastened by the presence of Theodore Roosevelt, who accepted Augusta's invitation to join her in her box. During intermission he met and congratulated the players. At the end of the evening, when he escorted Augusta from the box, "We found the whole route to the door packed, just a narrow lane we could walk through, and everyone taking off hats and looking at him with real reverence and affection. . . . It was an extraordinary kindness that he did us."

The third night the disturbance was minimal. Rowdies confined themselves to hanging around the stage door and insulting the actresses as they appeared: " 'Ah, ye sluts, ye,' 'Ah, ye bitches, ye,' 'Ah, ye whores, ye.' " For the first time the audience could hear the play in peace, and they laughed throughout.

John Quinn was so impressed he took Augusta to Tiffany's and bought her a watch. (Augusta did not tell him that in Ireland the gift of a watch was a symbol of engagement.) She reported to Robert: "Quinn has given me a very small and simple gold watch bracelet, I like it, though it doesn't look the 180 dollars I saw on the ticket when I tried it on. . . . Quinn won't go bankrupt at present anyway over it."

Moving on, the players were arrested in Philadephia (which created sympathy for them in Dublin) under a law permitting the city council to suppress immoral plays. Augusta had written beforehand, "I should like to avoid arrest, because of the publicity; one would feel like a suffragette," but once it happened, she wrote, "I feel like Wilhelm Meister going through ever-fresh adventures with the little troupe." Quinn arrived dramatically from New York just as witnesses were being examined. One of the actors described Augusta: "She sat amongst us, looking like a queen. She placed all her trust in our lawyer, John Quinn, who was a tower of strength." Afterward she wrote Bernard Shaw:

I am furious! Philadelphia is so pompous—and lets itself be governed by little political cliques of publicans and the like. Our

230

whole tour has been very amusing and successful. I like America very much indeed in spite of it all—it is a great excitement seeing a new country at my time of life, and since Philadelphia I feel any romantic adventure possible!

Romantic adventure was in fact, immediately at hand. John Quinn returned to New York while she and the players waited in Philadelphia for the verdict. Her next letter to him begins with a new salutation: "Dear, dear John:"

The company are still stammering when they speak of you, even [Lennox] Robinson says you "came like an Angel." I never think I felt prouder in my life, and I have had my proud days, when you made that wonderful attitude of deference and proclaimed yourself a friend.

The tour was so successful that Liebler and Company extended their engagement three months. The players moved on through Pittsburgh, Richmond, and Indianapolis to Chicago, where Augusta received a letter decorated with a sketch of a revolver and a coffin, telling her, "*Your fate is sealed.* Never again shall you gase [sic] on the barren hilltops of Connemara. *Your doom is sealed.* Irelands make believe friends cannot parade in sheeps clothing under my scrutinizing eye. I scent them to the lair. . . ." She carefully saved the letter and reproduced it and the sketch in her history of the Abbey Theatre. She continued, however, to walk to the theater alone through the snowy streets, explaining in a letter home, "I don't feel anxious, for I don't think from the drawing that the sender has much practical knowledge of firearms."

The players stayed on in Chicago until the end of February. Augusta reported to Robert on the accommodations: "I have nice rooms now on the 9th floor, there are 22 floors altogether, the place riddled with telephones and radiators, and I was glad to hear the voice of a fat housemaid from Mayo a while ago." She had written earlier that "There is not much for the housemaid to do, there is a brush attached to a hose that sucks up the dust in no time."

Augusta spent the last few days of the tour visiting John Quinn in his New York apartment. The players presented Quinn with a silver cup, a replica of the famous Ardagh Chalice, engraved with lines from Augusta's *Image* about Dan O'Connell: "He had a gift of sweetness of tongue. Whatever cause he took in hand it was as good as gained." They gave a last matinee in Boston and sailed for home on March 6, to be welcomed in Dublin with speeches and a banquet. The Dublin public wanted a performance too, and, as Augusta wrote John Quinn, "I was luckily there for the opening show which would not have come off otherwise, some of the players ill, and no clothes and everything upside down, but a great success in the end, and the greatest enthusiasm."

Augusta was back at Coole on March 16, 1912, the day after her sixtieth birthday, unpacking her suitcases and typing a letter to John: "We all landed safely. But, oh, John, I don't think I want you to land at Queenstown when you next come!" She described the carelessness and inefficiency which "came with rather too sudden a shock even for a returned Irishwoman, and I was thankful there were no returned Americans with us!" In the same envelope she sent a handwritten letter on small blue Coole stationery beginning, "My very dear John," and ending, "How good you were to me! How happy I was with you! How much I love you!"

John Quinn wrote her the same way, typed letters, the carbons of which he carefully saved, and handwritten letters he asked her to burn. A note of hers to him says, "Your dear letter goes into the fire tonight. I must keep it till then." It was unusual for John Quinn to write any love letter—following the advice of nineteenth-century Irish playwright Dion Boucicault: "Never fornicate through an inkbottle." His biographer writes that he "had a considerable contemporary (and surviving) reputation as a pursuer and conqueror of women . . . but I could find little evidence of it." Augusta, apparently, was a sufficiently reliable correspondent to be trusted to burn his love letters. With his lawyer-like inclination to keep his files complete, he, however, kept her love notes to him—and they are now in the Manuscript Room of the New York Public Library with the rest of his papers.

She wrote him the second day after her return:

My John, my dear John, my own John, not other people's John, I love you. I care for you. I know you. I want you. I believe in you. I see you always. Everything I ever said to you I say over again. Don't think I am fretting. I am proud. I am glad. You are nearer to me than anything, everything else a little far off. Where is the use of writing. You know all this do you not? AG

What had happened? She tried to explain:

Why do I love you so much. It ought to be for all the piled up goodness of the years. . . . Yet it is not that. It is the call that came in a moment. Something impetuous and masterful about you

232

that satisfies me. This gives me perfect rest. . . . You surrounded me with thought and care.

Whatever the sexual implications of "I want you," it should be fairly safe to say that if Augusta, after more than twenty years of celibacy, had begun an affair at sixty with a man eighteen years her junior, whatever else she might say of the relationship, she would not say, "This gives me perfect rest." However, Augusta in the matter of affairs was, particularly when she was far from home, incalculable. In a typed letter she called her American visit a "rapture of friendship that so possessed and satisfied me." She had found someone "impetuous and masterful," someone who was strong enough to take responsibility for her loving him. (Mary Colum described Quinn as "very dictatorial, of the type lately depicted in books as Nazi.")

Augusta knew his interests and his affairs were many and far-ranging, but, like a child to a parent, she insisted on her exclusive relationship: "My own John, not other people's John." He had rescued the players and taken care of her. He had given her a watch that kept getting broken and that he kept getting repaired. He acted as trustee for the fund she set up for Richard's education. He thought she was a wonderful woman, and he lived in America, from whence he was not likely to change her life. Though she wrote him on her return to Robert and Margaret and their children at Coole, "I have felt more profound loneliness than I have felt for many a year!" there was more room in her life for loneliness than for intimacy.

Within a day of her return she had her house in order and had started a new comedy. She wrote John in the typed letter that accompanied her second love note:

I am the principle of order in the house, and while I stay here I must keep things orderly. Don't think I am complaining. Richard and Margaret are as nice as possible and really glad to see me. But I am taking the burden of "him that commandeth" and whether that is right or wrong I don't know.

I am in terror of sawdust and idleness. I have set to work in the middle of bills and servants, to write a little comedy.

The play was *Damer's Gold*, a two-act comedy produced at the Abbey in November 1912. Damer the miser has spent his life collecting a crock of gold that is nearly full:

To take it and to shake it I do. It is often I gave myself a promise the time there will be no sound from it, I will give in to nourish

233

myself, I will rise out of misery. But every time I will try it, I will hear a little clatter that tells me there is some space left; some small little hole or gap. . . . I thought to stop it one time, putting in a fistful of hayseed; but I felt in my heart that was not dealing fair and honest with myself, and I rose up and shook it out again, rising up from my bed in the night time. I near got my death with the cold and the draught fell on me doing that.

His young nephew Simon plays cards with him for the crock of gold and wins it all. Simon hides the crock; Damer finds it, but he does not keep it. He has changed, and he goes out the door with Simon, exclaiming in the last speech of the play:

If I was tossed and racked a while ago I'll show out good from this out. Come on now, out of this, till we'll face to the races of Loughrea and of Knockbarron. I was miserable and starved long enough. I'm thinking as long as I'll be living I'll take my view of the world, for it's long I'll be lying when my eyes are closed and seeing nothing at all!

Augusta, with her full crock of good works, her success as a playwright, a fighter, and a public speaker, her triumphant trip to America, and her love for John Quinn, was saying the same thing.

Damer's Gold is the final development of the idea expressed in her previous two plays. In *The Bogie Men*, the chimneysweeps accept themselves as they are—with all their poverty. In *McDonough's Wife*, McDonough recognizes and uses his great gift of music, but in the service of the dead. In *Damer's Gold*, Damer takes his gold and uses it in the service of life and pleasure.

After *Damer's Gold*, Augusta wrote *Our Irish Theatre*, a history of the Abbey, to save herself the trouble of going over it for reporters. In America, away from people who knew better, she had expressed the bias in favor of her exclusively central position that pervades the book. When reporters asked how she became identified with the movement, she laughed and replied, "I didn't become identified. Mr. Yeats and I started it, I think. We were the movement."

Reverting to the pose of dutiful woman she had first adopted while editing her husband's autobiography and her husband's grandfather's letters, Augusta dedicated *Our Irish Theatre* "To Richard Gregory— Little Grandson." (Writing and receiving surreptitious love notes from a notorious womanizer apparently rekindled her need to appear submissive to her family.) The history contains, at the beginning of most chapters, several italicized paragraphs full of solicitous motherliness. These are addressed not to the general reader but specifically to her three-year-old grandson. In them she condescends and coddles at the same time she asks his approval as the male representative of the family. She says she is writing the book to explain why she must sometimes stop playing with him and go write letters, and why in the fall she must again go away to America "instead of waiting for your Christmas stocking and your tree." She tells him of an old man who said to her, "They tell me you are going to America, and says I, 'Whatever the Lady does, I am certain she is doing nothing but what she thinks to be right.' "

Having established her dependence on male approval and family approval, she goes on to establish herself as a friend and dutiful servant of high ideals. Many of her associates referred with envy, wonder, and malice to her great gift for self-advertisement. *Our Irish Theatre* is a delightful example. Almost all the good stories in it are about her and illustrate her courage, tenacity, and devotion to high ideals. The first chapter, "Theatre in the Making," tells of her meeting with Yeats when "things seemed to grow possible as we talked." She writes of encouraging the actors with "the homely proverb, heard I know not where, 'Grip is a good dog, but Hold Fast a better!' " She reprints a letter to Padraic Colum, in which she lectures him about her devotion to the theater and about the importance of Yeats's work:

> Remember, he has been for the last eight years working with his whole heart and soul for the creation, the furtherance, the perfecting of what he believes will be a great dramatic movement in Ireland, I have helped him all through, but we have lost many helpers by the way. . . . It is always sad to lose fellow-workers, but the work must go on all the same. "No man putting his hand to the plough and drawing back is fit for the Kingdom of God." He is going on with it. I am going on with it as long as life and strength are left to me. . . . It is hard to hold one's own against those one is living amongst, I have found that; and I have found that peace comes, not from trying to please one's neighbours but in making up one's own mind what is the right path and in then keeping to it. And so God save Ireland, and believe me your sincere friend.

She goes on in the second chapter, "The Blessing of the Generations," to list the people, both Nationalists and Unionists, who approved her work: Sir Frederic Burton, Aubrey de Vere, John O'Leary, William Lecky, and Douglas Hyde.

Having established herself as everyone's dutiful servant, she finally presents herself, in the chapter on "Playwriting," as an independent creator. As usual, she says she began writing comedy because the attention required for Yeats's verse plays was so great "that ear and mind crave ease and unbending, and so comedies were needed to give this rest." But she discusses her plays seriously: "Neither Mr. Yeats nor I take the writing of our plays lightly." And she, who was usually so reticent about her own feelings, described her progression from short comedies to historical plays: "Perhaps I ought to have written nothing but these short comedies, but desire for experiment is like fire in the blood."

The remainder of the book is devoted to the fight over *The Playboy* in Dublin, the fight over *Blanco Posnet* in Dublin, and the fight over *The Playboy* in America. She places herself exactly in the center of the action, with Yeats somewhere beside her. There is no doubt she is fighting in a good cause and has come a long way from her beginnings to join that fight. When she writes of Abbey supporter and Irish rebel John O'Leary, she recalls the attack on Roxborough defended by her father with gunshots from the windows, and wonders at finding herself on the other side of the lines with "so wild and dangerous a rebel." It is clear she is on the winning side. She says of the Irish people who tried to suppress *The Playboy*: "They had not realized the tremendous support we had, that we were not fighting alone, but with the intellect of America as well as of Europe at our back." The book ends with a last appeal to her grandson to approve the battle, and reminds him of a bribe:

Now, little Richard, that is the whole story of my journey; and I wonder if by the time you can read it you will have forgotten my coming home with a big basket of grapes and bananas and grapefruit and oranges for you, and a little flag with the Stars and Stripes.

Augusta reprinted the press clippings about her various battles in the Appendices at the end of the book. The final words, as she arranged the book for publication, are of an anonymous poem to her:

Nay, great and simple seer of Erin's seers,
How we rejoice that thou wouldst not remain
Beside thy hearth, bemoaning useless years,
But hear'st with inner ear the rhythmic strain
Of Ireland's mystic overburdened heart
Nor didst refuse to play thy noble part!

Augusta created a character for herself comparable in stature to Cathleen ni Houlihan and, safe within it, a small picture of herself as an independent creator.

In 1912 Augusta also published two volumes of her folk-history plays. She dedicated her *Irish Folk-History Plays: First Series* to Theodore Roosevelt: "These three plays concerning strong people of the world I offer to Theodore Roosevelt, one of the world's strong men." (At the time of Roosevelt's death she wrote John Quinn, "You know how I used to feel that the mere touch of his hand put some force into one.") The three plays were *Grania*, *Kincora*, and *Dervorgilla*, all superior to *The Canavans*, *The White Cockade*, and *The Deliverer*, which were published as *Irish Folk-History Plays: Second Series*, and dedicated to: "Dear John Quinn, best friend, best helper these half-score years on this side of the sea." Though she loved him, she did not let her love deflect her continuously acute judgment of who was the strongest.

The warmth of Quinn's admiration stayed with her through the spring of 1912 at Coole: "I am but too glad to see Robert and his wife wrapped up in each other. I also once lived in Arcady!" She had the pleasure of telling him about a lady who admired her watch: "She thinks it the most delightful one she has ever seen. She says, 'Who gave it?' I say, 'Mr. John Quinn.' She says, 'He must be an admirer of yours.' I say, 'Not more than I of him.' " She sent him a signet ring (and a rosary for his sister) that went down on the *Titanic*. He wrote her cautiously that "the ring that you so generously gave me and the Joseph Conrad MS of 'Karain' which were on the way to me were real personal losses." (To Augustus John he wrote, "Perhaps I am as well off without the ring.") Finally, in October, the washing machine she had commissioned him to buy with some of her American earnings arrived at Coole, to the delight and mystification of her servants.

In June, Augusta went to London with the Abbey players—who gave her *Bogie Men* its first performance at the Court Theatre. Katherine Tynan Hinkson, one of Yeats's oldest friends, saw him at lunch with Augusta for the first time in many years: "but it was a jerky meal. Willie was always rushing to the telephone. Afterwards in the drawing-room, after a little conversation, Lady Gregory asked that they might be excused as though life were not long enough for the affairs of the Abbey Theatre."

Augusta stayed with Hugh Lane, who had been knighted in 1909, at his beautiful Lindsay House in Chelsea, which caused her to say, as she had said of Quinn's apartment filled with beautiful paintings,

237

"I have had the great privilege through my life of living with beautiful things." That summer she admired Titian's portrait of "The Courier" and Ingres's portrait of the Duc d'Orléans. (When Margot Asquith asked her about Lane's background and career, Augusta replied, "I used to be his rich relation and now he is mine.") Lane further endeared himself to her by buying one of Robert's paintings.

Her visits to the elegance and luxury of Lindsay House were also replacements for her visits to Ca Capello, though no replacement for Enid Layard's friendship, which had ended with her death earlier that year. Augusta's other English friendships were kept in good repair, so much so that in 1920 she would write of her paradoxical preference for Ireland though "I am made more of in England, live better, kinder friends there." Earlier in 1912 she had read Wilfrid Blunt's *Gordon at Khartoum*—which, as she told John Quinn, contained "a very good letter of my own"—but her visit to Wilfrid was postponed by a death at home. As she explained to him: "My sister's husband died yesterday, in Galway, and I must go to her for a day or two. He was old and not very interesting, but after all, as an old cousin of mine used to say, 'When a woman loses her husband, she loses her crown.' " Arabella retreated into widowhood in her Galway house, surrounded by ministers and curates, and in December, Augusta sailed again for America.

This time there was no trouble over *The Playboy*. She spent most of her energy raising money for a Dublin gallery for Lane's paintings. In January 1913, while she was in America, the Municipal Council finally agreed to give £22,000 for the building, provided a site and at least £3,000 were given by the public.

The Americans were generous. She wrote Yeats from Chicago:

> Oh, my dear Willie, "The help of God is nearer than the door"—and hardly had I put up my letter when the telephone rang and said there were gentlemen downstairs waiting for me, and there I found nine or ten businesslike people, Judge Cavanagh, Judge McGowan, Mr. McCormack (just going to receive three million dollars at his bank), Mr. Ira Morris, Mr. Dillon (my old enemy), and others.

They promised £1,000.

She even cajoled the Abbey company, who had nothing but their small salaries, into contributing and wrote Yeats again from Philadelphia:

> . . . this morning we had a consultation, Company and I, and decided to cable guarantee for £1,000 inclusive of £180 already

sent. I guaranteed against personal payment and they will work it out by matinees, New York, Boston, Dublin, London, Oxford, etc. I am sure you will approve. It was very nice of them. . . .

When she considered guaranteeing an even larger sum, Quinn wrote her indignantly, "You should not even think of doing such a thing. It would not be fair to yourself or your family." So she turned her guns on him and asked him to promise a picture to the gallery. He replied, "Someday in the future, if I live longer than you. I had thought of it myself." To her he wrote, as she toured with the players, "I hope you will not work too hard. You never seem to worry. You are a philosopher as well as a soldier and a general." To Margaret back at Coole, he wrote, "She seemed to have been worrying a good deal and giving a great deal of time to raising funds in Chicago and Canada for the gallery." Lane wrote her, "It may be some satisfaction to you to know that if the pictures are saved to Dublin it is entirely owing to you and the generosity of your American friends."

Before she left America, Quinn took her (along with John Butler Yeats) to the Armory Show in New York, which he had helped organize, to which he had loaned seventy-five works of art (including pieces by Gauguin, Van Gogh, and Cézanne), and from which he purchased some thirty pieces (including works by Walt Kuhn, André Derain, Raymond Duchamp-Villon, André Dunoyer de Segonzac, Auguste Renoir, and Odilon Redon). Quinn's championing of the show, which presented 1,500 pieces of European and American Post-Impressionism and early abstractionism to a generally uncomprehending and occasionally offended public, could be compared to Augusta's championing of The Playboy's first presentation to audiences offended by its amorality and lack of a conventional resolution. And Augusta, who never really liked The Playboy, did not like the modern art either—disoriented by the strong colors and unusual forms.

She returned to Ireland in April 1913. On the voyage home, a heavy door slammed on her hand, injuring it severely. As soon as it was healed, she started making notes for The Golden Apple, a completely new kind of "wonder play" for children. On August 21 her third grandchild, Catherine Frances, was born at Coole. Margaret was very sick, and Augusta wrote Wilfrid Blunt, "I must take good care of her."

Since 1911 George Moore had been annoying all his Irish acquaintances by his account, in the first two volumes of his three volume Hail and Farewell, of his excursion into the Irish Renaissance. Violet Martin had sympathized with Augusta about his treatment of her in Ave, which appeared in 1911: "There is a leisurely superiority that

239

must be trying as much as the franker impertinence"—which was forthcoming, as far as Augusta was concerned when, in 1913, Moore circulated the manuscript of the final volume in which he alleged that Augusta had, along with her older sisters, tried to convert Catholics to Protestantism. Augusta wrote John Quinn, "I have taken up public work, and I hate the notoriety of it . . . I have so often the feeling of being slapped with a dirty hand." Quinn recommended slapping back. Augusta threatened to sue Moore and the specific charge of prose-lytizing did not appear in the published volume of *Vale*, though the leisurely superiority continued, Moore writing, "I have the pleasure in stating here, for my statement is implicated in an artistic move-ment, the Abbey Theatre, that the Gospels were never read by Lady Gregory round Kiltartan." (After Augusta's death, Yeats wrote that she had once said to him, "I have longed . . . to turn Catholic, that I might be nearer to the people, but you have taught me that paganism brings me nearer still," which was as much a flight of private fancy as Moore's contrary allegation.)

There were other disappointments and worries. In September 1913, after a vehement and ignorant campaign in the newspapers, the Dub-lin Corporation rejected the site over the River Liffey that Lane wanted for his gallery, rejected the employment of Sir Edwin Lutyens as ar-chitect because he was English, and rejected Lane's gift of the pic-tures. Augusta wrote him:

> I am glad in a way I was at that meeting. It took away some bit-terness, the aldermen were so far from any understanding of what was offered and what the gift would mean to the country. It is not their fault, it is the fault of the system that puts our precious things in the hands of a democracy.

She wrote in her biography of Lane, "I went back to my tree-planting at Coole; and Yeats went on through that September making those noble and indignant 'Poems Written in Discouragement.'"

She also went back to her notes for *The Golden Apple*, which was in typescript by October. John Quinn wrote her about it:

> It is a great thing for you that you are able to turn from that de-pressing gallery mess to your new play. You are a wonderful woman. I often think of you over there with the two grand-children, and your work and your success and the full rich life you lead, and how empty are the lives of so many women I know who eat and go out and dress and grow fat and grow old like marionettes.

The Golden Apple, written in the midst of "that depressing gallery mess," is delightful and light-hearted. It exhibits a new kind of humor, a combination of fantasy and pragmatism, of nonsense and realism, that is based not on the stupidity of her characters but on a delighted appreciation of their humanity. The plot, taken partly from the story of "The Three Sons" in her *Kiltartan Wonder Book*, published in 1910, is the traditional story of the young prince's journey to restore his dying father to health, and find his bride. Prince Rury, in search of the golden apple, goes through the perils of the Wood of Wonders and the giant's house with little difficulty. He meets the lovely Princess of Spain, who has been imprisoned by the not too wicked witch and her beautiful but selfish daughter, both of whom fall in love with him. In the end he finds the apple, cures his father, and frees the princess from the witch's power. The witch voluntarily breaks her Three Rods of Mastery because "There is coming some change in the world, and why would I go on battling? I am tired remembering the string of years behind me, where I made no great hand of my life." When the old king offers his kingdom to his son, the prince does something unusual in fairy tales—he refuses: "I will not take it, where I am well able to go out and win a country for myself."

The play, like most fairy tales, is about overcoming obstacles and evil so that order and peace may prevail. This is the first of Augusta's plays in which lovers marry happily, the wife is not soon killed or recently dead, or the woman does not have to run off with a young lover or marry an old man for shelter and safety. Two young people who love each other marry, which is of course the traditional ending for a fairy tale, but a great departure for Augusta. What had happened? She loved John Quinn and found it exhilarating and comforting rather than dangerous, primarily because it would not change her life. In accepting love as part of the social structure, she was no longer considering it in regard to herself but rather in regard to her children and her grandchildren. Part of the happiness of her little kingdom, and most of her claim on her grandchildren, depended on the continuing bond between her son and daughter-in-law. And no matter what fears she may have had about the dangers of love as a young woman, as far as her grandchildren were concerned, she could only hope for happy loves for them.

The force behind the play is her cherishing of her little kingdom, her son and his wife, their children. The two young women in the play, the beautiful, gentle princess and the witch's selfish daughter, reflect her vision of Margaret, who was beautiful, charming and, artistic (she illustrated this play and the *Kiltartan Wonder Book*), as well as vain, snobbish, and difficult. Also in accord with Augusta's wishes for herself, the old king recovers and keeps his kingdom while the young people go off to find one of their own.

Her little kingdom was in danger.

X

The Swallows Scatter

PARTING AND DEATH: 1914–1922

*Wherefore seeing we also are compassed
about with so great a cloud of witnesses,
let us lay aside every weight, and the sin
which doth so easily beset us, and let us
run with patience the race that is set before us.*

HEBREWS 12, 1

AUGUSTA'S one-act comedy *The Wrens* was produced at the
Abbey on June 1, 1914, twenty-seven days before Archduke
Ferdinand was assassinated at Sarajevo. In September 1914, Augusta
wrote John Quinn that "Robert all but joined the army and started
off and is much inclined to do so still." *The Wrens* seems to have been
written out of a premonition of that decision. The play is about the
age-old conflict between a wife who wants her husband and her home,
regardless of the political consequences, and the husband who wants
to be part of the action. The wife in the play is Margy; Augusta's
daughter-in-law was Margaret. The husband in the play is William,
as her son was Robert William.

The play is set in Dublin in 1799, on the day the Bill of Union with
Great Britain was passed and the Irish parliament abolished. Two
strolling singers, a man and a woman, are quarreling in front of the
parliament door, at which several servants are lounging. The man is

243

a drunkard, and in favor of union with Britain. The woman desperately wants a sober husband and a little home. She is against union with England. A servant suggests that the husband take the pledge against drink until the Bill of the Union is defeated, as it is sure to be. The husband agrees. Margy then realizes that if the bill is passed, she will have a sober husband; she changes her politics completely: "Isn't it better to me Parliaments to go to wrack in the clouds than my man to go live blazing drunk!" The bill passes by one vote because one of the servants was so interested in their quarreling he forgot to call his master, who would have voted against it. The husband, pledged to sobriety for life, moans, "I never enjoyed a worse day. There was nothing in it but was wrong." Margy replies, "No but the best day ever came before you. We'll have great comfort in the bye-and-bye and a roof to put over the child."

In this play the woman wins. In Augusta's life the man won. In August she wrote in her diary, "Too heavy-hearted to write, since I found Robert thought of joining the war." He joined the 4th Connaught Rangers in 1915. The war would be devastating to his generation and his class. Eleven of his first cousins served; six of them were killed.

In 1912 Augusta had noted hopefully that someone said to her, "He is developing late like his mother." In May 1914 he had a successful showing of paintings in London. She wrote Quinn about it, "You will know how pleased I am, because it shows that Robert is not an idler, that he can create." Yeats wrote about his painting: "Robert Gregory painted the Burren Hills, and thereby found what promised to grow into a great style, but he had hardly found it before he was killed. His few finished pictures, so full of austerity and sweetness, should find their way into the Irish public galleries." Like his mother, Robert Gregory was not a whole artist. But, being a man, he was expected to have a profession. In choosing art, he put more weight on his slender talent than it could bear.

At thirty-three, married, the father of three children, the owner of Coole Park, he was, as a contemporary described him, "an uneasy man." He was a good shot and an excellent horseman. He had played cricket for the Phoenix Cricket Club of Dublin and for the Gentlemen of Ireland. He had boxed for Oxford against Cambridge. When living in Paris he had boxed for the Amateur Championship of France.

He did not, however, find his true work until he joined the Royal Flying Corps in 1916. He was leader of his squadron, beloved of his men. In 1917 he received the Legion of Honor for "many acts of conspicuous bravery" and the Military Cross for "having invariably displayed the highest courage and skill." Bernard Shaw wrote Augusta about a visit with him during a training session:

> . . . in abominably cold weather, with a frostbite on his face hardly healed, he told me that the six months he had been there had been the happiest of his life. An amazing thing to say considering his exceptionally fortunate circumstances at home, but evidently he meant it.

J. B. Yeats, away in America, gave his opinion: "The way to be happy is to forget yourself. That is why Robert Gregory was happy."

Augusta's reaction to her son's enlistment was one of stunned endurance. In September 1914, with the news hanging over her, she wrote on a little cardboard card:

> What shall I do?
> Keep home healthy and peaceful for the children.
> Keep Coole for the children's children.
> Keep the Abbey going and don't give up its purpose.
> Keep my own work up to its highest possible,
>   as far as will can do it.
> Keep courage and patience through all.

The card, the back of a receipt for clipping hedges, had a little drawing of a tree beside her words.

Playwriting was low on her list of priorities at the time, and a matter of will rather than inspiration. She wrote Willie, "There is only half of me here while Robert is in danger." *Shanwalla*, a three-act play written in the fall of 1914, appears to be the work of an author who applied only part of her mind to its writing. In the play a young wife and an old blind man talk about ghosts who come back "to give help, that is what they do be doing. Believe me, if it is good to have friends among the living, it is seven times better to have them among the dead." Then, when the wife is murdered and her husband accused, she comes back to save him.

The main point of the play being the great power of spirits to protect those they love, it is as if Augusta, who was only half alive over worry for her son, felt she herself was a kind of ghost or spirit who could protect him. (Before the play was produced in April 1915, Augusta's brother Alfred's only son had died of wounds received in Belgium; Algernon's oldest son was killed at Ypres; and within the year Frank's oldest son would die at Gallipoli.)

Augusta's kingdom was also threatened financially. The reduction of rents and escalation in taxes continued. Augusta's jointure, the right to receive a percentage of the annual income from Coole assigned her at her marriage by Sir William, was down by half by 1917. Expenses were heavy. Robert and Margaret had an apartment in Paris and a house in London, and Robert earned nothing by his profession. Coole was rented occasionally for the Christmas shooting season. And Augusta's earnings improved with the 1910 reorganization of the Abbey that provided for the payment of royalties to its playwrights. She also earned money lecturing in America.

She went to America for the third time from January to April 1915 and wrote to Wilfrid Blunt about her lectures: "My voice carries and people sometimes cry and it is easy to make them laugh. It is strange to discover a gift so late in life." Hugh Lane was also in America at the time, selling pictures and raising money for the Red Cross. Augusta spent her last two weeks in Quinn's New York apartment. When she made reservations to come home, he made sure she sailed on an American rather than an English ship. He put her on board with armloads of presents and a copy of Conrad's *Victory*. She wrote him that as a result of the trip she had "a few dollars to keep things going, and your encompassing kindness gave me a pleasant feeling as of having lived in summer time."

In the spring of 1915 Augusta was at Coole with Robert, who was on leave, Margaret, the grandchildren, Bernard Shaw and his wife, and Augustus John, who was painting and repainting Shaw's portrait.

The products of this visit were a portrait, which Shaw subsequently gave to the Fitzwilliam Museum at Cambridge, a portrait he kept himself, and which remains at Ayot St. Lawrence, though Shaw said "to keep it in a private house seems rather like keeping an oak in an umbrella stand," and a final portrait with eyes closed called "When Homer Nods" (and called by the subject "Shaw Listening to Someone Else Talking").

During this visit to Coole, John asked to paint three-and-a-half-year-old Anne Gregory, whom he described as "a very pretty little child with pale gold hair." Augusta, who "had from the time of his birth dreamed" that Richard "might one day be painted by that great Master, Augustus John" would not hear of her pretty little granddaughter being preferred to the male heir. Requested to paint Richard instead, John produced what Anne later described as "a very odd picture . . . he had painted in enormous sticky-out ears and eyes that sloped up at the corners." She added that John "had been very annoyed at being thwarted, and had given Richard that funny look to pay Grandma out!" Augusta was pleased nevertheless: "I longed to possess the picture but did not know how I could do so without stinting the comforts of the household, and said no word. But I think he must have seen my astonished delight when he gave it to me, said it was for me he had painted it. That was one of the happy moments of my life."

But on May 7, 1915, she felt a profound depression and remembered feeling the same the day her sister Gertrude had died in childbirth so long ago in Cornwall. Shaw's chauffeur had frightened Richard when cutting his hair, and Augusta was upset, remembering her grief at parting with Robert when he was a child. She thought her depression was caused by the fear that "this roughness might be a foretaste of his school life among strangers." When she heard the mail boat had been torpedoed, she commented that she was "glad Hugh Lane was still in New York and remembered afterwards that Robert said nothing but turned away." When the cable came confirming that Lane had been on the *Lusitania*, Shaw asked what he could do to help. "I said I longed to be alone, to cry, to moan, to scream if I wished. I wanted to be out of hearing and out of sight. Robert came and was terribly distressed, he had been so used to my composure." She left for London to open the Abbey season there not knowing whether Lane was alive or dead. Within days his body was washed ashore in Ireland within sight of his birthplace. Augusta wrote John Quinn, "He was one of the very few outside my own children whose death would make a great difference in my life."

Losing Hugh Lane, she also gained a burden that would last the rest of her life. When Lane's gift of pictures to Dublin was refused, he had written a will leaving them to the National Gallery of England. In January 1914 he had been appointed director of the National Gallery in Dublin, and had told many people he had changed his mind about the pictures and would leave them to Dublin. The will in which he left them to England was found immediately. Shortly afterward, at Augusta's suggestion, his co-workers searched his desk at the Dublin National Gallery and found a codicil in which he bequeathed the disputed pictures to Dublin. Augusta was named trustee. Because the codicil was unwitnessed, British officials refused to honor it, saying it would take an act of Parliament to permit them to relinquish paintings legally bequeathed to them. What Lane had intended as a brief and deeply satisfying legal formality became a thankless task that was not completed at her death sixteen years later. The dispute was not settled until 1957, when an agreement was reached whereby half the pictures are kept in Dublin, the other half in London, and they are rotated every five years.

247

In September 1915 she was writing a lecture on "Laughter in Ireland," and on October 15 she sailed again to America for the fourth and last time. This time her three-month lecture tour took her up and down the east coast, where, among other engagements, she lectured to Professor George Baker's writing class at Harvard. She then moved on to Minnesota, Montana, Oregon, and California. She wrote, "It is a great thing to have seen the Pacific and to have had days of travel through forest and snowy peaks." She cleared £700. Her watch would not run and Quinn got it fixed. (He told her it was rusty inside and in the future to take it off when she washed her hands.) In New York she planned to stay with him at his Central Park West apartment, but his sister and niece were visiting. She went instead to the St. Regis as his guest and sailed for home on January 15, 1916.

She never saw John Quinn again. Her modulation away from her first delighted love for him reveals a genuine tact that was available automatically to her in regard to those she loved. She occasionally asked for a letter—"Please let me know how you are"—and complained that "You will never condescend to write a postcard," but she never asked for love.

Augusta was at Coole with Margaret and the grandchildren on Easter 1916 when the Irish Volunteers took over the Dublin Post Office and proclaimed the Irish Republic. Home Rule for Ireland, with the exclusion of the six northern counties, was already on the statute books—having finally been passed in 1914—to be implemented at the end of the war with Germany. Following a long tradition of looking only to the glory and not to the practical consequences, the Volunteers rebelled anyway. They and the British Army fought for a week in the center of Dublin. The Volunteers, having made their point, and having put in the history books another rebellion that would be more glorious in poetry and song than it was in fact, then surrendered.

Almost no one, including Augusta, knew what was going on. Telephone and telegraph lines were down; trains did not run. There were rumors of arrests and killings, most not true; of an arms-landing on the coast, also not true. Augusta made the best of it: "I have had so much extra time without papers or letter-writing that I am reading Shelley straight through and am going through Hugh Lane's letters and all the Gallery correspondence." Finally, she had a message from outside: Willie wired asking if they were all right. She could not answer; police in Gort were restricting the use of the telegraph to police business.

The death of acquaintances and fellow workers during the Rising, and the execution of their leaders afterward, turned her sympathy to their cause. In August she wrote Yeats, who was in France seeing Maud Gonne MacBride, "I have been a little puzzled by your apparent indifference to Ireland after your excitement about the Rising." She wanted him to make a statement and take a position. "You have a big name among the young men." Yeats wrote "Easter 1916," concluding that "A terrible beauty is born," and Augusta wrote *The Dragon*, the second of her delightful fairy-tale plays in which evil is conquered and harmony reigns.

The Dragon is one of her best plays, her only long one that is as good as any in her *Seven Short Plays*. Her alternate title was "Change of Heart," and most of the characters in it learn to accept responsibility for themselves in a way that is healthiest for them individually and for society as a whole. It has been prophesied that the young Princess Nuala "will be ate and devoured by a scaly Green Dragon from the North!" The princess's stepmother sets out to stop it: "I don't say I give in to your story, but that would be an unnatural death. I would be scandalized being stepmother to a girl that would be swallowed by a sea-serpent!" She decides Nuala must be married—for who ever heard of a dragon devouring a married woman?

The princess, not knowing at first why she must marry, is presented with the timid young Prince of the Marshes. She refuses him, telling her father in the same words that Grania used to describe her reaction to marrying Finn, "I felt the blood of my heart to be rising against it! And I will not give in to you again! It is my own business and I will take my own way." Losing patience, her father swears he will marry her to the first man to come through the palace gates. She cannot understand his determination until finally she learns that marriage is to save her from the dragon whose coming had been prophesied for many years. Having this knowledge, Nuala takes responsibility for herself. Like Grania, she refuses marriage as a means of protection. "As long as I am living I have a choice. I will not be saved in that way." Like many greater works of art, this play is a masterpiece of ambiguity, of characters' saying one thing that is correct, and doing another that is also correct, and so satisfying all the conflicting demands made on them by the author, who wants one thing and believes another.

Luckily, the first man to come through the palace gates is the young King of Sorcha disguised as a cook so that the princess, as he says, would not "feel tied and bound to live for if I live, or to die with if I should die." The old king, who is delighted to see him because his own cook has just quit, asks what sort of a dinner he can make. The queen, very sparing of food, prompts him:

Queen: There are sheeps' trotters below; you might know some
tasty way to dress them.

Manus: I do surely. I'll put the trotters within a fowl, and the
fowl within a goose, and the goose in a suckling pig, and the
suckling pig in a fat lamb, and the lamb in a calf, and the calf
in a Maderalla . . .

King: What now is a Maderalla?

Manus: He is a beast that saves the cook trouble, swallowing all
those meats one after another.

Manus learns the king has promised the princess to the first man to
come through the gate and attempts to claim her. The princess, true
to the class distinctions of her world, rejects him angrily.

The quarrel is cut short by a messenger who rushes in with news
that the dragon is on his way. The timid Prince of the Marshes tries
to stop the dragon; the supposed cook goes out and tames him. When
Princess Nuala learns that the champion who saved her is the cook,
she, apparently, dies of shame: "I have no respect for myself. . . . My
grief! The man that died for me, whether he is of the noble or the
simple of the world, it is to him I have given the love of my soul!" The
conflict between love and the social structure no longer exists for her,
but, fortunately, she is not called upon to test her new resolution,
since the cook is really a king.

The young King of Sorcha comes in very much alive—he had only
stumbled—to find her dead. The Prince of the Marshes gives him his
healing herbs, good to save one life only, to revive the princess. The
dragon comes to the window begging for food. The young king gives
him a coconut, for which the dragon thanks him: "I give you my word,
I'd sooner one of them than to be cracking the skulls of kings' daughters, and the blood running down my jaws. Blood! Ugh! It would disgust me! I'm in dread it would cause vomiting. That and to have the
plaits of hair tickling and tormenting my gullet." He leaves quickly
before anyone can discover that the young king has changed his
dragon's heart into a squirrel's heart.

This play, bright and happy, is a replay of *Grania*. But the characters in it are happy while Grania is sad, not because of some inherent
virtue in themselves but because their world is less constricted and the
evil in it is less powerful. There is a great difference between the
charming, docile dragon and the old, angry Finn. Augusta had revised
the possibilities for happiness. What she could not do for herself, she
could do for her children and grandchildren. (The play is dedicated

to Anne and Catherine; Catherine's nickname, like that of the princess, was "Nu.")

While working on *The Dragon*, Augusta wrote *Hanrahan's Oath*, a one-act comedy that is a description of her relationship with Willie. For several years their companionship was not so close or constant as it had been. Augusta was busy with her family and her trips to America. Willie had spent the last three winters in Sussex, revising, as he pompously put it, his style. Through Ezra Pound he had become fascinated with the Japanese Noh plays and, forgetting the needs of the Abbey, had written several esoteric dramas inspired by them.

When Major John MacBride's execution as one of the participants in the Easter Rising left Maud free to remarry, Yeats gathered his courage and proposed to her. But he first consulted Augusta, who made the uncharacteristically unrealistic suggestion that he insist she give up politics. Maud refused him. (Though not bereaved by the death of Major MacBride, Maud took to the wearing of mourning—and nearly equaled Augusta's record, dressing in black for thirty-seven years, until her death at eighty-seven in 1953). Willie then proposed to Maud's daughter Iseult, but she too refused him. Augusta and Olivia Shakespear had been looking for a wife for Willie since an alarming day at Coole in 1913 when Yeats received a telegram from a woman with whom he was having an affair telling him she was pregnant. She was not pregnant; Yeats ended the affair, but everyone was anxious to put him in safekeeping.

On October 21, 1917, Yeats, then fifty-two, married Miss Bertha Georgie Hyde-Lees, a young Englishwoman of twenty-four, a relation by marriage of Olivia Shakespear. Yeats gave careful instructions to Ezra Pound, who was best man: "Send a telegram to Lady Gregory. NOT one that will be talked about in Coole for the next generation. It's a place where the parson goes down to the post office every day to get the news off postcards." Outwardly, all was joyful. Augusta wrote him: "It is really an ease to my mind your going into good hands, I had so often felt remorseful at having been able to do so little for you now, with the increasing claims here." And Willie wrote her, "My wife is a perfect wife, kind, wise, and unselfish. I think you were such another young girl once. She has made my life serene and full of order." Augusta wrote John Quinn, "His wife has money, though perhaps not so much as he was led to believe, and they live in extreme comfort and ease."

Augusta must have felt she had lost him. In *Hanrahan's Oath* the poet Hanrahan—the character from Yeats's early stories in *The Celtic*

251

Twilight, which he and Augusta had revised together—leaves Mary Gills, at whose roominghouse he had been staying, and goes off with Margaret Rooney. Hanrahan resembles Yeats in his native indiscretion (Yeats's wife called him "William Tell"), which causes him to take an oath of silence he cannot keep. Mary Gillis resembles Augusta in that she is a widow and her roominghouse has greatly benefited from the poet's presence. She scolds him for leaving "after the good treatment I gave you this five weeks past, beyond any lodger was in the house!" Finally, after trying to trick him back, she loses patience and curses him. Hanrahan exits with his arm around Margaret Rooney, shouting curses at Mary Gillis.

In 1919 Yeats wrote his famous open letter to Augusta rejecting the Abbey Theatre:

> Of recent years you have done all that is anxious and laborious in the supervision of the Abbey Theatre and left me free to follow my own thoughts. . . . We set out to make a "People's Theatre," and in that we have succeeded. . . . its success has been to me a discouragement and a defeat. . . . I want to create for myself an audience like a secret society where admission is by favour and never to many. . . . Instead of advertisements in the Press I need a hostess, and even the most accomplished hostess must choose with more than usual care.

Like Hanrahan, Yeats appeared to be exiting—going toward England to write his esoteric plays for dancers, with his arm around his English wife, uttering curses at Augusta as he went. But the letter, while it was partially true to his feelings, was as much a drama as Augusta's play. Yeats's involvement with the Abbey continued; his rejection of it, and of her, were absorbed by Augusta in her capacity as friend to a great poet. She had built her life on service and acceptance, and in the coming years they served her well.

A year before Robert's death Augusta had written to Yeats:

> I am really suffering from the long strain of anxiety about Robert, and his ever-increasing danger. He is kept very hard at work now leading patrols and his squadron in these air-flights, his promised leave has been twice withdrawn, and there is no doubt the German machines are ahead of ours. I try to do what work comes my way as well as I can, and not to be a nuisance, but my mind is not free for a new task. I sometimes awake feeling as if some part of me was crying in another place. And all the war seems horrible and interminable.

In her memoirs she tells of the daily dread of a telegram bringing news of Robert's death. Finally, it came. On January 23, 1918, his plane was shot down in error by an Italian pilot as he returned from a flight over enemy lines in northern Italy.

I was at my writing table when I heard Marian come in, very slowly, I looked up and saw she was crying. She had a telegram in her hand and gave it to me. It was addressed to Mrs. Gregory, and I thought, "This is telling of Robert's death, it is to Margaret they would send it." The first words I saw were "killed in action" and then at the top, "Deeply regret." It was on the 23rd he had died. I said, "How can I tell her? Who will tell her?" For Margaret was in Galway with her children. I tried to stand up but could not. I said to Marian, "Who is there to go and tell Mrs. Gregory?" I felt that I must not cry or think, I must fix my mind on that one thing. I said, "I cannot go. Who is there? You may have to go." I asked about the train. There was time to get it, and I told her to order some vehicle to meet it. I sat there as if frozen. She came back and said, "There is no one to go but yourself, Mrs. Mitchell sent me a note from the Post Office saying you would know how to break it to Mrs. Gregory." I got up and went upstairs and put up my things for the journey, even changing my dress. Then I came down and got into the carriage and drove to Gort. As I went to dress I had seen John, his head hanging, leading the donkey back to the yard, and I knew he had heard it. I stayed in the brougham till the train came in, I forget how I got my ticket, I think the porter got it. When the train came and I went on the platform, Frank (my brother) called to me from a carriage and asked me to get in. I could not, I could not speak. I went to another carriage where there was some lady, a stranger. The terrible thought was still, "How shall I tell her?" At Craughwell, Frank came to the window, and I tried to tell him but could not speak and held out the telegram, but he said, "I know all about it." He had guessed from my face that some dreadful thing had happened, and had sent young Daly to the carriage to ask John D. As the train went on, a few tears came. The stranger, an Englishwoman, made tea for herself and got out her lunch-basket and offered me some. I could but shake my head. I wondered she did not know she was near so much grief. I changed into the Galway train. Daly, the porter we knew, was not there, or he would have known. I was glad there was no one who guessed. In the train, I felt it was cruel to be going so quickly to break Margaret's heart. I wished the train could go slower. I took a car at Galway and drove to the house, giving the man his fare. A maid opened the door. It was agony knowing the journey was at an end. I asked if Mrs. Gregory was in, she said, "Yes, in the study with the mistress." I went to Arabella's room and told the maid to send her to me there. I stood there, and Margaret came in. She cried at once, "Is he dead?" . . . Then I sat down on the floor and cried. . . .

Each year afterward, the anniversary of his death is marked in her diary by sad reminders: "Now I am typing this, seven years all but ten days since his death" . . . "This day ten years ago my child left this earth." A few months afterward she wrote, "I have lost my one great fear of losing his affection. Now there is nothing that could hurt me so much to dread."

To John Quinn she wrote, "My heart breaks when I think of little Richard and the others without their father." She was, she told him, comforted that he had been buried in Italy, in Padua, in a portion of the cemetery reserved for "those who have come to die for Italy."

Three days later she was writing:

Oh, my dear John. Just now a telegram came, and I thought, "I am not afraid of telegrams now," sadly enough, and then when I found from it that you had been through a surgeon's operation which I had not yet heard was to be, I felt what a new grief that telegram might have been.

He had survived a serious operation for a bleeding ulcer—and would survive for six more years as her dear friend and confidant. (In the letter he had written her in anticipation of the operation, he had told her again, "I have always said that you were the most wonderful woman I have ever met" and concluded, "I hope that I shall write you many, many more letters. I am not depressed. But I send you, my dear, dear friend, my best love and good wishes for you and yours.") She continued to share her grief with him. "The awakening every morning is the worst. I try to keep myself asleep—to hold onto dreams—to believe the weight of sadness is a dream. I am just doing all I can for his wife and his children." Quinn wrote, "I know you won't mind my adding, that I wish I could be there with you for a time, and do something to keep your mind off your sorrow."

In her rare published references to her son's death (aside from the autobiography, which was not published during her lifetime) she presents herself as an epic heroine bearing up under an archetypal, communal grief. In her preface to *The Kiltartan Poetry Book*, in preparation at the time of his death, she writes that it had seemed strange to her that the songs of sorrow so far outnumbered the songs of joy:

> But before that month was out news was brought to me that made the keening of women for the brave and of those who are left lonely after the young seem to be but the natural outcome and expression of human life.

During that year news was brought to her three more times of the death of young men close to her: her brother Frank's second and last son, her brother Edward's fifth and sixth sons.

In her everyday life she compartmentalized her grief and turned her care to the living. Sean O'Casey, who visited Coole in 1924, recalled pausing before a picture

> of a young, broad-shouldered man with an open courageous fàce.
> —My dear son, she murmured softly, my dear, dear son, lost leading his air-squadron over de [Sean O'Casey insisted Augusta had a lisp] Italian battlefield. For months and months I had dreaded it, for I knew de German planes were well ahead of ours in design and swiftness.
> He wished he hadn't paused before the picture. What the hell could he say to her. He gave a quick glance, and saw that holy tears were racing down the wrinkled channels of her cheeks. . . . We must be brave, she said, forcing her head higher, we must fence our sorrow away so no shadow falls on those left singing and dancing around us. Come, let us doh for a walk in de woods.

She did not, as did her character McDonough, have the power to honor appropriately the memory of her dead. But Yeats, whom she had been feeding all these years on the best wine, did. And though he had once feared that Coole might slip away from the Gregorys through Robert's "weakness of will," by the time of his death he had revised his opinion and wrote John Quinn, "He was the most accomplished man I have ever known." Augusta wrote Quinn, "Yeats has written a beautiful poem in memory of him. I am so grateful to him—it makes an extraordinary difference to me knowing my darling will be remembered." And because of the poem we see her beloved son, who found himself only in the dangerous enterprise leading to his death, as a symbol for all youthful power that develops so quickly and thoroughly it does not last long:

> Soldier, scholar, horseman, he,
> As 'twere all life's epitome.
> What made us dream that he could comb grey hair?

But Yeats also realized that Robert Gregory had suffered, like his wild uncles, like the heroes of the Irish rebellions, from having nothing better to do. In "An Irish Airman Foresees His Death" he described that emptiness:

> I balanced all, brought all to mind,
> The years to come seemed waste of breath,
> A waste of breath the years behind
> In balance with this life, this death.

Yeats also wrote "Shepherd and Goatherd" using Robert Gregory's death to expound his theory of the cycles of the soul. He begins by having the goatherd discuss the mother's reaction to her son's death, because

> how can I
> That found when I had neither goat nor grazing
> New welcome and old wisdom at her fire
> Til winter blasts were gone, but speak of her
> Even before his children and his wife?

In this poem he notes that she immediately substituted her grandson for her son in the structure of her life:

> She goes about her house erect and calm
> Between the pantry and the linen-chest,
> Or else at meadow or at grazing overlooks
> Her labouring men, as though her darling lived,
> But for her grandson now. . . .

She herself wrote John Quinn in her first letter after Robert's death that very little in her outward life had changed: "Last month I was planting for Robert, now I am planting for Richard."

Like all Augusta's grandchildren, Richard was born at Coole. From his childhood she had focused on him an intense but almost impersonal emotion. She described the effect of a slight cold of his on her, saying he was well "except for a sneeze or cough now and again, very seldom, but each time having a curious physical effect on me, as if all my bones had gone or melted." After his father's death she made Richard a kind of symbol: "Love, the solution of life, of living in heaven while on earth. I seem to grasp it sometimes; it would set

256

everything right if I could feel to all as I do to, say, Richard."

Her love was founded on family feeling and Richard's importance to her as an object of service. Her two granddaughters spent most of their early life at Coole. They adored their grandmother. She taught them their lessons, played games and read to them, let them climb to the tops of the tallest trees without flinching. But the male heir had first place in her affections. She wrote John Quinn, "I am so thankful Richard has the two little sisters. You know what a difference that makes"—giving them the same subsidiary value she herself had been assigned as a child. Later, when all three were away at school, she would note in her journal, "Have written to them and sent Richard cakes." She used her devotion to Richard, as she had used her devotion to his father, to protect her while she did what she wanted to do. When her brother Frank "grew grumpy after lunch, attacked me for having spent money (my own, earned!) on planting instead of 'keeping it for Richard to spend,'" she protested, "But Richard may love trees too and they can't be grown in a minute."

Possibly she now felt more attached to Coole than to any person. Her role as mistress gave her a position with the country people that suited her exactly:

> Looking back on the day my mind dwells with much happiness on a few friendly words with Hanlon and Coppenger who I met by the lake; grateful to me for my advice about Old Mrs. Coppenger's pension. It is to these people I am drawn, it startled me to find how much. Guy and Olive and Rita [in-laws and relatives] seem shadowy beside them. I would, as in the early days, wish to serve them, wish to have them for my friends.

She wrote—in one of the great recognition scenes of her life—after rereading the old diaries that recorded her boredom at Coole during the years of her marriage, "I see now how the cards have been shuffled. In my later life it is I who have been the gainer. It is my work that owes so much to the people."

Perhaps she now loved trees more than she loved people. Sean O'Casey said of her, "Books and trees were Lady Gregory's chief charmers; the one nearest her mind, the other nearest her heart." He described her gardening technique and costume:

> In her working overalls, which were an old black dress, an older, wide-brimmed, black straw hat, leather gauntlets over her able, wrinkled hands, one of which clutched a keen, chisel-edged stick, the Old Lady walked beside him, or a little before when the go-

ing got bad. Here, in the Wood of the Nuts, right in their way, callous and impudent, rose a mighty thistle, fully eight feet high, thrusting out its savage barbs toward their breasts, daring them to come on. Then, with the fire of defiance in her eyes, her ladyship charged down on the foe, hissing angrily, one gauntleted hand seizing a spiked branch, while the other stabbed the main butt of the thistle with the chisel-end of the stick, till the branchy spikes tottered, bent back, and fell to the ground, the victory celebrated by an uplifted stick and fierce mutterings of So perish all de king's enemies!

Her granddaughter Anne wrote that "one of the few times I saw her really furiously angry was when she found that several of her beautiful young larches had been cut down and taken away. . . . I had never heard her speak like this of anyone before—not even when the Black and Tans killed Malachi Quinn's young wife." Augusta wrote, "These woods have been well loved, well tended by some who came before me, and my affection has been no less than theirs. The generations of trees have been my care, my comforters. Their companionship has often brought me peace."

Besides the spacious and often lonely life at Coole, Augusta had her work with the Abbey and her fight for Hugh Lane's pictures, both of which required her presence in Dublin. Exchanging the green world of trees, children, and creative work at Coole for the active life of theatre management in Dublin gave a psychological wholeness as well as an aesthetic beauty to her life.

The first play she wrote after her son's death is about combining two very different ways of life into a whole that is healthier and more beautiful than either one alone. *The Jester*, written because Richard asked her for a play for his school to perform, is about two sets of princes, one cared for in great luxury but obliged to study, the other ruled by a cruel ogre but allowed to run wild in the woods. The two change places, conclude that the best life would be a combination of the two, and agree to live together and share their knowledge. The changes are presided over by a ragged jester, really Manannan, in Irish mythology a great mischief maker and powerful god. In her earliest versions she wrote in brackets "G.B.S." beside the first appearance of the jester. The play, dedicated to a nine-year-old child who had recently lost his father, written by a mother who had lost her beloved son, ends with these words spoken by the jester:

> And so I follow after
> Lycurgus who was wise;

> To the little god of laughter
> I pay my sacrifice!

In 1919 the latest Abbey manager, Fred Donovan, quit for many reasons, among them Yeats's wife's interference with his management. Augusta rather reluctantly agreed to the rehiring of Lennox Robinson, who had been manager from 1909 to 1913, and whom she blamed for the financial failure of the Abbey's last tour to America. (She once sympathized with John Quinn's difficulty in finding a suitable law partner: "I know from Robinson how hard it is to have a half-alive person to work with.")

As Robinson could not immediately take on all responsibilities, Augusta herself assembled a cast and rehearsed Shaw's *John Bull's Other Island*. When actress Mary Walker could not get to Dublin in time for a scheduled performance of *Cathleen ni Houlihan*, Augusta, rather than cancel the play, volunteered to take the part: "After all, what is wanted but a hag and a voice?" On March 18, 1919, three days after her sixty-seventh birthday, she played the old woman who turns out to be a "young girl with the walk of a queen" whom she and Willie had created together fifteen years before, and who in some ways epitomized her own metamorphosis from obscure widow to guiding spirit of the Irish Renaissance. After two curtain calls and an enthusiastic hug from the Abbey charwoman, she went back to her hotel, "very tired and hungry, and the fire out, and had stale bread with butter and a glass of milk."

Maud Gonne MacBride, "another Cathleen," went, with Willie, to see her second performance. Willie "said coldly that it [her performance] was 'very nice, but if I had rehearsed you it would have been much better.'" She gave one more performance before Mary Walker returned. After seeing Mary's performance someone asked Augusta if Mary "hadn't grown very poor and theatrical? I said she had so struck me, but I had thought it was perhaps professional jealousy."

In the daytime Augusta worked at *John Bull's Other Island*, the rehearsals "like Alice in Wonderland's game of croquet." In the midst of this Margaret wired from London asking her to meet Anne and Catherine, then seven and five, at the boat train—she was sending them to Augusta because their maid had been called home. Augusta met them, "gave them their bath and put them to bed (my bed, taking an attic one upstairs) and went for a while to the Abbey." The next day at rehearsal "Anne stayed quietly listening, but Catherine was all over the theatre and made friends with everyone, and I finally found her in the Box Office having a telephone conversation with Millington in the Office upstairs." The next day Augusta got a friend to take them to the zoo.

The following month, in April 1919, *The Dragon*, written two years earlier, enjoyed a successful first performance, "And at the end great applause and many calls for 'Author'—and I made my bow more confidently than when I had last done so as Kathleen ni Houlihan." She returned to Coole; no one there was interested in her triump, and Richard was upset because she had not brought him a fountain pen he wanted, "so the Tuesday night seemed a long time away!"

Augusta went on putting together her folklore collection, and in 1920 she published the two volumes of *Visions and Beliefs in the West of Ireland*, begun in 1896 under the impetus of Yeats's *Celtic Twilight*. At last her "jealousy for Galway," inspired by Yeats's stories of Sligo, was satisfied. But she was still worried what impression the mysticism and irrationality of her fairy lore might make and twice held back publication.

Since 1915 she had been fighting unsuccessfully to get Hugh Lane's thirty-nine pictures back to Ireland. They were well worth fighting for, including "Les Parapluies" by Renoir, "Vetheuil: Sunshine and Snow" by Monet, "Le Concert aux Tuileries" and "Portrait of Mademoiselle Eva Gonzalès" by Manet, "Moonlight" by Rousseau, "La Plage" by Degas, "Duc d'Orléans" by Ingres, four paintings by Antonio Mancini, three landscapes by Corot, three landscapes and a self-portrait by Courbet, a still life by Fantin-Latour. Although Lane, during his lifetime and in undisputed legacies at his death, had given over two hundred fifty pieces of art to the National Gallery of Ireland and the Dublin Municipal Art Gallery, the thirty-nine were the finest of his collection, and in attempting to get them back to Dublin, Augusta felt she was fighting to preserve a source of inspiration for future Irish artists.

The fight was the dreariest, least rewarding entanglement of her life, and it took up the last seventeen years of it. She wrote hundreds of letters, called meetings, visited various possibly influential people, all the while suffering "the grittiness of official discourtesy." For those years she was a beggar—and an unsuccessful one. One friend described her thus:

How tenacious she was about Hugh Lane's pictures. I remember her trudging in the rain in London to come to see me, as she thought that I, being a friend of George Curzon, would be able to persuade him to hand over the Collection to Dublin. Her umbrella dripped all the time on my best Chinese carpet—and George Curzon refused to give up the pictures.

The list of Augusta's correspondents was very long and covered the spectrum of political persuasions. She was not above mild bribery, writing a friend, "I need not say I am not relinquishing such action as sending woodcocks to Lord Carson and other supporters as I have done for many years."

Getting help from friends was occasionally as wearing as trying to convince opponents. In the third year of the struggle she wrote, "I had again a sleepless night this business seeming too hard, and no one very helpful at hand. Yeats seemed to have lost his interest in it." Here is Yeats, in the fourteenth year of the fight, being helpful:

> I wrote you yesterday and asked on the back of the envelope if there was anything I could do. I could see somebody on the Tuesday or Wednesday for you. I have left these days completely free. I can't at present do a very great deal; I overtired myself yesterday—a lunch with Mrs. Hall and tea with Gerald Heard—and to-day I have coughed up blood again. That's why I am dictating, for I am in bed.

She wrote another helper, "It is wonderful having you strong and important men handling the matter!"

Her friends helped out of duty and friendship. She too took up the fight because she was dutiful and faithful, but the emotion she put into it was not required by duty. She put into it the same driving emotion she had put into the formation of the Abbey or her love of rebel Ireland as a child. All the pieces of mythology that had been important throughout her life played their part. She was serving Ireland, fighting against England, for art, in the service of the dead. But, unlike her work for the Abbey, which required poetry and drama, the fight for the Lane pictures involved trudging around in the rain to see people who did not want to see her. It may be that she kept at it because both the Abbey and Ireland were a disappointment to her—though she never said so in so many words—and this was a way of keeping the faith. She wrote in her diary, "Perhaps it is this picture business that keeps me living. I must hold onto that."

The Lane pictures also provided the occasion for her best work of nonfiction, a biography of Lane. The first person who had been asked to write it, and entrusted with most of the documents necessary to make it factual, refused to do it or to return the documents. Another friend who took it up died. In 1920 she wrote in her journal, "Well I have broadened my shoulders for another burden and will write the *Life*."

Hugh Lane's Life and Achievement, published in 1921, is the warmest, the most pleasant and natural of all her nonfiction. She is not remote or artificial, as she is occasionally in her comments in the epic and folklore collections. She is not coy, as she is in her apostrophes to her grandson in *Our Irish Theatre*. Though the necessity of writing was a burden, the book was written with pleasure. It was about a person she liked, and it gave her a great opportunity for praising herself.

It is not, however, a great biography because she never forgets herself for her subject. An admirer told her, and she carefully recorded in her journal, "It shows *two* charming personalities, Hugh Lane's and Lady Gregory's own." She included numerous compliments to herself, among them Shaw's comment that "Lane had been wise to take to picture dealing; he would not have been fit for any useful job, whereas Lady Gregory if she had been a washerwoman would have been an excellent one!" Augusta's role in the book is double: she is one of the "cloud of witnesses" watching and approving Lane's struggle; she is a fellow fighter for Ireland.

What is missing from the biography is knowledge of Lane's character. She assumes he was motivated, as she was, by "the cloud of witnesses." She quotes her letters to him on the subject; she quotes no letters of his. She quotes Lane's friends. She incorporates poems by Yeats about several events in Lane's career. She uses Yeats's account of the Dublin dispute about building a gallery. Her approach was the same as her approach to folklore and epic. She was not interested in "the truth": she was interested in the story.

The central event of Lane's life, as far as one can tell from the biography, was his offer of the modern paintings to Dublin and Dublin's ungracious refusal of them. But Augusta's tendency to slur over unpleasantness prevented her from giving a clear account of the dispute. She is relieved that she does not have the newspaper clippings that would document it. She barely discusses Lane's principal opponent, William Martin Murphy, referring to him in Yeats's words as that "bitter-tongued man."

Only in his irritability and bad health does Lane achieve any depth. Augusta says she once called him Jephthah because his temper was so bad in the morning he would wound the first person he saw. She quotes Charles Ricketts's comment about him. "Everybody who is doing anything for the world is very disagreeable. The agreeable people are those for whom the world is doing something." She does not emphasize the central fact of the struggle for the pictures: that the whole trouble was caused purely by his own carelessness in not having a properly drawn and witnessed codicil leaving them to Ireland. Lane appears to have been his own worst enemy, but Augusta was not interested in understanding or drawing a moral. She preferred to cast him in the mold of her ancient heroes . . . who achieve great victories without internal struggle and die young, meeting their predestined fate.

In some ways Lane did fit the pattern. Augusta described his great ability to recognize Old Masters, an ability not achieved but simply possessed, like Cuchulain's strength or Deirdre's beauty. She quoted him: "You may set your judgment against me in anything else, but this knowledge of pictures is my gift." Certain abilities can be accepted as given. But to describe the change in his character from get-rich-quick picture dealer and social climber to public benefactor as "like the turning of an oyster-shell from black to white"—though it corresponds to her picture of him as essentially irresponsible—is completely insufficient if the object of biography, unlike that of the epic, is to inform and explain rather than to entertain and charm.

After finishing the Lane biography, Augusta returned to her interrupted notes for the play that became *Aristotle's Bellows*, produced in March 1921. It is another three-act "wonder play" written for children as well as adults. Conan, a cranky Trinity College graduate, makes himself unpleasant and unhappy by constantly wishing for perfection. He finds a magic bellows which, for seven times only, will change the things they are blown upon. The changes turn out to be unpleasant. He reverses the magic spell and uses the last blow to make himself content. Augusta says the moral was given by the mother in the play: "It's best to make changes little by little, the same as you'd put clothes on a growing child."

It is a very sensible moral, and one that coincided with the practical, accepting side of Augusta's nature. But it is an interesting change because so many of her plays are based on sudden miraculous changes. In a letter to Lennox Robinson she commented on the theme, "I don't think the philosophy is really sound. I only felt that it is the sudden wishing pedantic changes, as going on in Russia and in President Wilson's dreams that works the mischief."

Aristotle's Bellows in noteworthy too because of Augusta's extensive use of music and song to create atmosphere. She was running short of extra emotion and turned to music to obtain it ready-made. She recognized the lessening of her vitality. Writing to John Quinn, she quoted Wilfrid Blunt, who said he would write no more poetry because "that needs an overflow of vital power that cannot be renewed." She added, "I understand that now. That 'overflow' is, I think, gone."

XI

The End of the Renaissance

PERSISTENCE—*CON SPIRITO*: 1920–1927

Augusta Gregory seated at her great ormolu table,
Her eightieth winter approaching: "Yesterday he threatened my life.
I told him that nightly from six to seven I sat at this table,
The blinds drawn up."

W. B. YEATS, "Beautiful Lofty Things"

Two years after Robert's death Margaret told Augusta she wanted to sell Coole—house, land, everything—which she, as Robert Gregory's sole heir, had power to do. Margaret said she was afraid that if the children stayed at Coole they would grow up to "marry peasants." Except for a short visit to England during which they "were such a miserable and unattractive couple that we were allowed to go home sooner than had been arranged," Anne and Catherine had lived all their lives at Coole. Richard returned there from boarding school. Even before Robert's death Augusta had, in a letter to John Quinn, hinted at Margaret's dissatisfaction with life in the wilds of Ireland: "Margaret is young and beautiful, she is very much admired, and likes society." She concluded the entry in her journal containing the first news of Margaret's intention: "Oh, what can I do?"

From there on, her anxiety about Coole became a constant theme in her journals. For May 23, 1920, she gave a short history of all who had loved and worked there, ending:

265

Robert loved it and showed its wild stern beauty in his paintings; left it through high-mindedness and died fighting for a good cause. . . . I have lived there and loved it these forty years and through the guests who have stayed there it counts for much in the awakening of the spiritual and intellectual side of our country. If there is trouble now, and it is dismantled and left to ruin, that will be the whole country's loss.

I pray, pray, pray.

She tried to make herself believe she could be happy anywhere:

For myself I may buy a little home—Beach House, at Burren— that is to be with the children in the summer holidays. But for my sunset it doesn't much matter—I shall just work anywhere while mind and energy last—and after that—what does the last phase matter, except to be in no one's way.

Finally, she and Margaret agreed that Augusta could keep the house, surrounded by a "little" demesne of about 350 acres, paying all the expenses herself while all the income went to Margaret. The rest of the estate would be sold. She had asked her daughter-in-law what share of the expenses Margaret thought she should pay—since the children would be there part of the time—and Margaret replied, "Nothing."

Margaret wrote her about the arrangement, "Of course one is endangering the children's lives probably and certainly ruining them financially and socially by keeping on Coole but this is now entirely your responsibility." But later she wrote, "Thank you so much for your charming letter. I feel as if we are *each* doing what we believe right about the children's future. Such a happy time ought to be still there for all of us." The tension between them remained, as well as a desire on both their parts for peace and happiness. Augusta wrote, "Five of us only, and we might make such a harmony."

Margaret was not exaggerating when she spoke of the children's staying at Coole as "endangering their lives." Toward the end of World War I some Irish counties openly defied English law. Special British troops, often recruited from English jails, were sent in to maintain order. The Black and Tans, so called because of their peculiar mixture of uniforms, arrived in Ireland in January 1919 and did not leave until January 1922. The time of their stay was called The Terror. As in the days of the famine, as in the days of the Trouble in the north, Ireland presented the spectacle of civilized life juxtaposed with the extremes of human misery and depravity. Two local boys were killed, their bodies dragged behind a lorry. Augusta was told their bodies were unidentifiable: "The flesh was as if torn off the bones." A woman sitting on her doorstep holding her child was shot from a passing lorry. Looting and drunkenness were common. Augusta wrote a series of articles for the *Nation*, signed "An Irish Landlord," to let the English people know of the atrocities committed by their soldiers.

But even without the Terror, life at Coole required a great deal of energy. She wrote John Quinn, "I have been acting as governess, housekeeper, steward, forester, gardener." She described her sessions with Catherine, teaching whom was "like teaching a squirrel. A day or two ago when I pointed to a wrong line she said, 'Oh, Granma, I'm 'shamed of you!' and then stroked my face lest I should feel hurt." She worried about the hay lying out in the wet and a bull hired at stud whose services turned out to be worthless. The disorder around Coole encouraged personal lawlessness; remonstrating with a group of tenants about another tenant's being shot at, Augusta said she hoped "to see the day when murder will be looked upon as a crime as disgraceful as sheepstealing." To which they replied, "Oh, there is *no man* would do such a thing as steal a sheep!"

Yeats, in England during the worst of the Black and Tan outrages, wrote "Reprisals," in which he addressed Robert Gregory:

> Although your last exciting year
> Outweighed all other years, you said,
> Though battle joy may be so dear
> A memory, even to the dead,
> It chases other thought away,
> Yet rise from your Italian tomb,
> Flit to Kiltartan cross and stay
> Till certain second thoughts have come
> Upon the cause you served, that we
> Imagined such a fine affair:
> Half-drunk or whole-mad soldiery
> Are murdering your tenants there.

Yeats bids him, "Then close your ears with dust and lie / Among the other cheated dead." Augusta complained to her diary:

I cannot bear the dragging of Robert from his grave to make what I think not a very sincere poem—for Yeats knows only by hearsay while our troubles go on. . . . I hardly know why it gives me extraordinary pain, and it seems too late to stop it.

She did stop it, though. On the envelope containing the carbon copy of the poem sent to her by Yeats, she wrote, "I did not like this and asked not to have it published." In fact it did not appear until after both she and Yeats were dead, in an Irish university quarterly.

None of her own encounters with the soldiers was unpleasant. In Dublin, when she was returning in a tram from a rehearsal at the Abbey, "some trouble started between Irish and English, the tram had to stop, she climbed on the seat, looking keenly out, clapping her hands, and singing under her breath some patriotic ballad." Returning to Coole, the train on which she was riding was stopped and all passengers ordered out:

> . . . but the drop was so steep I saw I wouldn't get up again— so I sat down and stayed there, the only one who did. Soldiers passed and repassed and pulled out suitcases and parcels and threw them out for a search, but they passed as if I and my little fish bags (fresh mackerel for the workmen) were invisible.

She wrote, observing her usual sequence of priorities, "I have been praying very hard for this last night,—at least for peace and 'the coming of Thy Kingdom'—in Coole—in Kiltartan—in Ireland."

A part of her prayer was answered. In May 1920 she accomplished the sale of a small portion of the estate across the lake (which she had bought in 1901) to the Congested Districts Board, the representative of which had said to her, "You may write to me—but not Mrs. Gregory [Margaret]—she is too smart for us to deal with." Augusta believed the board would deal more fairly with ex-tenants who wanted land than would any private purchaser. In accordance with ancient custom and current legal practice, she and the government representative "walked over the farms, and each tenant gave me a piece of sod from his field, and I gave it to Edmonds, and so possession passed to the Board." The remainder of the land, by far the largest part, was sold in November to a group of tenants, her brother Frank arranging the sale, for £9,000.

Though the house and garden and some of the woods still belonged to the Gregorys, she felt greatly the diminution of her kingdom: "It is rather a shock, feeling I cannot cut a tree for firing or bring in a cart of maiden earth for the garden outside the white gates!"

In May 1921 Augusta was visiting Bernard Shaw in England. Margaret was at Coole. As Margaret was returning from a tennis party with English friends, the car in which she was riding was ambushed. The women were ordered to one side. One of the women, who was pregnant, refused to leave her husband. She and all the men were shot. After Augusta's first reaction of horror and relief, her second thought was for Coole: "It is impossible to know how it will affect her outlook and the life of the children and through them, of mine." A few days later she wrote, "All seems crumbling, yet I will not leave Ireland and will try to hold Coole for a while at least that the darlings may still think of it as home."

When she returned to Coole, she found that Margaret had been asked to look at pictures to identify the killers. Augusta was appalled and went immediately to Galway, where she finally succeeded in convincing the general in charge that Margaret could not identify anyone, "that she does not easily recognize a country face, and even finds it difficult with our own people." On her return to Coole: "M. was vexed because I had seen Mr. Sidley, and because 'they would think she was afraid.' So she was and so was I, and we'd have been superhuman if we had not been. But I feel, thank God, that her life is safe now; I believe it was in danger before."

Later she was told that the day after the ambush Margaret had received a message from "them" stating that she was safe, there would be no trouble "as long as there is a Gregory in Coole." Augusta believed Coole owed this immunity to her articles on the Black and Tan atrocities in the *Nation*—"though I did not think they were known of."

A month after Margaret's escape, in June 1921, Lloyd George proposed a peace conference, and a truce was made. During this time Augusta wrote in the privacy of the notes for her memoirs, "I wish to put myself on the side of the people, I wish to go to prison, I think even to execution (though I will not take a life)." In the next sentence she concluded, with a return to her usual practicality, "I think my name would serve the 'rebels' better than my life."

She was then writing "The Old Woman Remembers," a poem commemorating the leaders of rebellions against the English since the beginning of their occupation of Ireland:

> This is our rosary of praise
> For some whose names are sung or said
> Through seven hundred years of days
> The silver beads upon the thread.

When she read it to Willie, he said, "You have not the momentum you would have if you had given your life to writing poetry, but it has some charm."

On December 6, 1921, a treaty was signed with the British granting Ireland dominion status in the British Empire. Lennox Robinson sent Augusta a telegram with the news: "The little boy had fallen off his bicycle with excitement on the avenue and had shouted the news to the maids coming from Mass and they had cheered. He said, 'This is the first time I ever was sent with a message, and I brought the best message that ever was brought!' "

Most people were in favor of the treaty, as Augusta was, because it meant the departure of the Black and Tans. Augusta saw them leaving Dublin, with people lining the streets and no cheering, "just a sort of delighted murmur, a triumphant purr." However, the departure of the British permitted the explosion of local hooliganism, and disagreement about the terms of the treaty gave warning of the civil war to come.

Augusta was threatened by one of her tenants in a dispute about land—though she was now responsible for so much less land. "I referred him to Frank, and showed him how easy it would be to shoot me through the unshuttered window if he wanted to use violence." Fifteen years later, three years after her death, Yeats wrote about the incident in "Beautiful Lofty Things"; he did not transform it, as it needed no embellishment—though he did add ten years to her age.

No one shot at her. Someone did come knocking. A month later she was awakened by the gamekeeper's son saying men were downstairs pounding on the hall door.

"I think they are raiders."

I told him I would follow him down, put on my dressing-gown and a veil over my hair. He said they had called out to him to open the door. He said he had not the key.

"Where is it?"

"Upstairs in Lady Gregory's room," it being in the door all the time.

When I came to the door they were knocking again. I went to it and said, "Who is there?"

"Open or it will be the worse for you," a rough, unpleasant, bullying voice.

I knew one could not gain anything by speaking to such men, so I stood at the foot of the stairs. They kicked the door then and I expected every moment they would break in the unshuttered window and come in. I prayed for help though without much hope, and stood still. After a time the knocking ceased. . . .

After it was over she wrote, "It did shake the nerves. Yet at the worst moment I felt it was right, somehow, I should know what others had suffered in like cases, and that I might be glad later to have known it."

(Yeats's father once wrote her, "Courage with you is a gift of nature.") A few days later Yeats, who was at nearby Ballylee, went to the barracks and asked for Free State officers to patrol the grounds, which they did for a few days.

Whenever Yeats himself came to stay for a few hours or a day at Coole, she read him a few chapters of George Sand's *Consuelo* and a chapter of her memoirs. When she told him she feared she was putting in too many compliments to herself, he was prompt to reply:

> "But of course I can make a list of your faults if you like. You are autocratic."
>
> "I suppose when you say that," I said, "you are thinking of such a case as when I found you and Synge shivering disconsolately in the Abbey scene dock, because you were kept out of the green room by the uncleanly habits of the stage manager's little dog, and you were waiting for me to come and turn it out."
>
> "If you argue like that over every fault I give," he said, "how can I give any more? And I have plenty more on the list."
>
> "Oh," I said, "and when you first came here in your youth you said that I had but one fault, that was my enmity towards squirrels."

Actually, in calling Augusta autocratic, Yeats was thinking of the more recent instance of his having resolved to defy the rules of Coole by bringing his cat, Pangur, on a visit. He did not give Augusta the opportunity to enforce her rule because, driving up to the house with Pangur in a basket, he got cold feet and told the driver to take him on to the stables, where he left Pangur until late at night, when he came down in his slippers and carried the cat to his bedroom.

Willie was spending the summer of 1922 in his semi-ruined tower at Ballylee, whose purchase Augusta had negotiated for him with the Congested Districts Board in 1916. The price was £80, not a large sum even then, but, Augusta felt, unreasonably high for an uncomfortable ruin. Willie was delighted with it, though occasionally troubled by details of renovation. He had the window frames painted bright red, and she wrote in her journal that

> [Willie] gives me all the reasons why they are the only colour that is right with the old stones and I agree politely but not convincingly and at last I say "When one's friends marry one should make up one's mind to have done with telling the truth"; and he laughs, and says, "Quite right," but the bright red was his idea, George wanted bright blue.

He wrote a friend about the progress of the renovations:

> My wife and I had hoped to stay with her [Lady Gregory] next week as we were going down to superintend the finishing of another room in the Tower which will be necessary to us next spring, as we shall be liable in wet weather to a few hours' flood on the ground floor—perhaps twice in six months or so. However, we are not going as somebody has shot our builder and he is in hospital.

With his symbolic tower, hand-hewn furniture, running stream under the dining-room window, unheatable bedrooms, warlike neighbors, and comfortable Coole nearby, Yeats was like Thoreau at Walden Pond, who never wandered so far as to miss the ringing of Mrs. Emerson's dinner bell.

The house at Coole is gone, so one cannot compare it with the descriptions in Yeats's magnificent poetry; but, extrapolating from the contrast between his dilapidated tower and Yeats's glorification of it, we might expect that, were Coole still standing and were we not too dazzled by his poetry to feel anything but reverence, we would notice that, rather than being an architectural and sociological wonder, it was a large, overfilled, interesting house, and, rather than feeling the power of material things, we would have a lesson in the distorting power of the poetic vision.

By June 1922 the country was on the verge of civil war. Eamon de Valera, who headed the Irish delegation making the treaty with England, had repudiated the treaty immediately, his chief objections being the oath of allegiance to the British crown and the exclusion of the six northern counties (which intended to fight if included). In Gort, Free State (Irish government) forces occupied the barracks, and Republicans (the IRA—against the treaty) occupied the workhouse. A Gort shopkeeper commented on the young men on both sides: "Some that come to the counter that wouldn't be given the charge of a cat, talk as if they would take over the whole country."

Augusta's nephew Arthur and his family were forced to leave Roxborough when it was commandeered by the Republicans on the grounds he was a Freemason (which he wasn't) and a Unionist. Her brother Frank got most of the furniture away to Dublin in four vans and wrote asking Augusta to "ask Commandant L. to return my evening shoes (a new pair I had never worn) which he was seen parading about in at Roxborough." Roxborough was later abandoned, and was finally burned by mauraders. Countess Fingall, whose great house was threatened with burning several times, wrote of the year-long conflict:

"The country houses lit a chain of bonfires through the nights of late summer and autumn and winter and early spring." Coole was not harmed or threatened—which was explained by one of Augusta's workmen, who told her (she did not know whether "in praise or dispraise"): "But your ladyship gave the hand to good and bad."

Though elections to the *dáil* (the new Irish governing body) in June 1922 indicated that the majority of the Irish people were in favor of the treaty, De Valera declared that his Republicans constituted the true government of Ireland. Where possible, they took government into their own hands. Free State forces pushed the Republicans out of Gort; Republicans controlled the neighboring district of Burren. The two were carrying on a war against each other, and neither was able to prevent all sorts of personal lawlessness in the districts under its control. (Augusta had a session with a man suspected of stealing trees, "rather a verdict of 'Not Guilty but don't do it again.'")

Augusta, committed to and responsible for the ordinary good of life, could feel no sympathy for the continued violence. Unlike Augusta's, the self-respect of the young Irish patriots derived not from the practical benefits they brought their country but from their fight for a free Ireland. When, after seven hundred years, they found themselves soldiers of an Ireland that was more or less free, they had to find some flaw in that freedom to regain their equilibrium, to maintain their habitual attitude of devotion through resistance to authority.

All the horrors Ireland and England had inflicted on one another during their long conflict were reenacted by Irish against Irish—the executions, reprisals, floggings, kidnappings, hunger strikes. AE wrote of the civil war that "generations for 700 years fought for the liberation of beautiful Cathleen ni Houlihan, and when they set her free she walked out, a fierce vituperative old hag." And Augusta wrote mournfully in her journal, as the fabric of order in the neighborhood came apart around her, "I feel that my darling children will not come back this summer."

The bridge at Yeats's tower at Ballylee was blown up with charming civility. Yeats was warned by "a man, not in uniform" who said it would be safe for them to stay in the tower. Shortly after, Yeats saw men running away and one "called out it was coming, and went away saying 'Good night; thanks.'" Augusta, lonely for her grandchildren, wrote that perhaps

we are at the seamy side of the carpet, these burnings and breaking of bridges; and perhaps the pattern on the other side is growing to a harmony. And then, somehow I thought of those climbers

273

of Mount Everest going through so much hardship and peril for
the sake as it were of difficulties and dangers, and that we without
any effort of our own are confronted with—surrounded by—
both, and my courage rose.

Wilfrid Blunt died in England in September 1922. After his long
dalliance with Mohammedanism and with atheism, he saw a priest
and took communion before he died, and Augusta remembered Sir
William's prediction that "Wilfrid will die with the wafer in his
mouth." Dorothy Carleton, a distant cousin and Wilfrid's companion
in his last years, wrote Augusta that "at the end he drew some long
free breaths and a look of intense *interest* passed over his face and he
was gone." (He left Augusta the Bible he had had with him in prison
in Ireland, which was placed in her coffin at her death.)

In 1914 Augusta had helped arrange the edition of his collected
poems. In 1921 she had written the introduction to the American edition of his diaries, giving in it a charming picture of their last visit:

> We were out of doors all morning, he in his pony chair, in the
> beautiful oak woods that cover some five hundred of his Sussex
> acres. Our midday meal was set out nearer the house yet still
> under blossoming trees. Peacocks came to be fed and among them
> a Spanish lamb, black spotted, using its sprouting horns to butt at
> the watch dog in whose company it had been reared.

Though their surroundings were beautiful, Blunt was even then very
ill, and involved in an ugly quarrel about property and horses with
his daughter, Judith.

In her introduction Augusta shows how much he and she had in
common. She discussed his lifelong sympathy with nationalist causes,
in Ireland, in Egypt, in India: "An unusual and gallant record for a
Sussex gentleman of many acres, of inherited wealth and ease." She
shows how many claims he had on her admiration: "the adventure
of his personal life, the life of love, the romance of travel, the delight
in woods and fields and skies, the pride of ancestry and race . . . the
many gifts, the mastery of living that seem to belong to the heroic
ages of the world, that show him out as one of Plutarch's men." She
wrote John Quinn, "Wilfrid Blunt's death has been a grief to me and
I shall miss his forty years of friendship, and his welcome, if ever I
go to England."

She also told Quinn her anxieties about the sale of Coole, about the
Lane pictures, the local troubles. She did not, however, confide in him
about her operation for breast cancer in 1923. She wrote him only after

he had heard of it from Yeats, "Yes, I had rather a shock and a shake, but am quite well again and all is going well."

She was of two minds whether to confide in her journal. For May 27, 1923, she wrote, "The night before last I had a shock finding a hard lump under my left breast," then crossed out "finding a hard lump under my left breast." But she went on to describe the whole operation, her doctor saying,

> "Better have it out, and take the whole breast out"—another shock, nursing home, dreadful preparations. . . . They refused me a cup of tea in spite of Slattery's permission, but "would you like to see a priest before the operation?" . . . 11 o.clock, "theatre" and scaffold. No chloroform, local anesthetic. I was able to keep a face of courage and ask Gogarty about his feelings when kidnapped . . . some pain and at the last I fainted.

(Lennox Robinson wrote of her, "With much of the Spartan in her, she demanded the same qualities from others.") She recovered quickly and began writing her play on the life of Christ.

The violence and hatred corroding Ireland and the sorrows in her private life made her pray more fervently and believe more completely that only the surpassing love of Christ could triumph over such evil. She wrote John Quinn, "How can you doubt the Divinity of Christ? There is something of the divine in all of us, enclosed in the animal body, one conquering or being conquered by the other, and Christ's was the nearest to that completely divine nature we know of."

The Story Brought by Brigit, produced at the Abbey during Easter Week of 1924, was very popular. Though it retells the crucifixion story, the most interesting characters are those whose purpose is to show that the political atmosphere of occupied Jerusalem was similar to that of occupied Ireland. When a Pharisee worries that Christ will lead an uprising against the state, a Roman official says calmly: "To tell the clean truth, a little Rising now and then is no harm at all. It gives us an excuse to get rid of disturbers and to bring in our armies. A Rising too is very apt to lead to splits, and splits are a great help when you want to keep a country down."

Running through the play there is a particular note of grief, as appropriate to Augusta as to Christ's mother, over the death of a beloved son. "The worst of all is to think of the poor Mother. Why wouldn't they leave him to the death that is allotted by Nature? It is too soon his candle to be spent." And, finally, there is a serious questioning of the value of giving one's life for another. Two women discuss why Jesus does not save himself; one answers, "He is maybe weary of

serving the world, with the bad treatment and the abuse he was given."
And when a young rebel regrets that he turned against Christ, he exclaims bitterly: "That's the way of it! All the generations looking for
him and praying for him. We wanted him, and we got him, and what
we did with him was to kill him. And that is the way it will be ever
and always, so long as leaves grow upon trees."

Lennox Robinson believed Augusta was proudest of writing this
play. To his note of congratulation she replied, "I do not feel puffed
up by it because I have always a feeling that the plays I care most for
have been written not by me but through me."

By August 1923 most fighting between Free State soldiers and Republicans had stopped. The thousands of Republican prisoners in Free
State prison camps went on hunger strike (the last massive expression
of the death wish), demanding to be released. Augusta and Lennox
Robinson wrote a letter printed in a Dublin daily appealing to both
sides to give way. The strike was soon called off (though not because
of their letter). Almost all the prisoners were eventually released,
including De Valera, who in 1927 took the oath to the King and led
his followers into the *dáil*, declaring the oath was merely an empty
formula. Augusta wrote of the whole conflict, "All so sad and unsatisfactory and I think humiliating." But she too had her own habitual attitude toward authority, and once the active rebellion was over,
she began to feel that she was "more than ever a Republican, though
'without malice.' "

All during the Troubles and the Civil War, Augusta had been struggling with her memoirs. When she wrote Wilfrid Blunt asking for the
return of her letters, she said, "I am just well known enough for some
scribbler after my death to make a little book of me, full of stupidities,
and it will prevent that." She herself nearly wrote the book she feared.

Augusta wrote John Quinn more perceptive comments about her
life than ever found their way into her manuscript:

I am putting down memories and sometimes pages from old
diaries. I call it "My Education," for everything I have ever done
seems to have fitted me for something else—nothing to have
been wasted. But I should like to get it more coherent, a medita-
tion on my life.

A few months later she wrote:

It seems to me in looking through the old diaries and letters that
I must have started with a big stock in trade of energy, which
was always trying to turn some mill or another, and which only

276

found its proper uses when I had quite settled down here and took up only Irish things. . . .

She felt that "one hour's talk with Robert would put me on the right line."

She never found the right line. The 560 pages of her autobiography are a ragbag of interesting anecdotes, unconnected snippets from letters and diaries, brief insights, and trivia. (The parts she did not put in her final version are usually more interesting than those she did, and have been used extensively in this biography.) Her great-nephew Desmond Shawe-Taylor in reviewing the book wrote, "For all its incidental merits, however, there is something so odd as to be disconcerting, namely that it should be so little shaped, so little a work of art."

It is not even a work of intelligence. Augusta does for her life story the opposite of what she did for the Irish epics. Instead of untangling chronology, she muddles it. Instead of adopting a single style, she includes accounts by many people written at different times. Instead of clarifying her cast of characters, she mentions people she does not identify beyond a first name or initial. Instead of telling whole stories, she tells only part. She gives letters *from* Wilfrid Blunt in one chapter, and letters *to* Wilfrid throughout the book. All traces of their affair were eliminated. (Later, when she typed her diaries, she did not type the entries relating to their affair.) The part of her life most interesting to the public, the early years of the Abbey (when she was too busy to keep a diary), is dealt with most briefly.

Having kept half her motivation unconscious, and some of her actions under cover, Augusta was unable to analyze her fascinating, complex career. Unable to make a personal connection with her readers, and with no excuse for presenting herself as an epic heroine as she had done in *Our Irish Theatre* and *Hugh Lane's Life and Achievement*, her deepest instinct was to hide.

In November 1923 Yeats was selected to receive the Nobel Prize for Literature. In his acceptance speech he paid tribute to Augusta in words that were moving if not wholly accurate, saying he should be sharing the prize with John Synge, who was dead, and with Lady Gregory, "an old woman sinking into the infirmities of age." Though Augusta was seventy-one at the time, she was far from ready to accept his description. On the day she first read his speech, she had ridden across Ireland on the train and taken a cab to Yeats's house in Dublin. Finding no one at home, she ate her lunch, which she had brought in a basket across Ireland, in the hall. She then took a cab to the Abbey, where she found Willie, who gave her the first typed copy of his speech. As she commented in her diary, "He described me as 'an old woman sinking into the infirmities of age' (not even fighting against them!)." She and Lennox Robinson convinced Yeats that his description would detract from the drawing power of her plays, "and be considered to mean I had gone silly." Willie finally agreed to change it, then confessed he had already sent copies to the papers. And in his final version he changed the wording only slightly to read, "a living woman sinking into the infirmity of age."

Augusta and Willie were still tussling like an old married couple who find each other intractable but indispensable. Augusta was still bossing Willie. During a very crowded performance of Sean O'Casey's *Shadow of a Gunman*, "Two seats had been kept for Yeats and me, but I put Casey in one of them and sat in the orchestra for the first act, and put Yeats in the orchestra for the second." As she was about to introduce Yeats, then sixty-one, to a group of American journalists, she was heard to tell him, "Stand up, now, Willie, and do it properly."

Willie, who had won the Nobel Prize, could still get at Augusta about artistic matters. She wrote, "Yeats gave a cautious hearing to two acts of 'Sancho' beginning with a lecture on the faults of my dramatic method and the reason of my last play being so bad." And she, who had never been to school, could still get at him about intellectual matters. At the end of a reading of O'Casey's *Juno and the Paycock*, Yeats said that the play, and particularly the last scene, reminded him of a novel by Dostoyevsky. Augusta turned to him and in front of the assembled actors said, "You know, Willie, you never read a novel by Dostoyevsky." She promised to send him a copy of *The Idiot*.

Willie occasionally complained about Augusta to Olivia Shakespear. He wrote, "She hates all clergy though she never misses church and is a great reader of her bible and, as she believes, very orthodox—furthermore she is a great prude so far as what others say to her is concerned sometimes punishing me by half a days silence." In support of this, one notes that in her journal when she wrote that Moses must have had a "hell of a time" carving the ten commandments in stone, she crossed it out and wrote over it "the devil of a job," which seems not much different but was apparently less irreverent. But she wrote John Quinn about Yeats's "Leda and the Swan," a fairly explicit description of violent sexual intercourse, "When I left he had come to the conclusion it was not proper enough for the *Empire*. But it is a fine thing." She was prudish only for herself.

In 1925 Yeats published *A Vision*, his private mythology, in which he linked personality to phases of the moon. He placed Augusta, along with Queen Victoria, in Phase Twenty-Four. Such people serve a code:

All is sacrificed to this code; moral strength reaches its climax. . . . There is great humility— "she died every day she lived"— and pride as great, pride in the code's acceptance, an impersonal pride, as though one were to sign "servant of servants." There is no philosophic capacity, no intellectual curiosity, but there is no dislike for either philosophy or science; they are part of the world and that world is accepted. . . . They submit all their actions to the most unflinching examination, and yet are without psychology, or self-knowledge, or self-created standard of any kind, for they but ask without ceasing, "Have I done my duty as well as So-and-so?" "Am I as unflinching as my fathers before me?" and though they can stand utterly alone, indifferent though all the world condemn, it is not that they have found themselves, but that they have been found faithful.

She saw immediately what was lacking in this otherwise faultlessly correct assessment of her personality and exclaimed in her diary, "With Queen Victoria! . . . But I don't think she could have written 'Seven Short Plays!' "

Yeats, appointed to the Irish Senate in 1922, asked Augusta to stand for a seat in 1925, when she was seventy-three. Yeats, who was abashed by the bankers and businessmen who leaned over the backs of their chairs settling the affairs of state, would have been glad of her support. In 1925, when he was one of the few to oppose the abolition of divorce, Augusta's sister-in-law told her, "There is great indignation among the people at Yeats supporting *divorce*. 'Hasn't he a wife, and hasn't he two children? Why would he want divorce?' " Augusta let her name be put up for election but did no campaigning and, the morning after the election, read her name in the list of defeated candidates.

Her care for Yeats now extended to his children, Anne, born in 1919, and Michael, in 1921. But, unlike her care of her grandchildren, this was mainly a duty and not a pleasure. And the Gregory children were none too courteous, Anne Gregory remarking that

We didn't think much of them. . . . They were much too well dressed to start with, and didn't seem to be very keen on getting wet in the stream at the foot of the castle. Michael had pointed ears and looked like the elf in Puck of Pook's Hill, and we said to him we could see fur growing on the tips of his ears and sprouting out of them. We pretended to look inside for more fur, and I filled his ears with mud, and said all *I* could see was filth. He ran screaming into the cottage. . . .

Augusta wrote in her journal, "George Yeats and the children came here for the afternoon, made great friends with my children."

To Yeats, who wrote, "Friendship is all the house I have," she wrote an average of two letters a week throughout her life. She carried on the tremendous correspondence relating to the Lane pictures. She generally had "a letter in the writing" to Richard away at school. To Anne and Catherine during their first brief, unhappy visit to their mother in London she wrote wonderful letters and "sent great parcels of moss and little red toadstools on twigs from the Nut Wood" at which they "sniffed and sniffed the lovely wet mossy smell and imagined that we were back at our beloved Coole."

In March 1924 her sister Arabella, widowed since 1911, died in Galway. She reported in her journal, and to John Quinn, that she had written to Arabella *every day* since she became an invalid in 1917. Enid Layard's Remington was serving her well (though there is a sheet among her collected papers that reads: "This is a very torment-ing typewriter. Perhaps if Ict ut at fcy— Now let us see what will be the effect of— Perhaps it just wants to be taken notice of and made a fuss about   A great nuisance whatever it is and I wish I could have two, why does it go all right when I stand up and go wrong when I am typing?").

Her long and invigorating correspondence with John Quinn ended in July 1924. She had seen him last in January 1916, when she left America after her last lecture tour. He was in Europe in 1921 and 1923 visiting artists and buying art with Mrs. Jeanne Foster, the dear friend, confidante, and traveling companion of his last years. Augus-ta wrote, "The little trip to Paris will do you good though I feel sad that you pass so near our coasts and yet there is no chance of seeing you!"

At the time of her own operation she had written him that he must take good care of himself: "Fifty-three seems very young to me." In the spring of 1924 he sold his huge collection of books and manu-scripts, including many by Augusta and Yeats. He was in great pain through the spring and died of cancer of the liver on July 29. He was fifty-four.

At his death 1,500 pieces of modern art crowded his extensive Central Park West apartment. He was the first owner of a remarkable number of modern works that we now think of as masterpieces belonging to everyone: Rousseau's "Sleeping Gypsy," Brancusi's "Yellow Bird" and "Mlle. Pogany," as well as eighteen other sculptures by Brancusi, Picasso's "Three Women at the Spring" and fifty-one others, Matisse's "Blue Nude," Seurat's "The Circus." He had purchased Joseph Conrad's manuscripts when Conrad needed money. It was to him that T. S. Eliot gave the manuscript of *The Waste Land* in gratitude for his help. Quinn funneled money to needy geniuses through Ezra Pound, among them James Joyce. He defended *Ulysses* in court in New York in 1920. His biographer wrote of him, "Somewhere within the work of almost every major creative impulse in the art and literature of the early century, standing neither quite at the center nor quite at the edge, Quinn punctually appeared."

Augusta wrote in her journal, "A great blow yesterday. A cable from N.Y. 'John Quinn died this morning.' . . . America will seem very distant now without that warm ready sympathy and interest. The children will miss their Christmas apples. So my day and night have been sad and I am heavy hearted." As he was dying, Mrs. Foster asked him if he believed in reincaration, and if so, who he would like to be. He replied, "Cuchulain, of course!"

Augusta made a new friend that year. Sean O'Casey had submitted his first play, *The Frost in the Flower*, to the Abbey in 1919. It was returned with a note: "Not far from being a good play." He sent others. *The Crimson in the Tri-Colour* was returned with a note from Lennox Robinson, enclosing a detailed criticism of the characters by Augusta. She told him, "I believe there is something in you" and "your strong point is characterization." O'Casey persevered, and in 1923 the Abbey accepted his two-act tragedy *The Shadow of a Gunman*. The play was, to quote Augusta, "an immense success, beautifully acted, all the political points taken up with delight by a big audience."

Juno and the Paycock opened at the Abbey in March 1924, drawing even larger audiences. Augusta's journal is full of rejoicing. She walked around the corner to look at the long line of people waiting to get in, and after the performance she wrote: "That full house, the packed pit and gallery, the fine play, the call of the mother for the putting away of hatred, 'give us Thine own eternal love!' made me say to Yeats, 'This is one of the evenings at the Abbey that makes me glad to have been born.'"

Augusta sat with O'Casey often during performances and rehearsals. The seventy-two-year-old aristocrat and the forty-year-old labor-

281

er found they had much in common. They were both Protestants, though he no longer believed in religious forms. Like her, he was a great reader of the Bible. He, like her, had great sympathy for the working classes, though arrived at from a completely different direction. They were both dramatists; they were both moralists. The mother's cry at the end of *Juno*, "Sacred Heart o' Jesus, take away our hearts o' stone, and give us hearts o' flesh! take away this murdherin' hate, an' give us Thine own eternal love!" was an expression of exactly the same emotions, prompted by a similar experience of violence and hatred, that had made Augusta write her passion play.

O'Casey was invited to Coole in June 1924, a visit both he and Augusta thoroughly enjoyed. His description of Coole, written twenty-five years later in *Inishfallen, Fare Thee Well*, continually emphasizes her warmth and humanity. She met him at the station in Athenry to ride with him the last leg of the journey to Gort. He marveled at her composure in the third-class carriage (not knowing she traveled third-class frequently): "Look at her there, with all her elegance, well at ease among the chattering crowd of common people." He contrasted Yeats's retreat from common things with her acceptance:

> But Lady Gregory wasn't afraid of the child's cry or the creak of the lumbering cart; and she stayed to speak warm words to the ploughman splashing the wintry mold. She trotted fearlessly beside all these things, sad or merry; listened to their tales, sang songs with them when they were merry; and mourned with them when a silver cord was sundered or a golden bowl was broken. The taste of rare wine mingled with that of home-made bread on the tip of her tongue; her finely shod feet felt the true warmth of the turf fire, and beside its glow she often emptied the sorrows of her own heart into the sorrows of others. Out of her plush and plum, she came to serve the people, body and mind, with whatever faculties God had given her.

He characterized her role at the Abbey in a way that would have delighted her: "In the theatre, among the poets and playwrights, herself a better playwright than most of them, she acted the part of a charwoman, but one with a star on her breast." He went on to say of this mainspring of her character, "Ay, indeed, this serving eagerness of hers was a weakness in her nature."

She served him well. Knowing his eyesight was bad, she rigged up a special arrangement of shaving mirrors for him. Knowing his digestion was bad, she told him he "must ignore the formal table arrangements of the house and order his own particular likes—if he wanted poached eggs for dinner or tomatoes and fruit for lunch then these he must have and that was all about it." Knowing him unaccustomed to elegant surroundings, she quickly put him at ease:

> He hadn't been ten minutes at the table before he felt he had often been there, to eat soberly, and talk merrily of books and theatre, and of the being of Ireland; she in simple and most gracious ways showing how things were handled; pointing out that dese things were done, not because of any desire for ceremony, but because dey made one more comfortable, and made things easier to eat.

She did get him to wear a scarf around his neck because her house-keeper, Marian, refused to serve him "with the bare neck."

Lennox Robinson protested against O'Casey's rendition of Augusta's speech as a foolish exaggeration of a slight lisp. The exaggeration may have been his device for cutting her down to manageable size, for it is clear that O'Casey did feel threatened—even after his success—by those in positions of authority, and in regard to Augusta this uneasiness was in continual conflict with his real affection for her.

On his next visit in August of 1925 O'Casey brought his new play, *The Plough and the Stars*, later scheduled to go on at the Abbey in February 1926. The conflicts over its production were variations on most of the Abbey battles of the past. Michael Dolan, Abbey manager, began to protest immediately, writing, "Now, Lady Gregory, I respectfully beg of you to pause and think what it will mean. As you know, we cannot afford to take risks. . . ." He was especially concerned about the "bad language" that went "beyond the beyonds. The song at the end of the second act, sung by the 'girl-of-the-streets,' is unpardonable." As a further comment on Augusta's indifference to bad language when it was someone else's responsibility, when she read the play aloud at Coole, to Sean and her other guests, Jack Yeats and his wife, she read it straight through, bad language and all, even the song at the end of the second act.

Demands for censorship came from the actors, as well; one actress, who was to play a prostitute, objected to her line "I never had a child that was not born within the border of the Ten Commandments." Augusta remarked in her diary, "It had certainly not struck me as offensive, so I don't know what will happen. It was like one of our old storms in a teacup."

But this time there was a new twist, and demands for censhorship also came from one of the directors. In 1925, after long negotiations, the Abbey had been granted a government subsidy, and a government representative, Mr. George O'Brien, had been given a place on the board. True to the timid traditions of those opposing the Abbey, Mr. O'Brien wrote

> that to eliminate any part of it on grounds that have nothing to do with dramatic literature would be to destroy all our traditions. I feel, however, that there are certain other considerations affecting the production to which it is, in a peculiar way, my duty to have regard. One of these is the possibility that the play might offend any section of public opinion so seriously as to provoke an attack on the Theatre of a kind that would endanger the continuance of the subsidy.

Augusta and Yeats decided immediately, "If we have to choose between the subsidy and our freedom, it is our freedom we choose." But, as they had often done before, they negotiated their way around the objections. At a directors' meeting, certain passages, which Yeats and Augusta had already decided had to be eliminated, were eliminated. Directors had never forced actors to say lines to which they objected, so these were eliminated. Augusta gave a little lecture on the history of their past battles against censorship. "Yeats also spoke in the same sense. O'Brien sat up in his chair reiterating at intervals, 'That song is objectionable.' (We had already decided that it must go, but left it as a bone for him to gnaw at.)" Afterward she wrote, "Directors' meeting easy. O'Brien like a lamb, though after it he held back Perrin to say, 'I think Mr. Robinson has now given up that song.'"

With the actors pacified and the directors pacified, on the fourth night of the play the audience rioted. The play, about the Easter Rising of 1916, offended some patriots, particularly a group of self-consciously patriotic women, including Maud Gonne MacBride, because it showed the cowardice as well as the courage, the mixed motives, and, as Augusta described it, "the suffering that falls through war, and especially civil war, on the women, the poor, the wretched homes and families of the slums." She was not present at the disturbance. Yeats later told her he had been present only by accident, though he hinted cheerfully beforehand that he expected trouble. And after the disturbance he delivered one of his magnificent fighting speeches from the stage of the Abbey, beginning, "You have disgraced yourselves again. . . . Once more you have rocked the cradle of genius" and ending, "The fame of O'Casey is born tonight. This is his apotheosis."

Augusta formed her own opinion of the play several days later:

284

. . . there was no danger of riot and I could listen without distraction, it seemed to me a very wonderful play—"the forgiveness of sins," as real literature is supposed to be. . . . An overpowering play. I felt at the end of it as if I should never care to look at another; all others would seem so shadowy to the mind after this.

She was still a playwright herself. Her last translation of Molière, *The Would-Be Gentleman*, was produced at the Abbey in January 1926, a month before O'Casey's play. And even in her translation she was dealing with the themes most important to her. After Robert's death she had again become more conscious of "the invisible world," writing to John Quinn that she had been thinking about the religion of "Jacob Boehme and of Blake and his invisible city in which we may even now take up our abode." When the raiders were pounding on the door at Coole, she tried to "fix my mind on that high country." Her last three plays, *The Would-Be Gentleman*, *Sancho's Master*, and *Dave*, show a progression from the most banal social advancement to the attainment of a kind of heaven on earth.

The Would-Be Gentleman deals with the theme in a purely social context. Monsieur Jourdain, who wants his daughter to marry a lord, is attempting to jump from one social class to another. His wife wants to stay in their own world, and wants their daughter to marry an equal: "What I want is a man that will be thankful to me for my daughter, and that I can say: 'Sit down there, son-in-law, and eat your dinner with us!' " to which Monsieur Jourdain replies, "Those are the thoughts of a poor mean little mind, that never wishes to raise itself. Let me have no back answers! My daughter is to be a Marchioness in spite of everyone. And if you put me in a passion I'll make her a Duchess!" He is tricked into letting her marry the man of her own class whom she loves.

In *Sancho's Master*, Augusta's adaptation of *Don Quixote*, produced at the Abbey in March 1927, Don Quixote is trying to rise above the world of everyday reality into a realm of transcendent beauty and justice. She dwells on the theme of the attachment of the practical, reasonable man to the man of vision. The Duchess mocks Sancho for serving Quixote: "But something whispers in my ears, if Don Quixote de la Mancha is a fool or out of his mind, and Sancho Panza, knowing this, follows him, he must be yet more foolish than his master." Sancho defends himself: "It was allotted me to follow him. We are of the same townland. I have eaten his bread, I love him, he returns my kindness. He has promised me an island. And so it is impossible anything would part us, but the sexton's spade and shovel." (Augusta herself combined the two, writing in her journal, "I sometimes think my life has been a series of enthusiasms. But down to practical trouble today.")

During the writing of these plays and her last play, *Dave*, she was again anxious about the sale of Coole. Selling the land was not enough for Margaret. By her marriage to the son of Augusta, who loved Coole so dearly, and who had the right to live there rent-free throughout her life, she had become owner of a great house of which it was impossible for her to be mistress. The only way for her to assume that position was to sell Coole and buy another great house. Margaret began looking for a new mansion for herself and a buyer for Coole.

Margaret wanted the furnishings of Coole as well. Augusta wrote in her journal, "M. had never realized that I had been left the St. George's Place furniture and her surprise made me gasp and wonder if I could have been mistaken, but it was so." Margaret was anxious to assume *some* rights of ownership: "M. seems confident and has just put new pictures in some of the Grillion frames [frames that held pictures of Sir William's fellow members of the Grillion Club]." She crossed out, "That troubled my night." Margaret wanted to dismantle the library to take to the new house she would acquire. Augusta wrote, "I have given in to this but not to the flight of steps going down to the lawn being taken up, that the stones may be used for a wall and plateau at the new house. I was perhaps foolish but had a bad night thinking of it, the destruction being *begun* by us." The anguish she tried to deny kept breaking through: "One of those dreams in high company I've had of late, and awakening I lit the candle and wrote down: 'Moaning over the great changes.' "

Though Margaret fretted, she knew how to appreciate Augusta, writing her with a strange mixture of feeling and insensitivity, "I am so unutterably thankful you are alive. This sounds odd but I have seen so much lately of my generation suffering from selfish older generations that I feel terribly proud of you. I don't deserve you in the tiniest bit."

During this troubled period, in September of 1926, Augusta underwent a second operation for breast cancer, this time with a general anesthetic, and afterward grudged the £100 spent on "my poor body." Money continued to be a problem. Expenses rose and taxes, particularly income taxes, rose. She acquired a new friend and good helper in her tax man, Thomas J. Kiernan, later Ambassador to the United States, to whom she turned for help in financial matters. At one crisis she wrote, "I do feel ashamed to trouble you again but I am helpless!

So please forgive me . . . first a demand for a small amount, then £200–19–8. I should commit suicide but for having you as a rock to cling to!" Kiernan thought she was not nearly as helpless in financial matters as she claimed. He called her "a woman of great goodness, simplicity, and guile."

During these years she was aided, and delighted, by royalties, chiefly from her two collections of myths and her short plays. She reported to Kiernan that she earned £467 "as an authoress" in 1924, and exclaimed, "Is it not wonderful how these plays keep me afloat. I am always afraid the taste for them will dry up."

She practiced all sorts of little economies. And horrified her grand-daughters by her regular practice in restaurants:

> When we'd finished tea, Grandma took a used envelope out of her purse, and tipped all the sugar left in the sugar basin into it, folded it up, and put it back in her purse. . . . Grandma said that as she had paid for it and never took sugar in her tea, she didn't see why she should leave it for them to sell to someone else.

She rode third-class in trains. After a pleasant visit at the Viceregal Lodge in Dublin, a young aide-de-camp took her to the station and installed her in the third-class carriage:

> I said, "Are you shocked?"
> But he bent down and said, low and seriously, "I travel 3rd class myself."

When her travel was paid for by the Carnegie Trust, of which she was a board member, the secretary, her old co-worker Lennox Robinson, assured her it was not dishonest but accepted practice to travel third-class and claim reimbursement for first, which she did. One March 15 she wrote in her journal, "My birthday! No notice taken of it here but Margaret gave me my return ticket—first class for it. So I shall ride in luxury."

She was still laughing. She was asked to write an article on Sean O'Casey:

> They called me upon the telephone to ask if I would consent to do this. . . . I said I felt too tired to think of it, but might have more courage in the morning. Telephone said the Editor had heard me speak and was very anxious for it. I asked what payment I might expect, (calculating about £5) and the voice answered, "We thought of twenty guineas. Would that be satisfactory?" I could not help laughing at the preposterous amount as I answered it would, should I decide to write. Margaret was indignant when

287

I told her, said if I hadn't laughed they would probably have given more, but I would not have had the face to ask it.

However hard the times, she never regretted income lost from property given away. With money from her American lecture tours she had given Robert and Margaret a house at the Burren near the sea (which they named Mount Vernon after the Persse house there) and set up a trust fund for Richard's education. On the death of her sister Arabella, she renounced her share of the legacy in favor of her grandchildren.

She had the great pleasure of living in a world she had made, and made well. She was living with the grandchildren she had raised. The bookshelves, filled by previous generations of Gregorys, were overflowing with books by her and her friends. She was looking at trees planted by previous generations and by her. The flowers she had planted overflowed the garden wall in waves. She gave flowers to the Catholic chapel for feast days. The barracks, the workhouse, the Church of Ireland were all decorated with flowers from Coole. Once, when she had given away nearly every flower on the estate, she opened the grocer's order book that went back and forth between Coole and Gort and found a note from the grocer's wife asking for more: "So in the rain I went out and plucked at last the two little groups of tulips I had been sparing, just inside the gate, to have still some pleasure to the eye from their delicate pale tints." She feared losing this world.

In February 1927 she wrote in her journal, "I long for another summer in garden and woods, but perhaps a clean cut may be best." She wrote and then crossed out "I'm afraid I am being pictured to the children as an enemy because I had had the thought of putting off the auction for a while and living in a few rooms at Coole." She did not cross out "I have given up all but all. I can't need anything for long." (In the same journal entry she wrote, "Yeats said, 'With your help I have made *Oedipus* [his version of Sophocles's play] a masterpiece of English prose.'") A few years earlier she had written of her love of Coole:

Last night in the Library the firelight, the lamplight, shining on the rich bindings of that wall of books, and this evening, by the lake, so silent and beautiful, Crannagh so peaceful—"the tilled, familiar land"; and later as I went upstairs and looked from my window at the sunset behind the blue range of hills I felt so grateful, as I have often done of late, to my husband who brought me to this house and home.

In 1927 she began writing *Coole*, a room-by-room description of the house, the gardens, even the bookshelves, because "as seems likely I am now, through changes, to be divorced from these companionable shelves."

XII

The Happy Servant

LAST YEARS: 1927–1932

Fame is no plant that grows on mortal soil,
Nor in the glistering foil
Set off to the world, nor in broad rumour lies:
But lives and spreads aloft by those pure eyes
And perfect witness of all-judging Jove;
As he pronounces lastly on each deed,
Of so much fame in heaven expect thy meed.
                                        JOHN MILTON, "Lycidas"

ON April 1, 1927, Augusta wrote in her journal, "I have just put my name as witness to the sale of Coole—all—house, woods, gardens." The purchaser was the Ministry of Lands and Agriculture, which she preferred to any other because the estate would come under the care of the Forestry Department. That department would keep up and extend the plantings she and former generations had begun. She did not yet know if Margaret would take the furnishings, but on April 8 she wrote, " 'Weeds' [name of the house Margaret wanted] sale didn't go through. M. won't take over Coole." Once sure of the furnishings, she herself rented back the house and gardens from the Forestry Department for £100 per year. It was part of the great good luck that accompanied her through her life that she continued to live in her house until her death.

290

All through 1926 and her worry about the sale of Coole she had been struggling with her play *Dave*. When she read the final version to Willie, he said, "though without much enthusiasm, that it might be put on." It was produced at the Abbey in May 1927, one month after the sale of Coole. In some ways she gives a better picture of what motivated her entire life in the twenty pages of *Dave* than she gave in the 560 pages of her autobiography. The play is about someone treated as if he has little value and how he finds something to live for.

Dave, a seventeen-year-old bastard, had been brought as a servant to the house of Nicholas and Kate O'Cahan "from where he was standing, a *spailpin* [itinerant worker] with his spade in his hand, seeking work at the Easter fair." An old servant chose him because, having been brought up in the workhouse, he "would be easy brought on his back, having no kindred to be running to." The boy has accepted everyone's opinion of him, saying his name is "Dave, short and sharp like you would shout for a dog."

When the master and mistress are away, the old servant rifles through their chest, drinks their whiskey, and takes their gold. Dave, befuddled by whiskey and egged on by abuse ("Why would any Christian stretch a hand to you or the like of you?") asks, "What now is the worst thing and the most thing I could do to punish the world and the whole of ye?" and answers himself by deciding to burn down the house. When the master and his wife return unexpectedly, they are greeted by Dave with a lighted wisp in his hand: "Come in, come in, fellow law-breakers! There's a fire lighting will make you a ladder to the stars!" The old servant knocks him over the head and the two men bind him. They leave to get a magistrate to arrest him while Kate sits beside him.

Kate's situation is a less contricted version of Dave's. Like many wives in Augusta's plays, she is married to a man much older than she, but this is the first play in which the man is overbearing and rude. She loosens Dave's bonds and bathes his wounds with one of the fine towels from the chest. She sings to him and prays for him:

Astray in the lonesome world, he never met with kindness or the love of kindred, to make his heart limber. . . . Oh, King of Mercy come to his help! He is lonesome as a weaned lamb gone astray among the stones. It is as if he had lost his way in the world, and been bruised on the world's roads. The dust has darkened his eyes, it is hard for him to lift his head into the light. He is under clouds of trouble. Bring him to the dawn of the white day. Send a blessing on him from the Court of Angels!

291

XII: *The Happy Servant*

While unconscious, Dave sees a better place, and hears a voice telling him what to do, to which he replies, "I will, I will do your bidding as it is your will. I will go back till I have leave to come to you—till such time as you will beckon me to come." When Dave comes to, he describes his vision to Kate:

> Some good place it was—a very green lawn. It had no bounds to its beauty. . . . It was as if all the herbs of summer were in blossom—I think no one could be sick or sorry there. I would nearly say it had what should be the sound and the feeling of home. And a very laughable thing. It was nearly like as if I was a king's son or a great gentleman. I could not but laugh thinking of that.

Kate assures him he will reach this place someday and gives him advice on how to live until he does: "You have maybe brothers under trouble to reach a hand to, and to beckon them to it, as there was a hand reached out to you?"

He responds immediately, "I am going out as I came in, with my spade and my strength of my two hands that are all my estate. I am going in search of—to give help to—(*passes his hand over his eyes*) my people." He goes to help the people dying of famine in Iar Connacht:

> If it should fail me to earn a handful of meal to keep the life in them, I can show service to the dead. Those that die on the roadside I will not leave to be dragged by a dog, or swallowed down in a boghole. If I cannot make out a couple of boards to put around them, I will weave a straw mat with my hands. If the deadbells do not ring for them, I will waste a white candle for their wake!

He goes out saying, "I give you my word I never felt so merry or so strong. I am like one that has found his treasure and must go share it with his kin. Why wouldn't I be airy doing that?"

Unlike Augusta's religious conversion so many years ago, this glimpse of heaven is not an isolating vision. Augusta too had found her kin—no longer simply the Irish people; she had a sense of belonging to the wide world of those who, in the words of W. H. Auden, "show an affirming flame." She had worked too long for too many people and too many causes not to know that they were not simply a means of getting into heaven but actually part of her heaven.

Kate, the wife in the play, envies Dave his self-respect and happiness:

I've near a mind to go follow that poor lad that went out, not having a red halfpenny to handle, and wear out what is left of my life poor and banished like himself. And maybe get more respect than ever I got here, with my name not showing out in any old book!

Her husband realizes he has imposed on her with his exaggerated family pride, and offers to take her name in place of his. She refuses—his name is already engraved on their tombstone. The social structure is set too firmly around them. Augusta herself had left the little, narrow house; she was not going to lie under the family tombstone.

Since writing *McDonough's Wife* in 1911, Augusta had wondered if each new play would be her last. She ended the uncertainty in 1928 by publishing *The Would-Be Gentleman, Sancho's Master*, and *Dave* as *Three Last Plays*, announcing, "My decision that these three plays—or two, with one translation—must be my last has been made without advice save from the almanac, and rather from pride than modesty. . . ." But she did not stop writing plays. Her papers contain many scenarios, finished and unfinished, though none of great interest.

She was far from debilitated. A few days after her seventy-fifth birthday, "Nearly missed train but I jumped out and ran along the platform just in time! Without a rug, but I had my little evening coat in my suitcase and got that out, luckily for it was a cold morning, and wet."

She got a little deaf (so did Willie), and this deafness cut down on the pleasure of her contact with her immediate associates. Her eyes and memory were slower in putting together all the information she needed. She described an afternoon visit:

We had just gone down to the breakfast-room for tea when a motor was heard, and its occupants trouped in. I only recognized Mary Studd, but I brought them in and gave them tea. . . .

By degrees I made them out, a nice woman next to me was Lady Susan Dawney, and a pretty, bright girl Lady Blanche Beresford, engaged to one of the young men.

And, as usual, she took command of the situation:

Mary told me they were all Yeats enthusiasts, so after tea, in the library, I brought in his new poems "October Blast," and Yeats said "The Tower" and some others. . . . Then, Lady Blanche being disappointed that she could not buy a copy of "October Blast," (the edition had sold out), I found two pages of *The New*

Republic in which the same poems were printed, and Yeats gave it to her as a wedding present, and she wanted my name written on it also, but I said it must be on something of my own and gave her *Brigit* and the evening fell pleasantly.

Willie, who had been staying with his wife at Ballylee of the floods, got a bad cold that turned into congestion of the lungs. George took him to Spain and then to Cannes, where he had a general breakdown, caused, his doctor said, by "the overwork of years." Augusta remembered the long, dreary winters at Cannes with her brother Richard before his death.

Her brother Frank died in March 1928—the same month her husband, mother, brother Gerald, sister Arabella, and John Synge had died. Her brother Harry, just a year younger than Frank, died in May. When she visited him in the Dublin nursing home, he refused to believe she was his sister, asking, with some resentment of her success, if she were Lady Gregory, where were the photographers? She wrote, "He is the last of my brothers, and though the only one I had not felt much affection for, it upset me, and I came away tired and sad." (He was not really the last of her brothers; Augusta had simply lost interest in keeping track. Her youngest brother, Alfred, outlived her by fourteen years and died at 87 in 1946.)

She visited Roxborough:

. . . inside the front gate—the Grand Gate it was called by the people—all changed. . . . The chimneys and walls of the roofless house look gaunt. A very sad sight, the dairies, laundries, cowhouses, kennels, piggeries, all fallen to ruin or pulled down. The garden in rough grass, the pleasure ground rough grass, the walks overgrown. I should hardly have found my way about, all so changed and desolate. I thought of Oisin's return to desolate Almhuin. . . . For as he was the last of the Fianna, so am I of my generation, the brothers, the sisters; and now the homestead that had sheltered us all a deserted disconsolate ruin.

She dug up some phlox from the ruined garden, "a great enrichment to my borders."

Sean O'Casey submitted his next play, *The Silver Tassie,* to the Abbey in the spring of 1928. Augusta, Yeats, and Lennox Robinson all had serious criticisms of it. She injudiciously mailed O'Casey their comments and wounded him severely. He had gone to England temporarily and never returned. When Augusta wrote asking permission to visit him and his wife and then his new son, he refused, saying the bitterness he felt toward Yeats and Robinson would hurt her, "So knowing how I feel, and guessing what I would say about the many literary and artistic shams squatting in their high places in Dublin, I feel it would be much better to set aside for the present the honour and pleasure of seeing and talking with you." She asked again, humbly: "Your letter has grieved me—perhaps I deserve that—but I do ask you to change your mind and allow me to come and see your wife—and the boy—and the garden and the pictures and *yourself!*" He refused again. He later called his rejection of Augusta one of his "silly sins" and still later it was "a bitter memory."

The affection O'Casey felt for her stands in contrast to the indifference or dislike of many young playwrights. His rejection of her is, however, of a piece with their restiveness under the shadow of the old guard. Monk Gibbon, a young Irish poet, said that Yeats was like a great oak shutting out the sky, and Augusta was felt to be similarly oppressive, although it is doubtful she seriously harmed the career of any aspiring playwright. She helped many and believed herself to be of great help, writing proudly, "I am rather a good play doctor." Occasionally she went out of her way to be helpful, writing Robinson on one such occasion, "An old relative of mine used to say he 'never did a kind thing without regretting it,' and if S. O'N hadn't been poor and ill, I wouldn't have gone to the trouble of seeing and criticizing his play."

Until the last year of her life she read plays submitted to the Abbey, writing Robinson on one occasion, "I return a useless play. . . . I was sent 2 or 3 quite useless ones while you were away, nothing worth considering." It was easier for young playwrights to consider her useless. The Abbey rejected a play (partially a parody of *Cathleen ni Houlihan*) by Denis Johnston. Reportedly it was returned to him with "The Old Lady says No" scrawled across the cover. He renamed it accordingly and got it produced elsewhere. (Lennox Robinson insisted, rather improbably, that no one at the Abbey ever referred to her as "the Old Lady" and went on to say that Yeats, not Augusta, had rejected the Johnston play.) A later play by Johnston contains several insults to her, all indicating she had outlived her usefulness. One character offers to show another "the sights of the city, Guinness's Brewery—the corpses in St. Michan's—Lady Gregory." In the preface to his *Collected Plays* he says, "I was never invited to Gort." Her power to encourage, when not exercised, became a form of discouragement. Frank O'Connor, who was a director of the Abbey after her death, described her simply, but with feeling, as "a terrifying old lady."

The case of Dr. Oliver St. John Gogarty and Augusta is a study in the concealed resentment of success. In the 1920's Gogarty was neither poor nor aspiring nor a playwright, but his attitude toward Augusta had been formed in the early days of the Abbey when he was all three. The Abbey produced a few of his plays. He and Augusta were social friends: "I was in town for parties last week—Gogarty wanted me to go to him. . . ." He was her doctor, and during her first operation, performed with local anesthetic only, she was aware of "Gogarty rushing in now and again like a breeze." After her death he had nothing but contempt for her, the keystone of his dislike apparently being his unsuccessful attempts to ingratiate himself. He wrote that she "demanded servility of all her acquaintance. Neither Joyce nor I had pliant knees." (An early observer of the Abbey called him "a willing helper" who would "call cabs for Lady Gregory on a wet night with unequaled reliability.") Gogarty went on in several books to express his complicated opinion that Augusta's plays were no good: "her namby pamby humour deadens my spirits," and that Yeats, "who had a fine sense of humour," had written them but "did not want the comic to interfere with his fame as an outstanding poet . . . so he let Lady Gregory get away with the comics." Yeats, released at Augusta's death from the necessity of defending her in public, did nothing to refute Gogarty's opinion and so endorsed it in the minds of many who enjoyed her diminishment.

When St. John Ervine wrote his biography, *Bernard Shaw: His Life, Work and Friends,* he virtually ignored Lady Gregory, mentioning her only once as "that monumental widow who went about swathed in weeds and crape as if she were Queen Victoria's understudy." When O'Casey reproved him for slighting her, he replied that she had been overrated in the past and was best forgotten in the present. Before the players' refusal to work for him had forced him to leave the Abbey, Ervine had referred to her as "the first 'comic genius' who has been a woman."

Comparisons to Queen Victoria increased as fewer people knew what Queen Victoria really looked like. And, like many people who have been in the public eye for a long time, Augusta was no longer really seen by any but her closest associates, but was perceived to be acting out a role she had assumed years earlier. Many people who made the comparison to Queen Victoria considered it a compliment; she never liked it. When her dinner companion at a banquet made it, she choked on her food, and when she wrote in her journal, she was still choking, writing first "that overpowering analogy," then crossing that out in favor of "bewildering comparison."

It was not, however, a farfetched comparison, and she encouraged it by continuing to dress in black down to her toes. (She wore purple to weddings.) Her only concession to the flimsy twenties was the material of her clothes, not their design. She described an old outfit that, after many years of service in her wardrobe, continued its usefulness as a seat cover:

> But now the upholstery doesn't get any help from a wardrobe, and it seems to me that the result of a season and who knows what inflated dressmaker bills, ends with a little fistful of chiffon you could draw through a wedding ring.

She used to buy her clothes in Paris, but her insistence on maintaining her own fashion reduced her options. She was known to consult the Abbey wardrobe mistress about remaking dresses.

Like Queen Victoria, she was short and stout (Sean O'Casey wrote about having tea with her in her hotel room, "she eating bun after bun, murmuring that she was very, very hungry"), and she could have a rather stately bearing. People who had never been up close to her, or to Queen Victoria, did not know that her eyes were brown, a very lively brown, and that Victoria's were blue; and, most important, people who were not her friends did not know her face could be full of animation and vitality. O'Casey turns all the comparisons to Queen Victoria upside down with this description: "Lady Gregory, in the midst of her merriment and mourning, was ever running round, a sturdy little figure in her suit of solemn black, enlivened by gleaming eyes and a dancing smile."

When Anne and Catherine and Richard were not at boarding school, they were usually at Coole. Augusta gave Anne a gun for her eighteenth birthday, telling her, "A clean shot is the most merciful of executions." (This was the summer Yeats wrote "To Anne Gregory" and her golden hair.) Neither Richard nor Catherine enjoyed hunting as much as Anne. They also both wore glasses. When Augusta learned they needed them, she was as upset as only a grandmother could be: "Poor darling, it breaks my heart. . . . He and Catherine, so sound and flawless, and now wearing glasses."

Augusta continued to place Richard far above his sisters. Though money was a constant problem, she wrote with satisfaction about her £103 contribution toward a new motor car for him, a car that evidently did not satisfy him long, as three years later she wrote in her diary, "I've got the forms for Richard to draw out his deposits from the Savings Bank for his 'lovely sports car.' God bless him!" When she invited her tax man, T. J. Kiernan, to Coole, she asked, "Can you drive a Ford car? I've just purchased an old one for my granddaughter—rather a rattletrap (I have the loan of a good one from Richard) but does for knocking about."

Even Margaret, as it turned out, stayed in the neighborhood she had been so anxious to leave. In September 1928 she married Captain Guy Gough, the owner and occupant of Lough Cutra, one of the great estates near Coole. Margaret wrote Augusta about her marriage: "I feel it rather wonderful to have this second chance of making good." Augusta wrote in her journal, "I believe Robert would be, or is, glad." Augusta had "a lovely letter from Guy's mother" about the grandchildren, recognizing her primary role in their life: "I think how all these years you have housed and cared for them—may I share with you?"

Her beloved chicks now had another home nearby. She constantly lists their whereabouts as if she were telling a rosary, writing Sean O'Casey in 1928, "Richard at Woolich, Anne in Paris, Catherine at her mother's—Mrs. Gough—at Lough Cutra," and in 1931, Anne at Lough Cutra, Richard in the Royal Engineers at Trinity College, Cambridge, and "little Catherine is learning domestic and other work at a Dorset school." For a time Margaret rented Leixlip Castle near Dublin, of which Augusta wrote with delight, "This Castle—that was Sarsfield's!—is wonderful—the thickness of the walls, the old oak staircase, and all in beautiful order." The Goughs occupied the castle through Margaret's pregnancy and the birth of a stillborn child in 1930. They then moved on to Celbridge Abbey, the home of Swift's Vanessa in the eighteenth century, which they occupied for several years. All Augusta's people now had other homes.

She wrote about Richard's twenty-first birthday in 1930:

> I used to think and say—as a sort of vanishing point in the distance—that I should like to live to see Richard come of age. . . . That coming-of-age is not now the coming into ownership of his property and home that were owned by the generations before him . . . And although I am thankful it is in such good hands as those of the Forestry Department, there is a little sadness in this.

Willie was sick in Rapallo. She herself was not well enough to oversee the management of the Abbey. Free Ireland was a disappointment. Frank O'Connor when only eighteen had seen what was coming: "a new Establishment of Church and State in which imagination would play no part, and young men and women would emigrate to the ends of the earth, not because the country was poor, but because it was mediocre." Divorce had been abolished in 1925—Yeats's opposition meant little. Augusta wrote of a St. Patrick's Day celebration, "Very Catholic, shamrocks, etc. R.C.'s praising Ireland, 'no birth control . . . no divorce . . .' It seems as if nothing had been learned or forgotten." She was worried about censorship, writing on one occasion, "The Bishops in their pastorals for Lent haven't said anything about books or literature. A relief." There was opposition to spending the Carnegie Trust money on libraries: "The money better spent on bulls for farmers."

The fight for the Lane pictures continued, looking more and more like a losing one. Yet the detachment, the freedom of mind that made her an observer and creator as well as a participant was still with her. About one of the many meetings that were supposed to decide the fate of the pictures, she said, instead of describing her anxiety or hope, "I am torn with curiosity now the crisis is at hand." Yeats, recovered and back in Ireland, reported to her on a meeting about the pictures she could not attend. She wrote in her journal that

> Sarah Purser and Miss Horniman in such eager converse in the Hall they could hardly be got out when the door was to be closed, and when Yeats asked Miss Horniman what they were talking about she said, "We are agreeing that Lady Gregory is too stupid to be allowed to live." (Yeats did not agree to this opinion but I do sometimes.)

Coole was the last most important thing she had left. Her description of it in *Coole* is her account of what she had made of her life, summed up in a house and a garden. She described the downstairs rooms one by one, she described the woods and the gardens. She described the copper-beech tree engraved with the initials of famous visitors—another list of "witnesses" and companions. The book is full of compliments to her. She records that George Moore wrote, "I had no idea you were such a clever woman, I mean such an intellectual woman." She writes that Synge said of her *Cuchulain*, "I had no idea the book was going to be so great." *Coole* as it was printed by Yeats's sisters at Cuala Press in 1931 begins with Yeats's "Coole Park, 1929," in which he pays magnificent tribute to her as an inspiration to Douglas Hyde, John Synge, John Shawe-Taylor, and himself, asking "traveller, scholar, poet" to dedicate "A moment's memory to that laurelled head." She concludes with her own statement about her place in the world:

299

And as I sit here [in the garden at Coole] in the winter time or rough autumn weather I sometimes hear the call of wild geese and see them flying in the air, towards the sea.

I have gone far out in the world, east and west in my time, and so the peace within these enclosing walls is fitting for the evening of my days.

She was waiting for her death—off and on.

On January 23, 1928, four years before her death, she had written in her journal, "This day ten years ago my child left this earth. And it is time for me to go. So very tired this morning and scar throbbing. I am still working at those diaries, hoping to leave nothing that would give trouble." She was interested in doing more than not giving trouble. In one of her last entries she recalls that her mother's maid, when asked what her mother talked about, replied, "Praising herself mostly." Augusta added, "and I'm afraid I'm getting into this. Yet why should I let the good be 'interred with my bones'? And I feel ashamed and useless now, remembering all the work I did so easily in my time. But I don't want to give in to idleness."

By the end of 1929 her journal is again full of "wondering why I am so tired." A third operation was proposed but refused. Death, she felt, was "so much an easier thing to face than an operation—could but the poor body keep till then its sanity." In September 1930 she wrote, "Pain—pain—pain," and several days later, "Pain today. I am almost glad to have this excuse for idleness—for lack of power." In "Coole Park and Ballylee, 1931" Yeats described, much to her annoyance, her labored movements about the house she loved: "Sound of a stick upon the floor, a sound / From somebody that toils from chair to chair." She fell in the garden and was unable to get up, asking John Diviney, the workman who came to her aid, not to tell anyone.

She still received guests—Willie whenever he could come, and others. In the summer of 1931 Willie and AE met at Coole for the last time to plan for an Irish Academy of Letters. AE, however, more discouraged and bitter about free Ireland than any of them, wrote Willie afterward:

There is nothing to interest me in a nation run by louts and your Academy of Letters will not have the slightest affect in a country where all the papers are united in fears of clerical denunciation. I may think differently later on, but just now I feel alien to everything except the earth itself and if it was not for that love I would leave Ireland.

He did join the Academy, but a year later he left Ireland for good, and he died in England in 1935.

That summer Augusta also entertained Mario Manilo Rossi, Italian philosopher and teacher, who seems to have fallen in love with her. He described the approach to Coole Park as if it were the approach to Augusta herself: "The impression is of something intimate, something retired yet cordial. It is as though the house, not wishing to be directly seen, wished to hide itself in the depth so that only friends should find it." He wrote of her contribution to Ireland:

> You have never pretended to be a guide, to be a chief, to be a mother of Ireland and therefore you have been more than a guide, more than a national chief; you have created what did not exist, a common soul for the Catholic and the Protestant, for the poets and artists, for diverse and hostile spirits, and the living reality of the Irish soil—because all these could be your friends.

While greatly exaggerating her stature as a national figure, his praise correctly identified what had been one of her great strengths—a maternal, almost tribal identification with the people of Ireland. The Irish people, however, had bound themselves ever more closely to hypocrisy and fear while Augusta was going free.

Augusta was failing through the winter of 1931 and the spring of 1932. Willie stayed with her, occasionally serving as her secretary as she had served him. His duties included protecting her from prospective visitors, to one of whom he wrote, "I have been asked to stay with Lady Gregory who is now very old and infirm (private)." The love of mysteries and convolutions that flourished in his later years made him confidential about what was common knowledge. To Olivia Shakespear he wrote in his portentuously offhand way, "But I have told you enough of the Irish political underworld, the strange gallery I and mine play our part before, the 'dying chatelaine' and all the rest of it."

In February, when Willie was away briefly, Augusta sent him her blessing and farewell:

> Dear Willie,
> I don't feel very well this morning, rather faint once or twice. It may be the time has come for me to slip away—& that may be as well—for my strength has been ebbing of late, & I don't want to become a burden & give trouble. I have had a full life & except for the grief of parting with those who are gone, a happy one. I

301

do think I have been of use to the country. & for that in great part I thank you.

I thank you also for these last months you have spent with me. Your presence made them pass quickly and happily in spite of bodily pain, as your friendship has made my last years—from first to last fruitful in work, in service. All blessings to you in the years to come! A. Gregory

In March she agreed to take the pain-killing drugs brought her by Willie from Dublin, but only those "guaranteed not to contain morphia or to affect the mind." Her bedside books were her Bible from Wilfrid Blunt and *The Golden Book of Irish Verse* edited by Lennox Robinson. She had been living in two upstairs rooms, but one day in May she had herself helped downstairs and slowly went around the rooms she loved.

She died during the night of May 22, 1932 (two days after her son's birthday). Yeats, temporarily in Dublin, returned to Coole the next day. In their union, past and present had met, with Augusta believing in a well-ordered universe and Yeats continually remaking a universe to send back to him emotion and guidance. But in the end, Augusta leapfrogged over him toward the future, experiencing the beauty and validity of her everyday life without the necessity of an outside standard to give it meaning.

He lived seven years after her, but his long relationship with the woman he had called "my strength and my conscience" was not over. Publicly he had written warmly of her throughout her life. After her death he was still marveling at that part of her nature he had chosen to glorify, showing her defying a death threat in "Beautiful Lofty Things," describing her magnificent portrait in "The Municipal Gallery Revisited":

> Mancini's portrait of Augusta Gregory,
> "Greatest since Rembrandt," according to John Synge;
> A great ebullient portrait certainly;
> But where is the brush that could show anything
> Of all that pride and that humility?
> And I am in despair that time may bring
> Approved patterns of women or of men
> But not that selfsame excellence again.

He concludes, "Think where man's glory most begins and ends, / And say my glory was I had such friends."

He missed her bitterly, writing four years after her death, "I long for quiet; long ago I used to find it at Coole. It was part of the genius of that house. Lady Gregory never rebelled like other Irish women I have known, who consumed themselves and their friends; in spite of Scripture she put the new wine into the old bottles." But he did not know her well enough, he was too self-absorbed, to love her. Their relationship, founded on intellectual sympathy and her service to him, was immensely fruitful in the opportunities it gave each of them for individual achievement. But there had been no emotional union, and for Yeats there was no emotional bereavement.

Perhaps no one was bereaved by her death. Her grandchildren, Richard at twenty-three, Anne at twenty-one, and Catherine at nineteen, lost an unfailing source of love, but they did not lose part of themselves. Ireland did not feel her loss. What she had given—the Abbey, her epic collections, her plays—had been given completely. There was no sense, as there was in this country when Faulkner died, when Hemingway died, that some vivid sharer of our own time had gone, leaving us suddenly more alone. In fact, though the funeral was large, and though the obituaries were fairly accurate as well as long and complimentary, there was soon after a feeling of relief. And aside from her lack of personal appeal to many, she belonged, as a Protestant and a landowner, albeit a landowner without land, to a class that was rapidly losing power and prestige. The Republic of Ireland had no desire to glorify members of a class it was glad to be rid of. (The Church of Ireland in Gort, where she attended services, has been abandoned; the churchyard has been consecrated for the burial of Catholics.)

Nine years after her death the house at Coole was demolished for building stone. The gardens ran wild. The fields were planted over with quick-growing conifers. Oliver St. John Gogarty, discovering late that he and she were on the same side, wrote emotionally, though inaccurately:

All, all are gone, and the Big House is demolished. Not one of the Seven Woods remains, woods where on a tree you could find the initials G.B.S. or J.M.S.; but the tree may now be on a railway wagon going to supply the demand for building material, though it makes one wonder what can be worth building in a land where there is no reverence for great times and great men.

His comment on "great men" indicates that her sex also was a deterrent to proper recognition in a country where women are not thought much of except as symbols and troublemakers. (The autograph tree was not cut down, and recently a railing has been put around it. The

303

garden in which it stands has been weeded by the Forestry Department, and a nature trail leads visitors through the still existing Seven Woods of Coole. At Yeats's nearby Thor Ballylee there is a tearoom and a bookshop.)

At the Municipal Gallery in Dublin, Mancini's great portrait is stored in the basement along with portraits by J. B. Yeats and Nathaniel Hone. Her bust by Jacob Epstein is on display. (George Moore said she was the bravest woman he knew to allow it to be shown publicly.) At the Abbey, in a foyer containing large portraits of Yeats, Sara Allgood, Molly Allgood, Mary Walker, Frank Fay, Willie Fay, and Miss Horniman, there is a small portrait of her by AE in which she looks like an offended rabbit. When Sean O'Casey once protested against its "dull effrontery," she replied, with the exaggerated lisp he gave her, "I know, bery bad. We leave id dere because we don't want to turt poor A.E."

The meager recognition she received for her service would not necessarily be distressing to her. She got all sorts of rewards along the way, the most important being the opportunity to write her plays, and she looked for a different sort of reward later on. Though she worked at getting her diaries in order for future generations, she was working as she had always worked for "the cloud of witnesses," and she was flexible enough to shift about the constituents of the cloud to achieve a tribunal favorable to her—if not in life, then in death.

Though she served and glorified the Gregorys for fifty-two years, she—chosing the wider way—did not lie with them in the end. When Coole was sold in 1927, she had the family vault on the estate bricked up. At her request, she was buried beside her sister Arabella—actually wedged between Arabella and Arabella's unpleasant husband—on the Protestant side of the municipal cemetery in Galway. She chose the spot at the time of her sister's death: "It is a beautiful burying place, lying high, the sun shining on it, on the silver sea." Along with the dates of her life, a line from *Cathleen ni Houlihan*, changed from "They shall be remembered forever" to "She shall be remembered forever" was inscribed on her gravestone.

As far as she was concerned, this was not the end. She had written about the belief of the country people in immortality:

> none have yet been certainly aware of much more than shadows upon a veil, vague, intangible, yet making the certainty clearer every day that when the veil is rent for us at our passing away, or made thinner for us during our stay in this world, it is not death but life that is to be discovered beyond.

Besides, as she once wrote Wilfrid Blunt, "I believe we shall meet again after death . . . but if we don't you will have the worst of it, for you can't say anything to me, and if we do, I will say, 'I told you so!' " After her death Yeats thought he saw her arm at the edge of a door, moving slowly up and down, waving goodbye—

Tomorrow to fresh woods, and pastures new.

Chronology

ISABELLA AUGUSTA PERSSE GREGORY 1852–1932

1852   Born March 15, the twelfth of sixteen children, at her family's estate, Roxborough, County Galway, Ireland.

1857   Future husband, William Gregory, elected member of Parliament for County Galway.

1865   Future friend W. B. Yeats born in Dublin.

1867   Underwent religious conversion, felt she was "one of God's children, His angels were her friends."

1871   Future co-worker John M. Synge born in Dublin.

1872   William Gregory resigned as MP; married first wife; appointed Governor of Ceylon.

1873   William Gregory's first wife died.

1875   William Gregory knighted.

1876–79   Spent winters at Cannes with dying brother Richard.

1877   William Gregory resigned as Governor of Ceylon; returned to Ireland; met Augusta Persse.

1878   Father died.

1880   Married Sir William Gregory of Coole Park, County Galway, and Hyde Park Corner, London, on March 4.

1881   Son, Robert, born.

1882   Published pamphlet on Egyptian politics, *Arabi and His House-hold*. Love affair with Wilfrid Blunt began in December.

1883   Affair with Wilfrid Blunt ended in August.

1885   Trip to India and Ceylon, November 1885 through April 1886.

1888   Wilfrid Blunt imprisoned briefly in Ireland for leading tenants' meeting protesting rents.

1892   Sir William died March 6.

1893   Published pamphlet against Home Rule for Ireland, *A Phantom's Pilgrimage: or Home Ruin*.

1894   Edited Sir William Gregory's *Autobiography*. Met W. B. Yeats in London.

1896   Invited W. B. Yeats to Coole for visit. Began collecting folklore. Mother died. Oldest sister, Elizabeth Shawe-Taylor, died.

1897   Yeats spent the first of twenty successive summers at Coole. He and Lady Gregory and Edward Martyn began plans for the Irish Literary Theatre.

1898   Published selections from her husband's grandfather's letters in *Mr. Gregory's Letter-Box: 1813–1835*. Began to learn Gaelic. Wrote her first play, *Colman and Guaire*, not produced. Favorite brother, Gerald, died.

1899   Worked with Yeats, George Moore, and Douglas Hyde on plays for the Irish Literary Theatre. First performances of the Irish Literary Theatre in Dublin in May.

1900   Established *feis* at grave of Raftery, wandering country poet. Wrote scenarios for Hyde's Gaelic plays. Second performances of Irish Literary Theatre in February.

1901   Wrote *Cathleen ni Houlihan* and *The Pot of Broth* with Yeats. Edited collections of essays on Irish literary movement, *Ideals in Ireland*. Third performances of Irish Literary Theatre in October.

1902   *Cathleen ni Houlihan* and *The Pot of Broth* produced by the Irish National Theatre Society. Published retelling of Irish epics, *Cuchu-*

lain of Muirthemne. First visit of John Quinn, American lawyer and art patron, to Coole.

1903   First play under her name, *Twenty-Five*, a one-act comedy, produced by the Irish National Theatre Society. Published collection of folklore, *Poets and Dreamers*.

1904   Published second retelling of Irish epics, *Gods and Fighting Men*. Wrote one-act play, *The Rising of the Moon*, produced in 1907; wrote one-act comedy, *Spreading the News*, produced at the opening of the Abbey Theatre; wrote three-act historical play, *Kincora*, produced at the Abbey in 1906. The Abbey Theatre opened in Dublin on December 27.

1905   *Kincora* and three-act folk-history play, *The White Cockade*, produced at the Abbey.

1906   Published collection of folklore, *A Book of Saints and Wonders*. One-act comedy, *Hyacinth Halvey*; one-act tragedy, *The Gaol Gate*; three-act folk-history play, *The Canavans*; and translation of Molière's *The Doctor in Spite of Himself* all produced at the Abbey.

1907   Withstood disturbances at the Abbey over the production of J. M. Synge's *The Playboy of the Western World*. Her one-act comedy *The Jackdaw*; one-act tragedy *Dervorgilla*; one-act patriotic play *The Rising of the Moon*; revision of *The Canavans*; her translation of Maeterlinck's *Interior*; and *The Unicorn from the Stars*, a collaboration with W. B. Yeats, all produced at the Abbey. Son, Robert, married Margaret Graham Parry in September.

1908   Fay brothers left Abbey in January. Her translation of Molière's *The Rogueries of Scapin* and Sudermann's *Teja* and her one-act comedy *The Workhouse Ward* produced at the Abbey.

1909   Grandson, Richard, born at Coole in January. Lady Gregory nearly died of cerebral hemorrhage in February. J. M. Synge died in March. Her translation of Molière's *Miser*; revision of *Kincora*; and three-act comedy, *The Image*, all produced at the Abbey. Finished one-act wonder play, *The Travelling Man*, produced 1910. *Seven Short Plays* published. Defied British censor and produced G. B. Shaw's *The Shewing-Up of Blanco Posnet* at the Abbey. Published collection of folklore, *The Kiltartan History Book*.

1910   Her translation of Goldoni's *Mirandolina*; *The Full Moon*, a one-act wonder play; and *Coats*, a one-act comedy, all produced at the

309

Abbey. Wrote three-act tragedy, *Grania*, not produced, and one-act folk-history play, *The Deliverer*, produced 1911. Completed and produced Synge's *Deirdre of the Sorrows* with Yeats and Maire O'Neill. Published collection of folklore, *The Kiltartan Wonder Book*.

1911   Granddaughter Anne born at Coole. Went to America with the Abbey Players, October through March 1912. Withstood opposition to Synge's *Playboy*. Fell in love with John Quinn.

1912   One-act comedy, *The Bogie Men*; two-act comedy, *Damer's Gold*, produced by the Abbey players in London.

1913   Published history of the Abbey, *Our Irish Theatre*. Went to America with the Abbey players, January through May. Granddaughter Catherine born at Coole. Wrote three-act wonder play, *The Golden Apple*, produced at the Abbey in 1920.

1914   *The Wrens*, one-act comedy, produced by the Abbey players in London.

1915   Son, Robert, joined the 4th Connaught Rangers, transferred to Royal Flying Corps in 1916. Three-act ghost play, *Shanwalla*, produced at the Abbey. Went to America, January through April, with the Abbey players. Nephew Hugh Lane drowned on the *Lusitania* in May. Lady Gregory took up the fight to have paintings he bequeathed to Dublin in unwitnessed codicil returned to Dublin from London. Went to America in October on lecture tour.

1916   Easter Rising in Dublin. Wrote three-act wonder play, *The Dragon*, produced at the Abbey in 1919.

1917   Wrote one-act comedy, *Hanrahan's Oath*, produced at the Abbey in 1918. Yeats married Georgie Hyde-Lees in October.

1918   Son killed in January returning from flight over enemy lines in Italy. Published translations of Gaelic poetry in *The Kiltartan Poetry Book*.

1919   Wrote three-act wonder play, *The Jester*, for grandson's school. Acted part of Cathleen in *Cathleen ni Houlihan* at Abbey. Directed G. B. Shaw's *John Bull's Other Island* at Abbey. *The Dragon* produced at Abbey. Black and Tan terrorism in County Galway, 1919–21.

1920 Published collection of folklore, *Visions and Beliefs in the West of Ireland. The Golden Apple* produced at the Abbey. All of Coole, except house, garden, and 350 acres, sold to tenants.

1921 Published biography, *Hugh Lane's Life and Achievement.* Three-act wonder play, *Aristotle's Bellows,* produced at the Abbey. England granted Ireland dominion status in the British Empire. Civil war followed.

1922 Wilfrid Blunt died in England.

1923 Wrote poem on the heroes of Irish history, "The Old Woman Remembers," read at the Abbey. First operation for breast cancer. Yeats awarded Nobel Prize for Literature.

1924 Three-act passion play, *The Story Brought by Brigit,* produced at the Abbey. Sister Arabella died. John Quinn died. Began friendship with Sean O'Casey.

1926 Published expanded *Kiltartan History Book.* Her translation of Molière's *The Would-Be Gentleman* produced at the Abbey. Second operation for breast cancer.

1927 Wrote three-act adaptation of Don Quixote, *Sancho's Master,* and one-act wonder play, *Dave,* both produced at the Abbey. House, gardens, and remaining land of Coole sold to Forestry Department. Lady Gregory leased back house and gardens.

1928 *Three Last Plays* published.

1931 Published description of her estate in *Coole.*

1932 Died May 22.

Notes

I have referenced quotations and obscure facts—but not generally known ones. When no other reference is given, information on births, deaths, marriages, and other personal information of public record is from Burke's Irish Family Records *(London: Burke's Peerages Ltd., 1976).*

5 "WHY WOULDN'T WE": Isabella Augusta Gregory, *Lady Gregory's Journals: 10 October 1916–24 February 1925* (New York: Oxford University Press, 1978), I, 290.

"I SEEM POSSESSED": Augusta Gregory, Holograph Memoirs, Henry W. and Albert A. Berg Collection, New York Public Library, Vol. 8.

6 "NOT UNIVERSAL LOVE": W. H. Auden, "September 1, 1939," *Another Time* (New York: Random House, 1940).

"HAPPY IN THE THOUGHT": Isabella Augusta Gregory, *Seventy Years: The Autobiography of Lady Gregory* (New York: Oxford University Press, 1974), 28.

"I DOUBT I SHOULD": *The Autobiography of William Butler Yeats* (New York: Macmillan, 1965), 251.

"I HAVE HAD A FULL LIFE": quoted in *Theatre Business*, ed. Ann Saddlemyer, (Gerrards Cross: Colin Smythe, 1982), 12.

7 "SEIN FEIN, 'WE OURSELVES' ": Isabella Augusta Gregory, *Sir Hugh Lane* (New York: Oxford University Press, 1973), 61.

"FEW MEN OR WOMEN": Una Ellis-Fermor, *The Irish Dramatic Movement*, rev. (London: Methuen, 1954), 136.

8 PERSSE GENEALOGY: The exploration of Augusta Persse's ancestry begins with the entries for PERSSE, WADE, BARRY, and O'GRADY, paternal and maternal grandparents, in *Burke's Irish Family Records* (London: Burke's Peerage Ltd., 1976).

MILITARY OFFICER WITH ESSEX: This was John Crofton, whose great-granddaughter married the first Dudley Persse of Roxborough. (See CROFTON in *Burke's Irish Family Records*, which states that John Crofton's grandson, also John Crofton, had a daughter Sarah, unmarried in 1650; and see PERSSE, which states that the Very Reverend Dudley Persse of Roxborough married Sarah Crofton, daughter of John Crofton, after 1650.)

LORD DEPUTY OF IRELAND UNDER CHARLES I: This was Sir William Parsons, who with his brother Sir Laurence Parsons (from both of whom descended the

313

Earls of Rosse) arrived in Ireland during the time of Queen Elizabeth and became joint supervisors of all crown lands in Ireland. In 1640 Sir William became one of the two Lord Deputies under Charles I, and in 1643 the old English settler supporting the royalist party in the Civil War in England charged Sir William, who supported the parliamentary party, with treason and had him imprisoned. (*Burke's Peerage and Baronetage* [London: Burke's Peerage Ltd., 1893], entry for ROSSE, E.) Sir William Parsons had a great-great-great-granddaughter who married a Persse. (*Burke's Peerage and Baronetage*, entry for DOWNSHIRE, M, and *Burke's Irish Family Records*, entries for ORMSBY, BLAKENEY, PERSSE.) Sir Laurence Parsons had a great-great-granddaughter who married a Persse. (*Burke's Peerage and Baronetage*, ROSSE, E, and *Burke's Irish Family Records*, PERSSE.)

LEADER OF IRISH ARMY AGAINST CROMWELL: This was James Touchet, third Earl of Castlehaven, uncle of Frances Ankell, who married Thomas O'Grady, from whom descended Augusta's maternal grandmother. (*Burke's Dormant and Extinct Peerages* [London: Burke's Peerages Ltd., 1883], TOUCHET–Earls of Castlehaven, and *Burke's Irish Family Records*, O'GRADY.)

9 "FRANCES ALGOIN HER BOOK": Gregory, *Seventy Years*, 5. When no reference is given, information in this chapter on Augusta Persse's childhood and courtship is from *Seventy Years*, 1–32.

"GOD KNOWS MANY OF MY ANCESTORS": Gregory, Holograph Diary, Berg, Vol. 11, 8 April 1895.

"I HAVE KNOWN THE HILLSIDES ABLAZE": *Cornhill Magazine*, May 1900, 623.

10 STUFFED TURKEY IN A GLASS CASE: Gregory, Holograph Memoirs, Berg, Vol. 2.

ATTACK ON ROXBOROUGH: *Mr. Gregory's Letter-Box: 1813–1835*, ed. Lady Gregory (London: Colin Smythe, 1981), 22. (First published 1898.)

LORD GORT FEEDING THE POOR: Desmond Guinness and William Ryan, *Irish Houses & Castles* (New York: Viking, 1971), 180.

"I WELL REMEMBER THE POOR WRETCHES": William Gregory, *An Autobiography*, ed. Lady Gregory, 2nd ed. (London, John Murray, 1894), 140.

CONSPIRACY AGAINST DUDLEY PERSSE: Folklore Archives, University College Dublin, Ms. 538, 41.

11 "I HAD NO OBJECTION": William Gregory, *Autobiography*, 166.

"BRIGHT AND STRONG": Gregory, Holograph Memoirs, Vol. 10:

"A VERY PRETTY WOMAN": Sir William Gregory, *William Gregory, Autobiography*, 41.

12 FATHER GETS ESTATE FROM BROTHER: Gregory, Holograph Diary, Vol. 12, 11 April 1896.

DUDLEY PERSSE STAYS HOME: Elizabeth Coxhead, *Lady Gregory: A Literary Portrait*, 2nd ed. (London: Secker & Warburg, 1966), 3n.

"I NEVER MET AN INSTANCE": Charles Kickham, a leading Fenian, quotes the actual statement of an Irish judge in his novel about landlords and tenants, *Knocknagow or The Homes of Tipperary* (Dublin: James Duffy, 1887), Ch. 32.

"TREMBLE AT SIN": John Cuming, *Apocalyptic Sketches: Lectures on the Book of Revelation*, 14th edition (London: Hall, Virtue, and Co., 1851), 26.

"YOU MIGHT BE GREEDY": Gregory, Holograph Diary, Vol. 12, 11 April 1896.

13 SPITTING ON THE PICTURE OF VIRGIN MARY: Folklore Archives, University College Dublin, Ms. 455.

"THIS ORANGE RIP": Ibid., Ms. 602.

1862 CENSUS: J. C. Beckett, *The Making of Modern Ireland: 1603–1923* (London: Faber and Faber, 1966), 365.

"GRAND TRINE": Ronald Cole, Horoscope for Lady Gregory, August 1976.

14 "ISABELLA AND HER GINGHAM UMBRELLA": Isabella Augusta Gregory, *Coole*, ed. Colin Smythe (Dublin: Dolmen, 1971), 47.

15 "NOT BEAUTIFUL, QUITE THE REVERSE": Gregory, Holograph Memoirs, Vol. 3.
   DESCRIPTION OF ROXBOROUGH: Coxhead, *Lady Gregory*, 5.
   STREAM RUNNING THROUGH DEMESNE: *Lady Gregory's Journals: 1916–1930*, ed.
   Lennox Robinson (New York: Macmillan, 1947), 35–6.
16 "NOT RAIN BUT FOGGY DEW": Gregory, Holograph Memoirs, Vol. 8.
   "THAT STEADY PERSISTENCE": Charles Lever, *Jack Hinton: The Guardsman*
   (1847), Ch. 2.
   "QUICKLY STARTLED DEER": Gregory, Holograph Memoirs, Vol. 3.
   PLUMBING AT ROXBOROUGH: Based on George Moore's description of the plumb-
   ing at his family home in *Hail and Farewell: Vale* (New York: Appleton,
   1914), 325. As he was born the same year as Augusta, and born like her on
   an estate in the west of Ireland in a big house fronting a lake, it is assumed
   the arrangements were similar.
   MEAT CONSUMPTION AT ROXBOROUGH: Derived from the account given by Violet
   Martin (pseudonym: Martin Ross, Augusta's friend and contemporary, grow-
   ing up like her on a Galway estate) of her family's meat consumption in
   Irish Memories, written with her cousin Edith Somerville (London: Longmans Green, 1917), 24.
17 AUGUSTA NEVER SAW HER FATHER WALK: Gregory, Holograph Memoirs, Vol. 10.
   "A FIERCE-LOOKING MAN TO LOOK AT": Folklore Archives, University College,
   Dublin, Ms. 455.
   DUDLEY PERSSE DRIVING AROUND ROXBOROUGH: Ibid.
   "I AM GLAD HE DID NOT SEE THEM": Gregory, Holograph Memoirs, Vol. 14.
   WONDERFUL PAINTED BIRD: Gregory, Holograph Diaries. Berg, Fragment.
18 AUGUSTA'S EARLY EDUCATION: Gregory, Holograph Memoirs, Vol. 10.
19 SUMMERS AT NEWCASTLE: Ibid., Vol. 2.
   "ONE FISH, THEN ANOTHER": Like Augusta, George Moore was taken to see the
   salmon, and described the sight in *Hail and Farewell: Vale*, 144–5.
20 TIME AT CHEVY CHASE: Gregory, Holograph Memoirs, Vol. 9.
   BIBLE READING AT ROXBOROUGH: Ibid.
21 PERSSE FAMILY EVENINGS: Ibid., Vol. 10.
   "THE WEAKER SIDE": Ibid., Vol. 1.
22 "SEEMED TO LOOK WITH DISAPPROVAL": Ibid., Vol. 9.
   AUGUSTA WANTING TO SHOOT: Isabella Augusta Gregory, *Our Irish Theatre*
   (New York: Oxford University Press, 1972), 44.
23 "I DON'T KNOW IF YOU": Gregory, Holograph Memoirs, Vol. 2.
   "OF HIS ESCAPE FROM PRISON": Ibid., Vol. 3.
24 "WE THOUGHT YOU WOULD NOT DIE": quoted by Isabella Augusta Gregory in
   The Kiltartan Poetry Book (first published 1919), reissued in *The Kiltartan
   Books* (New York: Oxford University Press, 1971), 18.
   "BUT WE'RE SLAVES": *The Spirit of the Nation* (Dublin: James Duffy, 1845), 6.
25 "HOW THEY USED TO GO AWAY": Moore, *Hail and Farewell: Vale*, 43–4.
   WILLIAM GREGORY'S ELECTIONS TO PARLIAMENT: William Gregory, *Autobiog-
   raphy*, 161.
   TENANTS LOCKED IN A BARN: Gregory, Holograph Memoirs, Vol. 11.
   ADELAIDE TOLD TO WARN HER FAMILY: Ibid., Vol. 14.
26 "ALL WITNESSES REPORTED": Malcolm Brown, *The Politics of Irish Literature*
   (Seattle: University of Washington Press, 1972), 194.
   CHILDREN'S CHARADES: Gregory, Holograph Memoirs, Vol. 2.
   "OIVE GOT AN EXCUSE!": Ibid.
27 "WE HEARD THE MASTER'S VOICE": Ibid.
   "GOD SAVE IRELAND": quoted by Augusta in *Coole*, 38. She herself does not make
   a connection between the disturbances of contemporary Irish resistance and
   her religious conversion, but she gives enough of the chronology for the
   connection to be made.

28 "I IMAGINE HER WITHOUT": Moore, *Hail and Farewell: Vale*, 184.
"MY FIRST REAL MEMORY": Gregory, Holograph Diary, Vol. 12, 20 May 1896.
HER £30 ALLOWANCE: Gregory, Holograph Memoirs, Vol. 10.
"MORE GIFTED AS I THINK": Gregory, *Seventy Years*, 453.

29 MOTHER'S REACTION TO BROWNING: Gregory, Holograph Memoirs, Vol. 10.
FRIENDSHIP WITH THE MARTINS OF ROSS: Ibid.
LEARNING GERMAN: Ibid.

30 "HAD A GREAT DISLIKE": Gregory, *Kiltartan Books*, 19.
"SUPPORTING HIMSELF BETWEEN THE TABLES": *The Poems of W. B. Yeats*, ed.
Richard J. Finneran (New York: Macmillan, 1983), 303.
"THOSE THREE—WHAT SHALL I CALL THEM?": Gregory, Holograph Memoirs,
Vol. 8.

31 "HE REARED HIS FAMILY BAD": Folklore Archives, University College Dublin,
Ms. 455.
"THAT HE DID EVERYTHING": Ibid.
BROTHER SHOOTING THE CLOCK: Yeats, *Autobiography*, 263.
"THEY USED TO THROW AN OLD SHEET": Folklore Archives, University College
Dublin, Ms. 455.

32 "A ROSE AND APPLE-GREEN PEPLUM": Gregory, *Sir Hugh Lane*, 26.
"I HAVE ENOUGH OF EVERYTHING": Gregory, Holograph Memoirs, Vol. 3.
"FOR WHOM SHE HAD TO MAKE SMALL TALK": Gregory, *Seventy Years*, 100.
"I WAS NOT TO THINK MYSELF": Gregory, Holograph Memoirs, Vol. 10.
"WHO IS HE?": Gregory, *Sir Hugh Lane*, 26.
"A WILD SON OF THE HOUSE": Gregory, Holograph Memoirs, Vol. 10.
ENCOUNTER WITH MR. HENRY HART: Gregory, *Seventy Years*, 18, and Gregory,
Holograph Memoirs, Vol. 10.

34 VISITING CORNWALL: Gregory, Holograph Memoirs, Vol. 1.
"SO SHE WOULD NEVER": Gregory, Lecture, "Why the Irish Love Ireland," Berg.
BROTHER RICHARD AND HIS FRIENDS: Ibid., Vol. 10.
"I AM QUITE SURE": William Gregory, *Autobiography*, 214.

35 APPOINTED GOVERNOR OF CEYLON: Ibid., 256.
"A WOMAN OF MANY ACCOMPLISHMENTS": Ibid., 267.
"THE GREATEST SORROW OF MY LIFE": Ibid., 324.
GALWAY ELECTION: Gregory, Holograph Memoirs, Vol. 11.

36 MADNESS OF MATHEMATICS TUTOR: Ibid., Vol. 10.
"PUT SOMETHING IN THE POT": Gregory, *Seventy Years*, 97.
VISITING ITALY, LEARNING ITALIAN, TRANSLATING DANTE: Gregory, Holograph
Memoirs, Vol. 10.
DESCRIPTIONS OF THE COUNTRY PEOPLE: Ibid., Vols. 3 and 10.

37 "AND TO THINK THAT WHILE I LIVED AT HOME": Ibid., 10. In 1871, 22 percent
of all cottages in Ireland were only a single room, 6 percent were mud huts.
James S. Donnelly, Jr., *The Land and the People of Nineteenth-Century Cork*
(London: Routledge & Kegan Paul, 1975), 243.
DEATH OF MARY'S DAUGHTERS: Gregory, Holograph Memoirs, Vol. 10.
"SHE HAD BEEN A PART OF OUR LIFE": Ibid., Vol. 3.
THE BARON "MEANT BUSINESS": Ibid., Vol. 10.

38 SIR WILLIAM'S MOTHER'S DEATH: William Gregory, *Autobiography*, 355.
ADELAIDE'S UNHAPPY MARRIAGE, CHILDHOOD OF HUGH LANE: Gregory, *Sir Hugh
Lane*, 27–9.

39 DUDLEY PERSSE'S DEATH: Gregory, Holograph Memoirs, Vol. 10.
FRANCES PERSSE LEAVING ROXBOROUGH: Ibid.

40 "I MARRIED YOU BECAUSE": Gregory, Typed Memoirs, Folder 27.

41 BAD WINTER OF 1879–80: Donnelly, 253.

42 "A GRAND HOUSE": Elizabeth Plunkett, Countess of Fingall, *Seventy Years
Young* (London: Collins, 1937), 31.

"MINISTERING TO THE POOR": Augusta Gregory to Lennox Robinson, Manuscript Room, Morris Library, Southern Illinois University, Carbondale, Illinois, No. 24.

"I MUST HAVE HAD SOME BELIEF": Gregory, *Journals*, I, 506.

"GRANDMAMMA'S HYMN": Gregory, *Coole*, 25–6.

43 RICHARD'S DEATH, HER LACK OF BELIEF: Gregory, Holograph Memoirs, Vol. 10.

"SOMETHING LIKE MINE": Ibid.

"HOW GOOD OF HIM": George Eliot, *Middlemarch* (London: 1872), Ch. 3.

"HE HAD DETERMINED": Gregory, Holograph Memoirs, Vol. 10.

44 MRS. GALBRAITH HEARS OF THE ENGAGEMENT: Ibid.

"BOSWELL, TAKE THIS": Ibid.

46 "SO GAY IN ITS OUTLOOK": Gregory, *Seventy Years*, 263.

"MY WIFE, WHO WAS": William Gregory, *Autobiography*, 368.

"AND I CAN ASSURE YOU": Ibid., 367.

"WHO WAS SO ASTONISHED": Gregory, Holograph Memoirs, Vol. 2.

PRESENTATION TO THE QUEEN: Ibid., Vol. 12. A typical presentation described by Anne Fremantle in *Three-Cornered Heart* (New York: Viking, 1948), 81.

47 FIRST FORMAL DINNER: Gregory, *Seventy Years*, 32.

"VERY CLOSELY BUT HE NEED": Gregory, Holograph Memoirs, Vol. 12.

A "WHORL" FROM TROY: Gregory, *Seventy Years*, 32.

"THE MAN THAT MADE THE BIBLE TRUE": Ibid., 153.

48 "A SORT OF HUMOROUS GRUMBLE": Ibid., 154.

"DINNERS, RECEPTIONS, THE MARLBOROUGH HOUSE GARDEN PARTY": Ibid., 32.

"CUT TO THE BONE": Ibid., 98.

"HALF-VEXED, HALF-AMUSED": Ibid., 101.

CONVERSATION WITH FROUDE: Ibid.

WELCOME TO COOLE: Ibid., 32.

"REPROBATING THE EVIL DOINGS": William Gregory, *Autobiography*, 368–9.

"HAVE BEEN SO PERSECUTED": Ibid., 370–1.

49 "A CERTAIN DISTINCTION ABOUT COOLE": Gregory, *Seventy Years*, 25.

EARLY HISTORY OF COOLE: William Gregory, *Autobiography*, 2–5.

"CERTAINLY YOU MUST BEGIN": Gregory, *Coole*, 68.

OLDEST SON DISINHERITED: William Gregory, *Autobiography*, 3–4.

RICHARD GREGORY'S CAREER AND MARRIAGES: Ibid., 6–9.

50 "THE REAL GOVERNOR OF IRELAND": Ibid., 10–11.

SIR WILLIAM'S MOTHER'S EXCLUSIVENESS: Gregory, *Seventy Years*, 25.

"I HAVE NEVER READ OF A RACE": quoted in Edmund Downey, *Charles Lever: His Life in Letters* (London: Blackwood, 1906), II, 398.

"A ROBBER AND ASHAMED": William Gregory, *Autobiography*, 158.

SALE OF PART OF COOLE: Ibid., 154–8.

51 LADY MOLESWORTH'S CAREER: Millicent Fawcett, *The Life of the Right Hon. Sir William Molesworth* (London: Macmillan, 1901), 240.

AUGUSTA'S OPINION OF LADY MOLESWORTH: Gregory, *Seventy Years*, 106.

"A MYSTERIOUS POWER OF DRAWING OUT": Lady Dorothy Nevill, *The Reminiscenses of Lady Dorothy Nevill* (London: Edward Arnold, 1906), 146.

52 "TO ENTER INTO RELATIONS": Lady Dorothy Nevill, *Leaves from the Note-Books of Lady Dorothy Nevill* (London: Macmillan, 1907), 228.

CONVERSATION ABOUT WALKING STICKS: Gregory, *Seventy Years*, 120.

"WAS ABSORBED INTO A STRONGER ONE": Ibid., 106.

"MY SHYNESS KEPT ME DUMB": Ibid., 181.

"IT IS DELIGHTFUL": Ibid., 185.

"BOOMING OF A GUN": Ibid., 201.

MEETING FREDERIC BURTON: Ibid., 139.

53 "HER LITTLE SALON": Frank Lawley, "Racing Career of the Late Hon. Sir William H. Gregory," in *The Racing Life of Lord George Cavendish Ben-*

tinck, MP, by John Kent, ed. Frank Lawley (Edinburgh & London: William Blackwood & Son, 1893), 423.

NAMES ON FAN: A second fan, which took her through the 1920's, was signed by Sir Edwin Arnold, Henry James, Theodore Roosevelt, William Lecky, James Froude, John Morley, William Orpen, Paul Bourget, Mark Twain, Antonio Mancini, Horace Plunkett, Thomas Hardy, Ellen Terry, Augustus John, Rudyard Kipling, Fridtjof Nansen, Bernard Shaw, Jack Yeats, Edward Martyn, John Synge, John Eglington, Sean O'Casey—and George Moore. Coxhead, *Lady Gregory*, 31.

MOORE'S FIRST MEETING WITH AUGUSTA: Moore, *Hail and Farewell: Vale*, 184–6.

"THEY SEEMED DELIGHTED": Gregory, *Seventy Years*, 88.

54 "I REALLY THINK": Ibid., 81.

"IF THE YOUNGSTERS' ATTENTION": Ibid., 85.

"THE BEST DINNER HE HAD": Gregory, Typed Diary.

"THE DOUBTFUL GOOD OF SUCCEEDING": Gregory, *Seventy Years*, 208.

55 BIRTH OF SON: Gregory, Holograph Diary, Emory, 20 May 1881.

"LIFE'S BEST GIFT TO ME": Gregory, Holograph Memoirs, Vol. 10.

"THE WEAK POINT IN MARRIAGE": Gregory, Holograph Diary, Vol. 13.

56 "BUT STILL CARRYING IN HIS MAIMED POSITION": Michael Davitt, *The Fall of Feudalism in Ireland* (London: Harper & Brothers, 1904), 321.

£37,000 GIFT TO PARNELL: Barry O'Brien, *The Life of Charles Stewart Parnell*, 3rd ed. (London: Smith, Elder, 1899), II, 26.

"AN ABSOLUTE REIGN OF TERROR": William Gregory, *Autobiography*, 369.

"TELL THE PEOPLE": quoted by Anita Leslie in *The Marlborough House Set* (New York: Doubleday, 1972), 98.

"BESIDES ASSASSINATIONS SUCCESSFUL": William Gregory, *Autobiography*, 369–70.

57 "TUMBLED INTO A REVOLUTION": Gregory, *Seventy Years*, 34.

"STRONG, SELF-RELIANT, HARD": Wilfrid Scawen Blunt, *Secret History of the English Occupation of Egypt* (New York: Knopf, 1922), 151.

WILFRID BLUNT'S CAREER: see Elizabeth Longford, *A Pilgrimage of Passion: The Life of Wilfrid Scawen Blunt* (London: Weidenfeld and Nicolson, 1979).

58 CAREER OF "SKITTLES": see Henry Blyth, *Skittles: The Last Victorian Courtesan* (London: Rupert Hart-Davis, 1970).

"I WAS VERY MUCH AFRAID": Gregory, *Seventy Years*, 35.

"I DEFY YOU": Blunt, *Secret History*, 153.

"VERY HAPPY BY SAYING": Gregory, *Seventy Years*, 101.

"A QUIET LITTLE WOMAN": Longford, 191.

59 "HE IS BECOMING IMPRACTICABLE": Gregory, Holograph Diary, Emory, 2 January 1882.

"NOTHING COULD HAVE BEEN PLEASANTER": William Gregory, *Autobiography*, 375–6.

"YOUNG ENGLISHMAN STRUCK DATZEL": 28 March 1882.

60 SERVANTS AT CRABBET: Longford, 123.

AUGUSTA'S MAID REVOL: Gregory, Holograph Diary, 17 June 1882.

61 "GREGORY HAS FAILED US": Blunt, *Secret History*, 286.

"I MUST TALK THE MATTER OVER": 19 May 1882.

"THEY SAY ALEXANDRIA": Gregory, *Seventy Years*, 44.

"THE QUEEN VERY GREY": Ibid.

"HER MAJESTY WAS LOOKING BEAMING": Blunt, *Secret History*, 280.

"YOU LOOKED SO WRETCHED": 19 July 1882.

"I HOPE YOUR TOOTHACHE": 25 July 1882.

COULD I FIND HEART: published in Wilfrid Scawen Blunt, *The Poetical Works* (London: Macmillan, 1914), I, 347.

62 "SEVEN SOLDIERS IN THE HARNESS ROOM": Gregory, *Seventy Years*, 44.

"WHO BEING LANDLESS PRESENTS NO MARK": 24 July 1882.

ROBERT MARTIN RECRUITING "EMERGENCY MEN": Somerville and Ross, *Irish Memories*, 38.

"ONE OF THEM CELEBRATED": Gregory, Holograph Memoirs, Vol. 3.

"BABY HOPPING ABOUT": Gregory, Holograph Diary, 2 August 1882.

"WENT DOWN TO CRABBET": Ibid., 9 August 1882.

"I USED TO SAY": Gregory, Holograph Memoirs, Vol. 9.

63 "TO DO ANY GOOD": Blunt to Gregory, 26 August 1882.

"A LADY MAY SAY": Isabella Augusta Gregory, *Arabi and His Household* (London: Kegan Paul, Trench, 1882), 5.

"RATHER TO MY SURPRISE": 29 August 1882.

"WHAT WILL YOU SAY TO ME": 17 September 1882.

"I WAS IN DESPAIR": Gregory, *Arabi*, 11.

"I SHOWED HIM A PICTURE": Ibid.

"PUZZLED AND TROUBLED": Ibid., 12.

64 "MADE EVERY WOMAN IN ENGLAND": Gregory, *Seventy Years*, 46.

"I KNOW YOU DIDN'T WRITE IT": Ibid.

"'TWAS THEN, HE SAID": Ibid., 49.

"SOME SLEEPY AND ASTONISHED WAITERS": Ibid., 50.

DEFENSE FUND FOR ARABI: Blunt, *Secret History*, 563.

"AND HAVE I EATEN": Edith Finch, *Wilfrid Scawen Blunt* (London: Jonathan Cape, 1938), 168.

"AT THE CLIMAX OF THE TRAGEDY": Longford, 191.

65 "... I DENIED THEE": in Blunt, *Poetical Works*, I, 351.

"WILFRID IN THE EVENING": 12 December 1882.

"THE JOYS I WAS SO LATE": in Blunt, *Poetical Works*, I, 347.

"QUITE A NEW EXPERIENCE": Longford, 191.

"I KISS THE GROUND": in Blunt, *Poetical Works*, I, 348.

"MOST TROUBLED HOUR": Ibid., 350.

66 "ALSO I FEEL VERY SORRY": 22 March 1883.

"A CORK STICK CUT": 30 April 1883.

"I LIKE BEING HERE": 23 April 1883.

DEATH OF HALF-SISTER MARIA: Gregory, Holograph Diary, 3 May 1883.

"SO, WHEN IT COMES": in Blunt, *Poetical Works*, I, 348.

"I EXPECT TO SEE YOU": 13 May 1883.

"YOU SAW F. BURTON": 17 May 1883.

"BEHOLD ME HERE TO-DAY": in Blunt, *Poetical Works*, I, 349.

67 "SEE A STRANGE WOMAN": Ibid., 351.

"COMPLAINING OF HEADACHE": Gregory, Holograph Diary, 1 June 1883.

"MAD THROBBING OF MY FOOLISH HEART": in Blunt, *Poetical Works*, I, 351.

"SHE IN HER RIDING HABIT": 29 August 1883.

"TOOK WILFRID AND LADY ANNE": Gregory, Holograph Diary, 12 July 1883.

LOUIE EDGAR'S PRAISE: Ibid., 12 April and 7 July 1883.

68 WILFRID CONSIDERS AUGUSTA BETTER JUDGE OF POETRY: Blunt to Gregory, 23 April 1883.

"WILFRID GETTING ON": Gregory, Holograph Diary, 20 July 1883.

"I WROTE A SONNET ONCE": Gregory to Blunt, 17 May 1883.

"WILD WORDS I WRITE": in Blunt, *Poetical Works*, I, 352.

"GO FORTH, DEAR": Ibid.

"FOR ME THE DAYLIGHT": Ibid., 352.

LAST NIGHT TOGETHER: Longford, 194.

69 "A WOUND YEARS AGO": Ibid., 196.

"IT WAS VERY GOOD OF YOU": August 1883.

"PLANT DEEPLY": 5 September 1883.

"TO SEE HOW THE GRASS": Gregory to Blunt, 22 August 1883.

"YOU HAVE NOT WRITTEN": 11 September 1883.

SIR WILLIAM'S LEGS ON DRAKE'S STATUE: Gregory, *Seventy Years*, 103.

"I AM GLAD OF THE SILENCE": Gregory to Blunt, 18 December 1883.

70 ARTICLE ON PORTUGAL: "Through Portugal," *Fortnightly Review*, 40 (1883), 571–80.

"FIRST EARNED MONEY": Gregory, *Seventy Years*, 206.

"HIS MOST BEAUTIFUL": Gregory, *Coole*, 58.

"AREN'T WE HAPPY": Gregory, *Seventy Years*, 210.

"MY HEAD IS SO TURNED": William Gregory, *Autobiography*, 385.

"I MADE UP MY MIND": Ibid., 333.

"ON MY ARRIVAL": Ibid., 385.

71 "THERE IS NOT AN HOUR": Ibid., 393.

"YOU AND WILFRID TALK": Gregory, Holograph Diary, 2 February 1884.

SOCIAL ACTIVITIES IN 1884: Gregory, Holograph Diary, Vols. 2 and 3.

"WITH PROFESSOR HUXLEY": Ibid., 11 June 1884.

"BEGAN TO THINK": Gregory, *Seventy Years*, 58.

"HAD MORE SYMPATHY WITH WOMEN'S EMANCIPATION": Gregory, Holograph Diary, 14 June 1884.

"TO SUFFER AT THE ROSEBERY'S": Ibid., 11 July 1884.

72 "WHAT DID I DO?": Ibid., 16 June 1887.

"PATSY REILLY WANTING": Ibid.

"ASSAULT CASE BETWEEN FARRELL": Ibid., July 1887.

"SUMMER IS OVER!": Ibid., 5 August 1887.

RED FLANNEL PETTICOATS: Ibid., January 1885.

"WAS THE ONLY MAN": Gregory to Blunt, 23 October 1885.

"SEVERE NETTLE RASH": Gregory, Holograph Diary, 9 October 1885.

"TO LEARN TO KNIT": Ibid., November 1885. Unless otherwise noted, information on the Gregorys' Indian journey is from Holograph Diaries, November 1885 through 19 April 1886.

77 "ALAS! A WOMAN MAY NOT LOVE!": Holograph Diary, inside back cover, Vol. 5.

"I SHOULD NOT HAVE KNOWN YOU": Gregory, Holograph Diary, 5 May 1886.

78 "I HAD GROWN": Ibid., 14 August 1886.

"NO DOUBT THE EDUCATED CLASSES": Ibid., 26 May 1886.

"IN SPITE OF THE DARK": Ibid., 22 April 1886.

DEATH OF PAUL HARVEY'S AUNT: Ibid.

GREGORYS' SOCIAL ACTIVITIES ON RETURNING TO ENGLAND: Gregory, Holograph Diary, April and May 1886.

"HE FUNNILY ENOUGH IN THOSE DAYS": Fremantle, 98.

79 "SCANDALIZED WILLIAM": Gregory, Holograph Diary, 9 October 1885.

"I MUST SEND YOU": 5 May 1885.

ROBERT'S REFUSAL TO GREET BLUNT: Gregory, Holograph Diary, 23 July 1886.

"A BRUTAL AND ABSURD SPECTACLE": Wilfrid Scawen Blunt, *The Land War in Ireland*, 2nd ed. (London: Herbert and Daniel, 1908), 87.

"BOOTS ON AND WAS SHAMMING": 30 July 1886.

"A VERY HANDSOME SALVER": Ibid.

"GLADSTONE DEFEATED BY THIRTY!": Gregory, *Seventy Years*, 74.

"BUT THINKING OF STANDING": Gregory, Holograph Diary, 11 June 1886.

"CALLED ON LADY GREGORY": Blunt, *Land War*, 146.

80 "BUT AS HE LEFT": Gregory, Holograph Diary, inside front cover, Vol. 4.

"I WOULD LIKE TO ATTEND": 24 August 1886.

"AT THE BACK OF THE NORTH WIND": Gregory, *Seventy Years*, 225.

"I MUST CONDOLE WITH YOU": Ibid., 226.

"A FINE DAY": Gregory, Holograph Diary, 26 September 1886.

"ANGRY AND UNJUST": Ibid., 27 August 1886.

"IN THE AFTERNOON DROVE LOUISE FRANK": Ibid., 11 August 1886.

81 TWENTY-EIGHT-PERCENT REDUCTION IN RENTS: Ibid., 10 and 15 November 1887.
"HE WAS BRIGHT": Ibid., 11 October 1887.
"OF THE NEWS IN TODAY'S TIMES": Gregory, Holograph Diary, 26 October 1887.
WILFRID'S ARREST: Longford, 25–51.
"HOW BAD OF YOU": 29 October 1887.

82 "DELIGHTED TO TELL ME": Gregory, Holograph Diary, 7 January 1888.
"RECEIVED COMPLIMENTS": Ibid., 25 December 1887.
"A GREAT SUCCESS": Ibid., 27 December 1887.
"I HAD A BRILLIANT PARTY": 23 December 1887.
"WRITTEN TO ME WHILE IN PRISON": Wilfrid Scawen Blunt Collection, Fitz-william Museum, Cambridge, Ms. 1156–1977.
"MY HEART IS IN A PRISON CELL": Ibid., Ms. 1156–1977.

83 "WITHOUT THE GATE": Ibid., Ms. 1157–1977.
"A MUMMERY AS USUAL": Gregory, Holograph Diary, 1 January 1888.
"FEEL MORE INDIGNANTLY": Ibid., 26 February 1888.
"LOOKING NONE THE WORSE": Ibid., 11 May 1888.
"TWO VERY INTERESTING DRAWINGS": 4 June 1888.
"UNRULY TENANT OF MY HEART": in Blunt, Poetical Works, I, 150.

84 "A FINE OLD LADY": Blunt, Land War, 443.
"AUGUSTA DESERVES TO HAVE GOOD COMPANY": Gregory, Seventy Years, 381.
"LIKE A HOTEL-KEEPER": Gregory, Holograph Diary, 7 August 1888.
"HARRY AND ADA DROVE OVER": Ibid., 8 August 1888.
"THE TRIVIAL ROUND": Ibid., 15 June 1888.
4.5 PERCENT INTEREST ON MORTGAGE: Gregory, Holograph Diary, Vol. 10, p. 65.
"CLEANING, PAINTING, WASHING": Ibid., 28 October 1888.
"VERY DILIGENT, MAKES HIS OWN": Ibid., 16 May 1887.

85 "NERVE CONNECTING THE STOMACH": Ibid., 6 March 1889.
"I FEEL THAT ONE": Gregory to Blunt, 22 November 1889.
"ARE WE NOT BUT AS PRISONERS": Gregory, Seventy Years, 121–2.
"KINGLAKE'S NURSE CAME": 25 January 1891.
"MOST THANKFUL": Ibid., 25 December 1890.

86 "NOT ABLE TO KEEP DOWN": Ibid., January 1891.
FRANK AGENT AT ROXBOROUGH: Ibid., February 1891.
ARABELLA'S ENGAGEMENT: Ibid., 9 February 1891 through 17 March 1891.
"MAMA, I'M NOT SO READY": Ibid., 25 April 1891.
"COULD NOT TAKE A LAST LOOK": Ibid.
CRYING AT BACK OF BOX: Gregory, Typed Journals, Berg, Book 27, 385.
"I FELT A SYMPATHY": Gregory, Holograph Diary, 27 April 1891.
"HE IS VERY FULL": Ibid., 25 May 1891.
"WE WEPT ALL AROUND": Ibid., 4 July 1891.
"THE OCCUPATION FOR WHICH": Gregory, Seventy Years, 181.

87 "LANGUID, SUSPECTING": Gregory, Kiltartan Books, 19.
"I AM TRYING TO WRITE": Gregory, Seventy Years, 243.
WILFRID'S AFFAIR WITH JANEY MORRIS: Longford, 278–80.
"I SHALL BE VERY GLAD": 14 October 1891.
"—TO-DAY YOU TAKE IT": in Blunt, Poetical Works, I, 346. This poem was not in the Morris edition, but appeared in Blunt's Poetical Works (which Augusta also proofread for him) just before her "Woman's Sonnets."

88 "POOR ROBERT RATHER": Gregory, Holograph Diary, 15 November 1891.
"I FELT STUNNED": Ibid.
"AND WILLIAM CAME IN TO DINE": Ibid., 22 November 1891.
"I MUST TELL YOU": William Gregory, Autobiography, 399.
"SIR WILLIAM KEEPS GAINING": 19 January 1892.
SIR WILLIAM'S FAREWELL TO ROBERT AND HIS DEATH: Gregory, Holograph Diary, 8 January 1893.

GOING WITHOUT SLEEP NINETEEN NIGHTS: Gregory to Blunt, 31 March 1892.
"HE OPENED HIS EYES": Gregory, Holograph Diary, 28 February 1892.
"AND I SAT THERE": Ibid.
89 "FOR THE FIRST TIME": Gregory to Blunt, 31 March 1892.
"I HAVE NEVER SEEN": Gregory, Holograph Diary, 28 February 1892.
90 "I TRUST THAT NOTHING": quoted in Gregory to Enid Layard, July 1894.
91 SIR WILLIAM'S WILL AND HER FINANCIAL ARRANGEMENTS: Gregory, Holograph Diary, 8 January 1893.
"I SOMETIMES READ ALOUD": Gregory to Blunt, 23 July 1893.
"THE ROCKS THAT": Ibid., 29 April 1892.
"THE HOUSE IS VERY EMPTY": Ibid., 29 April 1892.
"AS I HAD FOUND DUDLEY": Gregory, Holograph Diary, January 1893.
"NERVOUS DEPRESSION": Gregory to Blunt, 16 November 1892.
92 TURNED OUT OF ROXBOROUGH: Gregory, Holograph Diary, January 1893.
"IT IS BEST SO!": Ibid., 11 February 1893.
"ROSE AND THE GIRLS": Ibid., February 1894.
"GERALD ACCEPTED BY ETHEL": Ibid., 13 February 1894.
RATS IN THE WALLS: Description of a visit to the Croft by Violet Martin, quoted by Maurice Collis in *Somerville and Ross: A Biography* (London: Faber and Faber, 1968), 82.
93 RELIGIOUS NARROWNESS IN GALWAY: Gregory, *Seventy Years*, 267.
"AND THE PLEASANT TALK": Gregory Holograph Diary, January 1893.
"LECKY, BILLY RUSSELL": Ibid., 27 April 1893.
"A MORE WORLDLY WISE WOMAN": Gregory, *Sir Hugh Lane*, 28.
OVERSEEING ADELAIDE'S SEPARATION: Gregory, Holograph Diary, Vol. 10.
"FOUND HER SAD": Wilfrid Scawen Blunt, *My Diaries* (New York: Knopf, 1922), I, 65.
WILFRID'S AFFAIR WITH MARGOT TENNANT: Longford, 297–8.
"I CAN ONLY DRIFT": 29 April 1892.
"VERY HAPPY IN THE BEAUTY": Gregory, Holograph Diary, 15 May 1893.
94 "MY HEART RATHER FAILS ME": Ibid., 27 April 1893.
"MANY THINGS SEEM UNPLEASANT": 26 June 1893.
AUGUSTA'S FIRST VISIT TO ARAN: Gregory to Blunt, 16 October 1893.
"THEY ARE LIKE A MIST": Douglas Hyde, *Beside the Fire* (London: David Nutt, 1890).
"IT REALLY GIVES ME": 6 July 1893.
"HIS NAME, WHICH WAS KNOWN": Lady Gregory, Preface to William Gregory, *Autobiography*, iii–iv.
95 "MORE IN THE WORLD": Gregory, *Seventy Years*, 268.
"LITTLE TEA PARTY": Ibid., 289.
"I MIGHT POSSIBLY BECOME": Gregory, Holograph Diary, Vol. 10.
FURNISHING FLAT: Gregory, *Seventy Years*, 270.
"TEASED SIR F. TO SAY": Gregory, Holograph Diary, Vol. 10.
"THESE PARTIES COST ME": Ibid.
"HAD A SANDWICH AT THE STATION": Ibid.
96 FIRST MEETING WITH YEATS: Ibid.
"MURMURED END OF VERSE": Violet Martin's description of Yeats in *Wheel-Tracks* by E. OE. Somerville and Martin Ross (London: Longmans, Green, 1923), 230.
"HANDSOMEST AND MOST ROMANTIC-LOOKING": Mary Colum, *Life and the Dream* (Garden City, N.Y.: Doubleday, 1947), 179.
"MOTHER, FRIEND, SISTER AND BROTHER": W. B. Yeats, *Memoirs* (New York: Macmillan, 1972), 160–1.
SIR HENRY'S DEATH: Gregory, Holograph Diary, Vol. 10.
"CHILDLESS AND WITH SUFFICIENT WEALTH": Gregory, *Seventy Years*, 285.

BIRCH FAMILY VISIT TO COOLE: Gregory, Holograph Diary, 23 July 1894.
97 "GRAND AND HAPPY SUMMER": Gregory, Holograph Diary, Vol. 11.
"CLEAN AND COZY, WITH FIRES": Ibid., 16 October 1894.
"AS MANY AUTHORS LEFT": Ibid., 20 October 1894.
"I DID NOT FEEL THREE INCHES TALLER": Ibid., 20 October 1894.
"THIS BOOK BEING IN GREAT DEMAND": Gregory, Seventy Years, 271.
"I SHALL LOOK FORWARD": 13 October 1894.
"IT IS THE VERY BEST BOOK": 24 November 1894
98 AUGUSTA'S "FEW WORDS" AT END: William Gregory, Autobiography, 357–61.
"AN URGENT INVITATION": Gregory, Holograph Diary, 30 November 1894.
JOCELYN PERSSE'S FRIENDSHIP WITH HENRY JAMES: Leon Edel, Henry James: The Master: 1901–1916 (Philadelphia: J. B. Lippincott, 1972), 183–191.
"HAVING HAD HIS WRIST CUT": Ibid., 9 November 1894.
"HIS SECOND RATE FASHIONABLE TALK": Gregory, Holograph Diary, Vol. 10.
99 A RECUMBENT FIGURE CARVED ROUGHLY: "A Gentleman," Argosy, July 1894, 81.
"IT IS NECESSARY THAT": Gregory, Holograph Diary, April 1895.
100 "THE PERPETUAL TALK OF FOOD": Ibid., 11 March 1895.
"DELIGHTED TO BE HOME": Ibid., April 1895.
FRANK HAD HIS JENNET SEIZED: Ibid.
"VERY HOT, MY POOR LITTLE ROOM": Ibid., 9 July 1895.
101 "THE DRAMATIC IDEA": Gregory, ed., Mr. Gregory's Letter-Box, 18.
"THE STARS IN THEIR COURSES": Ibid., 158.
"I DEFY ANYONE TO STUDY": Gregory, Our Irish Theatre, 41.
"BUT EVEN IN CROSSING": Gregory, ed., Mr. Gregory's Letter-Box, 149.
"I NOT AT ALL WELL": Gregory, Holograph Diary, 19 September 1895.
"YOU WILL FIND IT": May 1895.
"TO PAY MORE ATTENTION": Gregory, Holograph Diary, 3 November 1895.
"VERY LOW AND TIRED": Ibid., November 1895.
102 "A SECOND-RATE SELF-SATISFIED LITTLE WOMAN": Ibid., 16 December 1895.
HENRY JAMES ADVISES PAUL HARVEY: Gregory, Seventy Years, 182.
AUGUSTA'S MATCHMAKING: See Fremantle, 263–6.
SURVEY OF BROTHERS AND SISTERS' DIFFICULTIES: Gregory, Holograph Diary, January 1896 and 26 March 1896.
"IN HIS LITTLE TAIL COAT": Ibid., 9 November 1895.
ROBERT NOT WRITING OFTEN: Ibid., 13 February 1896.
"AND THE THOUGHT FLASHED": Ibid., 26 March 1896.
103 "A STRANGE BLANK": Gregory to Blunt, 3 January 1898.
"HALF-ASLEEP, PROBABLY THE EFFECT": Gregory, Holograph Diary, 9 July 1895.
"WITHIN 48 HOURS": Ibid., 2 May 1896.
"ALSO FULL OF ENTHUSIASM": Gregory, Seventy Years, 287.
EDWARD MARTYN'S CAREER: See Denis Gwynn, Edward Martyn and the Irish Revival (London: Jonathan Cape, 1930) and Sister Marie-Thérèse Courtney, Edward Martyn and the Irish Theatre (New York: Vantage Press, 1956).
"YOU HAVE WRITTEN": Denis Gwynn, 46.
104 "THE LUNAR POWER": Yeats, Memoirs, 100–1.
105 "IT TOUCHES ME VERY MUCH": Gregory, Holograph Diary, July 1887.
"IF YOU GET OUR BOOKS": Yeats, Memoirs, 102.
"YEATS IS FULL OF CHARM": 14 December 1896.
FOLKLORE ARTICLE PUBLISHED ANONYMOUSLY: Gregory, Seventy Years, 390n.
"LOVE OF COUNTRY": Isabella Augusta Gregory, Poets and Dreamers (New York: Oxford University Press, 1974), 51.
106 "IF BY AN IMPOSSIBLE MIRACLE": Isabella Augusta Gregory, Visions and Beliefs in the West of Ireland (New York: Oxford University Press, 1970), 190.
"HE WAS ALWAYS PINING": Ibid., 143.
107 "THIS DISCOVERY, THIS DISCLOSURE": Gregory, Kiltartan Books, 19.

IRRATIONAL BROTHER-IN-LAW: Gregory, Holograph Diary, 14 December 1896.

"PAUL'S LITTLE ABERRATIONS": Ibid., 1 January 1897. As Irish interests and playwriting absorbed Augusta, Paul Harvey faded out of her life. He had a distinguished career in the Diplomatic Service, was knighted, and in later life edited *The Oxford Companion to English Literature*—which gives full play to Augusta, Yeats, and John Synge as leaders of the Irish Renaissance, but which makes little reference to Irish writers of second rank.

"A SAD BUSINESS": Ibid., 25 January 1897.

SPENDING TOO MUCH MONEY: Ibid., 14 December 1896.

108 "IT IS NOT GETTING THE MONEY": Gregory, *Seventy Years*, 330.

"I THINK I DID MY BEST": Ibid., 331.

GORT INDUSTRIES: Gregory, Holograph Diary, 24 March 1897.

"TAKEN WITH HIS SIMPLE": Ibid., 23 February 1897.

"AFRAID OF BREAKING THE SPELL": Ibid.

LECTURE ON MANGAN: Gregory, *Seventy Years*, 333–4.

"EVEN WITH ROBERT": Gregory, Holograph Diary, 13 April 1897.

109 APRIL FLOWERS AT COOLE: Gregory, *Journals*, ed. Robinson, 43–4.

PITS FOR RHODODENDRONS: Gregory, Holograph Memoirs, Vol. 11. In *Seventy Years*, on page 11, she said the pits were eighteen feet deep.

110 BEGONIA TUBERS "EXPERIMENTALLY COOKED": This misadventure was fictionalized in "A Gentleman" in *Argosy*, July 1894, 76.

"ROSY BLOSSOMS AND DELICATE GREEN": Gregory, *Coole*, 94.

HER GARDENER'S ATTIRE: Described by Augusta in "A Gentleman," 76.

WATER PUMP AT COOLE: Anne Gregory, *Me and Nu: Childhood at Coole* (Gerrards Cross: Colin Smythe, 1970), 37–8.

111 TRIP TO BIDDY EARLY'S CABIN: Gregory, *Visions and Beliefs*, 31–2.

COOLE IN FLOWER IN JUNE: Gregory, *Journals*, I, 362.

"JUST ARRIVED FROM DUBLIN": Gregory, *Seventy Years*, 309–10.

112 MAUD GONNE AND JUBILEE RIOTS: Yeats, *Memoirs*, 112–13.

MAUD GONNE'S CAREER: Maud Gonne MacBride, *A Servant of the Queen* (London: Victor Gollancz, 1938, reissue 1974); Nancy Cardozo, *Lucky Eyes and a High Heart: The Life of Maud Gonne* (Indianapolis and New York: Bobbs-Merrill, 1978).

YEATS'S FIRST MEETING WITH MAUD; HIS DESCRIPTION OF HER BEAUTY: Yeats, *Memoirs*, 40.

"THAT SURPRISES ONE": Ella Young, *Flowering Dusk* (New York: Longmans, Green, 1945), 53.

113 "BROKE UP HIS LIFE"; "WHILE STILL CHERISHING HER"; "TORTURES OF HOPE": Gregory, Holograph Diary, 30 November 1897.

AUGUSTA'S REFUSAL TO LIGHT A BONFIRE: Gregory, *Seventy Years*, 310–11.

"I THOUGHT THE COUNT": Gregory, *Our Irish Theatre*, 19.

YEATS'S CHARACTERS WITH HAWKS' FACES: Gregory, Holograph Diary, 23 February 1897.

"WE WENT ON TALKING": Gregory, *Our Irish Theatre*, 19.

114 PROSPECTUS FOR IRISH LITERARY THEATRE: Ibid., 20.

AUBREY DE VERE, LECKY, DUFFERIN'S RESPONSE: Gregory, Holograph Diary, 30 November 1897.

EMILY LAWLESS'S RESPONSE: Gregory, *Our Irish Theatre*, 21–2.

115 GEORGE RUSSELL'S EARLY CAREER: Gregory, *Seventy Years*, 311–12.

"WITH HIS WILD RED HAIR": Ibid.

AUGUSTA'S MEETING WITH GEORGE RUSSELL: July 1897.

"HIS CHIEF VIRTUE": Ibid.

116 YEATS'S FUNNY STORIES: Gregory, Holograph Memoirs, 30 November 1897.

"PURPLE CLAD DRUID": Ibid.

ROBERT DREAMED HE COULD SEE VISIONS: Gregory, *Seventy Years*, 385.

"I AM LIKE MARTHA": Ibid., 384.

"HE NEVER HAD": Katherine Tynan Hinkson, *Twenty-Five Years* (London: Smith, Elder, 1913), 191.

YEATS MISTAKEN FOR A MISSIONER: Coxhead, *Lady Gregory*, 46.

"I HAVE NOT LOST DESIRE": "A Song," *Poems*, 139.

117 "A SOUND AS OF A BURMESE GONG": Yeats, *Memoirs*, 40.

"PRIDE, SHYNESS, HUMILITY": Gregory, *Seventy Years*, 121.

"A MOST BRILLIANT, CHARMING": Gregory, Typed Memoirs, Folder 15.

CROSSES OUT "BRILLIANT" AND "SIMPLE": Gregory, *Seventy Years*, 313.

"THEN IF I WAS": Ibid.

"BEAUTIFUL TO LOOK AT": Hinkson, *Twenty-Five Years*, 114.

"A PLAINLY DRESSED WOMAN": Yeats, *Autobiography*, 237.

118 "THIS HOUSE HAS ENRICHED": Yeats, *Memoirs*, 226.

"WHERE WE WROUGHT": Yeats, "The New Faces," *Poems*, 211.

"SHE/ SO CHANGED ME": "Friends," Ibid., 124.

"SYMONS'S REACTION TO AUGUSTA": Joseph Hone, *W. B. Yeats*, 2nd ed. (London: Macmillan, 1962), 131.

"IN THE YEARS [YEATS]": Augusta Gregory to John Quinn, Manuscript Room, New York Public Library, 28 November 1923.

HORACE PLUNKETT'S TALK: Gregory, *Seventy Years*, 314.

119 "A HORRID LOT": Gregory, Holograph Diary, 9 May 1900.

"A SIXPENNY OR MAYBE A THREEPENNY"; "I HAVE IT IN MY HEART": Gregory, *Seventy Years*, 383.

"LADY GREGORY, THOUGH NOT": Denis Gwynn, 154.

"YOU? CHAIRMAN?": Gregory, Holograph Diary, 30 November 1897.

HYDE ARRIVES ON BICYCLE: Gregory, *Seventy Years*, 317.

120 HYDE'S CAREER: Dominic Daly, *The Young Douglas Hyde* (Dublin: Irish University Press, 1974); Gareth W. Dunleavy, *Douglas Hyde* (Lewisburg: Bucknell University Press, 1974).

"NO WOMAN HAS": Yeats, *Autobiography*, 304.

"AN ABSURD OBJECT": Gregory, Holograph Diary, 30 November 1897.

SHARP'S SOUL FLOWED INTO THE TREE: Yeats, *Memoirs*, 129.

"AN ODIOUS GERMAN": Gregory, Holograph Diary, 30 November 1897.

"SHE IS VERY KIND": *The Letters of W. B. Yeats*, ed. Alan Wade (London: Rupert Hart-Davis, 1954), 3 October 1897, 287.

ARGUMENT ABOUT GAELIC: Gregory, *Seventy Years*, 319.

121 AUGUSTA LEARNING GAELIC: Gregory, *Kiltartan Books*, 19; Gregory to Blunt, 30 April 1898.

"HOW EXTRAORDINARILY GOOD": Yeats, *Letters*, 1 November 1897, 288.

AUGUSTA LOANING YEATS MONEY: Yeats, *Autobiography*, 273.

AUGUSTA'S VISIT TO YEATS FAMILY: Gregory, Holograph Diary, 19 February 1899.

122 J. B. YEATS'S PORTRAIT OF NORA: William M. Murphy, *Prodigal Father: The Life of John Butler Yeats* (Ithaca and London: Cornell University Press, 1978), 249.

"SORT OF A MOTHER OF SORROWS": Gregory, *Seventy Years*, 412.

"ON THE WHOLE": John Butler Yeats, *Letters to His Son W. B. Yeats and Others* (London: Faber and Faber, 1944), 151–2.

"MY OWN LIFE IS HAPPY": 9 January 1898.

"BUT THE VISIT": Gregory, Holograph Diary, 2 April 1898.

"THE PERFORMANCE WAS": Blunt, *My Diaries*, I, 291.

123 DEATH OF MAUD GONNE'S CHILD: Cardozo, 99–100.

MAUD TELLS YEATS OF ADOPTED CHILD: Yeats, *Memoirs*, 133.

AUGUSTA'S REACTION TO MAUD'S PLAN TO RELIEVE FAMINE: Gregory, Holograph Diary, 14 February 1898.

"TO IRELAND WHERE I HOPE": Ibid., 9 March 1898.

"SHE DIDN'T THINK": Ibid., 14 February 1898.

"MY BOOK COMES OUT": Gregory, *Seventy Years*, 303.

"SO FULL OF INTEREST": Gregory, Typed Memoirs, Folder 14.

124 WRITING "LIKE DRINK": Gregory, *Seventy Years*, 279.

"BRILLIANT UNORTHODOXY": Ibid., 304.

"A GUSHING NOTICE": Ibid.

"I SAY THE WORST": Ibid., 305.

"OLD MR. GREGORY'S BUST": Gregory, ed., *Mr. Gregory's Letter-Box*, 12.

"I WISH I HAD NOT GIVEN": Ibid., 130.

"YOUNG GEE SAYS": Ibid., 65.

"TO-DAY IT IS MR. GREGORY'S GREAT-GRANDSON": Ibid., 214.

"FORMALLY REBUKED FOR IDLENESS": Gregory, Holograph Diary, 15 March 1898.

"A SPLENDID REVIEW OF ME": Ibid.

"GERALD DIED IN MY ARMS": Ibid., 26 March 1898.

125 GERALD SEEN BY COUNTRY PEOPLE: Folklore Archives, University College Dublin, Ms. 455.

"POOR CHILD, POOR BOY": Gregory, Holograph Diary, 26 March 1898.

"WHICH UPSET ME VERY MUCH": Ibid., 4 May 1898.

"WHERE I COULD LEARN IRISH": Ibid.

"I FIND IT FASCINATING HERE": Ibid., 5 and 7 May 1898.

"I FIRST SAW SYNGE": Gregory, *Our Irish Theatre*, 73.

"IT WOULD BE HARDLY POSSIBLE": David H. Greene and Edward M. Stephens, *J. M. Synge* (New York: Macmillan, 1959), 87.

126 SYNGE'S UNCLE ON ARAN ISLANDS: Ibid., 75.

"THEY CAME LIKE SWALLOWS": "Coole Park, 1929," *Poems*, 243.

127 "THERE WAS A CURIOUS ENCHANTMENT": Berg, 20 September 1909.

SYNGE'S GRANDFATHER'S BODY SEIZED FOR DEBT: Edward Stephens, *My Uncle John* (London: Oxford University Press, 1974), 11.

"A LIFE OF ORDER": Yeats, *Memoirs*, 101.

"EVERYONE IS USED IN IRELAND": Greene and Stephens, 89.

"I THINK HE GOT VITALITY": Gregory, *Seventy Years*, 388.

128 "I AM SO TIRED OF HOUSEKEEPING": Gregory, Typed Memoirs, Folder 18.

"LOOKING LIKE A CONVERTED MAORI": Gregory to Enid Layard, 23 August (no year given).

"I ASKED DID SHE UNDERSTAND": Ibid., 1898.

VISITING ENID IN VENICE: Gregory, Holograph Diary, October 1898.

WRITING "COLMAN AND GUAIRE": When this play was published thirty years later as *My First Play*, Augusta wrote in the Foreword that she wrote it *after* the "three years' experiment" of the Irish Literary Theatre (Gregory, *Collected Plays*, III, 371); however, the manuscript in the Berg Collection is dated 1898.

"OUGHTMANA, KILMACDUAGH": Gregory, *Collected Plays*, III, 17.

129 "DID NOT ASPIRE TO A STAGE PRODUCTION": Ibid., 371.

"MY NERVES ARE STILL FEELING": Yeats to Gregory, 15 December 1898.

"THE BODILY MOUTH": Yeats, *Memoirs*, 132.

"WITH EVERY CIRCUMSTANCE": Yeats to Gregory, 15 December 1898.

"YOU ARE ABOUT TO RECEIVE": Yeats, *Memoirs*, 134.

"A VISION OF BEAUTY": Gregory, Holograph Diary, 19 December 1898.

130 "I HAVE MORE IMPORTANT THINGS": Hone, *W. B. Yeats*, 165.

"POET BETTER THAN COULD HAVE BEEN EXPECTED": Folder 5 (no date).

"AND WOULD KISS ME": Yeats, *Memoirs*, 134.

"NO, I AM TOO EXHAUSTED": Ibid.

"SHE WAS NECESSARY TO HIM": Ibid., 133.

"I AM AFRAID": Berg, Folder 6 (no date).

"I AM RATHER DISCOURAGED": 15 January 1899.

CHRISTMAS OF 1898: Gregory, *Seventy Years*, 318–21.

131 "I SOMETIMES THINK": Ibid., 321–2.

ATTRIBUTES OF A GOOD FOLKLORE COLLECTOR: Gregory, *Visions and Beliefs*, 15.

THREE PHASES OF IRISH RENAISSANCE: Pound, *Pound/Joyce: The Letters of Ezra Pound to James Joyce*, ed. Forrest Reid (New York: New Directions, 1967), 105.

"HE CAN'T BE A GENTLEMAN": Gregory, *Seventy Years*, 382.

"LOST HER POSITION": Gregory, *Sir Hugh Lane*, 43.

132 "I HAVE SUFFERED A GOOD DEAL": 15 June 1899.

133 GETTING LAW CHANGED: Gregory, *Our Irish Theatre*, 24–5.

134 "I DO NOT WISH": *Letters to W. B. Yeats*, ed. Richard Finneran, George Mills Harper, William M. Murphy (London: Macmillan, 1977), I, 50.

" 'EDWARD MARTYN AND HIS SOUL' ": Yeats, *Autobiography*, 278.

PRODUCTION OF COUNTESS CATHLEEN: Gregory, *Our Irish Theatre*, 27–8.

135 "A WHITE GARMENT": Mary Colum, 107.

"A BOILED GHOST": 27 February 1899.

"A MIDDLE-AGED WOMAN": Moore, *Hail and Farewell: Ave*, 280.

"SOMEWHAT DIFFIDENTLY": Ibid., 283.

136 "SOMETHING ABOUT A MAN": Ibid.

"I MUST BE CAREFUL": Ibid., 297.

"THINKING OF HOW HAPPY": Ibid., 287.

"HIS SLANDER IN MISCALLING": Gregory, *Coole*, 97.

"AMONG ALL TREES": Ibid., 101.

137 "TO PUT YOU FREE OF CHARGE": Gregory, *Seventy Years*, 360.

"THE WHOLE PLACE": Ibid., 366.

"SAFETY PINS MADE": Ibid., 355.

"GIVE ME A TALKING TO": Gregory, Holograph Diary, 16 April 1900.

138 "I FELT LIKE A REVENANT": Gregory, *Seventy Years*, 368.

"A LITTLE DISAPPOINTED": 6 March 1899.

ROBERT "SENT DOWN": Gregory, Holograph Diary, 13 October 1900.

FINDING RAFTERY'S GRAVE AND ESTABLISHING FEIS: Gregory, *Poets and Dreamers*, 41–2; 248.

"IT HAS SCARCELY": Isabella Augusta Gregory, *Gods and Fighting Men* (New York: Oxford University Press, 1970), 355.

139 "AND I WAS QUITE SORRY": Gregory, *Seventy Years*, 406.

"AFTER A SHORT HESITATION": Ibid., 392.

AUGUSTA AT THE BRITISH MUSEUM: Ibid., 396–7.

140 "AN IMMENSE RELIEF": Ibid., 393.

"IT IS A LONG DAY": Ibid., 395.

"PATRICK VERY BOOZY": Ibid., 396.

141 "CUCHULAIN STOOD UP TO HIM": Gregory, *Cuchulain of Muirthemne* (New York: Oxford University Press, 1970), 31.

"WHEN HE DIED MANCHA": Ibid., 39.

"AND IT IS FOLLOWING THE LEAD": Ibid., 204.

AUGUSTA'S DEDICATION TO CUCHULAIN: Ibid., 5–6.

142 "I SMOKED, AND THE LITERARY CONVERSATION": Somerville and Ross, *Wheel-Tracks*, 231.

"IN SO FEW WEEKS": Gregory, *Our Irish Theatre*, 53.

YEATS'S DREAM OF CATHLEEN NI HOULIHAN: W. B. Yeats, *The Variorum Edition of the Plays of* (London: Macmillan, 1966), 232.

143 ADDITIONAL EVIDENCE OF AUGUSTA'S AUTHORSHIP OF CATHLEEN: Daniel J. Mur-

phy, after examining the dialect Augusta uses almost exclusively in her own work and which appears nowhere in Yeats's work except in those plays on which she collaborated, concludes that she is the author of *Cathleen*. He notes also that the manuscript of the play in the Berg Collection of the New York Public Library is "written in Lady Gregory's hand in the kind of 'penny copy book' that she ordinarily used for both the drafts and final manuscript versions of her own plays." "Lady Gregory, Co-Author and Sometimes Author of the Plays of W. B. Yeats," *Modern Irish Literature: Essays in Honor of William York Tindall*, ed. Raymond J. Porter and James D. Brophy (New Rochelle, N.Y.: Iona College Press, 1972), 47.

144 "I HOPE YOU WON'T ALTER": Gregory to Yeats, April 1902.

QUOTATIONS FROM CATHLEEN NI HOULIHAN: *The Collected Plays of W. B. Yeats* (New York: Macmillan, 1952), 50-7.

145 "AN EXPRESSION OF THE WORSHIP": Ellis-Fermor, x.

"THE WALK OF A QUEEN": In her girlhood Augusta had read the lines of James Clarence Mangan's "Kathaleen Ny-Houlihan":

Think not her a gastly hag, too hideous to be seen;
Call her not unseemly names, our matchless Kathaleen:
Young she is, and fair she is, and would be crowned a queen,
Were the king's son at home here with Kathaleen Ny-Houlihan.
(Mangan, *Poems*, 397.)

"I CAN REMEMBER AS IF IT WERE YESTERDAY": Ellis-Fermor, x.

146 QUOTATIONS FROM THE POT OF BROTH: Yeats, *Collected Plays*, 60-7.

148 "HOPING IT MAY BE": Gregory, *Seventy Years*, 338.

ARTICLE ON JACK YEATS READ BY JOHN QUINN: Ibid.

149 MAUD AT REHEARSAL: Cardozo, 219.

"I HOPE KATHLEEN NI HOULIHAN": March 1902.

"A GREAT MANY THANKS": April 1902.

"I HAD NO IDEA IT": Gregory, *Seventy Years*, 403.

"I SEE ROOSEVELT": Gregory to Blunt, 1904.

"I NEVER EXPECT TO READ": Gregory, *Cuchulain*, 10.

"I THINK THIS BOOK": *Cuchulain*, 11. Foreword.

"THE CHIEF THING IS TO SHOW": Ibid., 10.

"WHEN OUR NARROW ROOMS": W. B. Yeats, *The Celtic Twilight* (London: Bullen, 1893), 199-200.

150 "SCOFF AT OUR LITERATURE": Gregory, *Seventy Years*, 400.

"SUCH PLAYS SHOULD BE PRODUCED": *Irish Literature and Drama* (New York: Thomas Nelson, 1936), 158.

THE IRISH TIMES COMMENT: Cardozo, 220.

"THAT PLAY MIGHT LEAD": Gregory, *Seventy Years*, 444.

"MADE MORE REBELS IN IRELAND": Lennox Robinson, *Curtain Up: An Autobiography* (London: Michael Joseph, 1942), 17.

"DID THAT PLAY OF MINE": "The Man and the Echo," *Poems*, 345.

151 AUGUSTA'S REFUSAL TO TAKE CREDIT: Coxhead, 65.

153 "LONELINESS MADE ME RICH": Gregory, *Journals*, ed. Robinson, 338-9.

"THE TALK IS ALL": Gregory, *Seventy Years*, 412.

"THE VERY DIVIL TO TALK": Collis, 55.

"QUICK-FIRING, CUT TO THE BONE": Gregory, *Seventy Years*, 98.

"SWIFTNESS IN PUTTING THOUGHT": Gregory, *Journals*, ed. Robinson, 339.

"IT IS WONDERFUL IN PLAYWRITING": Gregory to Blunt, 26 July 1903.

154 "HE WHO LOSETH HIMSELF'": Gregory, *Seventy Years*, 412.

QUOTATIONS FROM A LOSING GAME: Isabella Augusta Gregory, *The Collected Plays*, I (New York: Oxford University Press, 1970), 279-89; and from the second version of *Twenty-Five*, Ibid., 3-11.

"I STAKED MY ALL": in Blunt, *Poetical Works*, I, 350.

155 "RATHER SENTIMENTAL AND WEAK": Gregory, *Collected Plays*, I, 259.

BOUGHT A FEW ACRES: Gregory, Holograph Diary, January 1901.

"TO KEEP HIS SPIRITS UP": Gregory to Blunt, 22 June 1902.

"BONEFIRES," SPEECHES AND PRESENTATIONS; "FOR THIS SHOULD BE": Gregory to Yeats, 1902.

156 "ROBERT IS GOOD AS GOLD": Gregory to Blunt, 23 December 1901.

"A BACHELOR OF THIRTY-TWO": B. L. Reid, *The Man from New York: John Quinn and His Friends* (New York: Oxford University Press, 1968), 3.

"AT ONCE AN AUTHENTIC ORIGINAL": Ibid., ix.

"PERSONALLY, I AM A MORRIS SOCIALIST": John Quinn to Lady Gregory, 25 November 1902. Manuscript Room, New York Public Library.

"THERE SEEMED TO BE MAGIC": in Gregory, *Seventy Years*, 378–80.

157 "AN ANGEL UNAWARES": Reid, 10.

"GRATEFUL THANKS TO JOHN QUINN FOR": 20 June 1908.

AUGUSTA SENDS QUINN DRAFT OF TWENTY-FIVE: The notebook, parcel, string, and red sealing wax are all in the Manuscript Room, NYPL.

"I AM GOING ALONE": James Joyce, *Selected Letters*, ed. Richard Ellmann (New York: Viking, 1975), 8.

158 "THAT OLD HAKE GREGORY": James Joyce, *Ulysses* (New York: Random House, 1961), 216.

"THEM BAGSES OF TRASH": James Joyce, *Finnegans Wake* (New York: Viking, 1939), 420.

"I CAN STILL SEE": William K. Magee (pseudonym: John Eglington), "The Beginnings of Joyce," *Irish Literary Portraits* (New York: Macmillan, 1935), 137.

"W.B.Y. OUGHT TO HURRY": Joyce, *Selected Letters*, 96.

"I FEAR HIM": James Joyce, *A Portrait of the Artist as a Young Man* (New York: Viking, 1956), 252.

159 "DON'T LET THE DUBLIN YOUNGSTERS": Gregory to Yeats, 1904.

"A SHORT FIGURE IN RUSTY BLACK": Marie nic Shiubhlaigh (pseudonym for Marie Walker), *The Splendid Years* (Dublin: James Duffy, 1955), 20.

160 QUOTATIONS FROM THE RISING OF THE MOON: Gregory, *Collected Plays*, I, 59–67.

162 THE BIG WIND AT COOLE: Gregory, *Coole*, 94.

"IN A SUDDEN IMPULSE": Yeats to Gregory, 11 November 1905.

AUGUSTA'S CONGRATULATIONS ON MARRIAGE: Cardozo, 230.

"BLEW DOWN SO MANY": *The Variorum Edition of the Poems of W. B. Yeats* (New York: Macmillan, 1940), 814n.

"SOMETHING HAS HAPPENED": Young, 76.

"THE RISEN WIND": Gregory, Holograph Diary, 6 January 1902.

"THE PLACE SADLY CHANGED": Gregory, *Seventy Years*, 427.

163 "IF HE WERE A RICH MAN": 23 December 1901.

"WOULD HE GIVE ME": 17 May 1903.

"IMPETUOUS MEN, SHAWE-TAYLOR": *Poems*, 243.

164 "A TERRIBLE INFLICTION": Blunt, *My Diaries*, II, 53.

"I RATHER GRUDGE": Gregory to Quinn, 5 May 1903.

"YOUR BEAUTIFUL PICTURE": Quinn to Gregory, 15 May 1903.

QUINN'S DISLIKE OF MOURNING: Reid, 12.

AUGUSTA'S DEDICATION OF GODS AND FIGHTING MEN: Gregory to Quinn, 27 May 1904.

165 INSCRIPTIONS IN STORIES OF RED HANRAHAN: *Complete Catalogue of the Library of John Quinn* (New York: Anderson Galleries, 1924), 1143.

"MY OWN [WORK] IS": Gregory, Typed Memoirs, Folder 25.

"I THINK I MUST HAVE BEEN": Gregory, *Seventy Years*, 475.

SCENARIO OF THE POORHOUSE: Gregory, *Collected Plays*, I, 260.

"LITTLE MIRACLE PLAY": Gregory to Yeats, 1903.

COLLABORATION ON THE SHADOWY WATERS, ON BAILE'S STRAND, THE KING'S THRESHOLD: See D. J. Murphy, "Lady Gregory, Co-Author and Sometimes Author of the Plays of W. B. Yeats," in *Essays in Honor of William York Tindall*, 48–9.

"DO YOU REALIZE": James Flannery, *Miss Annie F. Horniman and the Abbey Theatre* (Dublin: Dolmen, 1970), 14–15.

YEATS CRITICIZING COSTUMES: Joseph Holloway, *Joseph Holloway's Abbey Theatre*, ed. Robert Hogan and Michael J. O'Neill (Carbondale: Southern Illinois University Press, 1967), 49.

"INCREDIBLY GRACELESS AND UGLY": Robinson, *Biography of Lady Gregory*.

166 "A WOMAN PURSUING A QUARREL": Florence Farr, Bernard Shaw, and W. B. Yeats, *Letters*, ed. Clifford Bax (New York: Dodd, Mead, 1942), xi.

"YOU'VE GOT A FINE BIT": *The Complete Plays of John M. Synge* (New York: Random House, 1935), 118.

"A CRY FOR A MORE ABUNDANT": Yeats, *Letters*, 436.

"THE FIRST THING YOU": *Letters to W. B. Yeats*, I, 134–7.

"BEGAN WITH THE DARING": Gregory, *Our Irish Theatre*, 58.

"I AM GIVING MYSELF": 25 December 1903.

167 TWO PAPER DOLLS: Manuscript Room, Trinity College Dublin.

"DESIRE FOR EXPERIMENT": Gregory, *Our Irish Theatre*, 57.

"LET THEM MAKE MUCH OF THE LINNET": Isabella Augusta Gregory, *The Collected Plays*, II (New York: Oxford University Press, 1970), 345.

"YOU WERE ASLEEP"; "IT IS MYSELF": Ibid., 348.

"THE FIRST MONEY": Yeats, *Letters*, 8 February 1904, 431.

YEATS FAMILY WANTING TO BORROW: W. M. Murphy, 263.

168 "NOT UNTIL I THINK YOU": Yeats, *Autobiography*, 273.

"GREAT SYMPATHY WITH THE ARTISTIC": Gregory, *Our Irish Theatre*, 34.

"QUITE UNTRUE ABOUT THE": Gregory, *Journals I*, 247.

QUOTATIONS FROM SPREADING THE NEWS: Gregory, *Collected Plays*, I, 15–29.

169 "WE GOT A TREMENDOUS": William Fay and Catherine Carswell, *The Fays of the Abbey Theatre* (New York: Harcourt, Brace, 1935), 165.

171 "THE LAST SECRET OF MATERNITY": Mario Manilo Rossi, *Pilgrimage in the West* (Dublin: Cuala Press, 1933), 49.

"SHE DID NOT CARE": Mary Colum, 119.

172 "THERE IS NO EXCITEMENT": Gregory to Blunt, 1 October 1906.

"SOME RICH EMOTIONS": Mary Colum, 124.

"DOING TOO MANY THINGS": Sean O'Casey, *Blasts and Benedictions* (London: Macmillan, 1967), 207.

"THE INTELLECT OF MAN": "The Choice," *Poems*, 246.

173 THE KID BENSON: Yeats, *Letters*, October 1901, 355–6.

174 "THOUGH I LIVE": quoted in Young, 80.

"A SPIRIT FROM BEYOND": W. B. Yeats, *Explorations* (New York: Macmillan, 1962), 146–7.

"IT SEEMED TO ME": Sara Allgood, *Memories*, Berg.

"BLISS IT WAS": *Prelude*, Book II, lines 108–9.

"THOUGH THEY HAVE COME": Yeats, *Letters*, 26 July 1904, 436.

175 "GAVE HER EVIDENCE": Ibid., 4 August 1904, 437.

"LADY G. CAME IN": Reid, 25.

YEATS AS DIRECTOR: Holloway, *Abbey Theatre*, 39.

AUGUSTA AS DIRECTOR: Ibid., 45.

"MARCHED ALONG TOGETHER": Reid, 27.

176 MISS HORNIMAN'S TEA PARTY: Lennox Robinson, *Ireland's Abbey Theatre* (London: Sidgwick and Jackson, 1951), 45.

"HOW EASY DEATH": Gregory to Blunt, 16 January 1905.

"THE AUDIENCE WOULD LAUGH": Ibid.

"TALL AND DARK": Gerald Fay, *The Abbey Theatre* (Dublin: Clonmore & Reynolds, 1958), 93.

MISS HORNIMAN'S DRAGON: Ben Iden Payne, *A Life in a Wooden O* (New Haven and London: Yale University Press, 1977), 81.

"A PLEASANT IF AT TIMES": Shiubhlaigh, 30.

"AN EXTREMELY LIKEABLE": Ibid., 48.

"HOLE AND CORNER IRISH IDEAS": Gerald Fay, 109.

"I SHALL LOOK UPON IT": *Letters to Yeats*, I, 147.

"A SHILLING IN A TUB": Gregory to Yeats, 1 March 1906.

"A RATHER TRYING GUEST": Gregory to Quinn, 20 September 1905.

177 "WOULD SMOKE A CIGAR": Robinson, *Ireland's Abbey Theatre*, 67.

"LADY GREGORY BEHAVED": Mary Colum, 119.

"LADY GREGORY NEVER FORGOT": Robinson, *Ireland's Abbey Theatre*, 70.

"A LOVER OF PEACE": Gregory, *Our Irish Theatre*, 38.

"I FEEL AS IF": January 1905.

"SO I WANT YOU": 1905.

"IT WAS HER SON'S PART": Holloway *Abbey Theatre*, 54.

"AUGUSTA SWEPT ME": Somerville and Ross, *Wheel-Tracks*, 233.

178 "ESTATE BUSINESS HAS": Gregory, *Seventy Years*, 428.

"YOU SEE WE HAVE BEGUN": 19 April 1905.

"I DON'T LIKE LOSING": June 1901.

"I WAS ABOUT TO WRITE": Yeats, *Letters*, July 1905, 455.

"IF SHE IS IN TROUBLE": Gregory, *Collected Plays*, II, 242.

"THOUGH THEY CAN STAND": W. B. Yeats, *A Vision* (New York: Macmillan, 1965), 171.

179 "HIS HAND STILL TREMBLING": Gregory, *Collected Plays*, II, 254.

"LADY GREGORY KNOWS THE SOUL": Cardozo, 255.

"SET IN CLEAN LETTERS": Gregory, *Collected Plays*, II, 240.

"HE [HYACINTH] FOUND HIMSELF": Ibid., I, 255.

QUOTATIONS FROM HYACINTH HALVEY: Ibid., 33–56.

180 "WHO KNOWS I HAVE EVER": Gregory, *Seventy Years*, 442.

"INSTEAD OF MERELY DEDUCING": *Theatre Business*, Yeats to John Synge, 3 January 1906, 89.

"WHERE ARE YOU?": Ibid., 9 September 1905, 78–9.

"THIS IS THE SORT OF CASE": Ibid., 31 December 1905, 87.

"NO CHAPERONES OR NON-DANCERS": December 1905.

"OUR DANCE WENT SPLENDIDLY": *Theatre Business*, January 1906, 97.

181 "THE ENEMY"; "I HOPE THAT LITERARY SOCIETY": Gregory to Yeats, Spring 1906.

"NO NOTICE AT ALL": December 1905.

"I HAVE WRITTEN OLD YEATS": *Theatre Business*, 6 January 1906, 95.

"I FEAR IF SOME OF THE DIRECTORS": 16 January 1906.

"YOU ARE THOUGHTLESSLY": *Theatre Business*, 7 January 1906, 103.

"WHAT A POOR CREATURE": Ibid., 9 January 1906, 100.

"THERE IS PROBABLY": *Letters to Yeats*, December 1905, I, 152–5.

"WILL WEAR OUT THE WORLD": Gregory, *Coole*, 104.

182 "OFTEN FOR MONTHS": *Essays and Introductions* (New York: Macmillan, 1961), 319.

"OF THE THEATRE YEARS": Gregory, *Seventy Years*, 389.

"HE WAS UNGRACIOUS": quoted in Coxhead, *Lady Gregory*, 121.

"I DARESAY A WEEK'S REHEARSAL": June 1905.

183 "I THOUGHT THE STARS": *Theatre Business*, 29 November 1908, 293–4.

"I SOMETIMES WONDERED": Gregory, *Seventy Years*, 388–9.

"TOOK COMMAND, INVITED": Sara Allgood, *Memories*.

"SAYING HE COULD CLAIM": Gregory, *Seventy Years*, 417.

"ONCE SHE WAS INDUCED": Robinson, *Biography of Lady Gregory*.

184 "I CAME ROUND BEFORE MEALTIME": Gregory, *Seventy Years*, 416.

"IS SHE NOT A BORN LEADER?": *Letters to His Son*, 109.

"HOPING THAT IN THE DIMNESS": Gregory, *Our Irish Theatre*, 37.

185 PERFORMANCES OF AUGUSTA'S PLAYS: Holloway, *Abbey Theatre*, 283.

"UP ROSE LADY GREGORY": William Fay and Carswell, 193.

"A REVELATION OF WHAT CAN BE DONE": Ibid., 194.

"SOME OF THE AUDIENCE": Ibid., 196.

"I HAVE ANOTHER COMEDY": 5 May 1906.

QUOTATIONS FROM THE JACKDAW: Gregory, *Collected Plays*, I, 71–93.

187 "WE WERE ASTONISHED": Gregory, *Seventy Years*, 419.

"HE WOULD GO": Gregory, *Sir Hugh Lane*, 79.

"HIS PORTRAIT OF A WOMAN": Ibid.

"IT IS A WONDERFUL PICTURE": 11 December 1907.

"THE MISS O'DEMPSEY WHO WAS ENGAGED": Yeats to Gregory, 4 July 1906.

188 "I WOULD ESTABLISH MYSELF": *Letters to Yeats*, 22 July 1906, I, 164–5.

DATING OF THE GAOL GATE AND THE CANAVANS: Holograph copy, *The Gaol Gate*, unsigned, dated 20–23 August [1906], Berg; Holograph copy, *The Canavans*, signed, dated 27 August 1906, Berg.

QUOTATIONS FROM THE GAOL GATE: Gregory, *Collected Plays*, II, 5–10.

189 "I WANT TO THANK YOUR KINDNESS": Berg, 7 September 1906.

"I KNOW ALL YOU HAVE DONE": Gregory, Holograph Diary, 3 March 1886.

"LADY GREGORY WROTE": W. B. Yeats, *Letters on Poetry from W. B. Yeats to Dorothy Wellesley* (London: Oxford University Press, 1940), 51.

"THIS IS THE DIFFICULTY": November 1906.

"PIFFLE" NOT "MIFFLE": Ibid.

190 QUOTATIONS FROM THE CANAVANS: Gregory, *Collected Plays*, II, 179–216.

191 "THE PLAY SEEMS": Ibid., 298.

192 "IRISH NANNY NOTES": Geoffrey Grigson, "Synge," *New Statesman*, 19 October 1962, 528.

"THOSE PLAYS WERE OUR CHILDREN": *Theatre Business*, 202n.

"I WOULD NOT FOR A MOMENT": Ibid., 5 January 1907, 197.

"I AM TIED TO THE COMPANY": J. M. Synge, *Letters to Molly*, ed. Ann Saddlemyer (Cambridge, Mass.: Belknap Press of Harvard University Press, 1971), 21 March 1907, 114.

193 "SYNGE SELDOM DID": Mary Colum, 119.

"SYNGE IS INVALUABLE": quoted in Greene and Stephens, 302.

"IT DID MAKE ME": *Theatre Business*, 205n.

AUGUSTA'S ACCOUNT OF THE PLAYBOY RIOT: *Our Irish Theatre*, 66–70.

"IT'S PEGEEN I'M SEEKING": Synge, *Complete Plays*, 75.

194 HOLLOWAY ON PLAYBOY RIOT: *Abbey Theatre*, 84.

"LADY GREGORY STOOD": Walter Starkie, *Scholars and Gypsies: An Autobiography* (Berkeley and Los Angeles: University of California Press, 1963), 39.

AUGUSTA OFFERS TO PAY COLUM'S FATHER'S FINE: Greene and Stephens, 243.

"IT WAS A DEFINITE FIGHT": Gregory, *Our Irish Theatre*, 68.

"THE AUTHOR OF CATHLEEN": Mary Colum, 139.

"THE ODD THING IS": Holloway, *Abbey Theatre*, 105.

"I NEVER WITNESSED": Mary Colum, 139.

195 "I WAS SORRY": *Theatre Business*, 5 February 1907, 213.

"I DARESAY IT WAS": Gregory, *Seventy Years*, 419.

"YOU WILL I AM SURE": Berg, 29 August 1908.

"WHEN AN IDEA": Gregory to Quinn, 2 October 1912.

"FREED FROM THE LEADING-STRINGS": Reid, 120.

"A VERY CHARMING GIRL": Gregory to Quinn, 17 August 1907.

MARGARET'S ENGAGEMENT RING: Gregory, *Seventy Years*, 341.

196 CEYLON TEA STOCK: "Letters from Lady Gregory: A Record of Her Friendship with T. J. Kiernan," *Bulletin of the New York Public Library*, December 1967, 630.

"I SHALL FOR THE PRESENT": 17 August 1907.

"A SLIGHT NERVOUSNESS": Gregory, *Seventy Years*, 428.

"IF HE HAD": Moore, *Hail and Farewell: Vale*, 171.

"IN TERRIBLE TROUBLE": Blunt, *My Diaries*, I, 172.

DATING OF DERVORGILLA: Holograph draft, unsigned, dated 24 June 1907, Berg.

"I FELT AS IF": Gregory, *Our Irish Theatre*, 58.

197 "THE PATH OF EXPEDIENCY": Ibid.

QUOTATIONS FROM DERVORGILLA: Gregory, *Collected Plays*, II, 95–111.

"ONE SIN, MOST CERTAINLY": in Blunt, *Poetical Works*, I, 351.

"THE FELLOW KNOWS": Gregory, *Seventy Years*, 35–6.

198 "GIVEN BY W. S. BLUNT": *Complete Catalogue of the Library of John Quinn*, 73.

"GLAD FOR ROBERT": Gregory to Quinn, 17 August 1907.

"SINCE I HAD LAST": Gregory, *Collected Plays*, IV (New York: Oxford University Press, 1970), 362.

"RECEIVED WITH GREAT GLEE": Gregory, *Seventy Years*, 418.

199 "WE ALL HAVE 'ARTISTIC TEMPERAMENTS'": *Theatre Business*, 22 December 1907, 255n.

"I HAVE SEEN HIM TELLING": Ibid., 28 December 1906, 190.

"THERE IS NO GETTING OVER": 20 March 1908.

"I CAN SEE SYNGE": 20 March 1908.

"VERY DANGEROUS SEIZURE": C. Dumas, Horoscope for Lady Gregory, Berg.

"CURIOUS BREAKDOWN": Yeats, *Memoirs*, 140.

"IF LADY GREGORY": Ibid., 141.

200 "YOURS SINCERELY, W. B. YEATS": Gerald Fay, 138.

QUOTATIONS FROM THE WORKHOUSE WARD: Gregory, *Collected Plays*, I, 97–105.

202 "YOU WERE MAYBE MISLED": Ibid., II, 91.

"POOR IRELAND IS IN": Gregory to Quinn, 17 August 1907.

"ASTONISHING THE ANIMOSITY": *Theatre Business*, 6 January 1906, 95.

203 "MARGARET IS STILL": *Theatre Business*, 13 July 1908, 286.

"I HAVE HEARD THE PIGEONS": *Poems*, 77.

204 "NO ONE EVEN CAN HAVE HEARD": Hone, *W. B. Yeats*, 225.

YEATS DRINKING THE TORQUEY: Told to author by Richard Graham Gregory.

"I THOUGHT OF THIS HOUSE": *Memoirs*, 230.

205 QUOTATIONS FROM THE TRAVELLING MAN: Gregory, *Collected Plays*, III, 21–8.

206 "BUT WHY DIDN'T": Ibid., 374.

"YOU ARE MORE BEAUTIFUL": "Broken Dreams," *Poems*, 154.

"I AM VERY SORRY": Gregory, *Seventy Years*, 418.

207 "I DID NOT RECOGNIZE": *Memoirs*, 160–1.

"VERY NEARLY SLIPPED AWAY": Ibid.

"SICKNESS BROUGHT ME THIS": "A Friend's Illness," *Poems*, 97.

"I MEAN BY SICKNESS": Berg, 8 February 1909.

"ALL WEDNESDAY I HEARD": *Memoirs*, 163.

"I AM STILL DEEPLY": Gregory, Typed Memoirs, Folder 13.

"I LOOKED UPON THE JOY": Gregory, *Seventy Years*, 457.

208 "IN THE EARLY MORNING": Ibid., 439.

"THIS SUDDEN SILENCE": *Theatre Business*, 24 March 1909, 298.

"YOU DID MORE THAN ANY": Ibid., 299.

"IT IS I WHO OUGHT": 25 March 1905.

"I THINK I OUGHT TO HAVE BEEN": 14 April 1909.

MOLLY RELIEVED: Elizabeth Coxhead, *Daughters of Erin* (London: Secker & Warburg, 1965), 193.

"LADY GREGORY WHO": *Memoirs*, 219.

"LORD, CONFOUND THIS SURLY": Ibid., 202.

209 AUGUSTA IN VENICE: Gregory, *Seventy Years*, 440–1.
DATING OF THE IMAGE: Typescript, Berg, dated 22–29 June 1909.
"MY CHIEF PLAY": Gregory, *Journals*, I, 585.
"A BOG SLIDE!": Holloway, *Abbey Theatre*, 133.
QUOTATIONS FROM AND SUMMARY OF THE IMAGE: Gregory, *Collected Plays*, II, 131–76.

211 "BUT IF THE DREAMER": Ibid., 297.
DEDICATION OF THE IMAGE: Ibid., xvii.
RENT REDUCTIONS, TAX INCREASES: See Yeats, *Memoirs*, 226n.
"HOW SHOULD THE WORLD": *Poems*, 95.
"SO I FEEL THE RICHER": Gregory, *Journals*, I, 231.

212 "AN EXTRAORDINARY INTEREST": Gregory, *Our Irish Theatre*, 84.
"MR. YEATS, UNTIL HE JOINED": Ibid., 92–3.
"WHEN WE HAD LEFT": Ibid., 94.
"REALISING THAT ALL THE": Mark Amory, *Biography of Lord Dunsany* (London: Collins, 1972), 73–4.

213 "TO W. B. YEATS": Gregory, *Seven Short Plays* (Dublin: Maunsel, 1909), i.
"SEIN FEIN—'WE OURSELVES'": Gregory, *Sir Hugh Lane*, 61.
DATING OF GRANIA: Holograph copy, Berg, signed, dated 22–30 November 1909.
"LOVELY DEIRDRE, WHO WHEN": Gregory, *Collected Plays*, II, 283.

214 QUOTATIONS FROM MIRANDOLINA: Ibid., IV, 195–233.
QUOTATIONS FROM GRANIA: Ibid., II, 13–46.

215 "LOVE ITSELF, WITH ITS SHADOW": Ibid., 283.

216 "I AM MASTER OF ALL FIGHTS": Synge, *Complete Plays*, 80.
DATING OF THE DELIVERER: Holograph draft, Berg, dated 10–15 July 1910.
DATING OF THE FULL MOON: Typescript, Berg, dated 10 September 1910.
DATING OF COATS: Holograph draft, Berg, dated 14 September 1910.
DATING TYPESCRIPT OF GRANIA: Typescript, Berg, dated August 1910.

217 QUOTATIONS FROM THE DELIVERER: Gregory, *Complete Plays*, II, 257–77.
"I REMEMBER ONCE": Mary Colum, 119.
"THE DAILY SPITE": "The People," *Poems*, 150.

218 "I CANNOT EXPRESS": quoted in Yeats, *Memoirs*, 289–90.
"I AM AMUSED": Ibid., 256.
"I COME TO SEE": Ibid.
"SINCE I WAS FIFTEEN": Ibid., 256–7.
"I NEITHER DEALT": Ibid., 257.

219 "IS SO VIOLENT": Gregory, *Collected Plays*, I, 261.
QUOTATION FROM COATS: Ibid., 131.
QUOTATIONS FROM THE FULL MOON: Gregory, *Collected Plays*, III, 31–51.

220 "CALL OF SOME": Ibid., 374.
"DEAR MANAGING DIRECTOR": *Letters to W. B. Yeats*, I, 220.

221 "TIGER ON THE PLATFORM": Typed Journals, Berg, Book 32.
"SHOULD CLOSE THROUGH COURTESY": Peter Kavanagh, *The Story of the Abbey Theatre* (New York: Devin-Adair, 1950), 75.
"A REGRET THAT IT WAS NOT": *Letters to W. B. Yeats*, I, 228–9.
"I HAVE BEEN THINKING": 6 June 1910.
"UNLESS THE £1000": *Letters to W. B. Yeats*, I, 235.
"I FEEL SURE": Gregory, *Our Irish Theatre*, 34.
"WE HAVE CERTAINLY": 1908.
DATING OF THE BOGIE MEN: Holograph draft, Berg, dated 17 April 1911.
QUOTATIONS FROM THE BOGIE MEN: Gregory, *Collected Plays*, I, 109–18.

223 "THEY WANTED ME": 26 August 1911.
"THE GAP MADE": 13 June 1911.

224 AUGUSTA'S HOROSCOPES: C. Dumas and J. R. Wallace, Berg.

QUOTATIONS FROM MCDONOUGH'S WIFE: Gregory, *Collected Plays*, II, 115–25.

225 "... AND BEING STILL": *Complete Catalogue of the Library of John Quinn*, I, 363.

"IF I HAD KNOWN": Gregory to Robert Gregory, Berg, 3 October 1911.

"DRAWING UP HER SHORT": Shiubhlaigh, 31.

"ALTHOUGH SHE CONFESSES": E. H. Mikhail, *Lady Gregory: Interviews and Recollections* (London: Macmillan, 1977), 44–5.

"LADY GREGORY IS": Gregory, *Our Irish Theatre*, 162.

226 "UNDER THE SHADOW": Ibid., 166.

"IT WAS MY FIRST": Ibid., 99.

"SAYING THAT I HAD": Ibid.

"LADY GREGORY'S FACE": Ibid., 182.

"LADY GREGORY IS QUITE": Ibid., 175.

"I WENT TO THE PLYMOUTH": Ibid., 99.

"SHE ROSE TO HER FEET": Mary Colum, 118.

"SAY A FEW WORDS": Gregory, *Our Irish Theatre*, 106–7.

"MRS. JACK GARDNER": 3 October 1911.

227 "IN A PLAY YOU MUST": quoted in Anne Dedio, *Das dramatische Werk von Lady Gregory* (Bern: Francke Verlag, 1967), 114.

"AN AUDIENCE CANNOT": Gregory, *Our Irish Theatre*, 169.

"IF EVER THERE WAS": Mikhail, 45.

"HAD I NOT BECOME INTERESTED": Ibid., 67–8.

"I WANT TO CREATE FOR MYSELF": *Explorations*, 254.

228 "WE HAD ONE LIABILITY": Maurice Browne, *Too Late to Lament* (Bloomington: Indiana University Press, 1956), 117.

"SOME OF THOSE WHO": Mary Colum, 139.

"THE COMPANY WHICH INSISTS": Gregory, *Our Irish Theatre*, 223–4.

"WHEN A WOMAN CHOOSES": Ibid., 241.

"HAVING SEEN THEM ALL": Ibid.

"I WILL ADMIT": Mikhail, 42.

229 "NOTHING BUT HELL-INSPIRED": Gregory, *Our Irish Theatre*, 106.

"ALL WHO DO ANYTHING": Gregory, Holograph Memoirs, Fragment.

"WHENEVER THERE WAS A SIGN": Gregory, *Our Irish Theatre*, 102.

"AND THE ROAR": Ibid., 108.

"IN POSSESSION OF THE ORIGINAL": Reid, 117.

QUINN'S QUARREL WITH YEATS: See Yeats, *Memoirs*, 227n.

230 "SO CLEVER, WITTY": Gregory, *Seventy Years*, 497.

"ASTONISHED AT LADY GREGORY'S": Reid, 116.

"WE FOUND THE WHOLE ROUTE": Gregory, *Our Irish Theatre*, 113.

"'AH, YE SLUTS, YE'": Reid, 117.

"QUINN HAS GIVEN ME": 25 December 1911.

"I SHOULD LIKE TO": Gregory, *Our Irish Theatre*, 121.

"I FEEL LIKE WILHELM MEISTER": Quoted in Coxhead, *Lady Gregory*, 149.

"SHE SAT AMONGST US": Starkie, 84.

"I AM FURIOUS!": Gregory, "The Lady Gregory Letters to G. B. Shaw," ed. Daniel J. Murphy, *Modern Drama*, 16 (19 February 1968), 339–40.

231 "DEAR, DEAR JOHN": 20 January 1912.

"YOUR FATE IS SEALED": Gregory, *Our Irish Theatre*, 234.

"I DON'T FEEL ANXIOUS": Ibid., 135.

"I HAVE NICE ROOMS": 16 January 1912.

"THERE IS NOT MUCH": Ibid., 3 October 1911.

GIFT OF CHALICE TO QUINN: Reid, 118.

232 "I WAS LUCKILY THERE": 16 March 1912.

"WE ALL LANDED SAFELY": Ibid.

"MY VERY DEAR JOHN": Ibid., enclosure.

"YOUR DEAR LETTER": 2 April 1912, enclosure.
"NEVER FORNICATE": Reid, 81.
"HAD A CONSIDERABLE CONTEMPORARY": Ibid., x.
"MY JOHN, MY DEAR JOHN": 17 March 1912, enclosure.
"WHY DO I LOVE YOU": 2 April 1912, enclosure.
233 "RAPTURE OF FRIENDSHIP": 6 May 1912.
"VERY DICTATORIAL": Mary Colum, 215.
"I HAVE FELT": 6 May 1912.
"I AM THE PRINCIPLE": 17 March 1912.
QUOTATIONS FROM DAMER'S GOLD: Gregory, *Collected Plays*, I, 135–51.
234 "I DIDN'T BECOME": Mikhail, 42.
235 "INSTEAD OF WAITING": Gregory, *Our Irish Theatre*, 17.
"THINGS SEEMED TO GROW": Ibid., 19.
"THE HOMEY PROVERB": Ibid., 37.
"REMEMBER, HE HAS BEEN": Ibid., 38.
236 "THAT EAR AND MIND": Ibid., 53.
"NEITHER MR. YEATS": Ibid., 64.
"PERHAPS I OUGHT": Ibid., 57.
"SO WILD AND DANGEROUS": Ibid., 44.
"THEY HAD NOT REALIZED": Ibid., 138.
"NOW, LITTLE RICHARD": Ibid., 139.
"NAY, GREAT AND SIMPLE": Gregory, *Our Irish Theatre*, 319.
237 "THESE THREE PLAYS": DEDICATION OF IRISH FOLK-HISTORY PLAYS, FIRST AND
    SECOND SERIES: Gregory, *Collected Plays*, II, xvii.
"YOU KNOW HOW I": 12 January 1919.
"I AM BUT TOO GLAD": 6 May 1912.
"SHE THINKS IT": 31 March 1912.
"THE RING THAT YOU": Reid, 12 August 1912.
"PERHAPS I AM AS": Reid, 121.
WASHING MACHINE AT COOLE: Gregory to Quinn, 22 October 1912.
"BUT IT WAS A JERKY": Katherine Tynan Hinkson, *The Years of the Shadow*
    (Boston: Houghton Mifflin, 1919), 15.
238 "I HAVE HAD THE GREAT": Gregory to Quinn, 6 May 1912.
"I USED TO BE": Ibid., 26 August 1911.
LANE BUYING ROBERT'S PAINTING: Gregory, *Seventy Years*, 472.
"I AM MADE MORE OF": Gregory, Holograph Memoirs, Vol. 8.
"A VERY GOOD LETTER": 6 May 1912.
"MY SISTER'S HUSBAND": 1912.
MUNICIPAL COUNCIL AGREED TO GIVE £22,000: Gregory, *Sir Hugh Lane*, 87.
"OH, MY DEAR WILLIE": Ibid., 92–3.
" . . . THIS MORNING WE HAD": Ibid., 93.
239 "YOU SHOULD NOT EVEN": January 1913.
"SOMEDAY IN THE FUTURE": Ibid., 6 January 1913.
"I HOPE YOU WILL NOT": Ibid.
"SHE SEEMED TO HAVE BEEN": Manuscript Room, New York Public Library,
    7 February 1913.
"IT MAY BE SOME": Gregory, *Sir Hugh Lane*, 94–5.
QUINN AND ARMORY SHOW: Reid, 142–53.
"I MUST TAKE GOOD CARE": 26 June 1913.
"THERE IS A LEISURELY": 1 January 1912.
240 "I HAVE TAKEN UP": 24 December 1913.
"I HAVE PLEASURE": Moore, *Hail and Farewell: Vale*, 185.
"I HAVE LONGED": Yeats, *Autobiography*, 267.
"I AM GLAD IN A WAY": Gregory, *Sir Hugh Lane*, 103–4.

"I WENT BACK": Ibid., 106.

"IT IS A GREAT THING": 27 November 1913.

241 QUOTATIONS FROM THE GOLDEN APPLE: Gregory, *Collected Plays*, III, 167, 168.

243 "ROBERT ALL BUT JOINED": 1 September 1914.

244 QUOTATIONS FROM THE WRENS: Gregory, *Collected Plays*, I, 189–91.

"TOO HEAVY-HEARTED": Gregory, Typed Memoirs, Folder 23.

"HE IS DEVELOPING LATE": Ibid., Folder 25.

"YOU WILL KNOW HOW": 21 May 1914.

"ROBERT GREGORY PAINTED": W. B. Yeats, *Essays and Introductions* (New York: Macmillan, 1961), 209.

SURVEY OF ROBERT GREGORY'S CAREER: Colin Smythe, ed., *Robert Gregory* (Gerrards Cross: Colin Smythe, 1981), 9–10.

"AN UNEASY MAN": Ibid., 10.

"MANY ACTS OF CONSPICUOUS BRAVERY"; "HAVING INVARIABLY DISPLAYED": Gregory, *Seventy Years*, 555.

245 "... IN ABOMINABLY COLD WEATHER": Ibid., 558.

"THE WAY TO BE HAPPY": *Letters to His Son*, 247.

"WHAT SHALL I DO?": Gregory, Holograph Note, Berg.

"THERE IS ONLY HALF OF ME": Gregory, *Seventy Years*, 551.

"TO GIVE HELP": Gregory, *Collected Plays*, III, 57.

246 REDUCTION IN JOINTURE: Gregory to Quinn, 11 August 1917.

"MY VOICE CARRIES": 12 March 1915.

"A FEW DOLLARS": 3 April 1915.

"TO KEEP IT IN": Michael Holroyd, *Augustus John* (New York: Holt, Rinehart and Winston, 1974), 436.

"A VERY PRETTY LITTLE CHILD": Ibid., 434.

"HAD FROM THE TIME OF HIS BIRTH": Gregory, *Coole*, 54.

"A VERY ODD PICTURE": Anne Gregory, 47.

"I LONGED TO POSSESS": Gregory, *Coole*, 55.

247 "THIS ROUGHNESS MIGHT BE": Gregory, Holograph Memoirs, Vol. 15.

"GLAD HUGH LANE WAS": Ibid.

"I SAID I LONGED": Ibid.

"HE WAS ONE OF THE VERY FEW": May 1915.

248 "IT IS A GREAT THING": Gregory to Blunt, 13 December 1915.

QUINN FIXING WATCH: Quinn to Gregory, 20 December 1915 and 29 January 1912.

AT COOLE DURING EASTER REBELLION: Gregory, *Seventy Years*, 532–49.

249 "I HAVE BEEN A LITTLE": Ibid., 548.

"A TERRIBLE BEAUTY IS BORN": *Poems*, 182.

QUOTATIONS FROM THE DRAGON: Gregory, *Collected Plays*, III, 211–59.

251 AUGUSTA SUGGESTS MAUD GIVE UP POLITICS: Hone, *W. B. Yeats*, 303.

YEATS'S MISTRESS NOT PREGNANT: Richard Ellmann, *Yeats: The Man and the Masks* (New York: Dutton, 1948), 208n.

"SEND A TELEGRAM": quoted in Reid, 307.

"IT IS REALLY AN EASE": Gregory, *Seventy Years*, 551.

"MY WIFE IS A PERFECT": *Letters*, 16 December 1917, 634.

"HIS WIFE HAS MONEY": 2 January 1921.

252 YEATS CALLED "WILLIAM TELL": Ellmann, 164–5.

QUOTATION FROM HANRAHAN'S OATH: Gregory, *Collected Plays*, I, 163.

YEATS'S OPEN LETTER ON ABBEY: Yeats, *Explorations*, 244–55.

"I AM REALLY SUFFERING": Gregory, *Sir Hugh Lane*, 186.

253 "I WAS AT MY WRITING TABLE": Gregory, *Seventy Years*, 553–4.

254 "NOW I AM TYPING THIS": Gregory, *Journals*, I, 571.

"THIS DAY TEN YEARS AGO": Gregory, *Journals*, ed. Robinson, 49.

"I HAVE LOST MY ONE": Gregory, *Journals*, I, 571.

"MY HEART BREAKS": 10 February 1918.

"THOSE WHO HAVE COME": Ibid.

"OH, MY DEAR JOHN": 13 February 1918.

"I HAVE ALWAYS SAID": 28 January 1918.

"THE AWAKENING EVERY MORNING": 13 February 1918.

"I KNOW YOU WON'T MIND": 26 March 1918.

255 "BUT BEFORE THAT MONTH": Ibid.

"OF A YOUNG BROAD-SHOULDERED MAN": Sean O'Casey, *Inishfallen, Fare Thee Well* (New York: Macmillan, 1949), 188–9.

"HE WAS THE MOST": *Letters*, 8 February 1918, 646.

"YEATS HAS WRITTEN": 15 June 1918.

256 "SOLDIER, SCHOLAR, HORSEMAN, HE": "In Memory of Major Robert Gregory," *Poems*, 135.

"I BALANCED ALL": *Poems*, 135.

"HOW CAN I / THAT FOUND": *Poems*, 143.

"SHE GOES ABOUT HER HOUSE": Ibid.

"LAST MONTH I WAS PLANTING": 10 February 1918.

"EXCEPT FOR A SNEEZE": Gregory, *Seventy Years*, 430.

"LOVE, THE SOLUTION": Gregory, *Journals*, ed. Robinson, 36.

257 "I AM SO THANKFUL": 26 March 1918.

"HAVE WRITTEN TO THEM": *Journals*, I, 501.

"GREW GRUMPY AFTER LUNCH": Ibid., 195.

"LOOKING BACK ON THE DAY": Ibid., 270.

"I SEE NOW HOW THE CARDS": Ibid., 305.

"BOOKS AND TREES": O'Casey, *Inishfallen*, 191.

IN HER WORKING OVERALLS: Ibid., 189–90.

258 "ONE OF THE FEW TIMES": Anne Gregory, 93.

"THESE WOODS HAVE BEEN": Gregory, *Coole*, 98.

"G.B.S." WAS JESTER: Gregory, *Collected Plays*, III, 379.

"AND SO I FOLLOW AFTER": Ibid., 208.

259 "I KNOW FROM ROBINSON": 2 October 1920.

"AFTER ALL, WHAT IS WANTED": Gregory, *Journals*, I, 55.

"VERY TIRED AND HUNGRY": Ibid., 58.

"SAID COLDLY THAT IT": Ibid.

"HADN'T GROWN VERY POOR": Ibid., 59.

"LIKE ALICE IN WONDERLAND'S": Ibid.

GRANDDAUGHTERS IN DUBLIN: Ibid., 60.

260 "AND AT THE END": Ibid., 66.

"SO THE TUESDAY NIGHT": Ibid., 67.

"JEALOUSY FOR GALWAY": Gregory, *Visions and Beliefs*, 15.

"THE GRITTINESS OF OFFICIAL": Gregory, *Sir Hugh Lane*, 156.

"HOW TENACIOUS SHE WAS": Gregory, *Journals*, ed. Robinson, 288.

261 "I NEED NOT SAY I AM": "Letters from Lady Gregory: A Record of Her Friendship with T. J. Kiernan," Part II, ed. Daniel Murphy, *Bulletin of the New York Public Library*, January 1968, 45.

"I HAD AGAIN A SLEEPLESS": *Journals*, I, 28.

"I WROTE YOU YESTERDAY": *Letters*, 16 November 1929, 770.

"IT IS WONDERFUL": "Letters from Lady Gregory," *Bulletin of the New York Public Library*, January 1968, 41.

"PERHAPS IT IS THIS PICTURE": *Journals*, I, 536.

262 "WELL, I HAVE BROADENED": Ibid., 87.

"IT SHOWS TWO CHARMING": Ibid., 238.

"LANE HAD BEEN WISE": Gregory, *Sir Hugh Lane*, 133–4.

"CLOUD OF WITNESSES": Ibid., 99, 104, 164.

"BITTER-TONGUED MAN": Ibid., 98.

WOUND THE FIRST PERSON HE SAW: Ibid., 135.

263 "EVERYBODY WHO IS DOING": Ibid., 44.

"YOU MAY SET YOUR JUDGMENT": Ibid., 126.

"LIKE THE TURNING": Ibid., 132.

QUOTATION FROM ARISTOTLE'S BELLOWS: Gregory, *Collected Plays*, III, 394.

"I DON'T THINK": Gregory to Robinson, No. 143.

264 "THAT NEEDS AN OVERFLOW": Gregory to Quinn, 7 December 1918.

265 "MARRY PEASANTS": Gregory, *Journals*, I, 116.

"WERE SUCH A MISERABLE": Anne Gregory, 22–3.

"MARGARET IS YOUNG": Gregory to Quinn, 11 August 1917.

"OH, WHAT CAN I DO?" Gregory, *Journals*, I, 116.

266 "ROBERT LOVED IT": Gregory, *Journals*, ed. Robinson, 15.

"FOR MYSELF I MAY BUY": Gregory, *Journals*, I, 216.

A "LITTLE DEMESNE": Ibid., 218.

MARGARET REPLIED "NOTHING": Ibid.

"OF COURSE ONE IS ENDANGERING": Ibid., 137.

"THANK YOU SO MUCH": Ibid., 285.

"FIVE OF US ONLY": Ibid., 161.

267 "THE FLESH WAS AS IF": Ibid., 209.

"I HAVE BEEN ACTING AS": Gregory to Quinn, 13 June 1919.

"LIKE TEACHING A SQUIRREL": Gregory, *Journals*, I, 84.

"TO SEE THE DAY WHEN MURDER": Gregory to Quinn, 14 June 1919.

"ALTHOUGH YOUR LAST EXCITING YEAR": *Variorum Poems*, 791.

"I CANNOT BEAR": *Journals*, I, 207.

268 "I DID NOT LIKE THIS": Gregory to Yeats, 23 November 1920.

"SOME TROUBLE STARTED": Lennox Robinson, "Lady Gregory," in *The Irish Theatre*, ed. Lennox Robinson (London: Macmillan, 1939), 59.

" . . . BUT THE DROP": Gregory, *Journals*, I, 267.

"I HAVE BEEN PRAYING": Ibid., 179.

"YOU MAY WRITE": Ibid., 142.

"WALKED OVER THE FARMS": Ibid., 156.

FRANK ARRANGING SALE OF COOLE: Ibid., 191.

"IT IS RATHER A SHOCK": Ibid., 193.

269 "IT IS IMPOSSIBLE": Ibid., 256.

"ALL SEEMS CRUMBLING": Ibid., 257.

"THAT SHE DOES NOT": Ibid., 273.

"M. WAS VEXED": Ibid., 274.

"AS LONG AS THERE IS": Ibid.

"I WISH TO PUT MYSELF": Gregory, Holograph Memoirs, Vol. 8.

"THIS IS OUR ROSARY": Gregory, *Collected Plays*, II, 359.

"YOU HAVE NOT THE MOMENTUM": Gregory, *Journals*, I, 291.

"THE LITTLE BOY HAD": Ibid., 318.

270 "JUST A SORT OF DELIGHTED MURMUR": Ibid., 323.

"I REFERRED HIM TO FRANK": Ibid., 337.

"I THINK THEY ARE RAIDERS": Ibid., 354–5.

"IT DID SHAKE THE NERVES": Ibid., 355.

271 "COURAGE WITH YOU": Gregory, *Seventy Years*, 507.

"BUT OF COURSE I CAN": Ibid., 138.

PANGUR AT COOLE: W. R. Rogers, ed., *Irish Literary Portraits: Broadcast Conversations with Those Who Knew Them* (London: British Broadcasting Company, 1972), 13.

AUGUSTA NEGOTIATING FOR YEATS'S TOWER: Gregory, *Journals*, I, 15.

"[WILLIE] GIVES ME ALL": Ibid., 392.

272 "MY WIFE AND I HAD HOPED": *Letters*, 5 November 1922, 692.

"SOME THAT COME TO THE COUNTER": Gregory, *Journals*, I, 368.
A FREEMASON (WHICH HE WASN'T): Ibid., 361.
"ASK COMMANDANT L. TO RETURN": Ibid., 371.
273 "THE COUNTRY HOUSES LIT": Fingall, *Seventy Years Young*, 414.
"IN PRAISE OF DISPRAISE": Gregory, *Journals*, I, 497.
"RATHER A VERDICT OF": Ibid., 402.
"GENERATIONS FOR 700 YEARS": Ibid., 350.
"I FEEL THAT MY DARLING": Ibid., 379.
"A MAN, NOT IN UNIFORM": Ibid., 387.
"WE ARE AT THE SEAMY": Ibid., 383.
274 "WILFRID WILL DIE": Ibid., 451.
"AT THE END HE DREW": Berg, 19 September 1922.
WILFRID'S BIBLE TO AUGUSTA: Gregory, *Journals*, I, 451.
BLUNT BIBLE PLACED IN HER COFFIN: Robinson, *Biography of Lady Gregory*.
"WE WERE OUT OF DOORS": in Blunt, *My Diaries*, vii–xiv.
"AN UNUSUAL AND GALLANT RECORD": Ibid.
"WILFRID BLUNT'S DEATH": 1 August 1922.
275 "YES, I HAD RATHER": 27 September 1923.
"THE NIGHT BEFORE LAST": *Journals*, I, 459–60.
"WITH MUCH OF THE SPARTAN": *The Irish Theatre*, 58.
"HOW CAN YOU DOUBT": 28 November 1923.
QUOTATIONS FROM THE STORY BROUGHT BY BRIGIT: Gregory, *Collected Plays*, III, 303–45.
276 "I DO NOT FEEL PUFFED UP": Robinson, Biography of Lady Gregory.
REPUBLICAN PRISONERS' HUNGER STRIKE: For a firsthand account, see Frank O'Connor's autobiography, *An Only Child* (New York: Knopf, 1961), 265–71.
AUGUSTA AND ROBINSON'S LETTER: Gregory, *Journals*, I, 486–7.
"ALL SO SAD AND UNSATISFACTORY": Ibid., 485.
"MORE THAN EVER A REPUBLICAN": Ibid., 471.
"I AM JUST WELL KNOWN": 17 June 1918.
"I AM PUTTING DOWN": 7 December 1918.
"IT SEEMS TO ME IN LOOKING": 13 June 1919.
277 "ONE HOUR'S TALK WITH ROBERT": 13 June 1919.
"FOR ALL ITS INCIDENTAL MERITS": "A Woman Young and Old," *New Yorker*, 19 (July 1976), 94.
"AN OLD WOMAN SINKING": Gregory, Typed Journals, Book 26, 353.
278 "HE DESCRIBED ME AS": Ibid.
"A LIVING WOMAN SINKING": Yeats, *Autobiography*, 387.
"TWO SEATS HAD BEEN": Gregory, *Journals*, I, 445–6.
"STAND UP, NOW, WILLIE": Gabriel Fallon, "Profiles of a Poet," *Modern Drama*, December 1964, 343.
"YEATS GAVE A CAUTIOUS HEARING": Gregory to Robinson, No. 120.
"YOU KNOW, WILLIE, YOU NEVER": Gabriel Fallon, *Sean O'Casey: The Man I Knew* (Boston: Little, Brown, 1965), 22.
"SHE HATES ALL CLERGY": *Letters*, 21 June 1924, 706.
"HELL OF A TIME": Gregory, Typed Journals, Book 27.
"WHEN I LEFT": 5 October 1923.
279 "ALL IS SACRIFICED": Ibid.
"WITH QUEEN VICTORIA!": Gregory, Typed Journals, Book 31.
YEATS IN SENATE: Yeats, *A Vision*, 26.
"THERE IS GREAT INDIGNATION": Gregory, Typed Journals, Book 30.
AUGUSTA DEFEATED FOR SENATE: Gregory, *Journals*, ed. Robinson, 335.
WE DIDN'T THINK MUCH: Anne Gregory, 117.
280 "GEORGE YEATS AND THE CHILDREN": Gregory, Typed Journals, Book 34.
"A LETTER IN THE WRITING": Gregory to Quinn, 7 December 1918.

"SENT GREAT PARCELS OF MOSS": Anne Gregory, 22.

WROTE TO ARABELLA EVERY DAY: Gregory to Quinn, 29 May 1924.

"THIS IS A VERY TORMENTING": Berg, Miscellaneous Notebooks.

"THE LITTLE TRIP TO PARIS": 27 September 1923.

"FIFTY-THREE SEEMS VERY YOUNG": 23 November 1923.

281 "SOMEWHERE WITHIN THE WORK": Reid, vii–viii.

"A GREAT BLOW YESTERDAY": Gregory, *Journals*, I, 569.

"CUCHULAIN, OF COURSE!": Reid, 635.

"NOT FAR FROM BEING": Gregory, *Journals*, I, 446.

"I BELIEVE THERE IS SOMETHING": Ibid.

"AN IMMENSE SUCCESS": Ibid., 445,

"THAT FULL HOUSE, THE PACKED PIT": Ibid., 512.

282 "LOOK AT HER THERE": O'Casey, *Inishfallen*, 176.

"BUT LADY GREGORY WASN'T AFRAID": Ibid., 180–1.

"IN THE THEATRE, AMONG THE POETS": Ibid., 196.

"MUST IGNORE THE FORMAL TABLE": Fallon, *Sean O'Casey*, 81.

283 "HE HADN'T BEEN TEN MINUTES": O'Casey, *Inishfallen*, 187.

"WITH THE BARE NECK": Anne Gregory, 84.

FOOLISH EXAGGERATION OF LISP: Lennox Robinson, *I Sometimes Think* (Dublin: Talbot Press, 1956), 120.

"NOW, LADY GREGORY, I RESPECTFULLY": Gregory, *Journals*, ed. Robinson, 88.

"I NEVER HAD A CHILD": Ibid., 95.

284 "THAT TO ELIMINATE ANY PART OF IT": Ibid., 90.

"IF WE HAVE TO CHOOSE": Ibid., 91.

"YEATS ALSO SPOKE": Ibid., 91–2.

"THE SUFFERING THAT FALLS THROUGH WAR": Ibid., 98.

"YOU HAVE DISGRACED YOURSELVES": Gerald Fay, 147–8.

285 ". . . THERE WAS NO DANGER": Gregory, *Journals*, ed. Robinson, 97–8.

"JACOB BOEHME AND OF BLAKE": 7 December 1918.

"FIX MY MIND ON THAT HIGH COUNTRY": Gregory, *Journals*, I, 355.

QUOTATION FROM THE WOULD-BE GENTLEMAN: Gregory, *Collected Plays*, IV, 175.

QUOTATION FROM SANCHO'S MASTER: Ibid., 262–3.

286 "I SOMETIMES THINK": Gregory, Typed Journals, Book 38.

"M. HAD NEVER REALIZED": Ibid., Book 35.

"M. SEEMS CONFIDENT": Ibid.

"I HAVE GIVEN IN TO THIS": Ibid.

"ONE OF THOSE DREAMS": Ibid., Book 36.

"I AM SO UNUTTERABLY THANKFUL": Ibid., Book 33.

"MY POOR BODY": Ibid., Book 35.

"I DO FEEL ASHAMED": "Letters from Lady Gregory," *Bulletin of the New York Public Library*, December 1967, 629.

287 "A WOMAN OF GREAT GOODNESS": Thomas J. Kiernan, "Lady Gregory and W. B. Yeats," *Southerly*, 14 (1953), 240.

"AS AN AUTHORESS": "Letters from Lady Gregory," *Bulletin of the New York Public Library*, December 1967, 629.

"IS IT NOT WONDERFUL": Ibid., January 1968, 53.

"WHEN WE'D FINISHED TEA": Anne Gregory, 25.

"I SAID, 'ARE YOU SHOCKED?' ": Gregory, *Journals*, ed. Robinson, 229.

CLAIMING REIMBURSEMENT FOR FIRST CLASS: Robinson, *Biography of Lady Gregory*.

"MY BIRTHDAY! NO NOTICE": Gregory, Typed Journals, Book 35.

"THEY CALLED ME": Gregory, *Journals*, ed. Robinson, 258.

288 RENOUNCED ARABELLA'S LEGACY: Gregory, Typed Journals, Book 29.

"SO IN THE RAIN I WENT OUT": Gregory, *Journals*, ed. Robinson, 44.

"I LONG FOR ANOTHER SUMMER": Gregory, Typed Journals, Book 35.

"LAST NIGHT IN THE LIBRARY": Gregory, *Journals*, I, 507.

289 "AS IT SEEMS LIKELY": Gregory, *Coole*, 17.

290 "I HAVE JUST PUT MY NAME": Gregory, *Journals*, ed. Robinson, 37.

"WEEDS SALE": Gregory, Typed Journals, Book 35.

291 "THOUGH WITHOUT MUCH ENTHUSIASM": Ibid.

QUOTATIONS FROM DAVE: Gregory, *Collected Plays*, III, 349–67.

292 "SHOW AN AFFIRMING FLAME": "September 1, 1939," *Another Time*.

293 "MY DECISION THAT THESE THREE": Gregory, *Three Last Plays* (London: Putnam's, 1929).

"NEARLY MISSED TRAIN": Gregory, Typed Journals, Book 36.

"WE HAD JUST GONE DOWN": Gregory, *Journals*, ed. Robinson, 38.

294 "THE OVERWORK OF YEARS": Hone, *W. B. Yeats*, 391.

BROTHER HARRY'S DEATH: Gregory, Typed Journals, Book 36.

" . . . INSIDE THE FRONT GATE": Gregory, *Journals*, ed. Robinson, 42.

"A GREAT ENRICHMENT": Ibid., 34.

295 "SO KNOWING HOW I FEEL": Eileen O'Casey, *Sean* (New York: Coward, McCann & Geoghegan, 1972), 102.

"YOUR LETTER HAS GRIEVED ME": "The Lady Gregory Letters to Sean O'Casey," *Modern Drama*, May 1965, 107.

"SILLY SINS": Ibid., 96.

"A BITTER MEMORY": Coxhead, *Lady Gregory*, 192.

YEATS SHUTTING OUT THE SKY: Monk Gibbon, *The Masterpiece and the Man: Yeats as I Knew Him* (New York: Macmillan, 1959), 12, 220.

"I AM RATHER A GOOD PLAY DOCTOR": "Letters from Lady Gregory," *Bulletin of the New York Public Library*, January 1968, 26.

"AN OLD RELATIVE OF MINE": 28 February 1931, No. 4.

"I RETURN A USELESS PLAY": No. 145.

ROBINSON SAYS NO ONE CALLED HER "THE OLD LADY": *Curtains Up*, 117.

"THE SIGHTS OF THE CITY": Denis Johnston, "The Scythe and Sunset," *Collected Plays*, I, 24.

"I WAS NEVER INVITED": Ibid., 16.

"A TERRIFYING OLD LADY": Rodgers, ed., *Irish Literary Portraits*, 13.

296 "I WAS IN TOWN": Gregory to Robinson, 22 June 1929, No. 12.

"GOGARTY RUSHING IN NOW": Gregory, *Journals*, I, 460.

"DEMANDED SERVILITY OF ALL": Oliver St. John Gogarty, "Reminiscences of Yeats," *Mourning Became Mrs. Spendlove and Other Portraits, Grave and Gay* (New York: Creative Age Press, 1948), 213.

"A WILLING HELPER": Gregory, Typed Journals, Book 38.

"HER NAMBY PAMBY HUMOUR": Oliver St. John Gogarty, *As I Was Going Down Sackville Street* (New York: Reynal & Hitchcock, 1937), 291.

"WHO HAD A FINE": Oliver St. John Gogarty, *It Isn't That Time of Year at All!* (Garden City, N.Y.: Doubleday, 1954), 246.

"THAT MONUMENTAL WIDOW": St. John Ervine, *Bernard Shaw: His Life, Work and Friends* (New York: William Morrow, 1956), 264.

"THE FIRST 'COMIC GENIUS' ": Gregory, *Seventy Years*, 483.

"THAT OVERPOWERING ANALOGY": Gregory, Typed Memoirs, Fragment.

297 PURPLE TO WEDDINGS: Gregory, *Journals*, I, 617.

"BUT NOW THE UPHOLSTERY": Gregory, Typed Memoirs, Fragment.

CONSULTING WARDROBE MISTRESS: Robinson, *Biography of Lady Gregory*.

"SHE EATING BUN AFTER BUN": O'Casey, *Inishfallen*, 172.

"LADY GREGORY, IN THE MIDST": Ibid., 193–4.

"A CLEAN SHOT": Gregory to Robinson, No. 60.

"TO ANNE GREGORY": For account of its writing, see Anne Gregory, 29–30.

"POOR DARLING, IT BREAKS MY HEART": Gregory, *Journals*, I, 599.

£103 FOR RICHARD'S CAR: Gregory, Typed Journals, Book 35.

"I'VE GOT THE FORMS": Gregory, *Journals*, ed. Robinson, 340.
298 "CAN YOU DRIVE A FORD": "Letters from Lady Gregory," *Bulletin of the New York Public Library*, January 1968, 23.
"I FEEL IT RATHER WONDERFUL": Gregory, Typed Journals, Book 38.
"I BELIEVE ROBERT WOULD BE": Ibid.
"A LOVELY LETTER": Ibid.
"RICHARD AT WOOLICH": "The Lady Gregory Letters to Sean O'Casey," *Modern Drama*, May 1965, 104.
"LITTLE CATHERINE IS LEARNING": Ibid., 110.
"THIS CASTLE—THAT WAS": "Letters from Lady Gregory," *Bulletin of the New York Public Library*, January 1968, 29.
"I USED TO THINK": Gregory, *Journals*, ed. Robinson, 47–48.
"A NEW ESTABLISHMENT": *An Only Child*, 210.
299 "VERY CATHOLIC, SHAMROCKS": Gregory, Typed Journals, Book 35.
"THE BISHOPS IN THEIR PASTORALS": Ibid., Book 30.
"THE MONEY BETTER SPENT": Ibid., Book 31.
"I AM TORN WITH CURIOSITY": "Letters from Lady Gregory," *Bulletin of the New York Public Library*, December 1967, 626.
"SARAH PURSER AND MISS HORNIMAN": Gregory, Typed Journals, Book 42.
"I HAD NO IDEA YOU WERE": Gregory, *Coole*, 62.
"I HAD NO IDEA THE BOOK": Ibid., 64.
"TRAVELLER, SCHOLAR, POET": *Poems*, 243.
300 "AND AS I SIT HERE": Gregory, *Coole*, 105.
"THIS DAY TEN YEARS AGO": Gregory, Typed Journals, Book 37.
"PRAISING HERSELF MOSTLY": Ibid., Book 43.
"WONDERING WHY I AM SO TIRED": Ibid., Book 38.
"SO MUCH AN EASIER THING": Ibid., Book 42.
"PAIN—PAIN—PAIN": Ibid., Book 43.
"SOUND OF A STICK UPON THE FLOOR": *Poems*, 244.
FALLING IN GARDEN: Coxhead, *Lady Gregory*, 199.
"THERE IS NOTHING TO INTEREST": *Letters to W. B. Yeats*, II, 532.
301 "THE IMPRESSION IS OF SOMETHING": Rossi, 46.
"YOU HAVE NEVER PRETENDED": Ibid., 46–7.
"I HAVE BEEN ASKED": *Letters*, 4 December 1931, 787.
"BUT I HAVE TOLD YOU": Ibid., 10 March 1932, 793.
"DEAR WILLIE, I DONT FEEL VERY WELL": in *Theatre Business*, 12.
302 "GUARANTEED NOT TO CONTAIN MORPHIA": Yeats, *Letters*, 10 March 1932, 794.
AUGUSTA GOING AROUND ROOMS: Ibid., 6 June 1932, 796.
"MY STRENGTH AND MY CONSCIENCE": Ibid.
"MANCINI'S PORTRAIT OF AUGUSTA GREGORY": *Poems*, 320.
"I LONG FOR QUIET": *Letters*, 3 May 1936, 855.
303 "ALL, ALL ARE GONE": Oliver St. John Gogarty, "The Big House at Coole," *A Weekend in the Middle of the Week* (Garden City, N.Y.: Doubleday, 1958), 158.
304 MOORE ON EPSTEIN BUST OF LADY GREGORY: Gregory, *Coole*, 52.
"DULL EFFRONTERY": O'Casey, *Inishfallen*, 275.
"IT IS A BEAUTIFUL BURYING PLACE": Gregory, *Journals*, I, 517.
"NONE HAVE YET BEEN CERTAINLY AWARE": Gregory, *Collected Plays*, III, 376.
305 "I BELIEVE WE SHALL MEET": Finch, 372.
YEATS SEEING HER WAVING GOODBYE: *Letters*, 27 January 1934, 819.

Bibliography

PUBLISHED WORKS BY AUGUSTA GREGORY

Arabi and His Household (pamphlet). London: Kegan Paul, Trench, 1882.

A Book of Saints and Wonders. The Coole Edition of the Works of Lady Gregory, ed. T. R. Henn and Colin Smythe. New York: Oxford University Press, 1971 (first published 1906).

The Collected Plays, I, *The Comedies*, ed. Ann Saddlemyer. *The Coole Edition of the Works of Lady Gregory*, ed. T. R. Henn and Colin Smythe. New York: Oxford University Press, 1970.

The Collected Plays, II, *The Tragedies and Tragic Comedies*, ed. Ann Saddlemyer. *The Coole Edition of the Works of Lady Gregory*, ed. T. R. Henn and Colin Smythe. New York: Oxford University Press, 1970.

The Collected Plays, III, *The Wonder and Supernatural Plays*, ed. Ann Saddlemyer. *The Coole Edition of the Works of Lady Gregory*, ed. T. R. Henn and Colin Smythe. New York: Oxford University Press, 1970.

The Collected Plays, IV, *The Translations and Adaptations of Lady Gregory and Her Collaborations with Douglas Hyde and W. B. Yeats*, ed. Ann Saddlemyer. *The Coole Edition of the Works of Lady Gregory*, ed. T. R. Henn and Colin Smythe. New York: Oxford University Press, 1970.

Coole. Dublin: Cuala Press, 1931.

Coole, ed. Colin Smythe. Dublin: Dolmen, 1971.

Cuchulain of Muirthemne: The Story of the Men of the Red Branch of Ulster. The Coole Edition of the Works of Lady Gregory, ed. T. R. Henn and Colin Smythe. New York: Oxford University Press, 1970 (first published 1902).

"The Felons of Our Land." *Cornhill Magazine*, 47 (May 1900), 622–34.

"A Gentleman." *Argosy*, 58 (July 1894), 72–81.

Gods and Fighting Men: The Story of the Tuatha de Danaan and of the Fianna of Ireland. The Coole Edition of the Works of Lady Gregory.

ed. T. R. Henn and Colin Smythe. New York: Oxford University Press, 1970 (first published 1904).

"Ireland Real and Ideal." *The Nineteenth Century*, Vol. 44, (November 1898), 769–82.

The Kiltartan Books Comprising the Kiltartan Poetry, History and Wonder Books. The Coole Edition of the Works of Lady Gregory, ed. T. R. Henn and Colin Smythe. New York: Oxford University Press, 1971.

Lady Gregory's Journals: 10 October 1916–24 February 1925, Vol. I, ed. Daniel J. Murphy. *The Coole Edition of the Works of Lady Gregory*, ed. T. R. Henn and Colin Smythe. New York: Oxford University Press, 1978.

Lady Gregory's Journals: 1916–1930, ed. Lennox Robinson. New York: Macmillan, 1947.

Mr. Gregory's Letter-Box: 1813–1835. The Coole Edition of the Works of Lady Gregory, ed. T. R. Henn and Colin Smythe. New York: Oxford University Press, 1981 (first published 1898).

In *The Nation*, "A Week in Ireland," 16 October 1920, 63.
"Another Week in Ireland," 23 October 1920, 123–4.
"Murder by the Throat," 13 November 1920, 215–17.
"A Third Week in Ireland," 4 December 1920, 333–4.
"A Fourth Week in Ireland," 18 December 1920, 413–14.
"A Fifth Week in Ireland," 1 January 1921, 472–3.

Our Irish Theatre. New York: Putnam's, 1913.

Our Irish Theatre: A Chapter of Autobiography. The Coole Edition of the Works of Lady Gregory, ed. T. R. Henn and Colin Smythe. New York: Oxford University Press, 1972.

Over the River (pamphlet). London: W. Ridgway, 1888.

A Phantom's Pilgrimage: or Home Ruin (pamphlet). London: W. Ridgway, 1893.

"A Philanthropist." *Argosy*, 51 (June 1891), 468–83.

Poets and Dreamers: Studies and Translations from the Irish Including Nine Plays by Douglas Hyde. The Coole Edition of the Works of Lady Gregory, ed. T. R. Henn and Colin Smythe. New York: Oxford University Press, 1974 (first published 1903).

Preface. *My Diaries: Being a Personal Narrative of Events, 1888–1914*, by Wilfrid S. Blunt. New York: Knopf, 1921.

Seven Short Plays. Dublin: Maunsel, 1909.

Seventy Years: 1852–1922: Being the Autobiography of Lady Gregory, ed. Colin Smythe. *The Coole Edition of the Works of Lady Gregory*, ed. T. R. Henn and Colin Smythe. New York: Oxford University Press, 1974.

Sir Hugh Lane: His Life and Legacy. The Coole Edition of the Works of Lady Gregory, ed. T. R. Henn and Colin Smythe. New York: Oxford University Press, 1973 (first published 1921 as *Hugh Lane's Life and Achievement*).

"Through Portugal." *Fortnightly Review*, 40 (1883), 571–80.
Visions and Beliefs in the West of Ireland. The Coole Edition of the Works of Lady Gregory, ed. T. R. Henn and Colin Smythe. New York: Oxford University Press, 1970 (first published 1920).
"A Woman's Sonnets," in *Poetical Works* by Wilfrid Scawen Blunt, London: Macmillan, 1914, I, 347–52.
Ed. *An Autobiography* by Sir William Gregory. 2nd ed. London: John Murray, 1894.
Ed. *Ideals in Ireland*. London: At the Unicorn, 1901.

UNPUBLISHED WORKS BY AUGUSTA GREGORY

(Unless otherwise noted, unpublished works by Lady Gregory are in the Lady Gregory Archives of the Henry W. and Albert A. Berg Collection, The New York Public Library, Astor, Lenox and Tilden Foundations.)

The Canavans. Holograph copy. Signed. Dated 27 August 1906.
Coats. Holograph drafts. Unsigned. Dated 14 September and 7 October 1910.
The Deliverer. Holograph draft. Unsigned. Dated 10–15 July 1910.
Dervorgilla. Holograph draft. Unsigned. Dated 24 June 1907.
Diary. 4 March 1880 through 24 May 1882. Holograph notebook. Special Collections Department, Robert Woodruff Library, Emory University.
Diary. 3 June 1882 through 7 June 1910. 14 holograph notebooks.
Diary. Typescript. November 1881 through April 1894; fragments 1882–1916.
"Emigrant's Notebook." Special Collections Department, Robert Woodruff Library, Emory University.
The Full Moon. Typescript, unsigned, undated. Typescript, signed, dated 10 September 1910.
The Gaol Gate. Holograph draft. Unsigned. Dated 20–23 August [1906].
Grania. Holograph outline, signed and dated 22–23 November 1909. Typescript (carbon), signed, dated 6 August 1910.
Hyacinth Halvey. Holograph draft. Unsigned. Dated 21–26 September 1905.
The Image. Typescript. Unsigned. Dated 22–29 June 1909.

Laughter in Ireland. Holograph draft. Unsigned. Dated 8 September 1915.

Memoirs. 15 holograph notebooks, dated 29 July through 23 November 1921. Typewritten draft, dated October 1918 through July 1922.

Journal. Typescript. 44 books. Dated October 1916 through 2 November 1930.

Poems written to Wilfrid Blunt in Prison. Wilfrid Scawen Blunt Collection, Fitzwilliam Museum, Cambridge. Ms. 1156–1977, 1157–1977.

"What shall I do?" Holograph note. Dated September 1914.

Why the Irish Love Ireland (Lecture). Holograph draft. Signed. Dated February 1912.

LETTERS BY AUGUSTA GREGORY

(Unless otherwise noted, unpublished letters by Lady Gregory are in the Lady Gregory Archives of the Henry W. and Albert A. Berg Collection, The New York Public Library.)

To Wilfrid Scawen Blunt. June 1882–18 June 1922. 50 Folders.

To Robert William Gregory. 1906–26 February 1912. 2 Folders.

To T. J. Kiernan. "Letters from Lady Gregory: A Record of Her Friendship with T. J. Kiernan," ed. Daniel J. Murphy. *Bulletin of the New York Public Library*, Part I, 76 (December 1967), 621–61; Part II, 77 (January 1968), 19–63.

To Enid Layard. 28 March 1882–15 January 1899. 6 Folders.

To Sean O'Casey. "The Lady Gregory Letters to Sean O'Casey," ed. A. C. Edwards. *Modern Drama*, 8 (May 1965), 95–111.

To John Quinn. Manuscript Room, New York Public Library.

To Lennox Robinson. Manuscript Room, Morris Library, Southern Illinois University.

To George Bernard Shaw. "The Lady Gregory Letters to G. B. Shaw," ed. Daniel J. Murphy. *Modern Drama*, 16 (19 February 1968), 331–45.

To John M. Synge. Manuscript Room, Trinity College Library, Trinity College, Dublin. *Theatre Business: The Correspondence of the First Abbey Theatre Directors: William Butler Yeats, Lady Gregory and J. M. Synge*, ed. Ann Saddlemyer. Gerrards Cross: Colin Smythe, 1982.

To William Butler Yeats. 1898–1932. 957 Folders, 19 Boxes. *Theatre Business*. Gerrards Cross: Colin Smythe, 1982.

OTHER SOURCES

Allgood, Sara. Memoirs. Berg Collection, New York Public Library.

Amory, Mark. *Biography of Lord Dunsany*. London: Collins, 1972.

Auden, W. H. *Another Time*. New York: Random House, 1940.

Barlow, Jane. *Irish Idyls*. London: Hodder, 1892.

Beckett, J. C. *The Making of Modern Ireland: 1603–1923*. London: Faber and Faber, 1966.

Blunt, Wilfrid Scawen. *The Land War in Ireland: Being a Personal Narrative of Events*, 2nd ed. London: Herbert and Daniel, 1908.

——. Letters to Augusta Gregory (5 April 1882–4 July 1922). Berg Collection, New York Public Library. 173 Folders.

——. *My Diaries: Being a Personal Narrative of Events, 1888–1914*. 2 vols. New York: Knopf, 1921.

——. *The Poetical Works*. 2 vols. London: Macmillan, 1914.

——. *Secret History of the English Occupation of Egypt*. London: T. Fisher Unwin, 1907; New York: Knopf, 1922.

Blyth, Henry. *Skittles: The Last Victorian Courtesan: The Life and Times of Catherine Walters*. London: Robert Hart-Davis, 1970.

Boyd, Ernest A. "A Fensian Unionist: Standish O'Grady," *Appreciations and Depreciations*. Dublin: Talbot Press, 1917.

Brown, Malcolm. *The Politics of Irish Literature from Thomas Davis to W. B. Yeats*. Seattle: University of Washington Press, 1972.

Browne, Maurice. *Too Late to Lament*. Bloomington: Indiana University Press, 1956.

Brugsma, R. P. C. *The Beginnings of the Irish Revival*. Groningen-Batavia: P. Noordhoff, 1933.

Burke's Dormant, Abeyant, Forfeited and Extinct Peerages. London: Burke's Peerage Ltd., 1883.

Burke's Irish Family Records. London: Burke's Peerage Ltd., 1976.

Burke's Landed Gentry of Ireland. London: Burke's Peerage Ltd., 1958.

Burke's Peerage, Baronetage and Knightage. London: Burke's Peerage Ltd., 1970.

Cardozo, Nancy. *Lucky Eyes and a High Heart: The Life of Maud Gonne*. New York: Bobbs-Merrill, 1978.

Carleton, Dorothy. Letters to Lady Gregory (8 January 1914–22 June 1926), Berg Collection, New York Public Library.

Church of Ireland. *The Book of Common Prayer*. Oxford: Samuel Collingwood, 1828.

Collis, Maurice. *Somerville and Ross: A Biography*. London: Faber and Faber, 1968.

Cole, Ronald. Horoscope for Lady Gregory. Erected Phoenix, Arizona, August 1976.

Colum, Mary. *Life and the Dream.* Garden City, N.Y.: Doubleday, 1947.

Colum, Padraic. *Three Plays: The Fiddler's House, The Land, Thomas Muskerry.* Boston: Little, Brown, 1916.

Complete Catalogue of the Library of John Quinn Sold by Auction in Five Parts. 2 vols. New York: Anderson Galleries, 1924.

Courtney, Sister Marie-Thérèse. *Edward Martyn and the Irish Theatre.* New York: Vantage Press, 1956.

Coxhead, Elizabeth. *Daughters of Erin: Five Women of the Irish Renascence.* London: Secker & Warburg, 1965.

——. *J. M. Synge and Lady Gregory.* London: Longmans, Green, 1962.

——. *Lady Gregory: A Literary Portrait,* rev. London: Secker & Warburg, 1966.

Cuming, John. *Apocalyptic Sketches: Lectures on the Book of Revelation* (14th edition). London: Hall, Virtue, and Co., 1951.

Daly, Dominic. *The Young Douglas Hyde: The Dawn of the Irish Revolution and Renaissance: 1874–1893.* Dublin: Irish University Press, 1974.

Davitt, Michael. *The Fall of Feudalism in Ireland.* London: Harper & Brothers, 1904.

de Burgh, V. H. Hussey. *The Landowners of Ireland.* Dublin: Hodges, Foster & Figgis, 1878.

Dedio, Anne. *Das dramatische Werk von Lady Gregory.* Bern: Francke Verlag, 1967.

Donnelly, James S., Jr. *The Land and the People of Nineteenth-Century Cork: The Rural Economy and Land Question.* London: Routledge & Kegan Paul, 1975.

Downey, Edmund. *Charles Lever: His Life in Letters.* 2 vols. London: Blackwood, 1906.

Dumas, C. Horoscope for Lady Gregory. Berg Collection, New York Public Library.

Dunleavy, Gareth W. *Douglas Hyde.* Lewisburg: Bucknell University Press, 1974.

Edel, Leon. *Henry James: The Conquest of London: 1870–1881.* Philadelphia: J. B. Lippincott, 1962.

——. *Henry James: The Master: 1901–1916.* Philadelphia: J. B. Lippincott, 1972.

Eliot, George. *Middlemarch.* London: 1872.

Ellis-Fermor, Una. *The Irish Dramatic Movement,* rev. London: Methuen, 1954.

Ellmann, Richard. *Yeats: The Man and the Masks.* New York: Dutton, 1948.

Ervine, St. John. *Bernard Shaw: His Life, Work and Friends.* New York: William Monroe, 1956.

——. Foreword. *Miss Horniman and the Gaiety Theatre, Manchester* by Rex Pogson. London: Rockliff, 1952.

——. *Some Impressions of My Elders*. New York: Macmillan, 1922.

Fahy, Jerome. Letter to Lady Gregory. Berg Collection, New York Public Library.

Fallon, Gabriel. "Profiles of a Poet," *Modern Drama*, 7 (December 1964), 329–44.

——. *Sean O'Casey: The Man I Knew*. Boston: Little, Brown, 1965.

Farr, Florence, Bernard Shaw, and W. B. Yeats. *Letters*, ed. Clifford Bax. New York: Dodd, Mead, 1942.

Fawcett, Millicent. *The Life of the Right Hon. Sir William Molesworth*. London: Macmillan, 1901.

Fay, Frank. Letters to Lady Gregory. Berg Collection, New York Public Library.

Fay, Gerald. *The Abbey Theatre: Cradle of Genius*. Dublin: Clonmore & Reynolds, 1958.

Fay, William. Letters to Lady Gregory. Berg Collection, New York Public Library.

Fay, William, and Catherine Carswell. *The Fays of the Abbey Theatre: An Autobiographical Record*. New York: Harcourt, Brace, 1935.

Finch, Edith. *Wilfrid Scawen Blunt: 1840–1922*. London: Jonathan Cape, 1938.

Fingall, Elizabeth Plunkett. *Seventy Years Young: Memories of Elizabeth, Countess of Fingall*. Told to Pamela Hinkson. London: Collins, 1937.

FitzGerald, Mary Margaret. *The Dominant Partnership: W. B. Yeats and Lady Gregory in the Early Irish Theatre*. Unpublished Ph.D. dissertation. Princeton University, 1973.

Flannery, James W. *Miss Annie F. Horniman and the Abbey Theatre*. Dublin: Dolmen, 1970.

Folklore Archives. University College Dublin. Manuscripts 455, 538, and 602.

Fremantle, Anne. *Three-Cornered Heart*. New York: Viking, 1948.

Gibbon, Monk. *The Masterpiece and the Man: Yeats as I Knew Him*. New York: Macmillan, 1959.

Gogarty, Oliver St. John. *As I Was Going Down Sackville Street*. New York: Reynal & Hitchcock, 1937.

——. "The Big House at Coole," *A Weekend in the Middle of the Week*. Garden City, N.Y.: Doubleday, 1958.

——. *It Isn't That Time of Year at All!* Garden City, N.Y.: Doubleday, 1954.

——. "Reminiscences of Yeats," *Mourning Becomes Mrs. Spendlove and Other Portraits, Grave and Gay*. New York: Creative Age Press, 1948.

Greene, David H., and Edward M. Stephens. *J. M. Synge: 1871–1909*. New York: Macmillan, 1959.

Gregory, Anne. *Me and Nu: Childhood at Coole*. Gerrards Cross: Colin Smythe, 1970.

351

Gregory, William. *An Autobiography*, ed. Augusta Gregory. 2nd ed. London: John Murray, 1894.

——. Letter to Wilfrid Blunt (19 May 1882). Berg Collection, New York Public Library.

Grigson, Geoffrey. "Synge," *New Statesman*, 19 October 1962.

Guinness, Desmond, and William Ryan. *Irish Houses & Castles*. New York: Viking, 1971.

Gwynn, Denis. *Edward Martyn and the Irish Revival*. London: Jonathan Cape, 1930.

Gwynn, Stephen. *Irish Literature and Drama in the English Language: A Short History*. New York: Thomas Nelson, 1936.

Hinkson, Katherine Tynan. *The Middle Years*. London: Constable, 1916.

——. *Twenty-Five Years: Reminiscences*. London: Smith, Elder, 1913.

——. *The Years of the Shadow*. Boston: Houghton Mifflin, 1919.

Holloway, Joseph. *Joseph Holloway's Abbey Theatre: A Selection from His Unpublished Journal: Impressions of a Dublin Playgoer*, ed. Robert Hogan and Michael J. O'Neill. Carbondale: Southern Illinois University Press, 1967.

——. *Joseph Holloway's Irish Theatre*, ed. Robert Hogan and Michael J. O'Neill. 3 vols. Dixon, Calif.: Proscenium, 1968–70.

Holroyd, Michael. *Augustus John*. New York: Holt, Rinehart and Winston, 1974.

Hone, Joseph. *The Life of George Moore*. New York: Macmillan, 1936.

——. *W. B. Yeats: 1865–1939*. New York: Macmillan, 1943.

Howarth, Herbert. *The Irish Writers: 1880–1940: Literature and Nationalism*. New York: Hill and Wang, 1959.

Hyde, Douglas. *Beside the Fire: A Collection of Gaelic Folk Stories*. London: David Nutt, 1890.

Jeffares, A. Norman. *W. B. Yeats: Man and Poet*. New Haven: Yale University Press, 1949.

Johnston, Denis. *Collected Plays*, Vol. I. London: Jonathan Cape, 1960.

Joyce, James. *Finnegans Wake*. New York: Viking, 1939.

——. *A Portrait of the Artist as a Young Man*. New York: Viking, 1956.

——. *Selected Letters*, ed. Richard Ellmann. New York: Viking, 1975.

——. *Ulysses*. New York: Random House, 1961.

Kavanagh, Peter. *The Story of the Abbey Theatre*. New York: Devin-Adair, 1950.

Kickham, Charles. *Knocknagow* or *The Homes of Tipperary*. Dublin: James Duffy, 1887.

Kiernan, Thomas J. "Lady Gregory and W. B. Yeats," *Southerly*, 14 (1953), 239–51.

Lawless, Emily. *Grania: The Story of an Island*. New York: Macmillan, 1892.

——. *Hurrish: A Study*. New York: Harper, 1888.

——. Letters to Lady Gregory (15 October 1897–28 December 1904). Berg Collection, New York Public Library.

Lawley, Frank. "Racing Career of the Late Hon. Sir William H. Gregory," in *The Racing Life of Lord George Cavendish Bentinck, MP*, by John Kent. Edinburgh & London: William Blackwood & Son, 1893, 366–426.

Leslie, Anita. *The Marlborough House Set*. New York: Doubleday, 1972.

Letters to W. B. Yeats, ed. Richard Finneran, George Mills Harper, and William M. Murphy. 2 vols. London: Macmillan, 1977.

Lever, Charles. *Jack Hinton: The Guardsman*. Philadelphia: Jasper Harding, 1847.

Lewis, Samuel. *A Topographical Dictionary of Ireland*. 2 vols. London: Lewis, 1837.

Longford, Elizabeth. *A Pilgrimage of Passion: The Life of Wilfrid Scawen Blunt*. London: Weidenfeld and Nicolson, 1979.

Lytton, Anthony. *Wilfrid Scawen Blunt: A Memoir by His Grandson*. London: MacDonald, 1961.

MacBride, Maud Gonne. *A Servant of the Queen*. London: Victor Gollancz, 1938.

Magee, William K. (pseudonym: John Eglington). "The Beginnings of Joyce," *Irish Literary Portraits*. New York: Macmillan, 1935.

Mangan, James Clarence. *Poems*. New York: P. M. Haverty, 1859.

Marcus, Phillip L. *Standish O'Grady*. Lewisburg: Bucknell University Press, 1970.

——. *Yeats and the Beginning of the Irish Renaissance*. Ithaca: Cornell University Press, 1970.

Martin, Violet Florence (pseudonym: Martin Ross). Letters to Lady Gregory (4 July 1901–3 August 1915). Berg Collection, New York Public Library.

Martyn, Edward. *The Heather Field and Maeve*, with an introduction by George Moore. London: Duckworth, 1899.

——. *The Tale of a Town and An Enchanted Sea*. London: Unwin, 1902.

Micks, William L. *An Account of the Constitution, Administration and Dissolution of the Congested Districts Board for Ireland from 1891 to 1923*. Dublin: Eason & Son, 1925.

Mikhail, E. H. *Lady Gregory: Interviews and Recollections*. London: Macmillan, 1977.

Mitchell, Susan. *Aids to the Immortality of Certain Persons in Ireland*. Dublin: Maunsel, 1913.

Moore, George. *The Bending of the Bough: A Comedy in Five Acts*. London: Unwin, 1902.

——. *Hail and Farewell: Ave, Salve, Vale*. New York: Appleton, 1912–1914.

——. *Parnell and His Island*. London: Sonnenschein, Lowrey, 1887.

Murphy, Daniel J. "Lady Gregory, Co-Author and Sometimes Author of the Plays of W. B. Yeats," *Modern Irish Literature: Essays in Honor of William York Tindall*, ed. Raymond J. Porter and James D. Brophy. New Rochelle: Iona College Press, 1972, 43–52.

——. "Yeats and Lady Gregory: A Unique Dramatic Collaboration," *Modern Drama*, 7 (December 1964), 322–28.

Murphy, William M. *Prodigal Father: The Life of John Butler Yeats*. Ithaca and London: Cornell University Press, 1978.

Nevill, Dorothy. *Leaves from the Note-Books of Lady Dorothy Nevill*, ed. Ralph Nevill. London: Macmillan, 1907.

——. *My Own Times*. London: Methuen, 1912.

——. *The Reminiscences of Lady Dorothy Nevill*, ed. Ralph Nevill. London: Edward Arnold, 1906.

O'Brien, Barry. *The Life of Charles Stewart Parnell*. 2 vols. 3rd ed. London: Smith, Elder, 1899.

O'Brien, Maire and Conor Cruise. *A Concise History of Ireland*. London: Thames and Hudson, 1972.

O'Casey, Eileen. *Sean*. New York: Coward, McCann & Geoghegan, 1972.

O'Casey, Sean. *Blasts and Benedictions*. London: Macmillan, 1967.

——. *Collected Plays*. 2 vols. London: Macmillan, 1950.

——. *Inishfallen, Fare Thee Well*. New York: Macmillan, 1949.

O'Connor, Frank. *My Father's Son*. New York: Knopf, 1969.

——. *An Only Child*. New York: Knopf, 1961.

——. *A Short History of Irish Literature: A Backward Look*. New York: Putnam's, 1967.

O'Grady, Hugh Art. *Standish James O'Grady: The Man and the Writer*. Dublin: Talbot Press, 1929.

O'Grady, Standish Hayes. *Silva Gadelica: A Collection of Tales in Irish*. London: Williams and Norgate, 1892.

O'Grady, Standish James. *Selected Essays and Passages*. Dublin: Phoenix, n.d.

O'Leary, John. *Recollections of Fenians and Fenianism*. 2 vols. London: Downey, 1896.

Payne, Ben Iden. *A Life in a Wooden O: Memoirs of the Theatre*. New Haven & London: Yale University Press, 1977.

Pound, Ezra. *Pound/Joyce: The Letters of Ezra Pound to James Joyce*, ed. Forrest Reid. New York: New Directions, 1967.

Quinn, John. Letters to Lady Gregory. Manuscript Room, New York Public Library.

Reid, Benjamin L. *The Man from New York: John Quinn and His Friends*. New York: Oxford University Press, 1968.

Robinson, Lennox. Biography of Lady Gregory. Berg Collection, New York Public Library.

——. *Curtain Up: An Autobiography*. London: Michael Joseph, 1942.

——. *I Sometimes Think*. Dublin: Talbot Press, 1956.

——. *Ireland's Abbey Theatre: A History, 1899–1951*. London: Sidgwick and Jackson, 1951.

——. *The Irish Theatre: Lectures Delivered During the Abbey Theatre Festival Held in Dublin in August 1938*. London: Macmillan, 1939.

Rodgers, W. R., ed. *Irish Literary Portraits: Broadcast Conversations with*

Those Who Knew Them. London: British Broadcasting Company, 1972.

Rossi, Mario Manillo. *Pilgrimage in the West*, trans. J. M. Hone. Dublin: Cuala, 1933.

Russell, George. *Letters from AE*, ed. Alan Denson. London: Abelard-Schuman, 1961.

Saddlemyer, Ann. "Image-Maker for Ireland: Augusta, Lady Gregory," *The World of W. B. Yeats*, rev., ed. Robin Skelton and Ann Saddlemyer. Seattle: University of Washington Press, 1967, 161–68.

——. *In Defense of Lady Gregory, Playwright*. Dublin: Dolmen, 1966.

Schreiber, Charlotte Guest. *Lady Charlotte Guest: Extracts from Her Journal: 1833–1852*, ed. Earl of Bessborough. London: Murray, 1950.

——. *Lady Charlotte Schreiber: Extracts from Her Journal: 1853–1891*, ed. Earl of Bessborough. London: Murray, 1952.

Shaw, George Bernard. "John Bull's Other Island." *The Bodley Head Shaw: Collected Plays with Their Prefaces*, Vol. 2. London: Bodley Head, 1971, 807–1028.

——. "The Shewing-Up of Blanco Posnet," *The Bodley Head Shaw: Collected Plays with Their Prefaces*, Vol. 3. London: Bodley Head, 1971, 673–814.

Shawe-Taylor, Desmond. "A Woman Young and Old," Review of *Seventy Years* by Augusta Gregory. *New Yorker*, 19 July 1976, 93–95.

Shiubhlaigh, Maire nic (pseudonym for Mary Walker). *The Splendid Years*. As told to Edward Kenny. Dublin: James Duffy, 1955.

Sichel, Edith. "Emily Lawless," *Nineteenth Century*, July 1919, 80–100.

Smythe, Colin. *A Guide to Coole Park, Co. Galway: Home of Lady Gregory*. Gerrards Cross: Colin Smythe, 1973.

——, ed. *Robert Gregory*. Gerrards Cross: Colin Smythe, 1981.

Somerville, E. OE., and Martin Ross (pseudonym for Violet Martin). *Irish Memories*. London: Longmans, Green, 1917.

——. *The Real Charlotte*. London: Longmans, Green, 1894.

——. *Wheel-tracks*. London: Longmans, Green, 1923.

The Spirit of the Nation, ed. Charles Gavin Duffy. Dublin: James Duffy, 1845.

Starkie, Walter. *Scholars and Gypsies: An Autobiography*. Berkeley and Los Angeles: University of California Press, 1963.

Stephens, Edward. *My Uncle John*, ed. Andrew Carpenter. London: Oxford University Press, 1974.

Synge, John M. *The Aran Islands*. Dublin: Maunsel, 1907.

——. *The Complete Plays of John M. Synge*. New York: Random House, 1935.

——. *Letters to Molly: John Millington Synge to Maire O'Neill: 1906–1909*, ed. Ann Saddlemyer. Cambridge, Mass: Belknap Press of Harvard University Press, 1971.

——. *Some Letters of John M. Synge to Lady Gregory and W. B. Yeats*, ed. Ann Saddlemyer. Dublin: Cuala, 1971.

Theatre Business: The Correspondence of the First Abbey Directors: William Butler Yeats, Lady Gregory and J. M. Synge, ed. Ann Saddlemyer. Gerrards Cross: Colin Smythe, 1982.

Toksvig, Signe. "A Visit to Lady Gregory," *North American Review*, Vol. CCXIV (August 1921), 190–200.

Unterecker, John. *A Reader's Guide to William Butler Yeats*. New York: Noonday Press, 1959.

Wallace, J. R. Horoscope for Lady Gregory. Berg Collection, New York Public Library.

Yeats, John Butler. "John Butler Yeats to Lady Gregory: New Letters," ed. Glenn O'Malley and D. T. Torchiana. *Irish Renaissance: A Gathering of Essays, Memoirs, and Letters from The Massachusetts Review*, ed. Robin Skelton and David R. Clark. Dublin: Dolmen, 1965, 56–64.

——. *Letters from Bedford Park: A Selection from the Correspondence of John Butler Yeats: 1890–1901*, ed. Daniel J. Murphy. Dublin: Cuala Press, 1972.

——. *Letters to His Son W. B. Yeats and Others: 1869–1922*, ed. Joseph Hone. London: Faber and Faber, 1944.

Yeats, William Butler. *The Autobiography of William Butler Yeats*. New York: Macmillan, 1965.

——. *The Celtic Twilight*. London: Bullen, 1893; London: Bullen, 1902.

——. *The Collected Plays of W. B. Yeats*. New York: Macmillan, 1952.

——. *Essays and Introductions*. New York: Macmillan, 1961.

——. *Explorations*. New York: Macmillan, 1962.

——. *The Letters of W. B. Yeats*, ed. Allan Wade. London: Rupert Hart-Davis, 1954.

——. *Letters on Poetry from W. B. Yeats to Dorothy Wellesley*. London: Oxford University Press, 1940.

——. Letters to Augusta Gregory (23 January 1898–23 September 1931). Berg Collection, New York Public Library.

——. *The Poems of W. B. Yeats*, ed. Richard J. Finneran. New York: Macmillan, 1983.

——. *Memoirs*, ed. Denis Donoghue. New York: Macmillan, 1972.

——. *Mythologies*. New York: Macmillan, 1959.

——. *The Variorum Edition of the Plays of W. B. Yeats*, ed. Russell K. Alspach, assisted by Catharine C. Alspach. London: Macmillan, 1966.

——. *The Variorum Edition of the Poems of W. B. Yeats*, ed. Peter Allt and Russell K. Alspach. New York: Macmillan, 1940.

——. *A Vision*. New York: Macmillan, 1965.

Young, Ella. *Flowering Dusk: Things Remembered Accurately and Inaccurately*. New York: Longmans, Green, 1945.

Index

Abbey Theatre, 74, 174, 175, 185, 304; beginnings of, 113–15; and demands for censorship of O'Casey's plays, 283–84; Lady Gregory's history of, 234–37; management change, 259; management trio, 182; and Miss Horniman's financial demands, 220–21; opening of, 176; resignation of Fay Brothers, 199–200, and G. B. Shaw, 211–12; Yeats's farewell to, 227, 252; *see also* Irish Literary Theatre; Irish National Theatre Society

AE. *See* Russell, George

Ahmed Arabi. *See* Arabi Pasha

Algoin, Frances (great grandmother of Lady Gregory), 192

Allgood, Molly (pseudonym: Maire O'Neill), 182, 187, 192, 199, 208, 213, 304

Allgood, Sara, 174, 181, 183, 199, 304

Ankell, Frances, 314

"Arabi and His Household" (Lady Gregory), 62–63

Arabi Pasha, 57, 58, 59, 61, 62–64, 64, 76

Aran Isles, 94, 125, 142

Argosy, 86, 99

Aristotle's Bellows (Lady Gregory), 263–64

Arms and the Man (Shaw), 113, 165

Arnold, Sir Edwin, 53, 318

Asquith, Herbert Henry, 93

Athenaeum, 124

Atkinson, Robert, 138–39

Auden, Wystan Hugh, 6, 292

Ave (Moore), 239–40

Ballylee, 271–72, 273

Barlow, Jane, 94

Barrie, James Matthew, 164

Barry, Frances. *See* Persse, Frances Barry

Basterot, Count de, 78, 112, 137

Beadon, Ada. *See* Persse, Ada Beadon

"Beautiful Lofty Things" (Yeats), 30, 91, 270, 302

Bending of the Bough, The (Moore), 136

Beresford, Lady Blanche, 293

Beside the Fire (Hyde), 94

Biddy Early, 111

Birch, Sir Arthur, 90, 96, 97; sons of, 96–97, 130 131

Blake, Val, 20

Blakeney Family, 9, 22

Blanco Posnet (Shaw). *See Shewing-up of Blanco Posnet*

Bleak House (Dickens), 140

Blunt, Judith, 58, 66, 97, 274

Blunt, Lady Anne King-Noel, 57, 58, 65–66, 67, 69, 72, 78–80, 80, 81–82, 84, 159

Blunt, Wilfrid Scawen, 53, 76, 89, 93, 95, 96, 97, 140, 163, 196, 238, 264; affair with Lady Gregory, 61–62, 64–69, 77, 154, 155, 277; arrest and imprisonment 81–83; background of, 57–58; comments on plays, 164; death, 274; and Egyptian cause, 58–59, 60–61, 64; *In Vinculis* (prison poems), 85; and Irish situation, 80; meets Yeats, 122; publishes Lady Gregory's

Blunt, Wilfrid Scawen (*continued*)
sonnets, 87; religion, 60; on Sir William Gregory's *Autobiography*, 97–98; writes play for Irish National Theatre, 158
Boehm, Sir Edward, 69
Boer War, 137, 140
Bogie Men, The (Lady Gregory), 221–22, 234, 237
Bonn, Moritz, 120
Borrow, George, 94
Borthwick, Norma, 130–31
Boru, Brian. *See* Brian (King of Ireland)
Boston, Massachusetts, 225–29, 231
Bourget, Paul, 318
Boyle, William, 185
Brian (King of Ireland), 166–67
Bright, John, 53
Brown, Isabella Augusta, 13
Browne, Maurice, 228
Browning, Robert, 29, 52, 53
Burke, Edmund, 49
Burke, Father (Catholic priest), 42
Burke, Rick (steward), 44
Burke, Thomas Henry, 60
Burkett, Archdeacon, 26–27, 33, 147–48, 150–51
Burkett, Miss Samuella, 41
Burton, Sir Frederic, 52–53, 66, 93, 95, 108, 235

Canavans, The (Lady Gregory), 188, 190–92, 237
Cannes, France, 36, 37, 39–40
Carleton, Dorothy, 274
Casement, Roger, 96
Casey, W. F. 185, 200
Castleboy (estate), 12
Castlehaven, Third Earl of. *See* Touchet, James
Castle Taylor, 31, 33, 81, 102
Cathleen ni Houlihan (Yeats and Lady Gregory), 143–46, 148–49, 150–51, 159, 164, 176, 304; Lady Gregory plays leading role, 259
Catholics and Catholic Church, 4, 5, 13, 83, 101; and Irish Literary Theatre's plays, 134–35; reaction to plays in U.S., 229
Cavendish, Lord Frederick Charles, 60
Celtic culture, 3; *see also* Gaelic literature
Celtic Twilight (Yeats), 96, 100, 251–52
censorship, 283–84
Ceylon, 35, 37, 69–70, 76–77

Chevy Chase (lodge), 9, 20
Chicago, Illinois, 231
Chicago Little Theater Society, 228
Childe, Mrs. Lee, 78
Churchill, Randolph Henry Spencer, 53
Clanmorris Family, 22
Clanricarde, 2nd Marquis and 15th Earl of (Hubert George de Burgh Canning), 22, 56
Coats (Lady Gregory), 216, 219
Colman and Guaire (Lady Gregory), 128–29
Colum, Mary Maguire, 135, 171, 172, 177, 193, 194–95, 217, 226, 228, 233
Colum, Padraic, 181, 235
Colvin, Auckland, 57, 58, 75, 76, 95
Colvin, Sidney, 139
Connel, Norreys, 185
Conrad, Joseph, 281
Coole (Lady Gregory), 289, 299–300
Coole (Coole Park) (estate), 38, 48–49, 50–51, 72, 91, 96–97, 107, 299–300, 301; damaged by "Big Wind," 162, 162–63; demolition of, 303–304; Lady Gregory's fear of losing, 268–69; Lady Gregory's gardening at, 109–11; Lady Gregory's love for, 288–89, 290; and Richard Gregory's inheritance, 204, 206; and Robert Gregory's inheritance, 51, 84, 91, 298; as meeting place and inspiration for writers, 125–28, 142; unharmed in Civil War, 273; Yeats and, 105, 118, 203–204
"Coole Park, 1929" (Yeats), 163, 299
"Coole Park and Ballylee, 1931" (Yeats), 300
Cornhill Magazine, 137
Cornwall, England, 33–34
Countess Cathleen (Yeats), 114, 126, 134
Crabbet Park (estate), 60, 65
Cregroontha (estate). *See* Roxborough
Crimson in the Tri-colour, The (O'Casey), 281
Croft, The (home of Frances Persse), 92, 92–93, 100, 103
Cuala Press, 299
Cuchulain of Muirthemne (Lady Gregory), 140–42, 149–50, 299
Cuming, Reverend John, 12
Curzon, George, 260–61

Damer's Gold (Lady Gregory), 233–34
Darragh, Florence, 188, 189–90
Daughters of Erin, 148, 158
Dave (Lady Gregory), 285, 291–93

Davis, Thomas, 24, 52
Davitt, Michael, 42, 56
Deirdre (Russell), 148
Deirdre (Yeats), 189
Deirdre of the Sorrows (Synge), 200, 208, 213
Deliverer, The (Lady Gregory), 216, 217–18, 237
Dervorgilla (Lady Gregory), 196, 197–98, 198, 237
de Vere, Aubrey, 114, 235
Diarmuid and Grania (Yeats and Moore), 148
Dickens, Charles, 139–40
Diviney, John, 253, 300
Doctor in Spite of Himself, The (Molière), 185
Dolan, Michael, 283
Donovan, Fred, 259
Don Quixote, 285–86
Dowden, Edward, 114
Dragon, The (Lady Gregory), 249–51, 260
Dublin: and dispute over Hugh Lane's paintings, 262–63
Dublin *Daily Express*, 148, 157–58
Dublin Municipal Gallery, 260
Dublin National Gallery (National Gallery of Ireland), 202, 247, 260
Duff, Mountstuart Elphinstone Grant, 74
Dufferin and Ava, First Marquis of (Frederick Temple Hamilton-Temple-Blackwood), 75, 76, 114
Dun Emir Press, 164, 167

Edgar, Louie, 67
Edward VII (of Great Britain), 140, 221
Eglington, John (pseudonym for William K. Magee), 114, 318
Egypt, 57–61
Eliot, Thomas Stearns, 281
Ellis-Fermor, Una, 7
Epstein, Jacob, 18, 304
Ervine, St. John, 296
"Eviction, The" (Lady Gregory), 83–84

Fand (Blunt), 159, 198
Farr, Florence, 134, 178
Fay, Frank, 148, 149, 151, 155, 158, 167, 169, 173, 180, 181, 304; resignation, 199
Fay, Willie, 148, 149, 151, 155, 158, 167, 173, 176, 180, 185, 188, 304; marriage, 189; resignation, 199
Fay, Mrs. Willie. *See* O'Dempsey, Bridget

"Felons of Our Land, The" (Lady Gregory), 9, 137
Fenians and Fenian literature, 24–25, 26, 27, 159
Fingall, Countess, 72, 108, 272–73
Forster, William E., 53, 56
Fortnightly Review, 70
Foster, Jeanne, 280, 281
Frohman, Charles, 182, 200
Frost in the Flower, The (O'Casey), 281
Froude, James Anthony, 48, 52, 318
Full Moon, The (Lady Gregory), 216, 219–20

Gaelic American (newspaper), 228
Gaelic language, 30, 87, 94, 100, 107, 120–21, 131
Gaelic League, 100, 119, 138
Gaelic literature, 138–39
Gaelic Society, 229
Gaiety Theatre (Dublin), 135, 137, 148
Galway, Ireland, 19
Galway Blazers, 22
Gaol Gate, The (Lady Gregory), 83, 188–89, 213
Gardner, Mrs. Jack, 226–27
"Gentleman, A" (Lady Gregory), 99
Gibbon, Monk, 295
Gladstone, William Ewart, 53, 55–56, 71, 78, 79, 93
Gods and Fighting Men (Lady Gregory), 149, 164
Gogarty, Oliver St. John, 296, 303
Golden Apple, The (Lady Gregory), 239, 240–42
Golden Dawn Society. *See* Order of the Golden Dawn
Goldoni, Carlo, 213
Goldsmith, Oliver, 48
Gonne, Iseult, 251
Gonne, Maud (Mrs. John MacBride), 158, 165, 206, 284; background of, 111–13, 123; and *Cathleen ni Houlihan*, 143, 148, 149, 150, 259; death of husband, 251; on Lady Gregory's playwriting, 179; marital problems, 177; marriage, 162; resigns from Irish National Theatre Society, 166; and Yeats, 6, 101, 114. 116–17, 120, 123, 129–30, 134, 165, 249
Gordon at Khartoum (Blunt), 238
Gosse, Edmund William, 218, 219
Gough, George, 113
Gough, Guy, 298
Gough, Nora. *See* Persse, Nora Gough

Grania (Lady Gregory), 213, 214–16, 237, 250

Great Famine (1845–47), 10

Gregory, (Isabella) Augusta Persse, Lady Gregory: affair with Wilfrid Blunt, 57–58, 58–59, 61–62, 64–69, 71, 77, 277; aids poor, 41–42, 53–54; ancestry and birth, 8–12, 13–14; autographed fan, 53; birth of son, 54–55; and Blunt's arrest and imprisonment, 81–84; breast cancer operations, 274–75, 286; burial place, 304–305; cerebral hemorrhage, 206–207; childhood, 5, 14–15; collects Irish folklore, 105–108, 111, 131, 138; compared to Queen Victoria, 296–97; continues to wear mourning clothes, 6, 90–91, 96, 97, 109, 138; and Coole, 49–51, 91, 286, 288–89, 290; death of, 302; on death of W. Blunt, 274; death of Hugh Lane, 247; early education, 18–19, 29–30; early meetings and courtship by Sir William Gregory, 37–38, 39–40, 43–44; edits husband's *Autobiography*, 94–95, 97–98; effect of father's death on, 39; Egyptian situation, 57–61, 62–64; financial situation of, 286–88; fights for Hugh Lane's art collection to return to Ireland, 260–61; fundraising efforts for gallery for Lane's art collection, 238–39; husband's death, 88–89; interest in gardens and trees, 102, 109–10, 257, 258; and Irish epics, 139–42, 149–50; and London society, 51–53, 71, 78, 95, 95–96; marriage, 44; memoirs of, 276–77; migraine headaches, 82, 85, 86; and G. Moore, 239–40; is nurse and companion for her brother Richard, 35–37, 39–40; O'Casey's rejection of, 294–95; playwriting, 152–54, 171–72, 184–85, 212–13, 215–16, 227, 236; relationship with parents, 17; relationship with John Quinn, 164, 229–30, 231, 232–33, 237, 241, 248; relationship with Yeats, 6, 117–18, 143–48, 164–65, 218, 303; religious background and conversion, 20–21, 26–27, 28, 83, 159, 240; and resistance movement, 24–25, 27, 30; rheumatism, 206; and Roxborough, 91–92, 294; son's death, 252–58; on Synge's death, 208; theater management career, 175, 181–82, 184; translates Molière, 185, 206, 285; trip to India and Ceylon, 72–78; visits America, 223–31, 238–39, 246, 248;

writes biography of Hugh Lane, 261–63

Gregory, Augusta Anne (called Anne) (granddaughter of Lady Gregory), 223, 246, 251, 257, 258, 259–60, 265, 279–80, 297, 298, 303

Gregory, Catherine Frances (granddaughter of Lady Gregory), 239, 251, 257, 259–60, 265, 267, 297, 298, 303

Gregory, Charles (cousin of Sir William Gregory), 54, 91

Gregory, Elizabeth Bowdoin (first wife of Sir William Gregory), 35

Gregory, Elizabeth O'Hara (mother of Sir William Gregory), 38

Gregory, Margaret Graham Parry (Mrs. [William] Robert Gregory) (daughter-in-law of Lady Gregory), 195–96, 198–99, 203, 205, 206, 207, 211, 212, 223, 239, 241–42, 243, 246, 253–54, 265, 268–69; and Coole, 286, 290; husband's death, 253–54; remarriage, 298

Gregory, Richard (great-uncle of Sir William Gregory), 49

Gregory, Richard Graham (grandson of Lady Gregory), 206, 207–208, 233, 246, 254, 256–57, 258, 260, 265, 297–98, 303, 333; and *Our Irish Theatre*, 234, 235, 236

Gregory, Robert (great-grandfather of Sir William Gregory), 49

Gregory, Robert (father of Sir William Gregory), 10, 50

Gregory, (William) Robert (son of Lady Augusta and Sir William Gregory), 76, 77, 79, 80, 81, 86, 88, 89, 91, 92, 93, 94, 95, 96–97, 111, 116, 137, 138, 211; as artist, 162, 177, 200, 207, 238, 244, 246, 266; attends Harrow, 100, 102, 107, 108, 120, 121, 124, 138; birth, 54–55; comes of age, 155–56; and Coole, 203–204, 206, 266; death of, 252–53; engagement of, 195–96; marriage, 198–99; at Oxford, 138; serves in World War I, 243, 244, 244–45, 245; and Synge, 182, 200; Yeats's poems on, 255, 256, 267–68

Gregory, William (grandfather of Sir William Gregory), 49–50, 101

Gregory, Sir William, 6, 10, 11, 80, 110; on Augusta Persse as a child, 17; in Ceylon, 35, 69, 70; courtship of Augusta Persse, 37–38, 39–40, 43–44; death, 88–89; Lady Gregory edits autobiography of, 94–95, 97–98; as a

Gregory, Sir William (*continued*)
landlord, 50; marriage to Augusta
Persse, 44; political background, 25,
34–35; position on Egypt, 61; and
wife's affair with W. Blunt, 67
Grey, Angus (pseudonym), 86, 99; *see
also* Gregory, (Isabella) Augusta
Persse (Lady Gregory)
Guest, Charlotte (Lady Schreiber), 47,
72
Gwynn, Stephen, 150

Hail and Farewell (Moore), 134, 239
Hamilton, Sir Ian Standish Monteith,
204
Hanrahan's Oath (Lady Gregory), 251,
251–52
Hardy, Thomas, 318
Harrison, Frederic, 53
Hart, Henry, 32–33
Hartington, Lord (Victor Christian Wil-
liam Cavendish), 58
Harvey, Paul, 78, 80, 95, 98, 101–102,
103, 107, 121
Heather Field, The (Martyn), 113, 114,
126, 134
Hinkson, Katherine Tynan, 116, 237
Holloway, Joseph, 175, 194
Home Rule, 78, 79, 79–80, 93, 101, 108,
138, 163, 248
Homeward Songs by the Way (Russell),
115
Horniman, Annie E. F., 165–66, 168,
175, 176, 180, 187, 188, 192, 220–21,
299; on Lady Gregory's playwriting,
179
Houghton, Lord. *See* Milnes, Richard
Monckton
Hour-Glass, The (Yeats), 162, 164
Hugh Lane's Life and Achievement
(Lady Gregory), 262–63
Huxley, Thomas, 71
Hyacinth Halvey (Lady Gregory), 179–
80, 213, 219
Hyde, Douglas, 4, 94, 100, 107, 119–20,
130, 131, 138, 142, 154, 156, 157, 158,
165, 235, 299
Hyde-Lees, Bertha Georgie (Mrs. Wil-
liam Butler Yeats), 251, 259

Ideas on India (Blunt), 72
"Idler's Calendar" (Blunt), 68
Image, The (Lady Gregory), 209–11
India, 72–76
Inishfallen, Fare Thee Well (O'Casey),
282

"In the Seven Woods" (Yeats), 203
In the Shadow of the Glen (Synge), 158,
166, 182, 193
In Vinculis (Blunt), 85
Ireland: Blunt's arrest and imprison-
ment in, 81–83; Civil War, 270, 272–
74, 276; conditions in *1879–1880*, 41;
conditions in *1881*, 55–56; conditions
in *1886-87*, 79–80, 80–81; conditions
in *1908*, 202; conditions in *1919–22*
(Black and Tans in), 266–70; famine
in Kerry and Maud Gonne's action,
123; fighting in Dublin between Vol-
unteers and British Army, 248–49;
Land Purchase Act, 163; treaty with
England, 269–70; *see also* Home Rule
Irish Academy of Letters, 300–301
"Irish Airman Forsees His Death"
(Yeats), 255, 256
Irish Folk-History Plays: First Series
(Lady Gregory), 237
Irish Folk-History Plays: Second Series
(Lady Gregory), 237
Irish epics, 139–42, 149–50
Irish folklore, 105–108, 111, 131, 138,
158
Irish Idyls (Barlow), 94
Irish literature: idealism in, 114, 139
Irish Literary Society, 108, 136, 137
Irish Literary Society of New York, 164
Irish Literary Theatre, 108; first season,
133–35; Martyn leaves, 119, 181;
prospectus for, 113–14, 139; second
season, 135, 136–37; third season, 142,
148; trial period over, 148; *see also*
Abbey Theatre; Irish National The-
atre Society
Irish National Land League, 42, 48, 56,
62, 106
Irish National Theatre Society: begin-
nings of, 148, 158; performs in Lon-
don, 164, 168; reorganization of, 180–
81; and Synge, 166; *see also* Irish
Literary Theatre
Irish People (newspaper), 26
Irish Players from Dublin, 200
Irish Renaissance, 3, 30, 99–100, 105–
108, 148
Irish Times, 150
Italy, 36, 137; *see also* Venice

Jackdaw, The (Lady Gregory), 185–86,
195, 213, 219
James, Henry, 43, 52, 95, 98, 102, 164,
318
Jester, The (Lady Gregory), 258–59

John, Augustus, 198, 237, 246–47, 318
John, Mike, 100, 121
John Bull's Other Island (Shaw), 259
Johnson, Lionel, 116
Johnston, Denis, 295
Joyce, James, 157–58, 281, 296
Juno and the Paycock (O'Casey), 278, 281–82

Kelmscott Press, 87
Kickham, Charles, 314
Kiernan, Thomas J., 286–87, 298
Kildare Street Club, 103, 119
"Kiltartan", 131, 139
Kiltartan Wonder Book (Lady Gregory), 241, 242
Kincora (Lady Gregory), 166–67, 168, 175, 177, 200, 203, 237
Kinglake Alexander William, 52, 53, 85
King's Threshold, The (Yeats), 165
Kipling, Rudyard, 318

"Lament, A" (Lady Gregory), 82–83
"Lament for the Death of Eogan Roe O'Neill" (Davis), 24
Land League. *See* Irish National Land League
Land of Hearts' Desire, The (Yeats), 165
Land Purchase Act, 163, 178
Lane, Hugh (nephew of Lady Gregory), 39, 131, 163, 194, 210, 211; becomes successful art dealer, 131, 187, 237–38, 246; considered for curator of Dublin National Gallery, 202; death of, 247; gallery problems, 240; Lady Gregory's biography of, 261–63; Lady Gregory's fight for art collection to return to Ireland, 260–61, 299; Lady Gregory's fund-raising efforts for gallery, 238–39; starts art career, 93, 98
Lane, John (brother-in-law of Lady Gregory), 32, 38, 93
Last Feast of the Fianna, The (Milligan), 135
Lavengro (Borrow), 94
Lawless, Emily, 95, 114
Lawley, Frank, 53, 124
Layard, Enid, 47, 48, 64, 72, 93, 94, 95, 96, 101, 103, 108, 128, 130, 137, 209, 238
Layard, Sir Henry, 46, 47–48, 53, 55, 64, 81, 88, 93; death of, 96; and Sir William Gregory's *Autobiography*, 94–95
Laying of the Foundations, The (Ryan), 164

Lecky, William, 52, 93, 114, 120, 123–24, 133, 235, 318
"Leda and the Swan" (Yeats), 278
Leixlip Castle, 298
Lever, Charles James, 16, 22, 50
Liebler and Company, 221, 231
Lindsay House, 237, 238
Lloyd George, David, 269
Local Government Bill of *1898*, 133–34
London: Lady Gregory's social life in society of, 45–46, 48, 71, 78, 95–96, 137
London Times, 63
Losing Game, A (Lady Gregory), 154–55
Lowell, James Russell, 53, 67
Lutyens, Sir Edwin Landseer, 240
Lyall, Sir Alfred Comyn, 108
Lytton, Robert (Edward Robert Bulwer Lytton), First Earl of Lytton, 66
Lytton, Neville, 163

MacBride, John, 162, 251
MacBride, Maud Gonne. *See* Gonne, Maud
McDonough's Wife (Lady Gregory), 224–25, 234
Maeve (Martyn), 113, 135
Maguire, Mary. *See* Colum, Mary Maguire
Mancini, Antonio, 187, 302, 304, 318
Mangan, James Clarence, 108, 328
Marlay Abbey, 298
Marriage, The (Hyde), 165
Martin, Katherine, 29
Martin, Robert, 62
Martin, Violet (pseudonym: Martin Ross), 29, 127, 142, 153, 177, 223, 239, 315
Martyn, Edward, 44, 78, 103–104, 105, 111, 119, 121, 156, 221, 318; and Abbey Theatre, 113–14, 133, 133–35, 148; leaves Abbey, 181; *see also titles of individual plays*
Mill, John Stuart, 51
Millais, John, 53
Millevoye, Lucien, 123, 162
Milligan, Alice, 135
Milnes, Richard Monckton (Lord Houghton), 52, 53, 57
Mirandolina (Goldoni), 213–14
Miser, The (Molière), 185, 206
Mr. Gregory's Letter Box (Lady Gregory), 120, 123–24
Mitchell, Susan, 121
Molesworth, Lady, 51–52, 66, 69, 71
Molesworth, Sir William, 51

Molière: Lady Gregory's translations of, 185, 199–200, 206 285

Morley, John, 318

Moore, George Augustus, 4, 28, 53, 65, 78, 134, 135–37, 142, 149, 154, 176, 209, 221, 299, 304, 315, 318; on Lady Gregory, 239–40; and E. Martyn, 103–104; relationship with Yeats and Lady Gregory, 135–36

Morris, Anna Hughes (Lady Morris), 94, 120, 121, 124

Morris, Jane Burden, 87

Morris, Michael (Lord Morris), 82, 94, 96, 120, 124

Morris, William, 87

"Mosada" (Yeats), 112

Mount Vernon (home), 12

"Municipal Gallery Revisited" (Yeats), 302

Murphy, Daniel J., 327–28

Murphy, William Martin, 262

Murray, Sir John, 94

Nansen, Fridtjof, 318

National Gallery of England, 247

National Gallery of Ireland. See Dublin National Gallery

National Land League of Mayo, 42

National Theatre Society of Ireland, 200

Naughton, Malachi, 210

Nevill, Lady Dorothy, 51–52

Newcastle (estate), 19–20

New Pilgrimage, A (Blunt), 85

New Republic, 293–94

New York, 229–30

O'Brien, Barry, 108

O'Brien, George, 284

O'Casey, Sean, 172, 255, 257–58, 278, 281–83, 296, 297, 304, 318; rejection of Lady Gregory, 294–95; see also titles of individual plays

O'Connor, Frank, 295, 298–99

O'Neill, Maire (pseudonym). See Allgood, Molly

O'Dempsey, Bridget (Mrs. Willie Fay), 189, 199

O'Donovan, Fred, 184, 199

O'Grady, Katherine. See Persse, Katherine O'Grady

O'Grady, Standish, 11

O'Grady, Standish Hayes (cousin of Lady Gregory), 30, 99, 107

O'Grady, Standish James (cousin of Lady Gregory), 30, 99–100, 107, 118

O'Grady, Thomas, 314

O'Grady, William (cousin of Lady Gregory), 11, 14, 109

"Old Woman Remembers" (Lady Gregory), 269

O'Leary, John, 104, 112, 114, 235, 236

On Baile's Strand (Yeats), 165, 176

Order of the Golden Dawn, 165

Orpen, William, 318

Our Irish Theatre (Lady Gregory), 221, 234–37

Parnell, Charles Stewart, 42, 56, 60, 79, 87, 217

Parry, Margaret Graham. See Gregory, Margaret Graham Parry

Payne, Ben Iden, 192, 196, 197

Parsons, Sir Laurence, 313–14

Parsons, Sir William, 313–14

Pearse, Padraic, 174

Persse, Ada Beadon (Mrs. Harry Persse) (sister-in-law of Lady Gregory), 84

Persse, Adelaide (Mrs. John Lane) (sister of Lady Gregory), 13, 15, 21, 25–26, 31, 32; marriage and marital problems, 32, 38–39, 41, 93, 102

Persse, Alfred Lovaine (brother of Lady Gregory), 14, 41, 102, 245, 294

Persse, Algernon (brother of Lady Gregory), 13, 15, 41, 42, 43, 62, 70, 71, 81, 91, 102, 245; death, 223; marriage, 78, 79

Persse, Arabella (Mrs. Wainwright Waithman) (sister of Lady Gregory), 13, 14, 18, 21–22, 25, 26, 28–29, 31–32, 38, 40, 44, 67–68, 83, 102; death, 280; husband's death, 238; marriage, 86

Persse, Arthur (nephew of Lady Gregory): Roxborough, 92, 107, 272

Persse, (Isabella) Augusta. See Gregory, (Isabella) Augusta Persse, Lady Gregory

Persse, Burton (cousin of Lady Gregory), 22, 33, 34, 42

Persse, Dudley (d. 1700), 9

Persse, Dudley (father of Lady Gregory), 17, 50; death, 39; first marriage, 10–11; Lady Gregory likened to, 67; second marriage, 11–13

Persse, Dudley (half brother of Lady Gregory), 11, 15, 22, 39, 43, 44, 70, 91

Persse, Edward (brother of Lady Gregory), 13, 15, 41, 69

Persse, Elizabeth (Eliza) (Mrs. Walter Shawe-Taylor) (sister of Lady Greg-

Persse, Elizabeth (*continued*)
ory), 13, 15, 21, 38, 43, 81, 84, 88, 92, 102; death, 102, 107; marriage, 31, 41

Persse, Ethel (niece of Lady Gregory), 103

Persse, Frances Barry (Mrs. Dudley Persse) (mother of Lady Gregory), 11–13, 17, 18–19, 30, 31, 55, 84; children of, 13–14; death, 102; effect of husband's death, 39

Persse, Francis Fitz Adelm (Frank) (brother of Lady Gregory), 14, 31, 32, 41, 44, 76–77, 84–85, 245, 253, 257, 270, 272; death, 294; as land agent, 86, 91, 100, 102, 107, 268; marriage, 60

Persse, Gerald Dillon (brother of Lady Gregory), 14, 39, 41, 62, 70, 80, 98, 102; death, 124–25; engagement, 92; Roxborough, 91–92, 107

Persse, Gertrude (sister of Lady Gregory), 13, 15, 21, 29, 31, 32, 105; death, 33–34, 39, 41; marriage, 33–34

Persse, Henry (Harry) (brother of Lady Gregory), 14, 41, 77, 80, 102; death, 294; marriage, 84

Persse, Jocelyn (nephew of Lady Gregory), 98

Persse, Katherine (Katie) (half sister of Lady Gregory), 11, 13, 15, 31, 41

Persse, Katherine O'Grady (Mrs. Dudley Persse) (first wife of Lady Gregory's father), 11

Persse, Maria (half sister of Lady Gregory), 11, 13, 15, 41, 66

Persse, Nora Gough (Mrs. Algernon Persse) (sister-in-law of Lady Gregory), 78, 84, 122

Persse, Richard Dudley (brother of Lady Gregory), 13, 15, 21, 22; death, 42–43; Lady Gregory is nurse and companion to, 34, 35–36, 37, 38, 39–40, 41

Persse, Robert Henry (uncle of Lady Gregory), 12

Persse, Rose Mesham (Mrs. William Persse) (sister-in-law of Lady Gregory), 91, 92, 124

Persse, William (great-grandfather of Lady Gregory), 9–10, 24

Persse, William Norton (brother of Lady Gregory), 13, 15, 41; death, 92; inherits Roxborough, 91, 92

Phantom's Pilgrimage: or Home Ruin (Lady Gregory), 93

Philadelphia, 230–31

"Philanthropist, A" (Lady Gregory), 86

Playboy of the Western World, The (Synge), 223, 236; compared to *Grania*, 216; production and reaction to in U.S., 228, 236; public reaction to in Dublin, 192–93, 193–95

Player Queen, The (Yeats), 200

Plough and the Stars, The (O'Casey), 283–85

Plunkett, Horace, 108, 118, 142, 318

Poets and Dreamers (Lady Gregory), 164

Poorhouse, The (Hyde), 165, 200

Portrait of the Artist as a Young Man (Joyce), 158

Pot of Broth (Yeats and Lady Gregory), 146–48, 164, 175

Pound, Ezra, 131, 251, 281

Protestants and Protestant Church of Ireland, 5, 13

Purser, Sarah, 175, 299

Quinn, John, 148, 156–57, 164, 166, 175, 178, 195, 198, 200, 254, 255; and Armory Show, 239; art collection, 280–81; death, 280–81; Lady Gregory's romance with, 224–25, 229–30, 230, 231, 232–33, 237, 239, 240, 241, 246, 248, 254

Raftery (poet), 138, 156

Reform Bill of *1832*, 25

Reform Bill of *1868*, 35

Renan, Ernest, 53

"Reprisals" (Yeats), 267–68

"Ribbonmen", 10

Ricketts, Charles, 263

Riders to the Sea (Synge), 158, 162, 167

Rising of the Moon, The (Lady Gregory), 150, 159–61, 167, 168, 213

Roberts, George, 181

Robinson, Lennox, 150, 165, 168, 183–84, 231, 269–70, 275, 276, 278, 281, 283, 287, 295; and Abbey Theatre, 185, 200, 221, 259; O'Casey's rejection of, 294–95

Rockbarton, Baron of, Viscount Guillamore. *See* O'Grady, Standish

Rockford, Ethel, 92

Rogueries of Scapin (Molière), 185, 199–200

Roosevelt, Theodore, 149, 207, 224, 229, 230, 237, 318

Rosebery, Fifth Earl (Archibald Philip Primrose), 53

Ross, Martin (pseudonym). *See* Martin, Violet

Rossi, Mario Manilo, 301

Rowan, Hamilton, 14, 23–24, 159

Roxborough (estate), 9, 10, 41, 91–92; description of, 15–17; destruction of, 272; Lady Gregory's last visit to, 294; Lady Gregory's love for, 23

Roxborough Volunteers, 9

Ruskin, John, 67

Russell, George (AE), 142, 148, 149, 157, 174, 196, 304; background of, 115–16; bitterness toward Ireland, 273, 300–301; on Irish Academy of Letters, 300–301; theater management politics and, 158, 181

Ryan, Fred, 164

Saint Colman, 38

Sancho's Master (Lady Gregory), 285, 285–86, 293

Sarsfield, Patrick, 178–79, 298

Schliemann, Heinrich, 47

Secret Rose, The (Yeats), 115

Seven Short Plays (Lady Gregory), 212–13

Seven Woods, 38, 203–204

Shadow of a Gunman, The (O'Casey), 278, 281

Shadowy Waters, The (Yeats), 165

Shakespear, Olivia, 101, 251, 278, 301

Shanwalla (Lady Gregory), 245

Sharp, William, 120

Shaw, George Bernard, 150, 165, 166, 185, 211–12, 221, 227, 245, 259, 262, 268, 318; has portrait painted, 246

Shawe-Taylor, Desmond (great-nephew of Lady Gregory), 277

Shawe-Taylor, John (nephew of Lady Gregory), 163, 211, 223, 299

Shawe-Taylor, Walter (brother-in-law of Lady Gregory), 34, 107

"Shepherd and Goatherd" (Yeats), 256

Sheridan, Mary, 14, 23–24, 32, 37, 142, 143

Shewing-up of Blanco Posnet (Shaw), 211–12, 236

Sibby (governess), 19

Silva Gadelica (S. H. O'Grady), 30, 99

Silver Tassie, The (O'Casey), 294

Sinclair, Arthur, 184, 199

Sketches of Life in the West of Ireland (art exhibition), 148

Skittles. *See* Walters, Catherine

Somerville, Edith, 29, 315

Somerville and Ross, 29

"Sonnets" (Lady Gregory). *See* "Woman's Sonnets, A"

Spirit of the Nation, 25, 30, 52

Spreading the News (Lady Gregory), 168–71, 175, 176, 186, 187, 191, 213, 219

Stephens, James, 26, 159

Stories of the Red Hanrahan (Yeats), 164

Story Brought by Brigit (Lady Gregory), 275–76, 294

Stuart, Villiers, 59

Studd, Mary, 293

Sudermann, Hermann, 199

Sullivan, Arthur, 53

Symons, Arthur, 103, 105, 118

Synge, John Millington, 4, 134–35, 142, 149, 158, 158–59, 166, 167, 173, 174, 185, 194, 216, 277, 299, 318; and Molly Allgood, 187, 199; background of, 125–27; death, 208–209; illness of, 198, 203, 206; Lady Gregory on, 182; public reaction to plays of, 192–93; and theater reorganization, 180, 181, 188; *see also titles of individual plays*

Taft, William Howard, 229

Tale of a Town, A (Martyn), 135, 136

Teja (Sudermann), 199

Tennant, Margot Asquith, 93

Tennyson, Alfred, Lord Tennyson, 52, 53

Terry, Ellen, 318

Theatre of Ireland, 119, 181

Thompson, Sir Edward, 139

Three Last Plays (Lady Gregory), 293

"Three Sons, The" (story), 241

Tinker's Wedding (Synge), 193

"To a Friend Whose Work Has Come to Nothing" (Yeats), 211

Touchet, James, Third Earl of Castlehaven, 314

Travelling Man, The (Lady Gregory), 165, 204–206, 213

Trevelyan, George, 53

Trikoupis, Kharilaos, 47

Tulira Castle, 103, 105, 119–20

Twain, Mark, 137, 149, 318

Twenty-Five (Lady Gregory), 155, 157, 159, 162, 164

Twisting of the Rope, The (Hyde), 142, 148

Tynan, Katherine. *See* Hinkson, Katherine Tynan

Ulysses (Joyce), 281
Unicorn from the Stars (Lady Gregory and Yeats), 198
United Irishmen, 23
"Upon a House Shaken by the Land Agitation" (Yeats), 211

Vale (Moore), 240
Valera, Eamon de, 272, 273, 276
Venice, Italy, 64, 72, 103, 128, 209
Victoria (Queen of England), 46, 140, 279; Lady Gregory compared to, 296–97
Vision, A (Yeats), 279
Visions and Beliefs in the West of Ireland (Lady Gregory), 260

Waithman, Wainwright (brother-in-law of Lady Gregory), 86, 102, 238
Waldgrave, Frances Elizabeth Anne, Countess Waldgrave, 35, 51
Walker, Frank, 181
Walker, Mary (pseudonym: Maire nic Shiubhlaigh), 159, 175, 176, 181, 183, 259, 304
Walters, Catherine ("Skittles"), 57–58
Washington, George, 9–10, 12
Washington, D.C., 229
Waste Land, The (Eliot), 281
Watts, George, 71
Well of the Saints (Synge), 193, 200
West, Henry, 34
Where There Is Nothing (Yeats, Lady Gregory, and Hyde), 142, 198
Whistler, James, 53
White Cockade, The (Lady Gregory), 178–79, 179, 237
Wilde, Oscar, 194
"Wind and the Whirlwind, The" (Blunt), 68
"Without and Within" (Lady Gregory), 83
"Woman's Sonnets, A" (Lady Gregory), 61, 65, 66–67, 68, 87
Wordsworth, William, 174

Workhouse Ward, The (Lady Gregory), 200–203, 206, 213, 219
World War I, 243, 244, 245, 266
Would-Be Gentleman, The (Molière), 185, 285, 293
Wrens, The (Lady Gregory), 243
Wyndham, George, 163, 178
Wyndham, Madeline, 60

Yeats, Anne (daughter of W. B. Yeats), 279
Yeats, Jack Butler (brother of W. B. Yeats), 148, 156, 157, 318
Yeats, John Butler (father of W. B. Yeats), 121–22, 148, 149, 157, 175, 184, 230, 239, 271
Yeats, Michael (son of W. B. Yeats), 279
Yeats, William Butler, 4, 30, 85, 96, 100, 101, 103, 107, 108, 110, 158, 172, 173, 174, 185, 295, 304; attends ailing Lady Gregory, 301; awarded Nobel Prize, 277–78; background of, 104–105; and Civil List Pension, 218; effect of Lady Gregory's death, 302–303; and Maud Gonne, 111–13, 116–17, 123, 129–30, 134, 162, 177; on Miss Horniman, 175; ill health, 294; on Irish epics, 149–50; and Irish Literary Theatre, 113–14, 133–34, 135–37; lectures in U.S., 157, 166; marriage, 251; on men at Coole, 126, 174; O'Casey's rejection of, 294–95; participates in pro-Irish demonstrations, 112; playwriting collaboration with Lady Gregory, 142–46, 164–65, 198, 296; poems on Robert Gregory, 255–56, 267–68; rejects Abbey Theatre, 227, 252; relationship with Lady Gregory, 111, 117–18, 121, 204, 207, 271, 299, 302, 303, 305; and G. Russell, 115; and Synge, 208; theater reorganization and management, 180, 181–82, 188; tower at Ballylee, 271–72; *see also* Abbey Theatre; *titles of individual plays and poems*
Young Irelanders, 24, 110

MARY LOU KOHFELDT was born in Fort Worth, Texas, and grew up in Arizona. She attended Stanford University, holds a masters degree from Duke University, and a Ph.D. from the University of North Carolina at Chapel Hill, where she also taught English literature. Ms. Kohfeldt, her husband, and two children now live in Princeton, New Jersey. *Lady Gregory* is her first published work.